Postmodern Literary Theory
An Introduction

Niall Lucy

BLACKWELL
Publishers

First published 1997
Reprinted 1998

Blackwell Publishers Ltd
108 Cowley Road
Oxford OX4 1JF
UK

Blackwell Publishers Inc.
350 Main Street
Malden, Massachusetts 02148
USA

British Library Cataloguing in Publication Data

A CIP catalogue record for this book is available from the British Library.

Library of Congress Cataloging-in-Publication Data

Lucy, Niall
    Postmodern literary theory: an introduction / Niall Lucy.
        p.   cm.
    Includes bibliographical references (p.) and index.
    ISBN 0–631–20000–2 (alk. paper). – ISBN 0–631–20001–0 (pbk.: alk. paper)
      1. Criticism–History–20th century.   2. Literature–History and criticism–Theory,
ect.   3. Postmodernism (Literature)   I. Title.
PN94.L83   1997
801'.95' 09045–dc21   97-12841
                                                                             CIP

Typeset in 10 on 12.5 pt Sabon
by Best-set Typesetter Ltd, Hong Kong
Printed in Great Britain by MPG Books Ltd, Bodmin, Cornwall

This book is printed on acid-free paper

Contents

Preface

The history of literary criticism in the twentieth century is marked by disharmony (at times acrimonious), disagreement (at times bitter) and more or less constant dispute over the purpose of criticism and the meaning of literature. For the most part, though, literary critical quarrels over what literature means have tended to be less philosophical than practical, turning on whether this or that literary work should be deemed a masterpiece or a trifle, canonical or incidental, great or minor. The vexed question of literature as a question in its own right, as it were, is asked not by literary criticism, but by literary theory.

Different theories of literature, in contrast to different critical approaches to it, began to emerge institutionally in the 1970s, as of course everyone knows from Terry Eagleton's book. Suddenly, or so it seemed, university literature departments were having to engage with 'political' and 'philosophical' questions about what a literature department teaches. It was no longer enough to question whether *Little Dorrit* is a more complex and satisfying work of art than *Great Expectations*. Literary theory was putting fundamental questions to the discipline of literary studies about its very disciplinarity. What does literary studies study? What is literature?

Such questions aroused great hostility at first, but in time most literature departments responded to them by conceding just a little bit of ground. 'Critical' approaches were renamed 'theoretical' approaches, and most departments added a few courses on 'women and literature', 'postcolonial writing', 'literature and society' – that sort of thing. The incorporation of 'theory' became a routine feature of the English curriculum, with Eagleton's book becoming a familiar set text for undergraduates in literature and other humanities courses. Today, students still read and crib *Literary Theory* as they try to come to terms with semiotics, phenomenology or psychoanalysis for an assignment, while the book continues to find its way to a general readership outside the university.

The success of *Literary Theory* is some kind of measure, at least, of the success of literary theory. Ironically, though, the popular and institutional success of 'theory' has had a detrimental impact on the status of literary studies as a university subject. Since the publication of Eagleton's book in 1983, two things have happened to explain the 'demise' of the English department: Cultural Studies, and postmodernism. Both of these owe their formations, if only in part, to the disruptive effects of literary theory on the status of English as 'Queen' of the humanities.

The demise is by no means universal, but, in Australia at any rate, the strong English departments today tend to be those in which Cultural Studies – which is rumoured to have 'the word' on postmodernism – is an internally significant and at least semi-autonomous entity, with its own Chair and a separate quota of teaching staff. Other English departments, sans Cultural Studies and still looking more or less like the pre-*Literary Theory* model, seem to have to work a little harder every year at getting the student 'numbers' up to the budgetary bottom line.

What has happened to English, then? One answer could be that English has always been, as a discipline, fairly undisciplined; and that while perhaps this used to be its strength, it was always going to become its weakness. Literary studies' openness to a range of critical approaches left it wide open to the most critical approach of all: the theoretical question of what literary studies studies. This was not a question that was asked by any single theory, but that only helped to make it all the more devastating in its effects. The question arose from 'literary theory' as an assemblage, one made up of many different political and philosophical allegiances without any necessary commitment to literature as such. But the response, certainly at any rate from many professors of English, was often cantankerously blunt: go away! If you have to ask, 'What is literature?', you clearly do not have the vaguest understanding of what literature means and why it is important.

And, of course, go away they did. To Cultural Studies.

Word seemed to have got about by the late 1980s or so that literature was no longer a hip subject. You couldn't use terms like 'text' in an English course without incurring the disapproval of some crusty old moralist, who, chances were, voted to the right of Genghis Khan! But, over in Cultural Studies, you could kind of say what you liked and come out with a degree. Of course, that is how earlier generations had got their

degrees in English: they had been given a few plays and novels and poems
to read, and they were able to say some 'sensuous' things about them,
while making sure the verbs were in the right places, and after three years
they ended up with a BA. The difference now is that you don't have to
worry about the verbs.

Enter: the postmodern.

In a postmodern world, literature is just another text. You can forget
all that stuff about truth and value – and other alienating lies perpetuated
by a deliberately selective version of history controlled by crazy power
freaks and their lackey dupes. 'Truth' is only what *circulates* as such;
hence the importance of technology and the media to an understanding
of 'our' world today. 'Values' are only *effects* of cultural traditions; hence
the importance of becoming cynical today, in order not to be suppressed
under the suffocating weight of 'culture' and 'tradition'.

What I am suggesting is that the English department has never really
engaged with literary theory. Most departments now have a lit theorist or
two on staff and, in addition to courses on 'minor' literatures, they often
have a course called 'Literary Theory'. But as Eagleton pointed out,
literary theory is a very rough mix of philosophical, political, sociological, anthropological and many other modes of enquiry and practice.
Literary theory has no disciplinary 'purity', in short, unless we count its
purity in terms of a certain notion of interdisciplinary contamination.
How, though, could literary studies retain any sense of its own
disciplinarity if it were to become the 'discipline' that teaches *inter*
disciplinarity? Rather than confront this question, English departments
have tended to confine it to particular courses.

Enter: Cultural Studies.

Cultural Studies revels in the idea that it is a discipline without a
centre, seeing this as a strength. English, meanwhile, remains obstinately
true to the idea that literature has an essence, or at any rate some kind of
identity all its own. Literary studies cannot let go of the idea that its
legitimate object of study is *literature*, and no matter how broadly
'literature' is defined, it must always remain definable. Its definition,
moreover, has to include a sense of literature's value and importance
(however these might be conceived) or else literature will be reduced to
just-another-mode-of-cultural-production, like television. Even worse,
compared to television, it could be seen as out-moded.

In a sense, then, if literary theory had not come along and asked the
question, 'What is literature?', none of this might have happened. Unable
or unwilling to respond to that question as a challenge rather than a

threat, the English department has allowed a certain idea of 'text' to take over from a certain idea of 'literature' as the ruling idea of 'culture'.

The idea that everything is text, which denies any special value to literary texts, is taken usually for a central tenet of postmodernism. One should probably add immediately, of course, whether enthusiastically or sardonically, that the very notion of a 'central tenet' is precisely the kind of thing that the postmodern idea of text rejects! In a postmodern world, nothing is central and everything is a paradox. Compared, then, to the idea of literature, the idea of text is anti-foundationalist.

If works of literature have 'depth', texts are mere assemblages of 'surface' effects. So if it is true that postmodernism understands everything as text, and if postmodernism is indeed the contemporary *Zeitgeist*, then it cannot be only literature which is understood now as lacking in depth. Politics too, for example, must be no less 'unfounded' in its assumptions, and no less able to control the difference between intentions and effects, than a literary text. And as with politics, so with everything else.

Forget depth: think surface!

If – again – this is the message of postmodernism, one may wonder where it comes from. My argument here is that postmodernism comes out of a romantic tradition in which literature is understood in terms of the *question* of literature. For the German Romantics at Jena in the 1790s (see chapter 2), the literary was conceived as inseparable from the literary theoretical: literature presents itself as literary theory. In this way, though, literature is also what is 'unpresentable', since it can never quite be found 'outside' the effects of theoretical speculations which are both about it and internal to it. One form that the question of literature takes, therefore, is the problem of deciding what is inside and what is outside the space of the literary.

This, I think, is the basis of the postmodern idea that everything is a text. For postmodernism, the problem of inside/outside relations is not confined to the question of literature but extends rather across the whole field of culture and society. What was once the romantic space of the literary becomes, for postmodernism, a general plane of human existence, on which concepts of identity, origin and truth are seen as multiple and structureless assemblages rather than as grounds for understanding human 'being' and culture. This is why I have called this book *Postmodern Literary Theory*, since I think 'postmodernism' refers to the generalization or flattening out of the romantic theory of literature which marks it as a 'radical' theory of the nonfoundational, structureless 'structure' of truth. I do not think postmodernism is all that radical, in other words.

But while the standard response to postmodernism is either to wildly celebrate or vehemently denounce it, my own response is rather different and closer to a poststructuralist approach. One of my key points is that postmodernism and poststructuralism are not the same, though of course they are very often taken to be. They are separated, as I discuss in chapter 5, by their different alignments to what may be called the concept of 'structure': while poststructuralism offers a critique of structure, seeing structures as inseparable from the 'plays' within them, postmodernism thinks it is possible to replace the concept of structure with a concept of 'nonstructure'. It derives the concept of nonstructure from the romantic theory of unpresentable literature, although more recent analogues are the psychoanalytic concept of the 'unconscious' and the structuralist concept of the 'nonintentional' effects of language (see chapter 1).

Rather than preempt my argument here, however, by summarizing it chapter by chapter, I would prefer to say just a few things which are intended to be of help in reading the book. First a certain structure of suspense runs right through my argument. I don't mean by this that the book is a kind of detective novel, or an instantiation of what it critiques, but simply that, in a sense, the argument progresses convulsively rather than by following a continuum. But nonetheless it does progress. So I am not trying to say that the book is full of contradictions; but I am suggesting that it is full of interruptions. These interruptions are not merely incidental, moreover, to the argument: they are indissociable from it. At different times it will appear that I am saying different things about postmodern literary theory, and all I want to say here is that those differences need to be assessed in terms of the different contexts in which they appear. In the end I come down on the side of pragmatics rather than theory, which should help to explain why I do not think that anything counts as 'the' position to adopt towards postmodernism. Nevertheless it will not be giving too much away to admit that, when push comes to shove, I am really not all that enthusiastic about postmodern literary theory. Pragmatically speaking, though, push does not come to shove all that often.

Secondly, it should be clear from the chapter titles that my approach to the topic is by way of concepts and problems rather than through a systematic account of different currents of thought within postmodern literary theory. In order to historicize these concepts and problems, I discuss some of the ideas of several philosophers from the past (notably

Hobbes, Rousseau, Kant, Nietzsche and Heidegger) along with those of contemporary thinkers such as Baudrillard, Kristeva, Derrida, Lyotard, Barthes, and Deleuze and Guattari. Many of these ideas are quite complex, and, while I have tried to discuss them as clearly and directly as I can, it should not be supposed that all sections of the book are of a piece in terms of being 'easy' to understand. Nothing in the book is intended to be difficult, though, and readers who might be unfamiliar with some of the many names that appear will find that there is always some clue given to the historical identity, at least, of the various figures I discuss and of the various ideas, arguments and texts I introduce.

Thirdly, my main concerns with postmodern literary theory have to do with what I see as the limitations of its 'ethics', as I discuss in the later chapters. Whether I am right about this is to some extent beside the point. But the fact that I am interested here in the question of ethics, if not in ethics as a question, should show that the book is addressed by no means only to students of English. I hope that my discussion of postmodern literary theory will have something to say to anyone who is interested in questions of politics and culture, for example, and therefore to readers generally. Certainly I have tried to write the book in a way which is inviting rather than intimidating, though of course my intention is no guarantee of success.

While I hope the book will be of general interest, however, this should not be allowed to obscure its very particular interest in approaching literature and theory as *problems*. I do not think they are problems to which a general solution may be found; they are problems, rather, which present the problem of how to approach them. The problem of *how* to approach literature and theory (whether these are conceived as separate or inseparable) is a pragmatic one, and cannot occur outside specific contexts. In short, I think that instead of trying to preserve a notion of literature as a certain *kind* of writing, which either includes or is opposed to theory as another kind of writing or as a mode of thought, the disciplinary object of literary studies should be seen as *the pragmatics of writing*. Such an object is closer to a *text*, though not necessarily as given by postmodern literary theory. What is needed is an idea of 'text' that allows pragmatics to be understood as ethics, which is an understanding that I believe poststructuralism makes possible.

The final point I wish to make for now concerns the examples I use of postmodern literature. These are all American, though I might just as easily have given Australian and British examples. I chose work, however, which I think will be most familiar to the most readers, though obviously I do discuss some writers who are less 'famous' than others. This is especially the case perhaps in chapter 11, where I discuss Paul Auster's writing. Nevertheless the context (or the pragmatics) of that discussion should make it clear why Auster is an appropriate example at that point. Since this is an introduction to postmodern literary theory, moreover, it seems only fitting that I should introduce not only 'theorists' but also 'writers', given that what is being introduced is the very problem of the relations between theory and writing *as* the problem of theory and writing.

Fortunately, I was able to approach this problem with the help of many friends and colleagues. I am particularly grateful to Abigail Bray, Robert Briggs, Claire Colebrook, Carolyn D'Cruz, Garry Gillard, Alec McHoul (for whom this book comes with a free set of steak knives), Jeff Malpas, Horst Ruthrof and Tony Thwaites. For their support at a crucial early stage in the project, I thank John Frow, John Hartley and Christopher Norris; and I owe a great deal to my editor at Blackwell, Andrew McNeillie, for his trust and wit.

Murdoch University
February, 1997

1

Mind and Myth

Suppose there were just two ways of thinking about how literature is produced. One way might be to think that literature is produced by writers of genius, the other that writers themselves are produced (to varying degrees) by forces beyond their control. The first way of thinking could be called the liberal humanist 'theory' of literary production, while the second could be seen as leading to the development of postmodern literary theory. By comparison to the first way of thinking the second is revolutionary because it denies that a literary text is the expression of an author's intentions, feelings and linguistic mastery. What is revolutionary about this second way of thinking is that authors come to be understood not as people but as subjects, to which extent they themselves are no less produced by literature (and as literature) than literature itself.

Among the many candidate forces for producing authorial or writing subjects, two have stood out in the twentieth century as super candidates: language and the unconscious. Although language enables us to say things, it also constrains us to say them in certain ways. Even literary language use, which is licensed to press against the limits of such constraint, can never be utterly unique and fully personal or private insofar as it must respect (even if it aims to modify or reject) the conventions by which language enables and constrains the indefinite (but not infinite) possibilities for saying something. This is to think of language as a structure or system that precedes 'us' such that there can be no understanding of ourselves outside of language. 'We' are therefore subject to, and subjects of, language's structuring principles and effects, and this is no less the case if who 'we' are happens to be the author of a literary text.

Now it is true that literary criticism has always been mindful of the role played by convention (to use the term of Lawrence Manley's impressive study) in the production of literature, whether in the form of universal laws or historically contingent attitudes and values. As far back as the early eighteenth century, for example, Alexander Pope could attribute the production of literature to 'true Genius' *and* 'Unerring Nature', without a hint of contradiction in doing so.[1] Hence convention, 'as both timeless forms of order and changing social values',[2] has always been a force that literary works have been allowed to exemplify or to contest, making it possible to canonize a work of literature either for being exemplary or disruptive of conventions: a poem (say) can be valued for encapsulating the spirit of its age or the properties of a certain genre, or for radically transgressing that spirit or those properties. But either way the credit (whether for encapsulation or transgression) has gone to authors.

Therefore it is revolutionary to argue that the 'credit' should go to language. In an extreme sense this argument entails 'the death of man', as it has been called, associated with the structuralist theory of literary production (indeed of cultural production in general). But to the extent that 'man' stands for a concept of the conscious individual most often associated with liberal humanist theory, then the death of man is attributable also to psychoanalysis. The role of psychoanalytic theory in that death (or in transforming the concept 'man' to mean 'subject' rather than 'person') has to do with its 'discovery' of the unconscious forces underlying all cultural phenomena, including every instance of language use and our 'own' self-understanding as cultural beings. What goes on inside our heads and how we act in the world, then, may not necessarily be what we think is going on or be an effect of desires and motivations we presume to understand. The 'real' cause of who we are and what we do may lie in our unconscious.

One point at which a theory of the unconscious and a theory of the structuring effects of language come together (although psychoanalysis and structuralism are not by definition mutually dependent) is in their different accounts of the Oedipus myth as expressed by Sigmund Freud and Claude Lévi-Strauss. For Freud, all of us who might regard ourselves as fully socialized have been successfully 'Oedipalized'.[3] This occurs when our pre-Oedipal selves, utterly abandoned to the 'pleasure principle', convert to the sway of the 'reality principle' knowing that the fulfilment of our pleasures must be delayed in order to attend to the immediate demands of reality. This does not mean that we give up our desire to fulfil our every desire. It means that we agree to the *postponement* of our pleasures for the sake of doing reality's urgent bidding, which is actually in our best interests. Hence we go to work to be able to play, or we refrain from killing someone who annoys us because we know that in succumbing to that 'pleasure' the consequences may be such as to put at risk the full expression of our future pleasures.

We do not, however, simply agree as a matter of course to the postponement of our pleasures: we have to be coerced into agreeing. If you are a boy this happens when you feel threatened with the loss of your penis for desiring to sleep with your mother, who has been 'castrated', and so you submit to the authority of your father and learn his ways. If you are a girl it happens when you recognize that, like your mother, you too are defined by the 'lack' of a penis and so you transfer your affections to your father only to learn that your desire to seduce him must never be realized. You then return to a relationship (which is no longer sexual) with your mother and begin the process of identifying with her, settling for a life in which a penile supplement – a baby – will have to replace your real (forbidden) desire. Clearly this is a process favouring boys, who can at least look forward to becoming their own patriarch one day. But the point is not that Freud's theory can be criticized. It is that it opens up a whole other order of analytical possibilities for the explanation of culture in general and literature in particular.

Let us now consider some of these possibilities before moving on to a discussion of Lévi-Strauss's theory of the Oedipus myth. It is important to note that what Freud called the unconscious is not something we are born with, like our internal organs, but something we produce (if Freud is to be believed) as a consequence of the Oedipalization process. We activate our unconscious, bring it into being, when we repress our first sexual desire, which for girls obviously is homosexual (hence all 'heterosexual' women are in fact repressed lesbians). Having opened up our unconscious and buried our foremost sexual desire in its innermost depths we are ready to enter into society and gender. Gendered society, then, is the result of active and ongoing repression on the part of all its members, except for those 'neurotic' or 'pathological' individuals who have not successfully Oedipalized themselves. This does not mean that society is a bad thing. On the contrary, the social order offers protection in the form of the reality principle (otherwise we would all be running amok expressing ourselves as pre-Oedipal pleasure seekers, putting ourselves and everyone else at risk) and opportunities for creativity in the form of 'displaced' expressions of our unconscious desires. Once accepted in these terms, psychoanalytic theory becomes a powerful explanatory mechanism for revealing the 'hidden' truths of cultural phenomena.

This raises a problem, though. For it may be that these 'truths' are *produced* as 'hidden': produced by psychoanalysis itself. If so, then for the institution of literary criticism psychoanalysis may function as a licence to print meaning. Say, for example, I wanted to make a point about what I saw as the systematic mistreatment of Aboriginal people within Australian society, and so I wrote a story in which a young Aboriginal man is seen out holding hands with his non-Aboriginal girlfriend one night by a group of white teenagers driving past who decide to teach him a lesson for daring to have a white girlfriend by running him over in their car. Afterwards the car speeds off, and the girl – terrified – flees home. Because it happens late at night there are no witnesses, but eventually someone finds an Aboriginal boy lying by the side of the road and calls for an ambulance. When the ambulance officers arrive, thinking he's 'just another drunken Aborigine', they check the boy's wallet for an address and take him back to his parents' house. Later that night his brain haemorrhages and the boy dies.

Regardless of the point I may have wished to make, there would be nothing to prevent a psychoanalytic reading of this story from 'discovering' that it is really about an unresolved conflict with my father. Hence 'my' identification with the 'misunderstood' black hero of the story would place me in relation to my father as the boy is placed in a 'tragic' relation to white, male-dominated Australian society which responds to him only through indifference or violence. Significantly the only woman in the story (an underdeveloped character) abandons the boy, symbolizing the resentment I harbour towards my mother for failing to protect me from the excessive masculinity of my overbearing patriarch of a father and for her subsequent refusal to sleep with me by way of compensation. Abandoned by my mother, I unconsciously project the hostility I have for her onto all women and expect them to let me down. Emasculated by my father, I think of all men as uncaring authority figures out to get me, even when I haven't done anything wrong. Confused and unloved, I am a helpless outcast lying face down by the side of a road in existential darkness innocently awaiting his return to the scene of a dreadful torment – the family home – from which there is no escape.

But in fact it is psychoanalysis that offers no way out. Once texts are understood to be 'given off' by the unconscious, such that no producer of a text can be said to be any more responsible for producing it than a rotten egg is 'responsible' for emitting a foul-smelling gas, then there is no position from outside that understanding which could not be understood as having been given off unconsciously itself. So that now if I were to admit the story I just told is actually based on 'a true story' (but not the whole story) of what happened, in 1992, in Perth, Western Australia, to an Aboriginal teenager called Louis Johnson,[4] this would not have to negate the notional psychoanalytic reading I have based on a pretence that the story was something I made up in a way that Herman Melville, say, made up the story of 'Bartleby'. The psychoanalytic question would, after all, remain: why did I tell the story, *that* story, here? If my answer were that I simply wanted to record the name of Louis Johnson, lest we forget, this would not be an answer, becoming available instead as more text for psychoanalysis to read. In fact I could never given an answer to the psychoanalytic question, otherwise psychoanalysis would have no special claim to know the truth. For psychoanalysis, then, the reason I told that story (which is something quite distinct from an idea of what the story *means*) could never be clear to me since the things we say and do are always in principle the result of 'irrational' desires and fears locked away inside our unconscious.

If there were something positive to be said about this it would be that psychoanalysis helps to debunk the aura surrounding the cult of author-ship which is so important to liberal humanist theory, wresting from a text's producer the power to determine a text's meaning. But perhaps it wrests this power unto itself. Whatever psychoanalysis says, in other words (always in other words), goes. For example: all reading is coprophagic. That is what James Strachey, the esteemed English transla-tor and editor of the standard collection of Freud's work, said in 1930 to a gathering of the British Psycho-Analytical Society: 'a coprophagic tendency lies at the root of all reading.'[5] Whereupon, and without even bothering to disguise his class hatred, he proceeded (in his own meta-phor) to defecate on the poor for having learned to read at all:

> The author excretes his thoughts and embodies them in the printed book; the reader takes them, and after chewing them over [sic], incorporates them into himself. Perhaps the clearest evidence of these unconscious processes is to be seen in the orgies of newspaper reading which have accompanied the spread of literacy to the lower classes of the community. Inconceivably vast masses of ink-stained paper are ejected every day into the streets; there they are seized and devoured with passionate avidity, and a few moments later destroyed with contempt or put to the basest possible uses; no one can find bad enough abuse for the rags of this gutter Press, but no one feels he has breakfasted unless one of them is lying beside his coffee and his toast.[6]

Whether it had occurred to Strachey that a popular press may play an important democratizing role in societies (or whether this is why he despised it) seems too mundane a point to unsettle his 'theory' of reading as a displacement for eating shit. Perhaps, then, his conclusion should come as no surprise:

> For if the book symbolizes the mother [a transformation of Freud's belief that books are 'feminine'], its author must be the father; and the printed words, the author's thoughts, fertilizing and precious, yet defiling the virgin page, must be the father's penis or faeces within the mother. And now comes the reader, the son, hungry, voracious, destructive and defiling in his turn, eager to force his way into his mother, to find out what is inside her, to tear his father's traces out of her, to devour them, to make them his own, and to be fertilized by them himself.[7]

Without wishing to reify common sense (not to mention basic logic or good taste) as a touchstone of the truth, should we be forced to ignore it altogether? In other words, how might I protest that Strachey's explanation does not describe my experience of reading, nor, I think, the experience of most others? If I did not believe in flying saucers, for example, would I be compelled to believe in them if somebody said they saw one? If thousands of people said they did?

Given that it relies so heavily on the work of Melanie Klein, which continues to exert an influence on 'postmodern' psychoanalysis, Strachey's account of reading as a displaced enactment of grotesque desires should not be dismissed too readily as eccentric or out of date. Klein argues that our earliest intellectual and aesthetic development corresponds with an infantile venting of destructive impulses.[8] Strachey acknowledges, therefore, that his 'theory' of reading as an expression of a kind of Caligulan lust for possession of the other's body, which rather puts a twist on the notion of getting to the heart of the matter, is indebted to 'the phantasies that Melanie Klein has found in children during the oral- and anal-sadistic phases: phantasies of the child forcing his way into his mother, soiling and laying waste her inside and devouring her contents – among them his father's penis as well as babies and faeces'.[9] It could of course be asked whether these 'phantasies' belong to the analysand or to the analyst, to the 'patient' or the 'discipline', and on what basis the difference could be known. But nevertheless the positive effect of psychoanalytic theory as a counter-force against the 'self-evident' sovereignty of the conscious author, which grounds liberal humanist literary criticism, should not go unnoticed.

For this reason Freud's reading of the Oedipus myth as pointing to the discovery of our unconscious DNA, as a kind of detective story 'in which the long-past deed of Oedipus is gradually brought to light by an investigation ingeniously protracted and fanned into life by ever fresh relays of evidence',[10] serves as a radical intervention into overly positivist or rationalist theories of cultural production. Moreover, the radical alterity – the a-rational (as it were) rather than the ir-rational structure – of the unconscious as posited by Freud has had a direct influence on poststructuralism, while the relation of psychoanalytic theory to postmodernism has tended to be taken up in a more general form of the latter's perception of the psychoanalytic emphasis on 'irrationality' (sometimes coded as 'embodiment') as a productive but undervalued ground of signification. I will return to these points later, once a discussion of the differences between the two (and indeed within the many) 'posts' gets underway.

Beforehand, though, we need to consider the other super candidate for producing writing subjects – language – from which the often-touted slogan of the death of man primarily derives. Here then we turn from psychoanalysis to structuralism and leap forward several decades from Freud's lectures of 1915–17 to Claude Lévi-Strauss's first volume of *Structural Anthropology*, published in French in 1958 (although based on papers dating from 1944) and translated into English in 1963.

If psychoanalysis hastened the death of man by pathologizing him, structuralism dealt the fatal blow by turning 'man' into a linguistic construct. For structuralism, everyone is born into a particular language community such that anyone's perception of reality is predetermined by the particular 'grammar' through which they come to know the world. What is called 'reality' (by an individual, a culture or an epoch) is structured, therefore, as a language: reality is simply what is able to be classified as such according to a system – to structures – of regulations and prohibitions which produce objects, knowledges, feelings, values and events 'in' the world. But the very notion of a world is always going to be culturally and historically specific to specific language communities since the structure of structures, as it were, is language, and so the very concept of 'structure' itself is a linguistic metaphor. Consequently, as Lévi-Strauss puts it,

> language can be seen to be a *condition* of culture, and this in two different ways: First, it is a condition of culture in a diachronic way, because it is mostly through the language that we learn about our own culture – we are taught by our parents, we are scolded, we are congratulated, with language. But also, from a much more theoretical point of view, language can be said to be a condition of culture because the material out of which

language is built is of the same type as the material out of which the whole culture is built: logical relations, oppositions, correlations, and the like. Language, from this point of view, may appear as laying a kind of foundation for the more complex structures which correspond to the different aspects of culture.[11]

Nevertheless, as for Freud with psychoanalysis, the whole purpose of Lévi-Strauss's project of structural anthropology was to reach a better understanding of nothing less than the structure of the human mind. By studying the structure of language, then, or the structures of languages (especially via the principles of structural linguistics), structural anthropology aspired to access the very structure of 'the' human mind. The importance of structural linguistics (arising from the work of Ferdinand de Saussure)[12] to Lévi-Strauss's project lay in its having developed a set of prescriptive procedures (a 'scientific method') which gave it the means for 'doing things as well and with the same sort of rigorous approach that was long believed to be the privilege of the exact and natural sciences'.[13] So by adopting the scientific method of structural linguistics, the 'undertheorized' discipline of anthropology, made dull by its dependence on empiricism, might hope to garner a little prestige of its own.

As a model of the kind of work to be produced by the new discipline of structural anthropology, Lévi-Strauss offered his reading of the Oedipus myth. For him, myth was a very special form of language but for a reason that was the opposite of why literature (exemplified by poetry) is understood as special. 'Poetry is a kind of speech which cannot be translated except at the cost of serious distortions; whereas the mythical value of the myth is preserved even through the worst translations.'[14] While the essence of a poem may be said to be its *syntax*, in other words, the essence of a myth is its *semantics*. What Lévi-Strauss calls 'mythical value' (semantics) is independent, therefore, of any particular myth's syntactical realization that might lead to its appreciation as literature or simply to its recognition as a linguistic construct. Myth is never *not* language, and it is never *simply* language. 'Myth is language, functioning on an especially high level where meaning succeeds practically at 'taking off' from the linguistic ground on which it keeps rolling.'[15]

Consequently all versions of a myth contain the same mythical value that can be analysed according to the 'scientific' procedures of structural linguistics. Such a value comprises 'bundles' of relations between gross units of meaning known as 'mythemes', the equivalent of sentences in ordinary speech. In the case of the Oedipus myth, Lévi-Strauss arranges these mythemes into four columns whose relations to one another reveal the mythical value of the myth (which is quite independent of any particular version of it, such as Sophocles' or Freud's). The first column is made up of units referring to the overvaluing of blood relations (Oedipus marries his mother, Jocasta, for example); column two expresses the undervaluing of such relations (Oedipus kills his father, Laius); column three refers to the slaying of monsters (Oedipus kills the Sphinx); and the fourth column comprises names referring to some general order of human disability ('Oedipus' translates as 'swollen foot') or, more specifically, to 'difficulties in walking straight or standing upright.'[16] But it must be stressed that the meaning of the Oedipus myth is to be discovered in the interrelations of the columns and not in the columns themselves. So in any telling of the myth the columns would be disregarded, whereas 'if we want to *understand* the myth, then we will [...] read from left to right, column after column, each one being considered as a unit.'[17] From this it transpires that the relation pertaining to columns three and four corresponds to that pertaining to the first pair of columns, which is one of a simple inversion (undervaluation is the inverse of overvaluation and vice versa). But it is not quite as easy to identify what the relation comprises in the case of the second pair. This becomes clearer only when the columns are seen to encapsulate competing myths of the origin of humankind. According to myths of human auto-generation (or autochthony) we gave birth to ourselves by rising up from the Earth, becoming crippled in the struggle. Hence the references to lameness in column four of Lévi-Strauss's analysis can be seen as affirming the myth of our autochthonous origin. By contrast column three signifies the refusal of autochthony, insofar as monsters like the Sphinx tried to prevent humankind from being born. In this way 'the overrating of blood relations is to the underrating of blood relations as the attempt to escape autochthony is to the impossibility to succeed in it.'[18]

The mythical value of the Oedipus myth lies, then, for Lévi-Strauss in its transposition of a primitive human question – are we born of one (world) or born of two (parents)? – into the related question: 'born from different or born from same?'[19] And this question, since it is independent of syntactical variations, will hold as the mythical value for every version of the Oedipus myth:

> A striking example is offered by the fact that our interpretation may take into account the Freudian use of the Oedipus myth and is certainly applicable to it. Although the Freudian problem has ceased to be that of

autochthony *versus* bisexual reproduction, it is still the problem of understanding how *one* can be born from *two*: How is it that we do not have
only one procreator, but a mother plus a father? Therefore, not only
Sophocles, but Freud himself, should be included among the recorded
versions of the Oedipus myth on a par with earlier or seemingly more
'authentic' versions.[20]

The structuralist approach does away, therefore, with the literary critical
problem of having to judge the aesthetic worth of an 'imaginative' text.
It defines its specialism as analysing the 'mythical' value, not the 'literary'
value, of a myth, which it takes 'as consisting of all its versions; or to put
it otherwise, a myth remains the same as long as it is felt as such'.[21] So by
comparison to liberal humanist literary criticism, structuralism looks like
a science – in the same way as structural linguistics appeared in comparison to anthropology. Appearances may be deceptive, of course, but there
can be little doubt that structuralism's scientific 'look' lent it strong
appeal as a way of dressing up the drab moralism of liberal humanist
literary studies in the 1960s, both as a way of reinventing the English
department as a stylish option for uncommitted recruits and as a means
of better 'quantifying', for funding purposes, what literary studies
studied.

But to return to the issue of appearances sometimes being deceptive.
One of the problems with Lévi-Strauss's analysis may be that it borrows
all the syntax of a scientific method, but to very little purpose. (This is to
ignore for now the vexed question of whether a 'scientific method' could
ever have an essence – a semantics, say – that was anything more than an
effect of its methodology, or its 'syntax'.) In other words, on the basis of
the constituent mythemes identified by Lévi-Strauss as being present in all
versions of the Oedipus myth, it would not be difficult to write a version
of our own:

> One day Peter Blynde asked his sister for a loan of $10,000. She gave him
> the $5,000 she'd been setting aside to buy a new car, which was all the
> money she had. Peter thought his sister was holding out on him and went
> into a violent rage, but there was nothing he could do – she'd already given
> him more than she was really able to afford. That's when Peter knew he
> would have to kill the loan shark he owed the money to before the loan
> shark killed him, which is exactly what he did.

Each of the elements identified as being present in all versions of the myth
is present here. Blood relations are both overvalued and undervalued, a
character's name signifies a disability, and someone's life is threatened by

a 'monster'. But it is difficult to see how these elements contain 'the' mythical value of the Oedipus myth, which ought to be present in this or any version: the question of whether we are 'born from different or born from same'.

What this may point to is structuralism's *production* of 'mythical value', which may have no value of its own outside the syntax of a structuralist analysis or independent of the structuralist method. If it could be asked whether psychoanalysis did not produce the 'unconscious', so we might question whether structuralism has not produced mythical value (or some other transcendental signified or irreducible essence) in order to 'find' and then analyse 'it'.

An analogy may help to clarify the point. Suppose, on the basis of fairly scant and inconclusive evidence, some archaeologists were to claim that a clandestine society had existed in ancient Egypt devoted to the worship of philosopher cats. Initiation to the cult was strictly monitored and its knowledges were kept a closely guarded secret, which is why there are so tantalizingly few traces of it in the archaeological record. Nevertheless it seems that cult followers looked upon some cats (by no means all) as philosophers, whom they held in the kind of esteem accorded to the likes of Aristotle and Kant today. Exactly how the cult identified these cats is not known, but the basic assumption seems to have been that cat culture was no less likely to be varied (and to include philosophers) than human culture. So the philosopher cats were out there, and they had important questions to ask. The problem was knowing how to understand them. But somehow the cult had learned the rudiments of a feline grammar, which it kept secret, and this gave members access to the many different philosophical ideas the cats had to impart, including a lengthy dissertation on a simile and a cave, and elaborate critiques of reason, judgement and aesthetics. Suddenly, however, the cult disappears entirely from the archaeological record at around 650 BC, and with it (so it seems) does all its knowledge and any memory of the cult's existence – with one possible exception. In a manuscript dating from the late Middle Ages, written by a German monk, a vexing reference appears to a Felix Catspaw, who seems to have been associated with some kind of clandestine goings-on in the Bavarian Alps in the last quarter of the twelfth century AD. According to the manuscript, Catspaw (whose moniker must have been a pseudonym) was known locally for his 'strange ways' with cats, and was treated with some suspicion for keeping the company of others who had similar 'ways'. The monk's reference is unclear, but there is no doubting the suggestion that these 'strange ways' involved a belief on the part of people like Felix that cats had something to say to them. What that was cannot be known. But according to some archaeologists the medieval manuscript could indicate that the cult worship of philosopher cats may have survived long past the decline of ancient Egypt, and that it may be alive still. In any case, whether the cult is still around, why couldn't it be true that philosopher cats are still with us, and that the moggy lying in front of your fireplace right now, or sunning itself in the garden, limbs outstretched, deep in thought, might not be one of them?

Which comes first, in other words, the evidence or the finding? Put to the story of the cult worship of philosopher cats, this question seems particularly apt. But it could turn out to be no less applicable to many other kinds of text, including some discussed already. Finding that cats are capable of philosophical thought may not be of an entirely different order of 'discovery' than finding, for example, that all human infants want to have sex with their mothers, or that all reading is about wanting to eat shit, or that we are all spoken 'by' language or mythic structures. Insofar as any of these statements makes sense, it could be said to do so paranoically: in such a way that the sense made is inseparable from the sense-making. To say that reading is coprophagic can indeed make sense, then, but only within a particular mode of sense-making practice (or according to a certain syntax). In a word, it makes sense psychoanalytically to say that reading is coprophagic. Within that discipline (or that discourse, with its own special rules and procedures for knowing what objects to look at and what to say about them) it makes perfectly good sense to know that our unconscious harbours radically irrational forces that influence what we do in our conscious life. With this principle in place, it can then make sense to argue that because many people read a newspaper while eating breakfast, therefore reading is a type of consumption, and so on. At this point, evidence and finding fold into each other and can no longer be separated: the discourse is well under way. The object 'itself' has become indistinguishable from its transposition through and into a disciplinized (and disciplinizing) rhetorical system. Consequently the 'sense' made of reading by James Strachey, say, cannot be seen as independent of the sense-making metaphors used by him (as an agent of psychoanalytic discourse) to discipline that sense in terms of excretion, embodiment, mastication, seizure, devourment and the like. The same might be said of the senses made of the Oedipus myth by Freud and Lévi-Strauss.

For now, this can be termed a paranoiac process of making sense.

From within a particular discourse, such as psychoanalysis or structural-ism, particular senses that might otherwise be nonsensical outside the discourse seem valid. Even seemingly irrational statements are rational-ized by the legitimacy of certain discourses. Before psychoanalysis, it could not have made legitimate sense to claim that reading is coprophagic or that our primary sexual urge is directed at our mothers. Insofar as these things are sayable now, however, their credibility de-pends on accepting that the unconscious was always already there, before the emergence of psychoanalysis. It is only on the basis of such priority that the unconscious can be claimed by psychoanalysis as an affective force in people's lives. And once the claim is accepted, of course, this gives psychoanalysis the authority (and power) to 'know' the uncon-scious, to say how it operates and what counts as evidence of its manifes-tations and effects.

A feature of paranoia is its potential to become a totalizing discourse, a discourse with no 'outside'. For the paranoid, everything can count as evidence of a particular theory of the truth, a theory that is otherwise (from outside the space of paranoia, to which the paranoid is blind) understood to be grounded on a false assumption and so the 'truth' it sees is only a delusion based on a miscalculation or a misreading. But the theory itself, as a set of rules and procedures, is not necessarily wrong. This is why a paranoiac reading of any set of events is often plausible (or at least why it is not always manifestly not true); hence a lot of money continues to be spent on investigating UFO sightings, for example. The point is that even paranoiac truths can be expressed according to the most mundane principles of truth-production, particularly in the form of scientific observations or eyewitness reports. Syntactically, then, the claims *I saw a Qantas airliner in the night sky above my house* and *I saw an alien spacecraft in the night sky above my house* are identical, though they are of course quite different semantically (let alone ontologically). But to believe the second claim one would have to believe that knowledge is something that experience simply 'gives off'. In other words, despite its loftiness, it has to be seen as grounded on a prior truth (experience is the basis of knowledge) before it can be believed. By the same token someone who had never had an 'experience' of seeing an alien spacecraft might still believe in UFOs. For such a person, UFOs would be always already real (they would fit into a particular picture of the world) and so in principle it would be no less possible to see an alien spacecraft than it is to see an aeroplane. In short, the world of objects for the UFO believer includes, without him necessarily having 'seen' one, alien spacecraft, just as for many other people the world of objects includes many different animal species they need not have seen.

Now while we cannot say that 'language' and the 'unconscious' are able to be seen as objects in this way, they can be regarded as *forces* that are no less actual than gravity or wind power. On this model, the forceful effects of language and the unconscious appear natural and a priori. Structuralism and psychoanalysis stand in relation to these forces, then, as Newtonian physics does to the laws of nature, such that a certain 'scientific' order of authority underwrites both structuralist and psychoanalytic truth-claims. But there is nevertheless a difference between the truth-claims of these discourses and those of science: regardless of any form of cultural or other difference whatsoever, regardless of anyone's 'personal' perception of 'reality' or relationship with their mother or anxiety over the alienating effects of language, no one can walk out of a window of a thirty-storey building and not fall. From this it can be inferred that all forms of difference have something in common, which is not necessarily a knowledge of the laws of gravity, but at least the knowledge that if you try to walk out of (what is known as) a window of (what is known as) a thirty-storey building you will most certainly fall, and almost certainly die.

But truth-claims about the 'laws' of the unconscious or the 'laws' of language are not of the same order as those about the laws of gravity. The only sense in which the unconscious and language can be understood in terms of 'laws' is from inside the discourses of psychoanalysis and structuralism. From inside those discourses, those 'laws' function *as if* they were transcendental – as if they were as consensual or as noncontroversial as the laws of gravity and therefore 'true'. However, from inside paranoiac discourses, almost anything can function as the truth. Outside those discourses, those 'truths' are open to question, negotiation, rejection, opposition, modification, debate and so forth.

So how do we know that we are not inside, instead of outside, a paranoiac discourse? How do we know that what we think is true is not simply a paranoiac fantasy, a delusion produced by the operations of certain texts, an elaborate misreading of things as they 'really' are?

Well one answer might be (and the qualification is important) that we don't, and we can't. The very notion of 'things as they "really" are' is itself an effect of textual operations, such that 'reality' is never anything more than a textual projection: it is something that texts allude to, point at, grope for and search after but which they can never be identical with. 'Reality' is not just something that is there already, waiting to be represented textually. Instead of thinking of reality as coming *before* textuality, then, it is possible (again the precaution is advised) to think of this very notion as an *effect* of textuality.

Such thinking can lead to many different consequences, one of which is a *celebration* of textuality that often circulates as 'the' truth about postmodernism. This is not to say that that 'truth' isn't true, but rather that 'postmodernism' circulates also in other ways, according to other meanings attributed to it, which will be considered later. But for now the truth about postmodernism is that it celebrates the text, which is to say it celebrates a certain kind of text that makes a game out of searching for the truth. An exemplary instance of the type is *The Crying of Lot 49* by Thomas Pynchon, published in 1965.

Pynchon's short novel opens with the sudden revelation that Oedipa Maas has been named executrix of the estate of her former lover, Pierce Inverarity, a California property dealer. But in trying to untangle all the legal knots of the will, she becomes increasingly unsure of what she can be sure about. By the end there is no way of knowing whether Oedipa has stumbled upon a vast underground postal network known as Trystero (also spelt 'Tristero') that began in fourteenth-century Europe and by which millions of Americans are secretly communicating with one another today, or whether she has simply imagined all the 'evidence' pointing to it and so she could be mad. Or, for reasons Oedipa would never be able to guess, perhaps the Tristero (or Trystero) was an elaborate plot devised by Pierce himself to make her believe there was a secret communications system operating below the surface of contemporary America, or perhaps she only imagined that Pierce had invented such a plot. Or perhaps there was a plot to make her think that Pierce had invented a plot to make her think there was a secret postal system called Trystero, or Tristero. Or she could be mad. Either Trystero is real, or a fiction. Either there is a plot to make her think that Trystero is real, or Oedipa is mad. 'Those, now that she was looking at them, she saw to be the alternatives. Those symmetrical four.'[22]

But, in a brilliant reading of *The Crying of Lot 49*, Tony Thwaites shows that the apparent symmetry of Oedipa's four alternatives turns out to be, in fact, quite asymmetrical. Oedipa's choices – Tristero or plot, reality or madness – are reducible to a single recurring term: there is a plot. There is a plot called Trystero; there is a plot about a plot called Tristero; there is a plot, which is real, to make Oedipa imagine there is a plot; there is a plot, which Oedipa imagines, to make her think there is a plot that is real. Once the plot is set in motion, nothing can stop it – and so Oedipa finds herself in the hopeless position of having to decide whether 'there is a plot' or 'there is a plot that there is a plot' or 'there is a plot that there is a plot that there is a plot' and so on indefinitely.[23] Hence there is nothing outside the plot, since nothing could be used to confirm it that could not be used also to reject it. Everything just repeats: nothing counts as evidence that does not count also as a chance event. And so in the end, in the space of the novel's 'conclusion', nothing is resolved. Instead of resolution, there is repetition. As Thwaites points out, the final words of the text do not decide anything but only repeat the puzzle that begins as the novel's title: 'Oedipa settled back, to await the crying of lot 49.'[24]

In the space between *The Crying of Lot 49* and 'the crying of lot 49', however, other critics have found plenty of evidence for making very definite decisions about both micro and macro elements of the novel. More often than not, those decisions are based on prior decisions about the novel's author, as typified in the following remarks of Edward Mendelson:

> Pynchon writes at the end of an era in which the Freudian interpretation of an event served as a more than adequate succedanium [a substitute] for the event itself: it was an act of courage to name his heroine Oedipa [. . .] for the novel contains not even a single reference to her emotional relations with her parents or her impulses towards self-creation. The name instead refers back to the Sophoclean Oedipus who begins his search for the solution of a problem (a problem, like Oedipa's, involving a dead man) as an almost detached observer, only to discover how deeply implicated he is in what he finds.[25]

Here the novel's meaning is tied to Pynchon's 'courage', though there is 'not even a single reference' to it. Moreover, while there is 'not even a single reference' to Sophocles in the novel, this goes to show that somehow the novel is about his Oedipus and not about Freud's, to whom there is 'not even a single reference' either. So although the text is (as it were) full of absences, two of these are powerfully present. But it would seem that the present absences are separated out from the absent absences retrospectively: after Mendelson has decided what the novel is about, he then rewrites the text in order to 'find' the underlying evidence that supports that reading.

This method of reconstructing a text in line with a prior truth is common to all forms of textual analysis, including liberal humanist criticism, discussed in this chapter. This suggests that any 'radical' contribution to the study of literature by psychoanalysis and structuralism is confined to a heightened awareness of the importance of 'nonpresent' forces in the production of textual meanings. From this point of view, Mendelson's reading of *The Crying of Lot 49* does not appear 'radical' because it locates the novel's meaning in Pynchon's authorial consciousness (his 'courage'): the novel means what Pynchon meant. Therefore 'meaning' is defined in terms of what is 'present' in the text, despite (as we have seen) the absence of any evidence for it: references to Freud's and Sophocles' Oedipus alike are absent, but the latter is nonetheless present. It would not necessarily be a 'radical' reading of *The Crying of Lot 49*, however, to locate meaning somewhere else – in 'absence'. If the novel's meaning were to be found not 'in' Pynchon, but 'in' the unconscious or 'in' language, this would simply be to presentify 'nonpresence' as a determinate and determining structure of sense-production. In effect, the 'absent' irrational forces of the unconscious or the 'absent' structuring properties of language would be no less present in the novel than the absent references to Sophocles' Oedipus and Pynchon's courage.[26]

A certain version of postmodernism, as we will see in the following chapter, might conclude from this that there is nothing 'below' the surface of any text. There is no prior (authorial) or underlying (structural) source or mechanism controlling the flows of meanings between texts and recipients (or novels and readers): there is only a 'play' of textual surfaces. Instead of meaning-to-say, there is only meaning-as-play. It is not difficult to see how a text like *The Crying of Lot 49* might become canonical for this 'version' of postmodernism that often circulates as the whole truth. The lack of any unequivocal evidence for deciding whether Trystero (or Tristero – since even the very name of whatever it is that might be in question lacks solidity) is real or fictional can make *The Crying of Lot 49* look like a watershed text, an early example of an emergent 'tradition' that becomes apparent only retrospectively.[27]

But before 'Pynchon' (as the metonym of a distinctively different kind of textual performance) became synonymous with a postmodern literary canon, his reputation was already established. Published in 1978, Mendelson's edited collection of essays on his work is proof that 'Pynchon' was considered deserving of serious critical attention some time before 'postmodernism' gained currency (around the mid-1980s) as the name of a new or anti-tradition that was then able to claim 'Pynchon' as a cornerstone. Without that name being quite yet available to him, then, Mendelson was able to situate 'Pynchon' (or, for him, Pynchon) only 'at the end of an era', which was of course the modernist period dominated by the likes of T. S. Eliot, James Joyce, Virginia Woolf, Marcel Proust and Gertrude Stein. Significantly, for Mendelson, what distinguishes Pynchon from these modernist writers is his 'courageous' rejection of psychoanalysis.

Modernist literature is characterized by a loss of faith in human sensibility, which it portrayed as having been destroyed by industrialized mass culture. New mass production technologies in the 1920s enabled new cultural industries to form around the movie camera, the radio mike and the gramophone disc, homogenizing aesthetic taste and judgement in the process. Cheaper production costs meant that print culture too, in the form of newspapers, magazines, popular novels and comics (as well as works of literature, philosophy, theology, science, history and so on), was able to be widely disseminated as never before. But the increasing democratization of knowledge and art was scorned by the modernist avant-garde for devaluing authentic cultural traditions and deadening the aesthetic imagination. Modern industrial society was worthy only of disdain because it encouraged the gross reduction of art and knowledge to commodified objects and manufactured opinions for streamlined distribution to mass audiences at a quick profit. Given the very gloomy picture the modernist intellectual class painted of a world in which many people just happened to like pulp fiction, white flannel trousers and jazz music (hence its despair over the masses' critical indiscrimination), it is no wonder that modernist letters feature so many formal experiments with textual means for representing the disjunctured interiority of the modern subject. The most famous of these is stream-of-consciousness, used to express the fluidity of a character's thoughts and feelings, ideas and associations, memories and projections, as they swirl inside the mind. More generally, the typical features of the modernist literary text are its multiple points of view, discontinuous narrative, fragmentary structure, generic hybridity and absence of a moral (or authorial) centre. Together these features, these particular formalist aspects of the text, trope a world of abject alienation in which individual subjects are characterized by their 'dissociated sensibility', to use a famous term of T. S. Eliot's.[28] Akin to this notion was the general 'pathology' of culture which the new 'science' of psychoanalysis gave credit to, and so it is not surprising that (as Mendelson infers) the projects of psychoanalysis and modernist literature were highly complementary. Psychoanalysis, in other words, evolved and flourished as a vitally integral part of the modernist intellectual class, whose motto was certainly not that culture wants to be free. Indeed, only five years before James Strachey's veiled

expression of disgust at the reading habits of the poor, Eliot was lamenting the 'hollow' nature of the modern mass-conformist individual whose
cultural capital amounted only to a talent for reciting the latest popular
doggerel:

> This is the dead land
> This is cactus land [. . .]
> *Here we go round the prickly pear*
> *Prickly pear prickly pear*
> *Here we go round the prickly pear*
> *At five o'clock in the morning.*[29]

This then was the era at whose close some forty years later, supposedly, Pynchon was writing. But that is not to suggest that modernism
(or indeed any cultural period) should be understood as perfectly stable,
internally consistent and homogeneous. Such a periodization of cultural
history belongs to liberal humanist literary theory and, at least since
Foucault,[30] it can no longer be seen as anything less than problematic. So
it is not a matter of modernism having exhausted itself by the mid-1960s,
nor of postmodernism starting up with the publication of *The Crying of
Lot 49*.[31] Among other differences from the European modernists of the
1920s and '30s, Pynchon writes as an American and from within a
national literary tradition that includes Ralph Waldo Emerson, Edgar
Allan Poe, Herman Melville, Walt Whitman, Emily Dickinson and
William Faulkner. Nor is this to say that 'national' literary traditions are
unproblematic and self-contained, but simply that the European canon is
not the only game in town.

It may still be true, though, that a general questioning of the notions
of tradition and cultural value did arise in the 1960s, especially in the
United States. In this regard, Bob Dylan and The Beatles were probably
far more responsible for 'changing the world' than either poets or philosophers had ever been, at least insofar as they were able to function
within a more or less global mediascape and cultural distribution system
as 'spokespeople' for a new generation looking for a good time. The
cultural capital of that generation's intellectual class, unlike that of
modernism's, came to include its knowledge and appreciation not only of
canonical literature and philosophy, but also of Elvis records, TV shows
and Andy Warhol paintings. Its historical imagination included the 'politicizing' properties of drugs, flowers and long hair, and its social conscience was formed around the protest march, the civil rights and
women's movements, and *Rolling Stone* magazine.

But if that sounds like a list of clichés, it should not be supposed that the cultural icons and values of the modernist intellectual class are not clichéd by comparison, or that they could not be made to sound so. The point is simply that the intellectual class of today is far less internally coherent and draws on a far more diverse range of texts and backgrounds in establishing its many different kinds of cultural capital, and also interacts with an 'outside' world that is itself more disparate and less easily classified as 'mass' or 'other', than was the case with the modernist intellectual class. Insofar as this is true, it describes what has come to be understood as the 'postmodern condition'. The postmodern intellectual class, then, may be seen as radically discontinuous with its modernist predecessor, and the moment of the break might as well be located in (and as) the '1960s'. If so, then we should not overlook the influence on the formation of a postmodern intellectual class of that decade's counter-cultural revolution, even if we think of it as hot air and regardless of knowing that not every member of that class is old enough to have actually 'been there'. The importance of the revolution is discursive and whether it deserves to be called a 'revolution' is beside the point for now.[32] But there is no doubt that the Western world is more democratic – politically and culturally – today than when Eliot, Woolf and Ezra Pound were writing, which may be no thanks to them.

Nor is today's more openly democratic West attributable to the novels of Thomas Pynchon, of course, and nor should democratic progress (as the death of Louis Johnson testifies) be mistaken for completion. Nevertheless, the intellectual class of today is much more disparate than it was in the modernist era and far less dissociable from an 'outside' world. A consensual faith in the kind of differences – between say authentic and mass culture, literature and criticism, tradition and fashion, truth and opinion – that sustained European intellectuals earlier this century no longer holds, so that the postmodern intellectual is freer to indulge a more heterogeneous mix of knowledges and interests in pursuit of a career. The postmodern scholar who publishes a paper on *Batman* comics or *The X-Files*, for example, may also be a Wittgensteinian, have published on Kant or Joyce and produced 'creative' work using the latest hypertext software. Certainly there would be no reason nowadays to suppose that an academic knowledge of and interest in popular culture must preclude more traditional knowledges and interests, or that 'critical' practices preclude an aptitude for 'creative' ones and vice versa.

To the extent, then, that a rejection of psychoanalysis marks a loss of faith in underlying causal explanations of cultural phenomena, *The*

Crying of Lot 49 can be seen as a postmodern text.[33] This is not to suggest that psychoanalysis has no place within postmodernism generally or postmodern literary theory in particular (to retain that distinction for now). We will see in chapters 10 and 11, for example, that psychoanalysis is a vital (if negative) force in the emphasis on 'schizophrenia' in Deleuze and Guattari's work (though this could be a reason for regarding it as somewhat different from postmodernism); and vital also to a certain form of feminist theory. Nor should we think that postmodernism has forsaken structuralism either, if only in the sense that postmodernism would be unthinkable were it not for its acceptance of the basic Saussurean principle of the arbitrary nature of the sign, and its consequence, the differential nature of meaning. So there is no question of psychoanalysis and structuralism having been rejected out of hand by postmodern literary theory. Indeed, the merging of psychoanalytic and structuralist thinking in the work of Jacques Lacan in the 1950s and '60s turned out to be a very important move for the development of postmodernism. Lacan thought of the unconscious as being structured like a language, and I will now turn to a discussion of some of the implications of that idea for postmodern literary theory.

2

Simulation and the Sublime

Despite any scientific respectability it may have courted in the modernist era, psychoanalysis has always suffered from 'philosophy-envy'. For Freud, as Rosi Braidotti points out, 'philosophy is not just one cognitive system among others but rather the discipline which operates the hierarchical systematization of different stages of knowledge. It therefore creates conditions of possibility for the elaboration of other discourses.'[1] In a word, Freud understood that philosophy functioned as a master discourse and so his own project can appear as an attempt to usurp that status. Freud regarded philosophy (like religion) as 'neurotic' for believing in the myth of the unified subject whose self-determining sovereignty was grounded in rationality. From that perspective, philosophy is seen to deal only with those structures which are present to subjects in (and as) their rational thoughts and conceptions and to ignore the even more powerful absent structures of irrationality that undermine the subject's will to mastery. It is only psychoanalysis that understands these 'absent' structures to be actually present in the production of subjectivity, such that no subject can ever hope to achieve total self-control. Hence psychoanalysis is more 'scientific' than philosophy because it has a more seemingly 'objective' or encompassing theory of the subject, which is the object of speculation for psychoanalysis and philosophy alike.

Yet psychoanalysis is too easily discredited from science's point of view. Threatened with the loss of its authority by scientific debunking, the response of psychoanalysis has been to reinvent itself as philosophy. Such a desire to philosophize psychoanalysis (and to psychoanalyse philosophy) shows through in a famous paper of Jacques Lacan's, called 'The Insistence of the Letter in the Unconscious', which he delivered at a seminar for philosophy students in Paris in 1957. The paper is best

known within the field of Anglo-American literary studies, but its philosophical aspirations are undeniable.

Lacan's target is the rational Cartesian subject of Western philosophy,
who 'is' because he 'thinks'. In a radical challenge to Descartes' famous
Cogito ergo sum, Lacan writes: 'I am where I think not.'[2] That is to say,
the truth of subjectivity is not to be found in conscious rationality ('I think,
therefore I am', as Descartes put it)[3] but rather in the radically unthought
and unthinkable structure of the unconscious which, for Lacan, resembles
language. Based on the Saussurean principle of the sign, which is that the
relationship between the signifier (or quasi-material form) and the signified (or mental concept) is arbitrary, the structure of language for Lacan
is such that 'language' is always already cut off from 'reality'. What is
taken as the meaning (or the signified) of any word, for example, is always
going to be a result of that word's *difference* from all other words within a particular language. Meaning, then, is a result of difference, and
difference is a result of language as a *system*. In order to have a particular
meaning of any kind, there has to be a general system or structure of
differential relations within which particular meanings can arise and be
identified. Consequently the Saussurean-based theory of language (or of
signification in general) is radical because it erases 'reality' from the
system: reality is never present 'in' or 'to' the system of language and so
is never self-identical with any part of the system that acts to convey or
signify 'reality'. What is present in the system instead is only what
functions as reality. Lacan concludes from this that 'we are forced to
accept the notion of an incessant sliding of the signified under the
signifier',[4] or of reality under language or any other system of signification.

This is not to suggest – on the contrary – that the structure of language
could have been otherwise. The gap between word and thing (or sign and
referent) is a necessary one inasmuch as language can never be identical
with what it names, for example, and vice versa. Hence language must
always 'lack' what it names. Lack and division are essential to the
structure of language, the very structure in which absent reality is made
to function as if it were present. From this it follows that presence (truth,
reality, self-identity) is an effect of a system (language) that is constituted
by absence and separation. The very lack within language and the very
gap between word and thing is what makes reality possible, making it
seem present.[5]

So to say the unconscious resembles the structure of language is to
assert the power of negation, repression and absence in the production of
positive meanings. Language is full of emptiness, as it were, and that is

precisely (if paradoxically) why it is so full of excess. Because signifieds are merely the structural effects of a system of differential signifiers, language can be said to be empty: signifieds are precisely what are not in that system, though they may be of it. At the same time, signifieds are only ever arbitrarily or conventionally related to signifiers and so, in principle, any signifier can lead to an association (if only contingently) with any number of possible signifieds. An excess of signification is always possible. It is on the basis of this excess (which is based in turn on lack) that examples of stable, clear and rational signification can be identified. In the case of the story of Louis Johnson in the previous chapter, for example, it was possible to read the story 'against itself', or against my intentions, precisely because signifiers are not inextricably bound to signifieds. So the signifier 'ambulance officers' was able to be associated with the signified 'my father' on the basis of a contiguity between authority figures. It is only by repressing such an association, according to Lacan, that someone could read that story in the 'standard' way and link 'ambulance officers' to 'people in white clothes who are medically trained to transport casualties to a hospital'!

This suggests that standard readings are repressive and that what they repress are nonintentional associations or possible meanings. For Lacan, then, meaning does not reside in the Cogito but rather in what might be called the unCogito: just as linguistic meaning cannot be controlled by the intentions of any language user, so meaning of any kind cannot be controlled by rationality. Reason, no less than language, is prone to slippage. And of course it is in literature and dreams that the expression of the excessive powers of language and the unconscious is most evident. Any signifier in a dream text could have many possible signifieds, none of which has to be standard. As Terry Eagleton explains:

> If you dream of a horse, it is not immediately obvious what this signi-
> fies: it may have many contradictory meanings, may be just one of a
> whole chain of signifiers with equally multiple meanings. The image of
> the horse, that is to say, is not a sign in Saussure's sense – it does not have
> one determine[d] signified tied neatly to its tail – but is a signifier
> which may be attached to many different signifieds, and which may itself
> bear the traces of the other signifieds which surround it. (I was not aware,
> when I wrote the above sentence, of the word-play involved in 'horse'
> and 'tail': one signifier interacted with another against my conscious inten-
> tion.) The unconscious is just a continual movement and activity of
> signifiers, whose signifieds are often inaccessible to us because they are
> repressed.[6]

Similarly, no literary text can be grounded in authorial intention because language too 'is just a continual movement and activity of signifiers' that simply cannot be determined by any conscious act of meaning-to-say on the part of any person. In practice, however, the uptake within literary studies of Lacan's psycho-structuralist theory of meaning has led to the privileging of a certain kind of literary text (rather than literature in general) as the exemplary instantiation of language's excess. Not surprisingly the privileged text of Lacanian-inspired literary criticism is the one which most resembles the open, associative and discontinuous narrative structure of the dream – or the literary work that least resembles the classical realist text.

Realism, indeed, is the literary equivalent of the 'mirror stage' of human subjectivity through which Lacan claims that we enter into the 'symbolic' order. At an early age we see an image of ourselves reflected in a mirror and consequently develop a sense of subject/object, self/other relations. We recognize our mirror self as being different from our true self, although (and crucially) it is only on the basis of seeing ourselves in a mirror that we gain an understanding of a 'true' self-identity in the first place. Our sense of a true self relies, therefore, on our sense of a symbolic self, or on a sense of self-as-other: our true self is nonoriginary, in other words. Hence 'truth' depends on 'fiction', which is a proposition that is often attributed to postmodernism as a kind of slogan and used to question its political commitment. Before entering into selfhood we inhabit the 'imaginary' order of pre-linguistic, nondualistic and undifferentiated subject/object relations, since as infants we do not distinguish between notions of the self and others. In entering the symbolic order, however, we pass into a world of prohibitions and restraints organized through and as language, reason and society, all of which are dominated by patriarchal law. On this model it is possible to see the imaginary and symbolic orders as collecting terms for sets of associated oppositions along the following lines:

imaginary	symbolic
infant	adult
feminine	masculine
sensory	sensible
intuitive	rational
private	public
pre-Oedipal	Oedipal
holistic	dualistic

true   false
prior   post

In terms of a system of literary values and classifications, the Lacanian imaginary/symbolic opposition is organized around the following binary pairs:

poetry   prose
lyric   epic
romance   narrative
metafiction realism
aphorism   essay
parody   irony
art   theory
creativity criticism

From this it can be seen that Lacanian-style literary criticism is on the side of anti-linear, nonclosural, self-conscious(ly) literary texts. The privileging of a certain order of literary textuality is consistent with Lacan's transcendental celebration of the macrological order of the imaginary, such that the values of romance literature, for example, can be read off from the list of terms on the left-hand side of the imaginary/ symbolic opposition above. Hence romance literature is infantile (or childlike), feminine, sensory, intuitive and so on, while realism is by contrast adult, masculine, sensible, rational and so forth. This same structure of correspondence enables poetry and aphoristic texts to be associated with pre-Oedipal subjectivity and truth, and collects theory and criticism under the secondary or 'post-al' values associated with Oedipal repression and dissemblage or the lack of truth. Lacanian literary criticism has to be seen, in other words, as an analytical system generated by and subordinate to a macrological system of values, interests and judgements of a general order, although this relation is by no means confined to literary criticism inspired by Lacan. As social theory, nevertheless, this general system of values is highly speculative and produces some very odd results: while the feminine is on the side of truth, for example, it is also on the side of the infantile, and it is difficult to see how this association differs from the routine ways in which women and children are often collected as a single class in need of men's protection or from the kind of bigotry that constructs women as physically, emotionally and intellectually inferior to men.

But of course it could be objected that Lacan's philosophical speculations on the structure of the unCogito should not be mistaken for social theory, and so any reference to the feminine is not to be confused with women in society. The feminine is simply one form of a whole category of repressed or forgotten structures of meaning-production or ways of being (generalized as the imaginary) that cannot be reduced to socio-biological equivalents. In support of this objection, many feminist theorists continue to be influenced by Lacan's ideas and this would seem hardly possible if his theory were in fact reducible to the vulgar prejudice that men think and women feel. On the other hand, as the feminist literary and psychoanalytic theorist Shoshana Felman writes:

> Contrary to received opinion, Lacan's preoccupation is not with theory per se (with games of 'intellectualization'), but always with his practice as a psychoanalytical clinician. He is first and foremost a practitioner, who happens to be thinking about what he is doing in his practice. His *theory* is nothing other than his training practice – his practice as an educator, a training analyst who introduces others to the pragmatic questions of the practice.[7]

On the evidence of Felman's account at any rate, it is possible for feminism to regard Lacanian theory as important and helpful precisely because it does seek to explain the pragmatic complexities of socio-biological men and women. Since it comes out of his empirical, hands-on experience as a practising clinician, Lacan's theory is more scientific than philosophical, more explanatory than speculative. But in that case one might continue to wonder why its alignment of intuition and infancy with the feminine so closely resembles routine sexist assumptions about women.

It may not be the 'philosophy' but the banality of psychoanalysis that is most striking. Moreover, if Lacanian theory (and psychoanalysis generally) appears complicit with banal sexism, it may also be complicit with banal romanticism. The imaginary/symbolic opposition that organizes the Lacanian value system can be seen as reproducing not only an unsophisticated distinction between 'sentimental' women and 'rational' men, but also the crude antinomy of Romantic imagination versus Enlightenment reason.

According to the French philosophers Philippe Lacoue-Labarthe and Jean-Luc Nancy, 'romanticism' is both an inadequate name and an unfinished project. For them it has no historical use-by date and cannot be relegated to a superseded past because 'it "leads" us first of all to ourselves.'[8] If so, then it may not be saying very much to claim Lacan's imaginary/symbolic opposition as a romantic inheritance since nothing would seem to be 'post-romantic' if romanticism is understood as not yet over. But in terms of how 'romanticism' circulates, as opposed to some notion of the 'truth' about romanticism (even if that truth is that 'romanticism' is an imperfect name), it may still be the case that Lacanian theory is able to be described accurately as romantic. Even if the accuracy of that description does depend on the 'inaccuracy' of (mis)understandings that circulate on behalf of romanticism, this would not make the description inaccurate. Indeed, if the positive value of an accurate description turned out to depend on the nonpositive or illicit value of an inaccurate understanding, this would be perfectly consistent with Lacan's theory of the dependence of rationality and presence on irrationality and absence as exemplified in the structures of language and the unconscious. It would be consistent also with psychoanalytic theory generally and with structuralism.

Focusing on Lacan's theory for now, though, suppose we were to think of 'romanticism' as a set of narratives or texts conveyed through language. I do not mean only the texts that were written by accredited Romantic poets and philosophers in the late eighteenth and early nineteenth centuries in Europe, but the texts of all the statements about, commentaries on and interpretations of something called 'romanticism' or 'romantic' regardless of whether it names an aesthetic or a philosophical movement, a cultural epoch or simply an attitude, and irrespective of when the statements, commentaries and interpretations were produced. These statements and so on – these texts – are not confined only to those that have been made already, but include any such texts that might be produced in the future. In this sense the argument of Lacoue-Labarthe and Nancy is a romantic text: it is one of the signifieds of 'romanticism'. At the very least, in other words, 'romanticism' is a signifier. As with any signifier, there is no natural or predetermined signified attached to it. Whatever 'romanticism' signifies, then, is always going to have to be textual since it must always occur in the symbolic realm. Any truth about romanticism will always be symbolic: it will never be 'really' true and imaginary. It will never be really true because any signified of 'romanticism' will itself be another signifier, another statement, commentary or interpretation – another text. This is so because all signifieds are, in a strict sense, signifiers. Say, for example, someone did not know what 'signified' signifies or, more generally, that they did not know what 'signified' means, and so I were to give as its meaning that it signifies 'the mental concept of the sign'. Strictly, what I would have given is another signifier, since 'the mental concept of the sign' is not automatically or naturally meaningful: its meaning is not pregiven. At the limit, 'the mental concept of the sign' comprises at least six signifiers (the words 'the mental concept of the sign'), which is to ignore the grammatical signifiers that enable 'the mental concept of the sign' to signify and the contextual signifiers through which 'the mental concept of the sign' could signify many different things. To get to the meaning or truth of any signifier, in other words, we have to use other signifiers. Hence we can never quite get to 'the' meaning or 'the' truth at all: what we do instead is slide from signifier to signifier, potentially without end.

Now this does not mean that in the pragmatic course of our lives we never exchange what functions as meaning. But it does mean that anything which functions as a meaning does so on account of repression. It means that for 'the mental concept of the sign' to function as the signified of the signifier 'signified', the possibility that it could function as the signified of another signifier has to be repressed. Moreover, if the preceding sentence appears awkward or infelicitous at the level of syntax (or the signifier), so that its meaning is not immediately clear and lucid at the level of semantics (or the signified), this may only demonstrate Lacan's point that language and the unconscious do not produce coherent and fully congruous texts. While some sentences (here or elsewhere) can indeed appear more obviously 'difficult' than others, the possible meaning-effects of even simple sentences are no less excessive than for complex ones. Hence there is no sentence (or no sign) that could be predetermined to signify only one thing, which is of course a commonplace understanding with respect to literary texts. Lacan's point, then, is that literary language is not quite as special as it usually seems, for all language is fundamentally 'literary' in the sense of having to be associative rather than deterministic (or referential). Even the most scientific or legalistic text can be read aberrantly or misread totally, and it is only by virtue of this possibility that it could ever be understood to have been read correctly. In other words, the 'correct' reading of any text is grounded in a repression of possible alternative or incorrect readings, just as our 'true' self-identity depends on seeing an image of ourselves reflected in a mirror that we recognize as alien or other to us. Self-recognition is based, therefore, on misrecognition, just as reading is based on misreading. And since every act of recognition and every act of reading occurs in the symbolic realm, we can say that all recognitions are actually misrecognitions and all readings are misreadings. Linguistically, everything we say and write is a structural effect of uncontrollable word-play or slippage, and psychoanalytically everything is a Freudian slip, an instance of what Freud called 'parapraxis'.[9] The radical import of Lacan's psycho-structuralist theory, in short, is that it regards the irruption of 'repressed' (aberrant, unintended, counter or nonsensical) meanings not as a special or extraordinary event, and certainly not as a 'mistake', but as the most mundane occurrence imaginable. Because Lacan refutes the rationality of the Cartesian subject, his theory of the unCogito is committed to the utter banality of irrational, nonintentional, nonsensical 'meanings' as an everyday matter of course.

Lacan's insistence on the banality of nonsense, however, is not quite the measure of his importance to literary studies. On the contrary, the literary critical uptake of Lacanian theory has focused on the 'exceptionality' of a certain kind of linguistic performance, a certain kind of literature, as described earlier. This is clear from the influence of Lacan's ideas on 'French' feminism generally and on feminist literary theory in particular, especially in the work of Julia Kristeva. In *Desire in Language* (based on her published papers from 1969–77) Kristeva presents her theory and practice of what she calls 'semanalysis', a project linking Saussurean semiotics and Lacanian psychoanalysis with the aim of developing a general theory of the otherness or the 'uncanniness' of human subjectivity and meaning. In the Preface to that book she writes as follows on the question of what comprises the *object* of semanalysis:

> I envisioned [. . .] this analytical project as having to be made up of the *specific object* it needed to assign itself in order to emphasize the limits of a positivist knowledge of language and to induce research, harried by the specificity that the subject of the theory believes it can detect in that object, to attempt to modify its very theoretical apparatus. That uncanny object, pre-text and foil, weak link in human sciences and fascinating otherness for philosophy, is none other than art in general, modern art and literature even more particularly.[10]

Despite its presentation as a radically ambitious project, then, Kristevan semanalysis proceeds from a very familiar assumption: that art and literature are the highest forms of cultural expression. This assumption is perfectly consistent with the values of the modernist intellectual class discussed in the previous chapter, especially since it is avant-garde art and literature that Kristeva privileges above all other forms of aesthetic production.

So it is interesting that Kristeva the literary theorist turned psychoanalyst (some years after gaining her doctorate in literary studies, she took a degree in psychoanalysis and continues to combine her work as a practising therapist with her academic career) should more recently have tried her hand as a novelist. Her first novel, *The Samurai*, was published in 1990 (English translation, 1992). In an interview about her turn to fiction writing, which is included in one of her recent critical works, Kristeva responds to a question on the relations between therapy and literature:

> I felt that I could not continue listening to the novelty and the violence that my patients brought me – without reducing them to what I already knew or to what books written before had said – unless I chanced my own lot. A way of jeopardizing oneself is to reveal oneself by means of a fiction that shows facets of that private depth on the basis of which I understand others, their sorrow, their perverseness, their desire for death, which are in collusion with mine. For me, at the time of *The Samurai*, the novel was a prerequisite for continuing to have a live, interventive listening, one that would be receptive to changes in patients and their symptoms. Thus understood, fiction amounts to a rebirth of the analyst's very personality, a new awakening of her unconscious that ventures beyond sublimation and gives new life to her interpretative capability.[11]

As this is probably not the sort of thing that Stephen King would say, we need to see that Kristeva has a fairly specific sense in mind of what she means by 'fiction'. The signified of her 'fiction' is clearly not 'a rollicking good story written for entertainment, with an eye on Hollywood', but something closer to the signifieds of 'avant-garde writing', either in a positive sense of the self-theorizing or self-analysing text or pejoratively as precious and defiantly anti-popular.

There are several points to be noted from this. First, Kristeva's celebration of 'experimental' literature as the ultimate realization of what she calls 'the uncanny' quality and force of language and desire situates her work within a modernist tradition, which goes to show that modernism is not reducible to a historical period. Secondly, the notion of putting oneself at risk ('jeopardizing oneself') by means of writing fiction presumes that the self is as much an experiment as the text, which is consistent with Lacan's theory of the linguistic (or, more broadly, semiotic) structure of the unconscious. Thirdly, though, if Kristeva's work, while remaining modernist in some senses, can be seen also to break with the modernist tradition, then the break occurs in her positive lack of recognition of an absolute distinction between critical and creative practices. Her merging of therapy and theory, her blending of psychoanalysis and semiotics, her insistence on the self-consciousness and self-creativity of theory as well as of art and literature, and her identification of the self as a text of experimental fiction all combine to produce a body of work (a career or an agenda) that cannot be separated into primary and secondary, imaginative and analytical, creative and critical parts.

But this does not mean that Kristeva's experimental project is therefore radical and postmodern, since it may simply be neo-romantic and banal. This might be to rethink 'postmodernism' generally as a misnomer for 'neo-romanticism',[12] which could be to think of its conditions of possibility in terms of narratives of recovery and continuity rather than of rupture and change. For example, without claiming Lacan's work as postmodern, we should not suppose that the Lacanian critique of so-called Cartesian dualism is indebted only to Freudian psychoanalysis for having problematized the 'rational' subject. Nor should it be supposed that Kristeva's creative 'writing' subject is indebted only to Lacanian psycho-structuralism for having theorized the unconscious in terms of a language. The challenge to Descartes well and truly predates Freud, while the trope of radical risk associated with submitting oneself to the unknown powers of the creative imagination goes back far earlier than the modernist theory of the unconscious and the modernist science of language (or structuralism). In 1817, for instance, the English Romantic poet and theorist Samuel Taylor Coleridge wrote, in direct opposition to Descartes, 'I am, because I affirm myself to be; I affirm myself to be, because I am.'[13] This does not have to mean that Lacan (or Freud) was directly influenced by Coleridge, though it may support Lacoue-Labarthe and Nancy's claim of romanticism's incompletion (if not of the romantic project's very structure of incompleteness) such that even today everyone is still a 'romantic'. Moreover, the infusion of art and life associated with romantic poetry and projected as a risk both to society and to the poet himself or herself, is encapsulated for Lacoue-Labarthe and Nancy in the following statement from a letter written in the 1790s by Dorothea Schlegel, wife of the German Romantic philosopher Friedrich Schlegel: 'Since it is altogether contrary to bourgeois order and absolutely forbidden to introduce romantic poetry into life, then let life be brought into romantic poetry; no police force and no educational institution can prevent this.'[14] Such desire for a fusion of opposites (poetry and life), especially in defiance of the institutions of social normalization, may be seen to be repeated in Kristeva's desire to fuse theory and therapy and therapy and fiction in terms of plumbing a 'private depth' which is inaccessible to the Oedipalized, repressed, symbolic world order.

Further instances of the Romantic anticipation of psychoanalytic and structuralist principles and promises abound. Two examples will suffice for now. Keeping in mind Kristeva's claims for fiction – that it results in a 'rebirth' of the analyst and a 'new awakening' of her unconscious, giving 'new life' to the analytical process – it is worth comparing the claims made by Percy Shelley for the national literature of his day. In 'A Defence of Poetry', published in 1821, he writes:

> For the literature of England, an energetic development of which has ever preceded or accompanied a great and free development of the national will, has arisen as it were from a new birth. In spite of the low-thought envy which would undervalue contemporary merit, our own will be a memorable age in intellectual achievements, and we live among such philosophers and poets as surpass beyond comparison any who have appeared since the last national struggle for civil and religious liberty.[15]

Time has proven Shelley right, for the Romantic period in Europe, very roughly dating from the 1760s to the 1860s or so, certainly did produce many outstanding writers and thinkers. Among them are the English poets John Keats, William Wordsworth, William Blake, Lord Byron, Coleridge and Shelley himself; the essayists William Hazlitt and Charles Lamb; and the writers Mary Shelley, Thomas Love Peacock, Ann Radcliffe, Jane Austen, Thomas de Quincey, Emily Brontë and Horace Walpole. The major French Romantics include the novelists Honoré de Balzac, Stendhal, Victor Hugo and Gustave Flaubert; the poets Charles Baudelaire, François de Chateaubriand and Stephane Mallarmé; the cultural critic, Madame de Stael; the writer and libertine, Marquis de Sade; and the philosopher and raconteur, Jean-Jacques Rousseau. But it is probably the German Romantics, especially the philosophers, who deserve the most credit for having self-consciously theorized (if not idealized) the principles of romanticism in art and life. The term 'romantic' was first used by the German poet and dramatist Johann Wolfgang von Goethe in an essay of 1830 and later came to be applied to a short-lived but highly influential 'school' of literary philosophy at the city of Jena in southern Germany in the mid-1790s. It is the Jena Romantics (who never identified themselves as a movement and whose ideas and careers went in many different directions after 1800) whose work forms the basis of Lacoue-Labarthe and Nancy's study of the emergence of *literary theory* as the central and abiding concern of romanticism in general. As it happens, the most famous members of the group at Jena, which was very loosely organized around an experimental sexual and social morality that was meant to reflect the ideas of the group's journal, *Athenaeum*, all had the given name of Friedrich: Schlegel, Schleiermacher, Schelling and Novalis. As well as the philosophers 'Friedrich', the major German Romantics include the philosophers Arthur Schopenhauer and Johann Gottfried Herder, as well as the poets Friedrich Hölderlin, Heinrich Heine, Friedrich Schiller and of course Goethe.

However partial and problematic, that is quite an impressive list of names. Without suggesting they all held exactly the same views about everything (or even anything), it would be uncontroversial to argue that the names appearing in the previous paragraph belong together as markers of a common approach to the nature and value of literature. That approach, which Lacoue-Labarthe and Nancy claim is what characterizes romanticism as radical and incomplete, can be summed up as the acceptance of the always already *theoretical* nature of the literary text. Hence 'literature' (in its modern sense) and literary theory come into being at one and the same time: for romanticism, literature and the theory of literature are inseparable. This is especially true of the Jena Romantics but also of the English Romantics who came after them, as typified in the following remarks of Shelley which can be reapplied to Kristeva's comments on the contiguity of therapy and fiction:

> All things exist as they are perceived; at least in relation to the percipient. 'The mind is its own place, and of itself can make a heaven of hell, a hell of heaven.' But poetry defeats the curse which binds us to be subjected to the accident of surrounding impressions [. . .]. It makes us the inhabitants of a world to which the familiar world is a chaos. It reproduces the common universe of which we are portions and percipients, and it purges from our inward sight the film of familiarity which obscures from us the wonder of our being. It compels us to feel that which we perceive, and to imagine that which we know. It creates anew the universe, after it has been annihilated in our minds by the recurrence of impressions blunted by reiteration.[16]

For Shelley, then, poetry 'creates anew the universe' because it transforms the world, defined as 'the accident of surrounding impressions [. . .] blunted by reiteration', into a product of the sublime imagination. For Kristeva, in the same way, fiction 'gives new life' to the 'very personality' and the 'interpretative capability' of the writer-analyst whose imaginative work 'ventures beyond sublimation' or beyond the social injunction to repress so-called natural instincts. In a word, poetry and fiction are sublime because they lead to a higher truth about the self: poetry 'purges from our inward sight the film of familiarity which obscures from us the wonder of our being', while through fiction one can 'reveal oneself' as a universal ethical subject whose own feelings of 'sorrow', 'perverseness' and 'desire for death' are 'in collusion' with those of others.

According to the great eighteenth-century German philosopher Immanuel Kant, in opposition to whose ideas the Romantic period is often (wrongly) defined, the sublime is an order of judgement. The sublime, as distinct from the beautiful or the horrible, is not to be found in nature, but in the mind. While the sublime is both 'universally valid' and 'independent of interest',[17] the analytical process by which anything is judged to be sublime is a cultural achievement, not a natural a priori condition. Hence the universal and disinterested sublime is always a product of particular cultural interests: a stormy sea, for example, may be produced as sublime – and therefore universal and disinterested – in the mind of someone (the English Romantic painter J. M. W. Turner, say) whose cultural stock of images of the beautiful and the horrible includes 'the stormy sea' as an example of powerful forces, objects or events that induce powerful feelings of fear, delight or grandeur. In a heightened act of critical judgement, 'a' stormy sea can then be understood to express the *idea* of 'the' stormy sea and hence be sublime. But for a culture that looked upon storms at sea only as fishing hazards, a stormy sea could never be sublime.

In this sense of the sublime, the transcendental values of poetry and fiction as idealized by Shelley and Kristeva have to be seen as outcomes of a particular interest, a particular history of ideas. The idea that poetry shows us 'the wonder of our being' and that fiction is revealing of the self, in other words, has a history. If the argument of Lacoue-Labarthe and Nancy is accepted, that history is the history of romanticism. As they put it:

> romanticism implies something entirely new, the *production* of something entirely new. The romantics never really succeed in naming this something: they speak of poetry, of the work, of the novel, or [. . .] of romanticism. In the end, they decide to call it – all things considered – *literature*. This term, which was not their own invention, will be adopted by posterity (including their own, most immediate posterity) to designate a concept – a concept that may still be undefinable today, but which the romantics took great pains to delimit. They, in any case, will approach it explicitly as a new *genre*, beyond the divisions of classical (or modern) poetics and capable of resolving the inherent ('generic') divisions of the written thing. Beyond divisions and all de-finition, this *genre* is thus programmed in romanticism

as *the* genre of *literature*: the genericity, so to speak, and generativity of literature, grasping and producing themselves in an entirely new, infinitely new Work. The *absolute*, therefore, of literature. But also its *ab-solute*, its isolation in its perfect closure upon itself (upon its own organicity) [. . .].[18]

It is possible to see this literary work of the imagination as a macro-category that produces the sub-orders of the psychoanalytic work of the unconscious and the structuralist work of language. Hence the romantic 'poem' becomes the psychoanalytic 'dream' and the structuralist 'text'. In the dream, psychoanalysis finds the unconscious to be actively at work, in production – just as structuralism finds language to be productively at work in 'the text'. In a famous essay by the French semiotician and narratologist Roland Barthes (an essay that marks a turn towards a 'later', poststructuralist, Barthes), a definition of 'the text' emerges in opposition to 'the work':

> The Text is not to be thought of as an object that can be computed. It would be futile to try to separate out materially works from texts. In particular, the tendency must be avoided to say that the work is classic, the text is avant-garde; it is not a question of drawing up a crude honours list in the name of modernity and declaring certain literary productions 'in' and others 'out' by virtue of their chronological situation: there may be 'text' in a very ancient work, while many products of contemporary literature are in no way texts. The difference is this: the work is a fragment of substance, occupying a part of the space of books (in a library for example), the Text is a methodological field. The opposition may recall (without at all reproducing term for term) Lacan's distinction between 'reality' and 'the real': the one is displayed, the other demonstrated; like-wise, the work can be seen (in bookshops, in catalogues, in exam sylla-buses), the text is a process of demonstration, speaks according to certain rules (or against certain rules); the work can be held in the hand, the text is held in language, only exists in the movement of a discourse (or rather, it is Text for the very reason that it knows itself as text); the Text is not the decomposition of the work, it is the work that is the imaginary tail of the Text; or again, *the Text is experienced only in an activity of production*. It follows that the Text cannot stop (for example on a library shelf); its constitutive movement is that of cutting across (in particular, it can cut across the work, several works).[19]

Like the Romantic Poem, the Barthesian Text is both self-conscious and pro-ductive. It knows itself as text and so cannot be approached as an inanimate object but only as a producing subject. While the producing subject of the work is the author, the producing subject of the text is the text 'itself'. However, there is no pure 'itself' of the text, for like the authorial producing subject the text cannot be confined to a point, since it occupies a 'field', and cannot be described as static but only in terms of a 'movement'. This movement of the text, moreover, is never linear but always involves a 'cutting across', just as the authorial producing subject could be said to cut across many different fields or categories (father or mother, husband or wife, son or daughter, lover, gardener, sports fan, writer, humanitarian, Marxist, philanderer and so on) in the many different movements of his or her subjectivity.

But in so defining the Text as *an activity of production* that is endless, Barthes may be drawing not only on the more immediate influences of the psychoanalytic work of the unconscious and the structuralist work of language. He may be searching for another 'new' name after the manner described by Lacoue-Labarthe and Nancy of the romantic effort to name 'the *production* of something entirely new [. . .] an entirely new, infinitely new Work', which they call the literary absolute. If so, then one form of the distinction Barthes makes in this essay could be the difference between the 'answering' work and the 'questioning' text. The text that never stops producing itself as textuality (defined as its self-knowing subjectivity), in other words, is the text that never ceases to be a question, that is inexhaustibly questioning and questionable. While there is little question that such a theory of the text is indebted to the psychoanalytic theory of the inexhaustibility of unconscious meaning and the structuralist theory of the inexhaustibility of cultural meaning, the unacknowledged debt (in all cases) is to the romantic theory of literature as the *question* of literature. For romanticism, that is to say, the world as experienced through the faculty of the imagination is full of wondrous enigmatic things that can in no way be reduced to objects but which are what they are, like a poem or some other work of literature, only as the sublime *question* of what they are. Their true nature is that their true nature, like the true nature of literature, remains forever out of reach of rational, scientific or pragmatic systems of calculation and knowledge. Their true nature, as exemplified by the nature of the literary text in general and the poem in particular, is that their nature is to *be* a question. So, for example, it is *as* a question that a Grecian urn is addressed in a poem, published in 1820, by Keats:

> What leaf-fringed legend haunts about thy shape
>   Of deities or mortals, or of both,
>   In Tempe or the dales of Arcady?

> What men or gods are these? What maidens loth?
> What mad pursuit? What struggle to escape?
> What pipes and timbrels? What wild ecstasy?[20]

In the poem, then, Keats's urn poses the question of itself as a question. But if the urn's nature is to be a sublime enigma, that nature is provided by and in the text, and as the text, of the poem. Whatever the urn signifies is a consequence therefore of the *poem* as signifier. It is the 'poemness' of the poem, its textuality, that supplies a meaning for the urn and produces its essentially esoteric nature. Hence the urn is occultized – semiotized, made significant – by a textual process, which could be described romantically as an effect of the sublime imagination. Through his imaginative identification with the urn, Keats creates the urn anew: as a poem, as text. And in this re-signified capacity the urn cannot be explained or understood according to any system of rational logic, or even any system of thought in the broadest sense, for the urn as poem 'dost tease us out of thought'. The absolute truth of the urn, and of the poem, is something that has to be felt, that is wordless, imageless, beyond thought and language. But this 'wordless' truth exists only in and as the words of the poem, so that the nature of the absolute truth is in fact the nature of the literary absolute, a ceaseless movement of the text. Any attempt to demystify the urn by explaining it would be a betrayal of that absolute truth, the truth of the question of literature, and so the poem ends by reaffirming and exemplarizing the urn's positively abstract nature, the knowledge of which is absolute because it cannot be exchanged, which is the only thing worth knowing:

> When old age shall this generation waste,
>   Thou shalt remain, in midst of other woe
> Than ours, a friend to man, to whom thou say'st,
> 'Beauty is truth, truth beauty,' – that is all
>   Ye know on earth, and all ye need to know.

According to this reading of Keats's ode, the reading is not something that has been brought to the poem from somewhere outside but is argued to be contained by the poem as an inseparable aspect of its literary absoluteness. If this can be said to define the poem as a self-theorizing text, such that any commentary 'on' it is also always 'of' the poem, inhabiting its poemness, its textuality, and if this order of poetry can be said to be new by comparison to previous, non-self-conscious poetry, then we may agree (for now) with Lacoue-Labarthe and Nancy that the literature of the Romantic period is by definition theoretical. Hence, more generally, the romantic theory of literature can be seen to under-write Barthes' theory of the text as a key concept of postmodern literary theory. Barthes' 'text', however, remains in opposition to 'the work' and is defined therefore as a special category of semiotic performance which romanticism calls 'literature'. But for postmodernism the features of Barthes' text are not confined to a special (sublime) order of signification: they are typical of signification in general, so that what Barthes calls 'the work' is always already *textual* in his own terms.

Now: once the text is generalized beyond limit, as soon as everything becomes text, then what was understood previously as special becomes ordinary. Once the romantic theory of literature (as an important ana-logue of the psychoanalytic theory of the unconscious and the structur-alist theory of language) takes over as the theory of everything, so that there is no longer any specialness attaching to literature because every-thing is literary in the sense of being textual now, then there is no longer any possibility of the sublime. In its place, there is only simulation.

This is the view of the French cultural theorist Jean Baudrillard, whose name is virtually synonymous with 'postmodernism'. Indeed, if Baudrillard is right, then his name could never be anything other than 'virtually synonymous' (which would be its essence), given that virtuality has taken over from actuality in the endless precession not of signs, but of simulacra, that characterizes the postmodern version of the real which he terms the 'hyperreal'. Baudrillard's most explicit theorization of the 'hyperreality' that defines the postmodern experience is provided in his short book, *Simulations*, published in 1983. We will need to discuss this book more closely in the following chapter, but here I want to focus briefly on the final order of what Baudrillard calls 'the four successive phases of the image'. These phases have to do with the sign or image's successive distancing from the object of representation (or referent), so that the sign moves through the following stages of signification and value:

- it is the reflection of a basic reality
- it masks and perverts a basic reality
- it masks the *absence* of a basic reality
- it bears no relation to any reality whatever: it is its own pure simulacrum.[21]

Baudrillard's argument is that reality no longer appears as such, but rather has *become* its appearances. Social knowledge nevertheless contin-ues to be based on the reality (or the presence) of the real, because the function of the postmodern sign is to disguise the fact that reality is no longer with us. Hence the third-order sign, which conceals the *absence* of reality, is intimately connected to the final order or the real truth of the postmodern sign: that there is no reality outside the sign, or outside simulation. He gives the example of Disneyland, which is 'there to conceal the fact that it is the [...] "real" America'.[22] The fantastic appearance of Disneyland functions to make the rest of America seem real, as if there were still some way of distinguishing between appearance and reality. But in fact, for Baudrillard, there is not. Reality (as what can be distinguished from its signs) has disappeared and in its place there are only the signs and systems, the simulacra, of its (dis)simulation. Disneyland is not a fantastic funhouse cut off from real America: it is the very origin of the possibility of the appearance of America as 'real' in a postmodern world. 'It is meant to be an infantile world, in order to make us believe that the adults are elsewhere, in the "real" world, and to conceal the fact that real childishness is everywhere, particularly amongst those adults who go there to act the child in order to foster illusions as to their real childishness.'[23] Disneyland, then, is both a third-order sign and a simulacrum of the highest order, making it also completely ordinary.

It is not hard to imagine why this theory has been enormously seductive for literary studies. Once Barthes' theory of textuality turns into (or gets displaced by) Baudrillard's theory of simulation, the romantic theory of literature can be seen as having arrived at the status of a master discourse. At such a moment the romantic reconciliation of opposites turns into the postmodern transcendence of binaries, and suddenly there are no longer any differences between the imaginary and the symbolic, true and false, reading and writing, text and outside-text, literature and literary theory. And so we find that the postmodern 'novel' (or the postmodern fictional text), twenty-five years after *The Crying of Lot 49* and over a century-and-a-half after 'Ode on a Grecian Urn', comes to include not simply an immanent form of self-analysis but a style of commentary that is explicitly literary critical, or literary theoretical, through and through. An example is the following passage from a work of fiction by Kathy Acker, *Empire of the Senseless* (1988), which appears a part of a story being told by the narrator, Thivai, of his cyborg lover, Abhor:

The German Romantics had to destroy the same bastions as we do. Logocentrism and idealism, theology, all supports of the repressive society.

Property's pillars. Reason which always homogenizes and reduces, re-presses and unifies phenomena or actuality into what can be perceived and so controlled. The subjects, us, are now stable and socializable. Reason is always in the service of the political and economic masters. It is here that literature strikes, at this base, where the concepts and actings of order impose themselves. Literature is that which denounces and slashes apart the repressing machine at the level of the signified. Well before Bataille, Kleist, Hoffmann etc., made trial of Hegelian idealism, of the cloturing dialectic of recognition: the German Romantics sung brazenly brassily in brass of spending and waste. They cut through conservative narcissism with bloody razor blades. They tore the subject away from her subjugation to her self, the proper; dislocated you the puppet; cut the threads of meaning; spit at all mirrors which control.[24]

In terms of a simple content analysis, it may be noticed that there are many words and expressions in this passage that look out of place. 'Logocentrism', for example, is a term associated with the French phi-losopher Jacques Derrida, some of whose ideas I begin to discuss in chapter 5. Acker's text, however, is a work of fiction, in which (according to a certain theory of aesthetics) one does not expect to find specialist philosophical terms of the order of 'logocentrism', 'Hegelian idealism' and 'the cloturing dialectic of recognition'. So one effect of the appear-ance of these signifiers in *Empire of the Senseless* may be to interrogate the whole system of oppositions organized around a notion of the abso-lute difference between 'creative' and 'critical', 'fiction' and 'theory'. If that system was still very much in place for modernism, its attempted undoing (via concepts of the text and of simulation) is one of the most significant features of postmodernism and probably one of the most convincing reasons for considering this particular version of the post to be justified in having a marker of its own identity. In the following chapter, however, I want to discuss the various ways in which that 'post' may not be quite as legitimate as suggested by a text like *Empire of the Senseless*. My discussion will be based on the seemingly very loose theory of history underpinning the passage above, and which is present also in (and as) Baudrillard's theory of simulation. Hence the following chapter will address the vexed question of 'the death of history' that so often accounts (positively and pejoratively) for the truth about postmodernism, especially as applied to the work of Jean-François Lyotard, whose name is also virtually synonymous with 'the post'.

3

The Death of History

'History' is another very complex signifier with many meanings. While history as such cannot be 'dead' (any more than it can be 'alive'), it is possible to suppose that history as a *sign* has lost all meaning and that it no longer refers to anything outside itself, having been divided or become indistinguishable from its referents. In a word, 'the death of history' does not refer to the death of *history* but rather to the 'death' of 'history' as a sign. For signs to have any referential value they must exist under certain historical conditions, according to Baudrillard: conditions that, for him, no longer hold. In the absence of those conditions – in the absence of history – there can no longer be any signs, only simulacra.

On this model 'history' is a transcendental signifier: the sign of signs. Once emptied, it causes all other signs to be made empty too. This is because 'history' is not only a sign among signs, but also the immaterial stuff of which the signifier/signified relationship acquires a cultural (or a contextual) rather than a purely formal sense, what might be called the spirit as against the letter of the sign's meaning. Things that we call cultural values and institutions (love and marriage, for example) do not make only formal sense, if they make any formal sense at all. But the many different kinds and practices of 'loving' and 'being married' do make sense: they make sense culturally, though very often in ways that are quite incommensurable across different and within single cultures. This is why, if history were dead, Shakespeare's plays would be indistinguishable from other dramatic texts except in terms of structural or systemic variations. In this way 'Shakespeare' would be emptied of the values inhering in that name now. It is also why there tends to be a lot of resistance generally and from within specialist communities to any new practice, invention or movement that either promotes or necessitates breaking with tradition. Hence the widespread moral panics around the inventions of the electric light bulb, the telephone, television and, more recently, the home computer. Each of these new technologies points only to the future in the present, seemingly at the expense of breaking with the past. Within aesthetic traditions, too, 'new' kinds of textual practice enter the world as threats to 'the' established order of aesthetic values – and so impressionism in art and stream-of-consciousness in literature provoked as much scorn as excitement at different times, just as romantic poetry did for having broken so defiantly with the classicist tradition.

One way that romantic poetry defined its iconoclasm is best expressed by the English poet William Wordsworth, writing in the famous Preface to the second edition (1801) of his *Lyrical Ballads* which had appeared originally two years earlier:

> The Reader will find that personifications of abstract ideas rarely occur in these volumes; and are utterly rejected, as an ordinary device to elevate the style, and raise it above prose. My purpose was to imitate, and, as far as possible, to adopt the very language of men; and assuredly such personifications do not make any natural or regular part of that language. They are, indeed, a figure of speech occasionally prompted by passion, and I have made use of them as such; but have endeavoured utterly to reject them as a mechanical device of style, or as a family language which Writers in metre seem to lay claim to by prescription. I have wished to keep the Reader in the company of flesh and blood, persuaded that by doing so I shall interest him. [. . .] There will also be found in these volumes little of what is usually called poetic diction; as much pains has been taken to avoid it as is ordinarily taken to produce it; this has been done for the reason already alleged, to bring my language near to the language of men; and further, because the pleasure which I have proposed to myself to impart, is of a very different kind from that which is supposed by many persons to be the proper object of poetry. Without being culpably particular, I do not know how to give my Reader a more exact notion of the style in which it was my wish and intention to write, than by informing him that I have at all times endeavoured to look steadily at my subject; consequently, there is I hope in these Poems little falsehood of description, and my ideas are expressed in language fitted to their respective importance.[1]

The romantic project, then, as announced here by Wordsworth, is to reinvent poetry from the bottom up, or from the inside out. The abstractions of the mind, couched in a specialist diction, must be replaced with passionate sensations expressed in ordinary language. In a famous statement, for Wordsworth 'all good poetry is the spontaneous overflow of powerful feelings.'[2] This is the origin of those calls for art to become 'relevant' to 'the people' as heard frequently this century and exemplified in the Workers' Art, Photography and Film schemes of various trade union groups. But in truth the 'men' whose language Wordsworth wanted poetry to imitate comprised a very specific class, and in two senses: it was not the language of men, but the language of *rustics* on which poetic diction was supposed to model itself. Yet where does one find 'rustics' except in poems? The 'rustic', if ever there were, is an example of *poetic diction*: as a concept it exists only through the specialist grammar of poetry, the very system that Wordsworth (and it may be said, the Romantics) wanted iconoclastically to overthrow. When Wordsworth claimed to have written poems that simulated ordinary life, this then was the very special form of 'ordinary' life he had in mind:

> Humble and rustic life was generally chosen, because, in that condition, the essential passions of the heart find a better soil in which they can attain their maturity, are less under restraint, and speak a plainer and more emphatic language; because in that condition of life our elementary feelings co-exist in a state of greater simplicity [. . .] because in that condition the passions of men are incorporated with the beautiful and permanent forms of nature.[3]

My point here depends neither on an etymology nor on a sociology of the word 'rustic'. It depends on the concept of rusticity being 'poetic' through and through. The referent of the 'humble and rustic life' in which 'elementary feelings co-exist in a state of greater simplicity', in other words, can be found selectively in texts like *A Midsummer Night's Dream* or *As You Like It* rather than in what Wordsworth means by 'nature', which in turn has its referent in similarly poetic texts. The prelapsarian 'nature' that Wordsworth invokes (later to become the space of the Lacanian imaginary) has its roots in a form of anti-intellectualism that associates the city with superficial appearances and the country with deep eternal truths ('the essential passions of the heart'). Like the modernists of our own century, Wordsworth (and romanticism) could be said to have had a problem with modernity:

> For a multitude of causes, unknown to former times, are now acting with a combined force to blunt the discriminating powers of the mind, and, unfitting it for all voluntary exertion, to reduce it to a state of almost savage torpor. The most effective of these causes are the great national events which are daily taking place, and the increasing accumulation of men in cities, where the uniformity of their occupations produces a craving for extraordinary incident, which the rapid communication of intelligence

hourly gratifies. To this tendency of life and manners the literature and theatrical ambitions of the country have conformed themselves.[4]

Wordsworth's radical move is to assert and identify with an intellectual class that he defines by its anti-intellectualism: he is on the 'cutting edge' precisely because he is so disenamoured of the *pace* of modern life, one of the very signifiers of modernity.[5] The 'rapid communication of intelligence', presumably a reference to what might also have been seen positively as the democratic spread of ideas and news by means of a strong and diverse press, was the symptom of a kind of pathology ('a craving for extraordinary incident') that served only to dissociate urbanites from their real sensibilities or, more grandly, from 'our elementary feelings', because the speed of city life inevitably does 'blunt the discriminating powers of the mind'. In despising the press and lamenting the emptiness of modern living, James Strachey and T. S. Eliot did not, therefore, give expression to undemocratic and anti-intellectual commitments that were wholly new.

They were not even new in Wordsworth. The celebration by Wordsworth and virtually all of his Romantic contemporaries of the uncomplicated honesty of country life, as being closer to the 'natural' state of man, can be traced to the ideas of the French philosopher Jean-Jacques Rousseau of a generation before. In *Émile*, for example, published in 1762, Rousseau writes that '[m]en are not meant to be crowded together in ant-hills, but scattered over the earth to till it. The more they are massed together, the more corrupt they become.'[6] As we might say now, Rousseau wrote *Émile* to tell it like it is: his plain sincerity becomes the test of his own wisdom, in just the same way that, by having 'endeavoured to look steadily at [his] subject', Wordsworth was somehow guaranteed pristine access to its truth. To use another contemporary expression, we could say that Rousseau and Wordsworth told the truth because they cut through the crap. And what is meant by 'the truth', of course, is whatever an honest man would understand to be universal and natural – the kind of truth that is as plain as the nose on one's face. As Rousseau puts it: 'This is what I have tried to do. Lest my book should be unduly bulky, I have been content to state those principles the truth of which is self-evident.'[7] What is meant by 'the crap' therefore is everything that society teaches, especially when the teaching is confined to books:

> The misuse of books is the death of sound learning. People think they know what they have read, and take no pains to learn. Too much reading only

produces a pretentious ignoramus. There was never so much reading in any age as the present, and never was there less learning; in no country of Europe are so many histories and books of travel printed as in France, and nowhere is there less knowledge of the mind and manners of other nations. So many books lead us to neglect the book of the world; if we read it at all, we keep each to our own page.[8]

Notwithstanding this apparent attack on the printed word, *Émile* is among the most eminently quotable of eminently quotable books. On every page there is at least one beautifully couched maxim, or some delicious outburst of invective or other (very often directed at philosophers or Englishmen). But the legacy of its influence on a general romanticism can be summed up in two statements: '[t]he splendour of nature lives in man's heart; to be seen, it must be felt',[9] and '[h]uman institutions are one mass of folly and contradiction.'[10] Nature is good, culture is bad.

The expression of our romanticized prelapsarian (pre-civilized, pre-Oedipal, imaginary) true selves is in direct contrast to the political philosophy of someone like the Englishman Thomas Hobbes, in whose *Leviathan* the state of nature is such that 'every man is Enemy to every man' and (in a famous but often misapplied description) human life is 'solitary, poore, nasty, brutish, and short'.[11] For Hobbes, whose *Leviathan* was published in 1651, following a period of great political turmoil and social upheaval in England, civil society, if properly ordered, was the means of transforming the precarious existence of natural man into a life of artificially safe prosperity and longevity. Civil society, based on self-discipline (repression, Oedipalization), offered men and (in principle) women a *way out of* the 'nasty, brutish, and short' future that was all they could expect in nature. Civil society (culture) is good, nature is bad: the inverse of Rousseau's philosophy.

In this broad difference between Hobbes and Rousseau we can glimpse the shape of a chasm separating the Enlightenment from romanticism, which I will discuss more fully in later chapters. But the point for now is that Rousseau inverted Hobbes's estimation of the nature/culture binary; and that inversion remains intact as a romantic legacy (in further support of Lacoue-Labarthe and Nancy's argument). Rousseau's children nowadays are the new 'pagans', the 'ferals' and the other post-hippie romantics (including the psycho-feminists, or the 'corporealists') who think that thinking – mainstream, masculinist, patriarchal, Babylonian, oppressive, linear, phallic, institutional – is an act of self-deception and who advocate a 'return' to some lost notion of an original true self, through 'magic', 'the body', or 'nature' and sometimes all at once.

Rousseau's legacy is in evidence, then, wherever nature is romanticized. It inheres also in expressions of a loss of faith in human institutions (especially language) as exemplified by a great deal of postmodern literature. One outcome of this loss of faith, so that in effect life is seen to revert to being 'nasty, brutish, and short', is the contemporary dystopic novel, typified by Kathy Acker's *Empire of the Senseless*. What might be called the moral outlook of Acker's text can be summed up in a statement by Thivai: 'If reality is not my picture of it, I'm lost.'[12] But since 'reality' is no longer able to be pictured individually by an act of self-creating will, as it was for the Romantics, this leaves both Thivai and his lover, Abhor, with nothing to believe in and nothing to look forward to. In the dystopic world of Acker's novel (set predominantly in a Paris of the near future) no one has anything to look forward to because systems of value, which acquire meaning only out of some belief in the possibility of history, have been replaced by systems of exchange. Without value, the sign ceases to exist. Without the sign, there is nothing to believe in.

In spite of any first impression to the contrary, the postmodern dystopia is in fact continuous with the romantic conception of culture. Culture, for Hobbes, represents positive artificiality, while for Rousseau it is fraught with 'folly and contradiction'. The choice between civil society and the state of nature is not the one confronting Thivai and Abhor, however. For them, given that Acker is writing some two centuries after Rousseau and therefore not only after romanticism, but also after Marxism, psychoanalysis and structuralism, the choice is Baudrillardian: signs, or simulacra?

For romanticism, by being true to one's inner feelings it was possible to strike out of the 'mind-forged manacles' of social reality, as Blake puts it in his poem 'London',[13] into the intensity of real reality. As the brilliant British essayist Isaiah Berlin writes, with characteristic elegance, for the romantics 'the tidy regularities of daily life are but a curtain to conceal the terrifying spectacle of true reality, which has no structure.'[14] *Lack* of structure therefore was positive, and it was natural. But for Hobbes, of course, this was precisely what is wrong with nature: it is so positively lacking in structure that no one can be guaranteed enough food, shelter and security to stay alive.

Given its radical difference from the Hobbesian conception of nature, it is no surprise that romanticism took a very dim view of history. For romanticism, history is going in the wrong direction. The historical will to progress, or the drive towards further and better social development (which is only one version of history, of course), puts us at an ever increasing distance from 'the' nature of our true selves. Nothing could be more absurd from this point of view than arguing, as Hobbes did, that society should be modelled on the principles of geometry.[15] The proof indeed is performed by *Leviathan* itself: for all that Hobbes is critical of what he calls 'insignificant Speech', by which he means any form of linguistic 'extravagance', such as a metaphor or an abstract philosophical term for a speculative concept that has no reality outside a discourse, his own argument depends on the very kinds of excess it tries to exclude. In Part I of *Leviathan*, for example, he writes that

> The Light of humane minds is Perspicuous Words, but by exact definitions first snuffed, and purged from ambiguity; *Reason* is the *pace*; Encrease of *Science*, the *way*; and the Benefit of man-kind, the *end*. And on the contrary, Metaphors, and senselesse and ambiguous words, are like *ignes fatui*; and reasoning upon them is wandering amongst innumerable absurdities; and their end, contention, and sedition, or contempt.[16]

By careful attention to observable phenomena and the application of deductive reasoning, Hobbes hopes to explain, in plain English, the manifest superiority of artificial social institutions over natural anarchy and chaos. But in wanting to eradicate from words their tendency to excess and ambiguity, he wants to deny the very condition of language itself. Hobbes's own plain and simple prose is every bit as much a *style* of writing as the 'extravagance' he warns against in philosophical discourse. No matter how much he tries to confine words to a 'purely' denotative or descriptive function, they turn out to be never quite as docile as desired. Hence the endless qualifications, repetitions and degrees of clarification that Hobbes is forced to resort to throughout *Leviathan* in an effort to ward off the effects of 'insignificant Speech'. Every attempt at precision, in other words, results in an *excess* of clarification.

What is perhaps most striking, nevertheless, about Hobbes's appeal to the simplicity of truth is that the 'radical' convictions of Rousseau and Wordsworth seem hardly to differ from it. The belief that plain language contains plain truth is common to major figures of both the Enlightenment and the Romantic period. It is not the means but the ends that distinguishes them: for Hobbes, ordinary language is the basis of a just and reasonable society; for the romantics, as exemplified by Wordsworth's Preface to the *Lyrical Ballads*, ordinary language gives access to real or true reality, which is pre-social. One might conclude from this that ordinary language is valued not for what it 'is', but for its service-ability to a general theory or conviction.

In the absence of a general theory, therefore, ordinary language would cease to have any value at all. If it were believed that there is nothing to believe in, how could language continue to be used as if it were the means of arriving at the truth? This is the proposition posed by *Empire of the Senseless* and which is made explicit at many points throughout the text, for example in the following passage as narrated by Abhor:

> Here language was degraded. As daddy plumbed and plummeted away from the institute of marriage more and more downward deeply into the demimonde of public fake sex, his speech turned from the usual neutral and acceptable journalese most normal humans use as a stylus mediocris into . . . His language went through an indoctrination of nothingness, for sexuality had no more value in his world, until his language no longer had sense. Lack of meaning appeared as linguistic degradation.
>
> This is what daddy said to me while he was fucking me: 'Tradicional estiol de p . . . argentino. Q . . . es e. mas j . . . de t . . . los e . . . dentro d. la c . . . es m . . . indicado p . . . entablar g . . . amistades o t . . . tertulias a . . . es m . . . similar a. estilo t . . . : se c . . . la c . . . con l. palma de la m . . . y s. apoyan l . . . cinco d . . . se s . . . y s. baja l. mano, l . . . de e . . . manera y. el c . . . se h . . . hombre. origen e. profundamente r . . . y s. han h . . . interesantes t . . . en l . . . jeroglificos e . . . y m . . . Es e. mas r . . . para d . . . de l . . . comidas p . . . no c . . . la de . . .' He had become a Puerto Rican.[17]

Whether this is a parody or an accurate rendition of Puerto Rican Spanish, the 'words' of Abhor's father can function only at the level of the signifier for English-speaking readers. Insofar as they *look* like words, they appear to belong to a language. But this goes to show only that language is reducible to its appearance, that words are first and foremost quasi-material signifiers. For language to have meaning, culture has to have value and history has to matter. If the real truth, however, is that history is the lie by which culture disguises the fact of its naturally savage interests and practices (the Hobbesian 'warre [. . .] of every man, against every man')[18] in the name of human progress and welfare, then it cannot be possible to have faith in the power of plain language to convey plain truth. For the only plain truth is that human life is 'solitary, poore, nasty, brutish, and short': that is, for postmodernism, culture comes to be troped in terms of Hobbesian nature. In this respect a novel such as *Empire of the Senseless* can be seen as continuous with the romantic tradition of adopting a negative attitude towards the values of the city, modernity and progress. Although the chic cynicism of Lou Reed and The Velvet Underground, if not of the New York avant-garde in general, may be a more contemporary source of the dark despair that defines the human condition in *Empire of the Senseless*, Acker's dystopic vision belongs all the same to a tradition of romantic disillusionment with culture. Like Wordsworth, Acker too tries to keep her readers 'in the company of flesh and blood': the difference is that, for Acker, 'flesh and blood' has lost its value as a metaphor and become all there is to say about being human. Given as a premise that the world is totally lacking in the possibility of gentle feelings and good intentions, this places certain constraints on the possibilities for literature. In terms of content, there is only violence and pornography – while the choice of form is restricted to the fragment. The cool jibe. The surrealistic image:

> I laughed at myself and gave her what she wanted. I pierced myself through her belly-button. I thrust and pushed her own blood up her womb. As her red head rose out of the white fur, her mouth opened: monstrous scarlet. Tiny white shells appeared in that monster sea. 'My little dead shark. Better than dead fish.' I whispered to her while I fucked her in her asshole.[19]

Empire of the Senseless could be described as an attempt to set a record for the use of the words 'fuck' and 'cunt', which appear on almost every page. By constant repetition, however, they become decreasingly shocking, turning into 'senseless', empty signifiers. After a while they become no more noticeable than punctuation marks which seem to appear in the text only for the sake of some variety rather than according to a systematic set of rules for clarifying and communicating sense. Often, if punctuation marks serve any function at all in *Empire of the Senseless*, it seems to be as reminders of a time when punctuation marks were used for the disambiguation and control of linguistic meaning. In a word, they function here as simulacra rather than as signs.

According to Baudrillard, the sign's value is an expression of faith (or its opposite) in a notion of the real: its function is to represent or disguise some aspect of reality, or that faith. This is most evident in the sign's first stage, that of reflection, whereby it functions as a '*good* appearance' or a faithful image of a prior and independent referent.[20] This is the stage or order of the sign in the classical realist text, for example, such that the narrative as a whole can be taken as a kind of archaeological record of the life-world it accurately and verifiably depicts. But it is also how the sign can function on a far smaller scale: for example, at the level of the

comma. From the point of view of proper grammatical usage, the appearance of a comma indicates the necessity for a pause and helps to perform
the work of converting otherwise chaotic syntactical data (signifiers) into
orderly units of semantic sense (signifieds). The comma's appearance,
then, is underwritten by a faith in a theory of *proper* grammatical usage.
It is only because commas belong, in Saussure's terms, to a *langue* or
system of grammatical rules that their *parole* forms (the actual events or
appearances of commas) can convert syntax into semantics.[21] However,
since the *langue* is only ever inferrable from instances of *parole* (how
could there be direct access to the rules that commas perform in the way
it is possible to claim direct access to commas themselves?), the very
notion of 'proper' grammatical usage has to be seen as inferential. The
'properness' of 'proper' grammar, in other words, does not have the
status of an absolute value: it is an ideal that any actual grammatical text
can only hope to approximate. In this sense the ideal itself is textual
insofar as it has no status outside the texts of its approximate actuality or
instantiation, whether in terms of success or failure (use and misuse).
Hence the ideal of proper grammar is a text and may be understood
therefore in Baudrillard's terms according to different orders of the sign.
If the ideal is believed, proper grammar functions as a first-order sign the
value of which Baudrillard describes as 'sacramental'. Since the ideal of
proper grammar can never be identical with actual instances of grammatical usage, though, but must always be inferred to lie behind or
beyond them, then the ideal can be understood to function also as a
second- and third-order sign. It could be said that the inferred *langue* of
proper grammar disguises the overwhelmingly more frequent socio-
historical events of so-called 'ungrammatical' usage. In terms of the
everyday actualities of grammatical practice, 'proper' usage is exceptional. This could be taken to mean that 'proper grammar' is a lie, since
'improper' grammatical events are in fact far more common and ordinary
and in a sense more 'proper'. In that case the ideal of proper grammar
would be seen as a distortion of the real, acting as a second-order sign
with the value of 'malefice' or '*evil* appearance'. In the third stage the sign
passes beyond being a good or bad appearance to the order simply of
celebrating or playing at *being* an appearance. An example of this stage,
whereby the sign conceals 'the *absence* of a basic reality', is the performance of an inferred grammatical system which seemingly underlies the
appearance of Puerto Rican Spanish in the passage from *Empire of the
Senseless*. The actual black marks on the page that constitute what
Abhor's father is meant to have said while raping (or, as the text says,

'fucking') her serve as a performance, then, not as a reflection: without promising to reveal a 'hidden' meaning, they play at being a grammatical event, at being the sign *of* something.

Baudrillard's fourth-order sign, the simulacrum, breaks entirely with the logic of appearance or representation. In this final stage the sign refers only to itself. Consequently simulacra only *simulate* the 'old' relationships of signs to things, or the different differences between appearance and reality. On this model the whole of *Empire of the Senseless* and not simply some part of it could be taken to simulate the relation of literature to life as pertaining to liberal humanist theory, say, or the first order of the sign. In other words, as a dystopia, the novel could be read as being more real than the real. Through its simulation of human life as 'solitary, poore, nasty, brutish, and short', and through its idiosyncratic syntax (or experimental approach to narrative conventions), *Empire of the Senseless* constructs itself as a hyperreal event: a text that is indistinguishable from any outside-text (or 'real world') experience of pain and confusion caused by a loss of faith in the teleological progress of history.

In a famous statement, Baudrillard writes that '[t]he very definition of the real becomes: *that of which it is possible to give an equivalent reproduction.*'[22] Reality now is always already constituted in advance by its reproducibility as text, such that the condition of the real is no longer discernably different from what used to be able to be distinguished from it. 'At the limit of this process of reproducibility, the real is not only what can be reproduced, but *that which is always already reproduced.*'[23] Hence today the 'realest' (or the hyperreal) experience of a perfect childhood is to be had as an adult visiting Disneyland, where the opportunity for that experience has been reproduced as a fantasy for grown-ups to act out in the perfect simulation of an event that never happened but which is nonetheless indistinguishable from its having done so. Or, to choose another example, what is the difference between 'the war in Vietnam' and the Francis Ford Coppola film, *Apocalypse Now*? What is the difference between a war or a famine somewhere in the world and newsreel footage of those events on television? To answer such questions, one would have to believe in the rational subject's critical powers of discrimination which might allow for differences to be identified between structures of domination (power) and systems of representation (media). Then one might, as the Marxists used to do, point a finger at the dominant and lend a helping hand to the dominated. For Baudrillard, however, Marxism and other 'old-fashioned' systems of political correction based on a faith in human rationality can no longer act effectively in a world where the spheres of political and cultural economy 'fuse in the same marketing and merchandising of objects and ideologies'[24] and in which, for millions of TV viewers, soap operas fuse with documentaries. Not a day passes but something happens some-where, moreover, that defies imagination. In a word, for Baudrillard reality has become unreal:

> Today it is quotidian reality in its entirety – political, social, historical and economic – that from now on incorporates the simulatory dimension of hyperrealism. We live everywhere already in an 'esthetic' hallucination of reality. The old slogan 'truth is stranger than fiction,' that still corre-sponded to the surrealist phase of this estheticization of life, is obsolete. There is no more fiction that life could possibly confront, even victoriously – it is reality itself that disappears utterly in the game of reality – radical disenchantment, the cool and cybernetic phase following the hot stage of fantasy.[25]

If there is nothing left to fantasize about now, since reality is always already virtual reality, this rather robs the human imagination of any force. And since our rationality is ineffectual too, the very notion of the human subject comes to make no sense. Cool detachment and blank indifference are the only appropriate responses to the de-sensitizing 'simulatory dimension of hyperrealism'. Senseless and insensible, the 'postmodern' subject cannot rely on either consciousness (viz. Descartes) or affirmation (viz. Coleridge) to forge an identity, because nothing so sure as an identity is possible under the totalizing sign-hollowing, difference-levelling regime of the simulacrum.

Now if all this were to be believed, then the question of what kind of literature such a regime or epoch might produce would be answered by *Empire of the Senseless*, in which characters coolly say such desperate things as 'Sleep or ease is a priority the way love used to be'[26] and the code to the CIA Library reads: 'GET RID OF MEANING. YOUR MIND IS A NIGHTMARE THAT HAS BEEN EATING YOU: NOW EAT YOUR MIND.'[27] With the loss of passion and intellect, human identity reduces to the basely sexual or dissipates in the artificial – and so characters are routinely referred to not as people, but as 'fuck', 'cunt' and 'human construct'. The more the loss of faith in the real brings about dehumanizing effects in the simulated world of the novel, however, the more a romantic conclusion becomes inevitable. As Baudrillard writes: '[w]hen the real is no longer what it used to be, nostalgia assumes its full meaning.'[28] Or, as Abhor puts it at the very end, after being severely kicked by Thivai and a human construct called Mark:

I now fully knew what I didn't want and what and whom I hated. That was
something.

   And then I thought that, one day, maybe, there'ld be a human society in
a world which is beautiful, a society which wasn't just disgust.[29]

But this is not simply a romantic note to end on. There is nothing
indeed that qualifies *Empire of the Senseless* as postmodern that dis-
qualifies it from being romantic. If the romantic text is defined, as
Wordsworth defined romantic poetry, by its radical difference from all
other kinds of text, this must mean that it is virtually (ideally, it would be
literally) 'unreadable' in terms of established codes of textual production
and reception. For Wordsworth, the romantic poem differs from its
predecessors because of its refusal to reproduce a 'proper' poetic grammar or diction. Hence, ironically, romantic poetry is incommensurable
with poetry. If poetry is beautiful, romantic poetry is sublime. In this
capacity it is absolutely new and different, fusing poetics and experience:
the romantic poem, the romantic text of literature in general, is indistinguishable from what it is 'about' – in its sublime specificity it becomes the
universal and disinterested experience of what it describes. In imitating
the 'language of men', for example, Wordsworth aspires to keep us 'in
the *company* of flesh and blood', promising to reconcile through the
literary absolute the otherwise incommensurable domains of poetry and
life. Since it is not 'that which is supposed by many to be the proper
object of poetry' that he sets out to achieve, we can say that for
Wordsworth the romantic poem is radically and self-consciously *improper*: it is both incommensurable with and unreadable as 'poetry' at
all.

   Now in *Empire of the Senseless*, such unreadability is effected by the
appearance of foreign languages (Arabic features rather prominently)
and the inclusion of many drawings. Not just any foreign language but
Arabic especially appears 'unreadable' in the context of a novel written
in English. The drawings, moreover, are obviously incommensurable not
only with the conventions of written narrative, but with the very medium
of a story told in words.[30] At the same time, in their very difference from
the literary, the drawings serve to emphasize the literariness of the text in
which they appear: no less than the drawings it includes, *Empire of the
Senseless* is 'untranslatable'. The writtenness of the text cannot be exchanged for a spoken equivalent: its literariness is an effect of its being
written – that is the nature of the literary absolute. Literature, in other
words, is always writing, and so in a sense is always visual. It has to be

seen. What appears to make *Empire of the Senseless* 'look' different, then, is also what makes it a work of literature in the absolute sense. More generally, the text's overall difference from standard conceptions of the genre of the novel proper serves only to reinforce its status as a work of literature in romantic terms. What might be called its rejection of 'literary diction' in favour of imitating the rhythms and grammars of contemporary urban ideolects, for example, could be seen as an attempt to authenticate the experience of disaffection that the novel describes. After all, what room is there for 'literary' language when 'the principal economic flow of power takes place through black-market armament and drug exchange'[31] and the truth, as an old man puts it to Abhor, is that 'One must learn how to suicide in this world, for that's all that's left us'?[32] How can literature be both literary in the 'proper' sense and honest at the same time when just about everybody seems to be into drug-trafficking and incest nowadays? How can the genre of the novel proper, in other words, possibly tell it like it is if the way that things are now is so utterly improper and, according to standard codes of sense-making, so absolutely unrepresentable? In a word, the answer to these questions – the romantic solution – is to write *unreadable* literature. The logic is explained by Abhor in a passage that is worth quoting at some length:

> That part of our being (mentality, feeling, physicality) which is free of all control let's call our 'unconscious'. Since it's free of control, it's our only defence against institutionalized meaning, institutionalized language, control, fixation, judgement, prison.
>
> Ten years ago it seemed possible to destroy language through language: to destroy language which normalizes and controls by cutting that language. Nonsense would attack the empire-making (empirical) empire of language, the prisons of meaning.
>
> But this nonsense, since it depended on sense, simply pointed back to the normalizing institutions.
>
> What is the language of the 'unconscious'? (If this ideal unconscious or freedom doesn't exist: pretend it does, use fiction, for the sake of survival, all of our survival.) Its primary language must be taboo, all that is forbidden. Thus, an attack on the institutions of prison via language would demand the use of a language or languages which aren't acceptable, which are forbidden. Language, on one level, constitutes a set of codes and social and historical agreements. Nonsense doesn't per se break down the codes; speaking precisely that which the codes forbid breaks the codes.[33]

In trying to represent the unrepresentability of senselessness (the freedom of the unconscious), Acker's text defiantly (and romantically) violates the protocols of official or proper literary discourse. In doing so it can be seen as continuous with a romantic tradition of celebrating the 'forbidden' as the inexpressible expression of the truth. Its improperness from the point of view of the generic conventions of the novel makes it all the more proper in terms of literary absoluteness or from the point of view of the Barthesian Text: 'it is Text for the very reason that it knows itself as text.' In an even more radical departure from a proper sense of the literary, Acker's text finds an image of itself not in a radical form of 'writing' as understood normally, but in another kind of taboo: tattooing. As a writing on the body, the flesh made over into text, tattoos can be seen as the most forbidden form of literature and therefore, in romantic terms, as pure instances of the literary absolute. They serve no function but to violate a taboo, to *be* forbidden – just as the romantic function of literature is to defy, 'for our survival', whatever is prohibited socially and historically. Hence the tattoo can be seen as a postmodern form of the romantic poem: in its defiance of an 'imprisoning' taboo it achieves the same effect as desired by Dorothea Schlegel for romantic poetry – to stand against 'bourgeois order' and the 'absolutely forbidden', to become what 'no police force and no educational institution can prevent'.

As writing, then, *Empire of the Senseless* simulates tattooing. This is not only because the drawings in the text all look like tattoos, but because of the cartoonish or tattoo-like nature of the world the text describes – in which things do not so much 'happen' (according to any proper narrative logic) as rather just seem to 'appear' without any motivation or context. Just as it would be senseless to ask, *What is the sense of a tattoo?*, moreover, so it would be an admission of one's failure to be in tune with what is really going on to interrogate any of the starkly disjunctured episodes of *Empire of the Senseless* for a hidden meaning. To ask how it might be possible for swashbuckling pirates and computer analysts to exist in the same historical present, as they do in this novel, for example, would be like asking what a tattoo skull or dragon *means*. Of course, if you have to ask – you can never know.

Hence 'truth' turns out to be wordless. As we found in the case of Keats's Grecian urn, the real significance of the emblematic tattoo in (and as) Kathy Acker's text can never be given in terms of rational discourse. Its incalculability or senselessenss *is* its value – and one is either 'hip' to this, or not. In the same way, one either appreciates, with Keats, the beauty and truth that is contained in and animated by the sublimely enigmatic urn – or not. In both cases, however, it may not be sublime intuition (or romantic imagination) that is in question, but the power of community membership to determine and bestow significance.

One way of explaining such power involves a notion of 'language-games' as conceived by the Austrian-born, English-trained philosopher Ludwig Wittgenstein and taken up in the work of contemporary French philosopher Jean-François Lyotard. Wittgenstein developed the idea of language-games as a solution to the philosophical problem of deciding the relationship between any statement and the 'reality' to which it allegedly refers, or (as we might say now) between a discourse and its 'outside'. Instead of asking, for example as Socrates did, *What is knowledge?*, expecting there to be a single answer, Wittgenstein proposes that we should think of 'knowledge' (and 'truth') as internal properties of particular language-games.[34] Hence there is no such thing as absolute knowledge or truth: there are instead *many* things that will, under certain codified conditions, count as knowledges and truths according to the different rules and prescriptions of different language-games. For Wittgenstein, then, language-games constitute *criteria*. Relating to this point is his suggestion that philosophy should replace entirely its idea of 'essences' with a notion of 'family resemblances':

> – We are inclined to think that there must be something in common to all games, say, and that this common property is the justification for applying the general term 'game' to the various games; whereas games form a *family* the members of which have family likenesses. Some of them have the same nose, others the same eyebrows and others again the same way of walking; and these likenesses overlap. The idea of a general concept being a common property of its particular instances [. . .] is comparable to the idea that *properties* are *ingredients* of the things which have the properties; e.g. that beauty is an ingredient of all beautiful things as alcohol is of beer and wine, and that we therefore could have pure beauty, unadulterated by anything that is beautiful.[35]

For the language-game of literary criticism, the notion of 'family resemblances' is a much more flexible and practical tool than, say, the notion of 'genre', which expresses a far more Socratic faith in neat, essential differences. The notion of 'language-games', moreover, would do away with having to comprehend the nature of the wordless, unreadable truth of a text such as *Empire of the Senseless*, since 'unreadability' would be simply the desired effect of the particular language-game it performs. Readers for whom tattooing is an inexplicably profound art of resistance (despite the fact that tattoos have never been more popular and therefore less taboo) would form a community based on a family of language-games in which the synonymity of the inexplicable and the profound was coded as true.

Wittgenstein's ideas have been elaborated most recently and, from the perspective of the language-game of postmodern literary theory, most influentially, in Lyotard's *The Postmodern Condition: A Report on Knowledge*, which he prepared on behalf of the government of Quebec in 1979 and was translated into English in 1984. Lyotard thinks it is justifiable to refer to present history as 'the postmodern age' because, since at least the 1950s, a 'crisis' of 'legitimation' has come about with regards to all forms of knowledge, making it impossible for discourses to be legitimated by 'an explicit appeal to some grand narrative, such as the dialectics of Spirit, the hermeneutics of meaning, the emancipation of the rational or working subject, or the creation of wealth'.[36] Hence Lyotard calls discourses of self-legitimation 'modern' and defines 'the postmodern condition' as the *crisis* of legitimation. On this model 'truth' is seen as completely internal to the rules and procedures of a discourse, or a language-game, rather than being transcendental or outside a discourse. This explains why something can be true according to one set of rules and false according to another. Just as the games of baseball and cricket make sense to themselves but not to each other, so the rules of any discourse cannot be reapplied outside that discourse and expected to have any pragmatic effect. It would not help you to know how to drive a car in traffic, for example, if you happened to know the rules according to which stock market shares can fluctuate. So the rules of a game can be thought of as a 'pragmatics' for getting something done: whether the outcome is to win at chess or to win a date with someone you desire, the game has rules that must be followed.

Now it may be all very well to think of certain kinds of knowledge-production in terms of language-games, but surely some things are just true regardless of what rules are applied? And it is surely this order of truth that describes the outcomes of scientific research, making science a very different kind of 'discourse' from, say, narrative? But what Lyotard argues in *The Postmodern Condition* is that science actually requires the language-game of narrative for its own legitimation. His concern is not with the status of scientific truth, but with the legitimating rules and procedures of scientific discourse. This distinction is often misunderstood, leading to quite absurd claims about the nature of scientific truth being the same as that of narrative truth because Western science is the product of a classed, sexed and ethnocentric history. Since it is privileged white men who control the laboratories and the research funds, the law of gravity must be patriarchal.[37] This is not at all what Lyotard argues, however.

For him, the postmodern crisis of legitimation is revealed through science's inability to reconcile its difference from narrative with its dependence on it. In the first place, scientific knowledge is deeply invested in being different from narrative knowledge. Borrowing from the work of American speech-act philosopher J. L. Austin,[38] Lyotard distinguishes these different knowledges or language-games in terms of different speech-acts or utterances: scientific speech-acts are 'denotative' (a term Lyotard uses in place of what Austin calls 'constative' utterances), while narrative speech-acts are 'performative'. In such terms the whole of Lyotard's argument can be summed up as follows: *all* speech-acts are performative – there is no such thing as a denotative utterance.

If there *were* a hard and fast distinction between constatives and performatives, nevertheless, it would look like this: constative utterances would be those of which it could be said their referent is either true or false, independent of the utterance – hence, *It is raining*. A performative utterance, on the other hand, would be one of which it could be said that its referent is an effect of (or is performed by) the utterance: for example, *I like it when it rains*. On the face of it this looks like a distinction between the kinds of 'objective' statement associated with scientific discourse and the 'subjective' variety typical of narrative discourse. But for this to be so, certain rules and procedures have to be followed. Hence it turns out that the 'objectivity' of the utterance *It is raining* is not something that can be said to be independent of the pragmatic circumstances or contexts in which that speech-act could be made. Lyotard gives as an example of a denotative ('objective', constative) speech-act the statement 'The university is sick' and argues as follows:

> A denotative utterance such as 'The university is sick,' made in the context of a conversation or an interview, positions its sender (the person who utters the statement), its addressee (the person who receives it), and its referent (what the statement deals with) in a specific way: the utterance places (and exposes) the sender in the position of 'knower' (he knows what the situation is with the university), the addressee is put in the position of having to give or refuse his assent, and the referent is handled in a way unique to denotatives, as something that demands to be correctly identified and expressed by the statement that refers to it.[39]

For 'The university is sick' to be considered an objective statement independent of sender and context, in other words, it is utterly dependent on being made by a sender who is authorized to speak objectively about the referent and on a context in which the authority of the sender and the objectivity of the referent are legitimated. If uttered in the context of a language-game other than, say, a serious conversation or an interview, the speech-act 'The university is sick' would not be denotative but performative and of the order therefore of an utterance such as 'I like it when it rains.' Or if the statement were made by, say, a student (rather than a Dean or a Vice-Chancellor) who was participating in the language-game of a serious conversation or an interview, it would still be of the order of a performative speech-act. One might then want to decide if it was (in Austin's terms) a felicitous or infelicitous speech-act – that is, whether it was uttered in good or bad faith by the student – but in any case the statement could never carry denotative (or 'scientific') force unless it met all the requirements of a language-game whose outcome was agreed to be the production of statements that are objectively true. Moreover, efforts to decide the 'felicity' of speech-acts run into all the problems pertaining to the distinction between constatives and performatives: there simply are no transcendental grounds on which utterances can be judged as felicitous or infelicitous.

The suggestion then is that there are no grounds for distinguishing between utterances that are transcendentally true or false and those that are true or false only contingently. Instead, certain rules and procedures can *legitimate* the transcendental status of certain speech-acts. 'Objectivity', in other words, is something that has to be performed: scientific denotation depends on narrative performativity. While it may look as if a statement such as 'The university is sick' is more conjectural and less scientific (regardless of the sender's authority) than a statement such as 'It is raining' or 'Friday follows Thursday', none of these statements can avoid having to perform the truth status of the referents to which they refer. 'It is raining', for example, would not be taken as a denotative speech-act if it occurred as a line of poetry. Hence 'denotation' can be seen as a special kind of performance, which may be defined as *the performance of non-performativity*. It is in this way that the efforts of Thomas Hobbes to eradicate 'insignificant Speech' from his method of cultural theory and analysis can be seen as a particular speech-act vested with a particular style or performance.

This may seem to suggest, however, that romanticism has been right all along: that 'performativity' is simply another term for the literary absolute, and so the self-theorizing literary text is in fact the model and condition of all forms of textual production, including the seemingly least literary of forms – scientific discourse. But in that case performativity (or literary absoluteness) would function denotatively, as a very kind of context-free transcendental that the very notion of performativity (as argued by Lyotard) acts to thwart. The same might be said of Baudrillard's simulacrum: insofar as the simulacrum is a sign that produces its own referent, one would have to ask how it differs from the sign in general? Contrary to the chronology proposed by Baudrillard, the simulacrum would in fact have to come *first*, before the other 'stages' of the sign, in order to have signs that could be regarded as 'good appearances', for instance, or what could be described as denotative signs. In order to have denotation or representation, there has to be performativity or simulation. What can be called (after psychoanalysis) the 'repressed' term is the one that romanticism privileges: hence imagination, which is inimical to scientific reason, becomes the condition of rational thought, and so on. However, and we need to be quite clear on this, Lyotard is not arguing that narrative language-games are the condition of scientific truth as such (in an ontological sense), but rather that, in an age in which the grand narrative (or the metanarrative) of history has been rebuked, science is forced to seek legitimation in the rules and procedures of narrative performance. While he is not terribly forthcoming at giving his reasons for considering 'history' to be dead, this is emphatically not to say he thinks that scientific truth is 'untrue' and that somebody could, if they wished, step out the window of a thirty-storey building and fly.

Nevertheless we have found, in this chapter, that 'the death of history' is an animating force in postmodern literature and theory. The texts of Baudrillard, Acker and Lyotard all seem to require that 'history' is no longer able to function as the legitimating background to understandings of the sign, the literary text and knowledge. In the absence of history as a metanarrative, signs, literary texts and knowledges are able to be radically reconceived. Hence 'the death of history' is required to legitimate the 'radical' nature of Baudrillard's, Acker's and Lyotard's texts. In a word these writers could be said to have *performed* 'the death of history' as a particular set of utterances or language-games. As a totalizing speech-act, moreover, 'the death of history' is no less a metanarrative than utterances that express a belief in historical 'progress' or the 'spirit' of history. Hence the language-game of 'the death of history' is romantic: one of the moves by which 'postmodernism' legitimates itself is through a totalizing 'dehistoricization' of the contexts in which signs acquire values, just as Wordsworth legitimated romantic poetry through its rejection of 'poetic' language and themes as defined historically. I will now go on to discuss how this move is related to a general process of what I will call *totalizing negation*, and flag the possibility of a further move – one that romanticism never makes – as enabled by an enlightenment tradition discernible in the work of Jacques Derrida. Hence my argument will become that, if such a move is possible, 'poststructuralism' and 'postmodernism' should never be used interchangeably.

4

Literature and the Liminal

Attempts at defining postmodernism are notoriously unsatisfactory. So much so, that it has become a standard move in the game of defining postmodernism to say that attempts at defining it are notoriously unsatisfactory. In his *Postmodernist Fictions*, for example, the British literary theorist Brian McHale begins as follows: ' "Postmodernist"? Nothing about this term is unproblematic, nothing about it is entirely satisfactory.'[1]

According to Lyotard, 'every utterance should be thought of as a "move" in a game.'[2] Hence we might see such interrogative utterances as McHale's ' "Postmodernist"?' as a standard opening move in the game of legitimating postmodernism, helping to define its undefinability by invoking postmodernism as a question or a problem in advance. Such moves are closely related to other, seemingly more expository, utterances made on behalf of postmodernism. For example, in a famous passage towards the end of *The Postmodern Condition*, Lyotard offers a 'definition' of postmodernism that is kept from being denotative since it is couched in the future perfect tense. In moving to define postmodernism in this way (performatively rather than denotatively), the 'truth' about postmodernism is preserved (or manufactured) as being unpresentable and hence sublime:

> The postmodern would be that which, in the modern, puts forward the unpresentable in presentation itself; that which denies itself the solace of good forms, the consensus of a taste which would make it possible to share collectively the nostalgia for the unattainable; that which searches for new presentations, not in order to enjoy them but in order to impart a stronger sense of the unpresentable. A postmodern artist or writer is in the position of a philosopher: the text he writes, the work he produces are not in principle governed by preestablished rules, and they cannot be judged

according to a determining judgment, by applying familiar categories to the text or to the work. Those rules and categories are what the work of art itself is looking for. The artist and the writer, then, are working without rules in order to formulate the rules of what *will have been done*. Hence the fact that work and text have the characters of an *event*; hence also, they always come too late for their author, or, what amounts to the same thing, their being put into work, their realization (*mise en oeuvre*) always begins too soon. *Post modern* would have to be understood according to the paradox of the future (*post*) anterior (*modo*).[3]

If (with the exception of the final sentence) 'romanticism' and 'the romantic' were substituted for 'postmodernism' and 'the postmodern' in this passage, nothing would change: 'The romantic would be that which, in the modern, puts forward the unpresentable in presentation itself' and so on. To emphasize the point it is worth referring back to Lacoue-Labarthe and Nancy on the subject of the unnameable, unpresentable and undefinable 'Work' of (and as) the romantic imagination:

> romanticism implies something entirely new, the *production* of something entirely new. The romantics never really succeed in naming this something [. . .]. In the end, they decide to call it – all things considered – *literature* [. . .]: the genericity, so to speak, and the generativity of literature, grasping and producing themselves in an entirely new, infinitely new Work. The *absolute*, therefore, of literature [. . .].

So: on the one hand romanticism is defined as 'the *production* of something entirely new', while on the other postmodernism is defined in terms of 'working without rules in order to formulate the rules of what *will have been done*'. On this basis it is difficult to see how post-modernism and romanticism differ. For what could be of the order of 'something entirely new' that was not 'unruly' from the point of view of pre-established conventions or language-games, or whose organizing principles were able to be identified only after the event? Moreover, in each of these definitions, what is in question must remain so – it can never be resolved or come into being as an 'outcome' or a 'product'. Paradoxically, after all, the whole point is to present the unpresentability of the unpresentable. As Lacoue-Labarthe and Nancy put it, immediately following the passage above:

> At the same time, however, the stakes turn out to be even larger. The absolute of literature is not so much poetry [. . .] as it is *poiesy*, according to an etymological appeal that the romantics do not fail to make. Poiesy or, in other words, production. The thought of the 'literary genre' is thus less

concerned with the production of the literary thing than with *production*, absolutely speaking. Romantic poetry sets out to penetrate the essence of poiesy, in which the literary thing produces the truth of production in itself, and thus [. . .] the truth of the production *of itself*, of autopoiesy.[4]

From the Greek words meaning 'creation' and 'to make', from which our 'poetry' is derived, 'poiesy' is a noun of *process*. The Romantics had several names for it, one of which was 'inspiration': 'when composition begins', Shelley writes, 'inspiration is already on the decline, and the most glorious poetry that has ever been communicated to the world is probably a feeble shadow of the original conceptions of the poet.'[5] Inspiration, then, is unpresentable. It can never as it were 'materialize', or appear as a work of literature in the standard sense. Hence every poem 'always come[s] too late', as Lyotard puts it of the postmodern text, because, by definition, the insubstantiality and unpresentability of poiesy (or postmodernism) can never be presented in and as the substance of a poem or a text. Poiesy is unpresentable as poetry since by nature it is unpresentable in and of itself. Consequently for the Romantics, as Lacoue-Labarthe and Nancy observe, poetry means 'something entirely new' from the point of view of established literary critical language-games, and so (in Lyotard's terms, albeit via Kant, as we will see later) it 'cannot be judged according to a determining judgment, by applying familiar categories to the text or to the work'. For the Romantics, in short, 'poetry' means 'poiesy', which is why Shelley was able to conceive of poetry as a kind of auto-generative force:

> Poetry is not like reasoning, a power to be exerted according to the determination of the will. A man cannot say, 'I will compose poetry.' The greatest poet even cannot say it; for the mind in creation is as a fading coal which some invisible influence, like an inconstant wind, awakens to transitory brightness; this power arises from within, like the colour of a flower which fades and changes as it is developed, and the conscious portions of our natures are unprophetic either of its approach or its departure.[6]

It is this 'invisible influence' which is always unpresentable that the romantic poem and the postmodern text both fail (but gloriously) to capture. And in their failure, of course, they both succeed, given the initial aim of 'put[ting] forward the unpresentable in presentation itself'. In other words it is Lyotard's insistence on the rule-producing, as opposed to rule-imitating, force of postmodern language-games that situates his notion of postmodernism within a tradition of the romantic approach to literature as the *question* or theory of literature. Literature is always in question for romanticism, and for precisely the reasons Lyotard attributes to the nonscientific status of narrative, which 'does not give priority to the question of its own legitimation and [. . .] certifies itself in the pragmatics of its own transmission without having recourse to argumentation and proof'.[7] This is why postmodern theory is always postmodern *literary* theory, even when it is about architecture or television – in the sense that, in its similarity to romanticism, postmodernism privileges the self-reflexive, self-legitimating, auto-poiesic text over all others.

There are many questions of, let us say, an ethical and political nature that could be put to such a privileging. Before raising them, though, I want to clarify what Lyotard thinks the differences between narrative and scientific texts (or knowledges or language-games) comprise. The basic difference is that narrative language-games are heterogeneous as opposed to the more restrictive outcome-oriented, rule-governed game of science. Science, because it is dominated by rules, is ends-directed, whereas narrative (or more broadly art), because it produces rules only in and as itself, is completely free from having to legitimate what it 'is' according to any external criteria. A scientist could never, for example, justify a scientific experiment on the grounds that it must be scientific because he or she says so. The personal beliefs of scientists are not in themselves scientific and cannot be used to legitimate what scientists do in the name of science. But artists, on the other hand, can do almost anything and call it art. The display of a public urinal by Marcel Duchamp, the French surrealist, in a Parisian art gallery in the 1920s is the standard case in point. What is the answer to the question, *What is art?*, if a work of art can be a piss-pot? Surely this must mean that 'art' cannot be defined according to any language-games that define 'knowledge'. To ask, *What is art?*, and, *What will happen if you walk out the window of a thirty-storey building?*, is not to expect answers of the same order. You know the answer to the latter question is that you will most certainly fall, and almost certainly die. But the answer to the question of what is art is not something that you 'know' in the same way, although you might not think that art is *just* a matter of opinion and therefore *everything* is art at least potentially. Whatever you think art is, however, its ontology is very much more plastic than what you think most other things are. A table, for example, may take many different forms, but still far fewer forms than art can take. Compared to 'art', then, by whatever definition, just about everything else is *less* heterogeneous – least of all, 'science'.

Even so-called 'found' objects (a public urinal or the 'language of men') can become art since the rules for its production and definition are never fixed. So while it may look as if 'art' changes each time it makes an appearance as something entirely new, the positively dynamic unpresentability of art means that change is never an outcome but always a condition. Hence, as Lyotard puts it, we need to situate change in art within the space of the future anterior – for it is not presentable change as such but rather unpresentable changeability that makes art what it is.

Now it is clear from this that we cannot have a knowledge of art in terms of how 'knowledge' has come to be defined scientifically. 'Art' is a collecting term for a set of family resemblances between a heterogeneous mix of rules and procedures. In a word, art has many language-games. But (as Lyotard tells it) there is only one language-game of science: 'Scientific knowledge requires that one language game, denotation, be retained and all others excluded.'[8] So while many different kinds of move and utterance can be made in science, they are only 'turning points in the dialectical argumentation, which must end in a denotative statement'.[9] One way by which a statement can appear as denotative, or appear to approach degree zero performativity, is by warding off the kinds of utterance that count as art or as self-legitimating narrative knowledge. While heterogeneous narrative knowledge is inclusive and tolerant, then, regarding scientific discourse simply as another class of language-game or as 'a variant in the family of narrative cultures', this is not true in reverse: 'The scientist questions the validity of narrative statements and concludes that they are never subject to argumentation and proof.'[10] And so from science's viewpoint the family of narrative language-games derives from 'a different mentality: savage, primitive, underdeveloped, backward, alienated, composed of opinions, customs, authority, prejudice, ignorance, ideology'.[11] Due to such radical incommensurability between narrative and scientific knowledge, it is 'impossible to judge the existence or validity of narrative knowledge on the basis of scientific knowledge and vice versa: the relevant criteria are different'.[12]

It is important to remember that Lyotard's argument is presented against a background of the 'disappearance' of grand unifying narratives. Since there are no longer any binding consensual beliefs, or so Lyotard tells us, this frees art to 'be' whatever it keeps on becoming, while at the same time posing a crisis of legitimation for science. The questions, *What is art?*, and, *What is art for?*, are on the one hand unanswerable and on the other irrelevant. Art is self-legitimating and therefore it 'is' whatever 'it' is, and because it is self-legitimating it is non-utilitarian and does not

have to be 'for' any purpose other than 'to be'. So for art the loss of
metanarratives is positive, liberating it from the imprisoning rules and
procedures of traditional aesthetics. But for science the opposite effect is
true. When there used to be metanarratives, science was able to answer
the questions of what it is and what it is for without any difficulty.
Science was defined as the production of verifiable (denotative) statements, at the consent of experts, about referents, for the purpose
of leading human civilization through history to an ever closer sense of
absolute truth and knowledge. Science was 'for' the advancement of
freedom and justice, then, since in getting closer and closer to the truth
we were being liberated from the ignorance and prejudices of the past.
But nowadays, in the absence of grand narratives of progress, liberation
and justice, science's 'goal is no longer truth, but perfomativity' – it no
longer does what it does 'to find truth, but to augment power'.[13] In other
words, science has become self-legitimating: it has become like art. The
situation as Lyotard sees it is summarized nicely by Steven Connor, who
writes that the goal of science now is not 'what kinds of research will lead
to the discovery of verifiable facts, but what kind of research will work
best, where "working best" means producing more research along the
same lines [. . .] increasing the performance and operational output of the
system of scientific knowledge'.[14]

So for Lyotard the distinction between art and science is the difference
between production and what is produced, or between production and
knowledge. Quite romantically (and by now quite predictably) Lyotard
defines 'postmodernism' not simply in opposition to classical science, but
against knowledge. This is not quite to say that postmodernism comprises a family of anti-knowledges (although it could be to suggest that so
far as postmodernism is concerned, anything goes), but it does indicate
that if 'knowledge' is paired against postmodernism, postmodernism is
paired with 'truth'. In other words, performative, unpresentable truth is
superior to mere denotative knowledge. More broadly, though, the
postmodern break with the legitimating procedures of modern or
Newtonian science can be traced, as Fredric Jameson, the American
literary and cultural theorist, argues in his 'Foreword' to *The Postmodern Condition*, to an event that is usually considered to have to do
with the arts: 'I am referring to the so-called crisis of representation, in
which an essentially realist epistemology, which conceives of representation as the reproduction, for subjectivity, of an objectivity that lies
outside it – projects a mirror theory of knowledge and art, whose
fundamental evaluative categories are those of adequacy, accuracy, and

Truth itself.'[15] It is truth of this order, what might be called absolute truth, which can presume to be totalizing because it can presume to fully adequate and accurately re-present objectifiably real phenomena, that Lyotard calls 'knowledge'. Its opposite and higher form, what might be called true or transcendental truth (or romantic truth), he associates with postmodernism. In a word, postmodern truth is nontotalizing.

Hence what might be called the ethics of *The Postmodern Condition* can be summarized as follows: 'little' is better than 'big'. For it is not just narratives, but 'little' narratives, that Lyotard privileges over grand theories or metadiscursive systems. Micro-forms, because they are so unhindered by rules and contexts and therefore so open to so many indefinite interconnections, are superior to supposedly totalizing macro-forms. The Final Solution is a macro-narrative and it is bad, while 'Tune in, Turn on, and Drop out' is an example of a micro-narrative and so it must be good. The American counter-cultural leader Timothy Leary's famous little statement, because it qualifies as a fragment, can appear in multiple contexts and be interconnected with other statements in ways that are plural, local and impermanent. The Third Reich's 'solution' to the Jewish 'problem', however, is completely goal-oriented and therefore closed, intolerant and totalizing. Now while no one would disagree that The Final Solution is abhorrent, this does not make little narratives superior ethically or in other ways to big ones. For Lyotard nevertheless it is a case of the smaller the better, because it is the smallest little narratives whose rules and procedures are least determinable and determining. As David Carroll comments:

> A disbelief in metanarratives forces science to legitimate itself on its own terms (in terms of performativity) and also provides an explosion of non-totalizable 'little narratives' – the smaller and more diversified, in Lyotard's view, the better – whose conflictual multiplicity and heterogeneity resist all forms of totalization. Narrative, at least as long as it remains 'little,' is taken by Lyotard to be a kind of open, highly mobile form that, in each instance, determines on its own how the various elements it contains or refers to will be interrelated. The little narrative is, in this sense, a kind of 'zero degree' of differentiating discourse – the form discourse takes to express diversity and unresolved conflict and, thus, resist homogenization.[16]

Little narratives could therefore be said to allow for many language-games to be kept in play at the same time; hence they are heterogeneous. In a later book, *The Differend* (French 1983, English 1988), Lyotard turns his attention to what he regards as the ultimate micro-form – the phrase – in order to consider the problem of interrelation, or how it is that phrases provide so many potential links to so many different language-games at once but are yet, in practice, most often linked to specific 'regimens':

> A phrase, even the most ordinary one, is constituted according to a set of rules (its regimen). There are a number of phrase regimens: reasoning, knowing, describing, recounting, questioning, showing, ordering, etc. Phrases from heterogeneous regimens cannot be translated from one into the other. They can be linked one onto the other in accordance with an end fixed by a genre of discourse.[17]

The 'differend', then, describes the incommensurability between different regimens, such that any unresolved conflict or dispute would be the consequence of a 'lack of a rule of judgment applicable to both arguments'.[18] In this respect, differends are completely unextraordinary because there are in fact no transcendental rules for linking one phrase to another. But while there are neither any categorical nor formal rules for linking phrases, this does not mean that phrases are not always being linked: what is in question, in other words, is not a philosophy but a pragmatics of linkage. 'To link is necessary, but how to link is not.'[19] Moreover in the terms that Lyotard defines 'the phrase', it is impossible for there to be an end to phrasing:

> A phrase 'happens.' How can it be linked onto? By its rule, a genre of discourse supplies a set of possible phrases, each arising from some phrase regimen. Another genre of discourse supplies another set of possible phrases. There is a differend between these two sets (or between the genres that call them forth) because they are heterogeneous. And linkage must happen 'now'; another phrase cannot not happen. It's a necessity; time, that is. There is no non-phrase. Silence is a phrase. There is no last phrase. In the absence of a phrase regimen or of a genre of discourse that enjoys a universal authority to decide, does not the linkage (whichever one it is) necessarily wrong the regimens or genres whose possible phrases remain unactualized?[20]

The phrase therefore is what cannot fail to happen since it has to be responded to, and every response (even silence) must happen as another phrase. So there is always phrasing without end ('There is no last phrase'), and this is a process over which no one has any control because one phrase always leads to another and to another, indefinitely. But what we can control, if only minimally, is how we choose to link phrases – although even this cannot put a stop to phrasing. On the contrary, as

Carroll argues, far from producing closure a chosen linkage actually reopens the question of the differend:

> The choice, then, of one response, one linkage, over all the other possibilities, does not resolve the question of linkage, but reopens it; not only must another phrase follow every phrase, but there remains the problem of all the unphrased phrases that underlie what is actually phrased. On the most fundamental level and in terms of the slightest of relations, then, there is dispute, 'dissensus,' a *différend* [. . .]. The principle of disputation, of *dissensus*, is located on too basic a level ever to be completely overcome; to overcome it would be to give the last phrase and terminate linkage – both of which are, by definition, impossible.[21]

In the sense that it is always open and interminable, the differend can be seen as strikingly similar to what we have found to be the case with romantic 'literature': it is always open to further questioning – or in other words it is always in dispute. From the romantic point of view there is, literally, no end to literature as a question: just as for Lyotard there is no way to stop phrasing and linking. In each case it is the phenomenality of a *process* that is unstoppable, although the process never actually appears as such. One can cite as evidence a material instance of literature and of a phrase, but never of *literature* (in its romantic sense) or of *phrasing*. Yet for romanticism and (according to Lyotard) for postmodernism, the phenomenality of the literary absolute and the phenomenality of the differend are indisputable, even while being always in dispute. Hence, for Lyotard, there *is* something that is not in dispute, which is that *everything is in dispute*. And it is difficult to see how this statement differs from a metanarrative or from 'a genre of discourse that enjoys a universal authority to decide'. For all that Lyotard is on the side of difference and diversity, then, such that he advocates the necessity of responding to every phrase or language-game in its own terms, according to its own rules and statements, in order to prevent the 'injustice' of an inappropriate response, his insistence on the ethical nature of heterogeneity turns out to be indistinguishable from the sort of statements he regards as totalizing and therefore unethical (or 'unjust').

It might also be noticed that Lyotard seems to have no problem deciding between (or identifying) different language-games. Hence we might ask: what are the rules of the language-game Lyotard uses to decide the rules of any language-game? What is the language-game he plays, in other words, to know what a language-game looks like? Surely it must be that he plays the game of 'argumentation and proof' associated not just with science but with philosophy, which is another 'genre of discourse that enjoys a universal authority to decide'. This does not mean that because Lyotard argues and evidences his ideas, what he says is therefore true. It means that, because he presents his ideas in that way, what he says is legitimated from outside the things he says themselves: first, the rules of the game of academic discourse have been decided by a community of scholars. Lyotard has not invented the rules of 'argumentation and proof': he is merely practising them in order to win consent for his position within that community. Secondly, academic rules would seem to be a good example of non-self-legitimating procedures: their legitimation seems to derive from a belief in a metanarrative, which could be described as the slow advance towards absolute truth. So academics work within rules because they believe collectively that by doing so they will get nearer and nearer to the truth of whatever it is they are looking for, and this will be to the ultimate good of human societies in general.[22]

Lyotard believes, however, that the only 'just' way of working within rules is to work *against* them, and that this is how artists work. Art (by which he means avant-garde art, modelled on the romantic theory of literature as literary theory) knows no bounds because it knows no rules: it is forever working to find new rules by which something entirely different can be understood as art. Hence each time another new object becomes a work of art, 'art' (as the theory of itself) is remade. But one could just as easily say that this applies to scholarship. So instead of arguing that academic practices are legitimated externally, it could be argued that the whole 'point' of scholarship is to invent new rules for 'doing scholarship'. That is why scholars write books and papers: not for the 'cynical' or self-serving purpose of finding new ways to write books and papers (although that is certainly an available – if base – motivation), but in order to find new rules for thinking about 'intellectual' problems – just as artists are said by Lyotard to 'do art' in order to find new ways of thinking about or experiencing 'aesthetic' problems. In any case, what would be the rules of the language-game one would use to decide between these completely different forms of scholarly legitimation? On the other hand there may be no need even to ask this question, since the whole 'problem' of legitimation may not itself be either particularly postmodern or particularly interesting. What is noteworthy instead is that Lyotard's whole position rests on a seemingly a priori distinction between self-legitimating and non-self-legitimating language-games, and he is in no doubt that the former category is ethically superior. But how did these 'categories' get to *be* categories in the first place, if not through a decision, on Lyotard's part, according to the very rules of the game that he calls science? How, for example, did he get 'outside' phrasing and gaming in order to be able to see that complex phenomena are reducible to minimal components (phrases and language-games) unless he used the rule, familiar to the academic community, of proposing the denotative existence of some phenomenon or other in order to test (by verification or falsification, or some other means) the validity of the thing in question and of the proposition? What is 'postmodern' about that?

I am suggesting here that Lyotard's distinction is thoroughly romantic. His categories of self-legitimating art versus non-self-legitimating science depend on a prior and romantic categorization of literature as literary theory versus every other form of textual production (or 'knowledge'). But the question remains: who decides – and how – whether something is self-legitimating, or not? Say, for instance, that I were to claim that reading Kant stretches me 'creatively' far more than looking at a painting (just to invert the standard prejudice), and I saw no justification for believing that anyone else read Kant for reasons that were other than self-legitimating: what rule could be applied as the disproof of such a claim? Or what if I were to say that I read Kant only to find new rules for thinking with? Or that scholarship holds no other 'purpose' for me than to provide a space in which to push rules to their limits so that I might be able to think differently? In Lyotard's terms, this would make me an artist. I would have to be an 'artist' because my account of what I do is incommensurable with what Lyotard insists I do – namely that I try, although I am doomed to failure, to 'explain' the inexplicable. As a 'critic' or 'theorist', I try to find rules for presenting what is unpresentable. I try to force art (as a name for all forms of textual heterogeneity) to fit into my pre-established conception of what it must be. So, as a critic, I am the artist's enemy. But if it were true that what I am doing is the opposite of this – that I approach 'philosophical' texts as self-legitimating, rule-producing, open-ended language-games that supply no reason *for* approaching them – then, according to Lyotard, I must be an artist.

The creative/critical binary as determined by the romantic theory of the self-legitimating literary text (the auto-poiesic poem) lies at the heart of Lyotard's distinction between the micro-heterogeneous differences of and as the work of art versus the totalizing and totalitarian regimes of non-aesthetic discourse. We have encountered this opposition several times already now, with the 'radical' option appearing as the latter term in each of the following pairs: reason versus imagination, conscious sovereignty versus unconscious alterity, the symbolic versus the imaginary, individualism versus structure, culture versus nature, the author versus language, poetic versus ordinary language, constative versus performative speech-acts, science versus art, macro- versus micro-narratives, work versus text. This list could be expanded, but it is already of sufficient length to see that there is no absolute consistency between all the privileged terms. Wordsworth's celebration of so-called ordinary language, for example, does not seem obviously commensurate with Lyotard's privileging of perfomative utterances. This need not be seen as an instance of a differend, however, if Lyotard is seen as remaining onside with the romantic project of finding new rule-breaking moves to make in the name (or game) of taking a risk. Given what Wordsworth saw as the overly-formalized patterns that poetry had settled into, it was a risk to assert that real poetic truth resided in the unruly flux of 'ordinary' language – just as the risk for Lyotard was taken in his privileging of the unruly flux of performative speech-acts over rule-bound constatives. Despite such apparent inconsistencies in the list above, in other words, there does seem to be a repetition at work in the formation of all the pairs that binds them as one. It is that each privileged term looks upon its opposite (and is *required* to do so) as homogeneous and totalizing. Constatives are required to be rule-*bound*, for example, in order that performatives can be liberatingly heterogeneous. In the same way, 'poetic diction' has to be cast as over-determined stylistically in order for 'ordinary' language to become the true medium of free self-expression. So too does conscious sovereignty have to appear as repressive and monolithic for the unconscious to be marked as an emancipatory, lawless space and so on. In each case, what is 'unpresentable' requires that something else is very much presentable indeed. Hence, compared to, say, the literature of a realist epistemology, 'literature' in its romantic sense is always unpresentable – it is always on the threshold of coming into presentation and is therefore always *liminal*. It is the liminality of literature, then, or its conditionality of always being 'in between' one set of rules and another (in the space of the differend) that sets it apart as the romantic question par excellence. But the liminality of literature makes no sense unless its 'outside', for example realism, is marked as having *none* of the qualities associated with performative, heterogeneous, unruly little narratives or auto-poiesic texts. It is for this reason – for this same purpose – that Lyotard presents 'science' as utterly intolerant of narrative language-games, seeing them as 'savage, primitive, underdeveloped, backward, alienated, composed of opinions, customs, authority, prejudice, ignorance, ideology'.

A further instance of the type (namely of the romantico-postmodern game of totalizing the opposition out of any investment in stakes that might be called ethical, political or even critical) comes, again, from Roland Barthes. In his influential *S/Z* (French 1970, English 1974), where he develops a form of critical commentary that is highly 'creative' in its reading of a classical work of literature ('Sarrasine', a short story by Honoré de Balzac from 1830), Barthes introduces a distinction between what he calls 'readerly' and 'writerly' texts:

> the writerly text is not a thing, we would have a hard time finding it in a bookstore. Further, its model being a productive (and no longer a representative) one, it demolishes any criticism which, once produced, would mix with it: to rewrite the writerly text would consist only in disseminating it, in dispersing it within the field of infinite difference. The writerly text is a perpetual present, upon which no *consequent* language (which would inevitably make it past) can be superimposed: the writerly text is *ourselves writing*, before the infinite play of the world (the world as function) is traversed, intersected, stopped, plasticized by some singular system (Ideology, Genus, Criticism) which reduces the plurality of entrances, the opening of networks, the infinity of languages. [. . .] But the readerly texts? They are products (and not productions), they make up the enormous mass of our literature.[23]

Here we can see the operation of what may be called *totalizing negation* at work. When the radical new alternative is set against a standard that is made to look so terribly dull and commonplace, of course the new will appear desirable and 'sexy'. Hence the exciting 'plurality' of the writerly text opposes the monotonous singularity (or, one is tempted to say, the missionary positionality) of the readerly. The writerly is all mystery, passion and romance *because* the readerly is so dispassionately objectifiable and denotative. The writerly is heterogeneous and fluid because there *are* some systems that are 'singular' and stable to which it can be opposed. The writerly marks the space of desiring *because* the readerly marks the space of knowing. The unpresentability of the one depends on the presentability of the other.

For Barthes, then, unpresentable desire is opposed to presentable knowledge in the form of writerly and readerly texts, which is yet another opposition stemming from imagination versus reason. Nevertheless Barthes' form of this distinction did have some immediately positive consequences: in disturbing the difference between critical reading and creative writing, *S/Z* extended the rules of text–commentary relations to allow for literary critical writing to become more explicitly open, experimental and productive (to become, as it were, more like romantic literature). In short, *S/Z* provided some new rules for 'doing criticism' such that critical interpretations of literary texts could now include 'inventive' textual strategies on the part of performative writer-critics. This was no bad thing in itself, though it was not without some dubious effects (as I will discuss in the following chapter). Moreover insofar as Barthes recommends, as a mode of creative or performative criticism, the cutting up of literary texts into what he calls 'lexia' or 'units of reading' (that do not have to correspond to grammatical units), his writerly practices in and as *S/Z* may be seen as an analogue of Lyotard's ideas concerning the privileged status of little narratives and phrases. Barthes' critical recognition of the internally troublesome status of the sign (as conceived within a representational framework) in Balzac's story allows him to display (albeit with a certain virtuosity) that the same semiotic instability also functions *as* the story. For Barthes, then, even a classical realist text like 'Sarrasine' cannot quite control the semiotic energies of its own performance, just as the story itself can be said to be 'about' an always imperfect control over sexual energies. But in order to see this aspect of the text, in order to see what might be called its immanent or underlying openness to the freedom of nonrepresentational semio-sexual economies, one has to read the text differently – almost as if it remained unwritten. 'The more plural the text,' Barthes claims, 'the less it is written before I read it.'[24] So what has to be avoided at all costs is any acceptance that 'Sarrasine' is complete or finished, since the writerly approach requires that every text is 'a galaxy of signifiers, not a structure of signifieds; it has no beginning; it is reversible; we gain access to it by several entrances, none of which can be authoritatively declared to be the main one'.[25] Just as there is no single way of entering the human body, Barthes invites us to 'come' into the text by any of its many openings. To be opposed to difference as it applies to text–commentary relations, therefore, is to be constructed in opposition to sexual choice and freedom. The comparison is unavoidable, if it is also (perhaps despite itself) totalizingly prescriptive. It may also be seen as grounded in totalizing negation, in the sense that in order to assert the virtues of textual and sexual 'plurality' it presumes there *are* forms of textual and sexual practice that are 'singular'. Or at any rate it presumes that some forms of textual and sexual practice are 'denying' a heterogeneity within, just as 'Sarrasine' can appear as readerly only by repressing a tendency to writerliness. Hence 'difference' here is located on the side of nonrepresentational and non-heterosexual practices, on the presumption that their opposites are singularly monolithic (let alone on the presumption that they are in any way equivalent) and therefore totalizing and totalitarian. Since it is realism and heterosexuality which are singled out (by implication) for declaring there is only one 'main' entrance, then of course it is realists and heterosexuals who are the enemy. The fact that the imputed declaration may not be true, either in theory *or* in practice, is no impediment to Barthes' affirmation of the rule-breaking, risk-taking 'radical' nature of the writerly – just as later it will not be a hindrance to Lyotard's theory of the ethical superiority of little things over big ones that not all scientists might look upon artists as examples of 'primitive' forms of life.

Tolerance of difference is good. It may seem to be so manifestly good as even to count for a perfect instance of a metanarrative. Who would come out against difference today and not be met with resistance, where resistance is allowed? While racism, homophobia and misogyny (to name but a few undemocratic, unenlightened enemies) are by no means relegated to the past, neither have these problems been swept under the carpet in democratic societies. While it is certainly true that today's intellectual class is more heterogeneous and situated more problematically in relation to an outside than was the case for its modernist predecessor, this does not have to mean that 'postmodern' intellectuals are all invested in so many different micro-agendas that there is no hope of a consensus on anything at all. It does not mean that simply because there is debate among intellectuals as to the best or most appropriate rules to apply in given situations, therefore the very notion of 'rules' is unfoundational. It does not mean that because there is difference *within* the postmodern intellectual community, therefore there *is* no intellectual 'community' at all any more because wherever there are differences there must be differends – and so our heterogeneous interests, which are incommensurable, keep us from forming anything so nostalgic as 'alignments' or 'bonds'. Intellectuals can no longer talk among themselves because the different values they subscribe to are just products of the rules of different language-games, and there are no rules for communicating those completely localized, utterly situated, wholly game-dependent values from one discursive zone or playing field to another. Hence there are no rules for deciding which values are (provisionally, contextually and for different reasons) 'better' than others. Or to reduce all this to its base condition: *there is no truth*.

Now, as we have seen, Lyotard's response to this condition is to call for heterogeneity to be left alone, since for him 'justice' is done only when incommensurability has not been sought to be resolved but has been left intact. Justice is done, then, when a judgement has *not* been made. One may not be upholding the principle of tolerating differences, however, if what one does is to assign 'difference' the same value as 'incommensurability'. Yet, for example, the response of American postmodern philosopher Richard Rorty to the perceived absence or impossibility of truth is simply to call for more civility in performing the rules of a debate, with a view to arriving at 'pragmatic consensus'.[26] Hence the British philosopher Christopher Norris, whose work is positioned very much against the ideas of Lyotard and Rorty and very much closer to those of Derrida, argues that

> In fact there is little to choose, preferential idioms aside, between Rorty's pragmatist talk of consensus as the aim of civilized debate (treating truth as just a matter of what's currently and continguently 'good in the way of belief') and Lyotard's proposal that we should strive to maximize 'dissensus' as a means of furthering the interests of justice in a liberal-pluralist polity. For they are agreed on the following points: (1) that the Enlightenment project (or the philosophic discourse of modernity) has entered a phase of terminal decline; (2) that any attempt to revive that project is sure to have bad (ethically and politically retrograde) effects; and (3) that since 'critique' in the old (i.e. Kantian or Marxist) sense has now gone the way of all those other outmoded 'meta-narrative' concepts, therefore the best – indeed the only – alternative is an ongoing 'cultural conversation' which acknowledges its own strictly localized character and abjures any thought of truth and validity beyond its immediate sphere. Only thus, according to Lyotard, can a *certain idea* of Enlightenment – standardly equated with Western notions of reason, progress, political 'maturity' etc. – be prevented from continuing to impose its culture-specific norms under cover of a universalist rhetoric which easily translates into forms of cultural imperialism.[27]

Since we now have a number of different positions on offer, how should we decide between them? There would seem to be three options: either we decide to agree with Lyotard and, Bartleby-like, 'prefer not to' decide;[28] or we go with Rorty and find a consensual or middle-ground position, such that 'the community' decides; or we follow Norris and try to make a decision from somewhere other than within the space of transcendental heterogeneity or pragmatic contingency. Again: either there is nothing to decide; or the 'decision' (which is not quite the right word) is completely case-restrictive and self-legitimating; or what has to be decided is the relationship of any problem's 'inside' to some 'outside' standards or values which are not necessarily transcendental without having to be utterly contingent. In terms of the first option, decision making (or any closural move at all) is banned from being brought into play. All language-games are valid because they all have their own rules which must be respected: so any attempt to adjudicate between language-games is a violation of their inalienable right to be what they are, no matter how different they might be according to another set of rules. Language-games are incomparable because they are incommensurable. They cannot be compared or judged, because to do so would involve appealing to an outside (in the form of a metanarrative) whose own rules would be capable of comprehending only themselves. Now if in fact all meanings, knowledges and values were indeed restricted to parallel language-games, then of course there could be no hope of changing the world. This or that language-game might change, but 'the world' never could: because any notion of 'the world' would be locked inside a particular language-game. And if one such notion 'happened' to be invested in the spread of democracy, while another 'happened' to regard clitoridectomy as an essential part of its life-world – there would be no basis for choosing between them. Imagine, then, the sort of ethico-political tunnel-vision that a theory of language-games implies: strictly, indeed, it has to be wondered how a theory of language-*games* (in the plural) could ever arise in the first place. For how could one get outside any language-game to know that there are other rules, other language-games, in the world – unless one claimed to have access to the rules of what must be called a 'metalanguage-game' (or a metanarrative)? Perhaps, though, one could 'know' of other rules as an *effect* of the rules of a particular language-game that just happened to produce this as a thinkable proposition. But in that case, for all those who played it, there would be only *one* – universal – language-game, and so the distinction between self-legitimating and non-self-legitimating language-games could never count as a 'report' on knowledge in the way that Lyotard must surely have intended his 'Report on Knowledge' to count as a set of verifiable statements about an agreed object or problem. The distinction between language-games (or the 'theory' of language-games) could be only an effect of a set of local contingencies that just happened to make possible the idea that there is more than one language-game. But if the academic community did regard *The Postmodern Condition* as an utterance that is fully circumscribed within contingent limits, then it would never have any status as knowledge. Here there are two possibilities:

either Lyotard and the academic community are playing different language-games or we are playing the same language-game. If the former is true, how could anyone know it? If the academic language-game and Lyotard's language-game are different, neither side could be aware of this. And so it is possible that Lyotard is right – that there is something outside and higher than 'knowledge', something romantically unpresentable, that we should all know about. But of course we could never know what Lyotard was referring to, because we couldn't even know that he was talking about something different from what we think we know already. On the other hand, if Lyotard and the academic community *are* speaking the same language – then what counts as 'knowledge' is just what happens to get agreed upon among equals or interested parties.

This brings us to the second option, as mentioned above. If anything can count as knowledge so long as a community agrees to it, then we cannot say that modern chemistry is better than medieval alchemy. All we could say is that these different systems, based on different knowledges of the properties of elements, are both results of a 'shared conversation' (as Rorty puts it) between members of different communities. For different reasons of 'social pragmatics', the modern and medieval communities talked among themselves about different things and came to different agreements. That is all. In some African and some Islamic communities today, they are still having a 'shared' conversation in which it is still being 'agreed' that clitoridectomy is a good thing. In liberal democratic communities, the talk is that we continue to agree that clitoridectomy is not for us. That is all. Even when the members of a community agree to disagree, this too, as Norris points out, is able to be accommodated by Rorty's principle of pragmatic consensus: 'No doubt (and here again he is on a wavelength with Lyotard) there is room for quite a measure of internal "dissensus" within any given community. But in the end such differences only make sense – only register as part of a meaningful dialogue – on condition that all parties subscribe to the wider conversational rules of the game.'[29] Like the first option we discussed, then, this one also rules out the possibility that any knowledge or value could ever be other than fully situated within certain limits. For Lyotard the limits are defined by language-games, for Rorty by communities. Either way, one would have to be attached to some prehistoric notion of the Enlightenment to believe there is a way of *evaluating* differences.

This is the third option, though it is not necessarily 'prehistoric'. Once again, to be outside Lyotard or Rorty's views – to be outside the postmodern life-world – is to be placed, by an act of totalizing negation, on the side of monolithic, imperialist, intolerant, outmoded ways of thinking. One would have to be either stupid or dogmatic to want to be somewhere other than where it's all happening, where today's ideas are really at. One would have to be very dull indeed to think there *are* ways of thinking that cannot be ruled out so easily by acts of totalizing negation. Far better to occupy the space of liminality and to write with proselytizing fervour on the margins of the literary/critical divide. But critical practices and categories of critical thought might not be reducible to romantic evaluations of the mundane and the glamorous, as I will argue in the following chapter. The discussion there will proceed around a comparison of the American postmodern literary scholar Ihab Hassan's project of 'paracriticism' with some of Derrida's ideas (especially, at first, his notion of 'play') as associated generally with poststructuralism.

5

Interpretation as Invention

Although the term 'postmodernism' did not gain currency in English until around the mid-1980s, by which time it was well and truly on the road to cross-over fame through more widespread general usage, it was certainly in circulation academically before then. If one were tracing its points of entry into academic discourse, then the publication in 1975 of Ihab Hassan's *Paracriticisms: Seven Speculations of the Times* should not be overlooked. Hassan's reputation as a literary scholar of considerable standing in America was well established by 1975, based on such works as *Radical Innocence* (1961) and *The Literature of Silence* (1967). From the outset his critical project can be discerned as the attempt to develop an understanding of, and a vocabulary for, the 'new' literature that had begun to emerge in the United States from the mid-1950s, associated at first with such writers as Truman Capote, Norman Mailer and William Styron. Somewhat later, Hassan started using the term 'postmodern' to describe the new directions in American writing that, by the time his book *The Dismemberment of Orpheus: Toward a Postmodern Literature* was published in 1971, were being shaped by (among others) Pynchon, Susan Sontag, John Barth, William Gaddis, Donald Barthelme and John Hawkes. Despite the appearance of the term 'postmodern' in the title of that book, however, it did not catch on immediately as a critical marker of the literary concerns and practices of the period. While several neologisms were then in use ('surfiction' and 'fabulation', for example) to describe the 'new' writing, it was the term 'metafiction' that was in vogue. This was the term employed most widely to describe the peculiar self-legitimating features of the 'new' literature (confined almost exclusively to prose writing) and, as the prefix 'meta-' suggests, what it marked as 'new' was a perceived preoccupation among American fiction writers of the time with the nature of fiction: 'metafiction' refers, in short, to fiction that is 'about' fiction.[1]

So it was generally accepted (although not without dissensus) by American literary scholars of the 1960s and '70s that new rules for doing literature had come into play in the 1950s, and that the writing through which this had occurred deserved a name of its own. However, as we found with the literature of the Romantic period, one of the perceived qualities of the 'newness' of this 'new' American writing was that it resisted being named, because its very newness kept it a kind of secret from the old orders of literary exegesis. The 'new' literature was 'new' because, in a word, it was unpresentable. What was important was not whether it was called metafiction or postmodernism, then, but that it was acknowledged as 'new'. In an early attempt to catch the tenor of such writing, Hassan suggested there were five distinguishing features of 'the hero' in the new American novel of the 1950s: these were the hero's acceptance that (1) human actions are ruled by 'chance and absurdity', (2) there are no norms of moral conduct, (3) alienation is the condition of human life, (4) human motives are characterized by 'irony and contra-diction' and (5) human knowledge is 'limited and relative'.[2] In other words, as Lyotard does in *The Postmodern Condition*, Hassan assumes that the new literature (or new forms of self-legitimation, for Lyotard) can be understood as a response to a change in the background life-world. The five distinguishing features of the American novelistic hero of the 1950s are a 'reflection', then, of alterations in the life-world 'outside' the novel. By a similar logic, Lyotard argues that the heterogeneity of the postmodern text corresponds to what he calls the postmodern 'condition' itself. And so, just as Rousseau and Wordsworth had called for a change in art as a necessary response to a changing world, Hassan and Lyotard both explain what they see as new kinds of textual practice in terms of a response to new epistemic conditions. For Hassan, then, formal experi-mentation in fiction is intimately bound up with vital questions of 'life', which is why he sees what he calls 'a new *introversion of form*' in American writing of the 1950s as 'the fictional correlative of the self in recoil'. Thereafter he explains (among other issues) the return to promi-nence of the American short story at that time in the following terms:

> The rifeness of the novelette and short story form is thus seen not merely as evidence of our frenetic and accelerated mode of existence, and of all the distractions created by our mass media. That rifeness is evidence, on a more basic level, that our lives can take shape only in sudden epiphanies or isolated moments of crises [sic], and that, indeed, since our world may

come to end without notice, we lack those powers of anticipation and development which longer novels imply. Likewise, the current fashion of symbol, ritual, and archetype is not simply a compliment we pay to Sir James Frazer and all the anthropologists who have gilded the primitive past; it is rather an admission that we seek an order which reason and science have failed to provide, and look for verities which are not distorted by the conscious or sophisticated mind. Finally, the dandyism and refinements of style in some recent fiction do not only reflect our concern with, even our reliance on, sheer sensibility; they are also an attempt to preserve the integrity of language by removing it, perhaps too rashly, from the corruption of discursive speech in our age. As poetry aspired to the condition of music in the work of the French Symbolists, so does fiction now aspire, in certain instances, to the condition of poetry.[3]

Hassan's emphasis here is on 'the little'. Short fiction, symbols and stylistic detail: these are among the markers of the new formalistic 'introversion' which is really a sign of the alienated self recoiling from the metanarratives of reason, science and the mass media, as well as from the debilitating 'corruption of discursive speech'. Hence we might notice that the passage both looks back (through a glazy modernist perspective on the dangers of popular culture) to a romantic insistence on the vitality of the literary life-world, and forward to the postmodern conceit of the ethical superiority of little to big. For it is actually little narratives (which 'aspire', significantly, 'to the condition of poetry'), according to Hassan, that define the literary preference of 'our age' at that time.

A decade later, in his remarkable *City of Words*, a study in excess of four hundred pages of just about everyone of any significance who was publishing fiction in America in the 1960s, the English literary critic Tony Tanner makes an argument that is similar to Hassan's. Although it is not a new idea that social reality is a construct, 'an inverted superstructure which man the engineer has erected on "natural" reality', Tanner maintains that nevertheless 'it is one which seems to have been entertained by American novelists of the past two decades to an extent that makes it begin to look like an obsession.'[4] So for Tanner, too, the 'new' forms of American writing in the 1960s are explained against a background in which, as Lyotard might say, there is no longer a belief in the grand unifying narrative of 'society'. Typically, then, a disbelief in metanarratives succeeds to an intensity of faith in the truthfulness of the literary text – so long as literature is understood as heterogeneous and unpresentable. Time and again the point is made by Tanner that the 'new' writing of the 1960s cannot be categorized in terms of standard generic types. In such texts as *Snow White* (1967), for example, the American storyteller Donald Barthelme writes 'a curious kind of prose, sometimes feeling hard and shellacked, like plastic, at other times fluttering like gay ribbons over the contemporary landscape, like the bunting over used car lots', while Richard Brautigan's *Trout Fishing in America* (1967) could be described as 'an idyll, a satire, a quest, an exercise in nostalgia, a lament for America, or a joke – but it is a book which floats effortlessly free of all categories and it is just this experience of floating free which is communicated while one is reading the book'.[5]

As generic boundaries blurred, so too did the distinction between fiction and nonfiction. Any account of the 'new' American writing of the 1960s and 1970s therefore has to include works of nonfiction – in the form of 'the new journalism' associated with the likes of Tom Wolfe, Hunter S. Thompson and Michael Herr, and also as 'the nonfiction novel' associated with Capote's *In Cold Blood* (1965) and Mailer's *The Armies of the Night* (1968). Hence the notion of literature expanded to become a kind of 'writing' in general, a point I will return to when discussing Derrida's work later in this chapter. The impetus for this expansion, or this loosening up, was often given as a response to changing attitudes and values of the time. As early as 1961, for example, the American novelist Philip Roth argued that 'the American writer in the middle of the 20th century has his hands full in trying to understand, and then describe, and then make *credible* much of the American reality. It stupifies, it sickens, it infuriates, and finally it is even a kind of embarrassment to one's own meager imagination.'[6] But earlier still, in 1958, the critic Norman Podhoretz was claiming that novelists were no longer even the most important of literary figures. According to him, the novel flourished in Victorian England 'because it remained in touch' with its times, but in what he calls 'the spiritual dislocation of the Cold War period' the novel has lost its sense of purpose because it has been overwhelmed by the task of having to make America 'credible'. 'And what the novel has abdicated', Podhoretz maintained, 'has been taken over by discursive writers'[7] – that is, by essayists.

But what had been posed, by Podhoretz, as a choice between fiction and nonfiction was not really an issue for many other critics later in the period. For example, in the first book-length study of the nonfiction novel, *The Mythopoeic Reality* (1976), the literary theorist Mas'ud Zavarzadeh placed fiction writers alongside nonfiction writers as kindred spirits in the struggle to make America credible. What he calls 'the modal ambiguity' of *In Cold Blood*, then, is claimed by Zavarzadeh as the narrative equivalent of 'the inherent complexity of contemporary reality'.[8] Hence the book's account of events surrounding the real-life murders of a rural family by two young drifters in the small town of Holcomb, Kansas, on 15 November, 1959 turns Holcomb – by means of Capote's 'mythopoeic' approach – into 'a crisis city: a state of existence reflecting contemporary America, which, having failed to cope with emerging urban reality, is immersed in a total communal fear, estrangement, and paranoia'.[9] For Zavarzadeh, though, the explanatory powers of the imagination are not confined, as they were for Podhoretz, to contemporary writers of nonfiction: they are displayed by writers of fiction too, albeit by those who write in the manner of what Zavarzadeh (who is rather fond of neologisms) calls 'transfiction' (a term for what most other critics of the time were calling metafiction). Hence he puts together Pynchon's Lot 49 with Oscar Lewis's nonfiction novel La Vida (1967) as examples of writing that responds to an epistemic change, a change he defines in literary terms as the shift from 'the totalizing novel' of the early nineteenth to mid-twentieth centuries to the 'supramodernist' narratives of today:

> The difference between Middlemarch and To the Lighthouse is basically a matter of quantitative changes in such aspects of the novel as the psychological analysis of the character and the retardation of the plot: both are still operating within the narrative framework of the totalizing novel. However, The Crying of Lot 49 or La Vida, which are widely known supramodernist narratives with overall narrative concerns relatively similar to those of George Eliot's and Virginia Woolf's novels, are entirely new kinds of narratives which are not understandable in terms of the criteria used to approach traditional novels. The narrative configurations in Pynchon's and Lewis's books are the function of a technologically induced reality and a reorientation of literary tradition itself.[10]

Here we find a typically romantic (and at the same time strangely materialist) explanation of literary change: Pynchon and Lewis write the way they write because the world is the way it is. While being romantic, though, it is also (as we have found before) a typically postmodern explanation. Without saying there is no such thing as literary change, however, since there patently is, this does not have to mean that literary changes are effects of epistemic shifts. If we followed the American philosopher of science Thomas Kuhn,[11] for instance, we could think of different theories or estimations of literature in terms of 'paradigms', such that, for whatever reasons, at any time one paradigm can always give way to another. But paradigmatic shifts, or a shift in any culture's understanding of what literature means (say the shift from classicism to romanticism), would not be seen as a 'response' on the part of the literary community of the time to actual or perceived changes in the epistemic life-world. It may be (as we have seen repeatedly) that literary communities often *explain* shifts in this way to themselves, but that is another matter. The point is that such explanations may miss the point: that change is, in a sense, naturally occurring and hence chaotic. It happens, randomly and for a variety of reasons, whenever someone gets an idea and enough other people (who are specialists, and therefore in a position to act on that idea) think it is a good one. So it could be that romanticism started not because city life was actually dispiriting and therefore some noble souls decided to dedicate themselves to the reanimation of the human spirit through poetry, but because enough people who wanted to be poets thought it was a good idea to think that city life is dispiriting and that would be a good thing to write poems about. On this model the prolixity of many American novels of the 1960s – for example Barth's *The Sot-Weed Factor* (1960) and Pynchon's *V.* (1963) – and the general heterogeneity of literary forms at that time would be explained as the uptake of such 'good' ideas as that novels ought to be extremely long and wordy and that literature ought to mean many things, including nonfictional writing.

But a problem we seem to keep encountering is that these keep being presented as the only choices. Either literary change is an outcome of socio-historical change, or literary change is an effect of change within the system (or language-game) of literature. For all that Lyotard's account of postmodernism would seem to support the latter option, however, it remains the case that (for him) the very notion of postmodern literature or art belongs to a particular historical moment (the present), and for this reason his account of the nature of 'postmodern' textuality has to be seen as inseparable from what he thinks the nature of the postmodern historical present is (even if that nature is defined in terms of future anteriority). In other words, Lyotard's account of literary change would seem to be that it *is* an effect of change within the literary system, but that this effect is nevertheless temporal and contingent. The idea that literature is just a language-game, then, is historical – including the idea that this idea is 'ahistorical'. So even the notion of literary change as an internal effect of systemic change relies on a model of some external field as the impetus for change in any language-game.

Things change, certainly. But the values that attach to different changes are obviously not value-free themselves. It might even be said that changes change according to the added values ascribed to a notion of change in general. Hence for a theory of literature as a system that is driven by change, the event of every literary change itself would be, in a sense, quite unremarkable. However, because consensus is always rent by dissensus, there is never a single literary theory or paradigm that has complete control of the meanings of 'literature' and therefore of the values that attach to changes within, to, or as literature at any time. Perceptions of literary changes differ, then, as do actions proceeding from those differences. So change can be embraced or rejected, or responded to in many other ways. One response to changes that are said to have been brought about through and as 'postmodernism', for example, might be that – in the very questions which are raised concerning what 'it' is, or even *whether* it 'is' – some positive changes have occurred in the loosening up of such categories as knowledge, literature and culture. Whether postmodernism marks an actual change from other modes of cultural experience, then, it could be said to do so virtually: in the sense that it is more common now than ever to come across expressions of the 'otherness' of contemporary experience. After a certain point, perhaps it is not worth trying to separate the experience from the expression. Kroker and Cook, for example, in a tone that is no doubt ironically breathless, and as if writing the floor-plan for a text such as *Empire of the Senseless*, refer to the 'edge of delirium and doom' on which postmodern experience is situated. 'The cultural signs', they say, 'are everywhere': among which they cite as examples the video clip by Dire Straits for their single, 'Money For Nothing' (1985), which is 'a brilliant satire on Baudrillard's implosion of experience in the simulacrum', and the cover of Joni Mitchell's album, *Dog Eat Dog* (1985), showing

> a wrecked car and a stranded victimized woman surrounded by a pack of vicious dogs as a metaphor for postmodern culture and society in ruins. But what gives away the game of the double-reversal going on in this album cover is that the psychological sensibility evoked by *Dog Eat Dog* discloses itself to be both *piety* (an ethics of concern for the welfare of the woman as victim) and *idle fascination* with her coming death. In *Anti-Oedipus*, Deleuze and Guattari, repeating Nietzsche's insight that the coming fate of suicidal nihilism would be the production of a culture oscillating between the mood lines of a little voluptuousness and a little tedium, said that the main emotional trend lines of the '80s are now *piety and cynicism*: piety to such a degree of intensity that it flips into its opposite sign – a cynical fascination fueled by *ressentiment* with the fate of those who fall outside the fast-track of mediascape '80s style.[12]

Notwithstanding its ecstatic tone, the similarities between this passage and the one quoted above from Hassan's *Radical Innocence*, published a quarter of a century earlier, are striking. What Kroker and Cook refer to as the postmodern mood of 'delirium and doom' corresponds to Hassan's assertion in 1961 of 'our frenetic and accelerated mode of existence' at a time when 'our world may come to end without notice.' Moreover the cultural significance that Kroker and Cook give to micro-texts (the music video and the album cover) makes the claim by Hassan – that 'our lives can take shape only in sudden epiphanies or isolated moments of crises' – seem almost prophetic. The differences between these passages, then, emerge against a shared background. But the differences are no less conspicuous all the same. Hassan's quietly melancholic tone is in marked contrast to the ecstasy of Kroker and Cook, and this distinction is in keeping with Hassan's allusion to Scottish anthropologist Sir James Frazer's *The Golden Bough*, a massive twelve-volume encyclopedic narrative of human development from 'symbolic' to 'scientific' thought, published from 1890 to 1915, which became a standard reference for writers and critics of the first half of the twentieth century, compared to Kroker and Cook's citation of French philosopher Gilles Deleuze and clinical psychoanalyst Félix Guattari's *Anti-Oedipus*, a lengthy, uncompromising study, published in French in 1972 and in English five years later, which is both profuse and ecstatic in its presentation of the political role of desire across the history of Western culture, and which is now a standard reference for postmodern scholars.[13] But the difference in the references to *The Golden Bough* and *Anti-Oedipus* is not simply that Frazer's book belongs to the cultural capital of an older generation while Deleuze and Guattari's book seems almost to bring the future into the present. Nor is it simply a disciplinary difference between the literary anthropological explanation of culture offered by Frazer, based on the importance of epistemological evolution, and the psycho-philosophical explanation of Deleuze and Guattari, based on the importance of dynamic desire. There is something in the different *moods* of relating to the present in these passages that distinguishes them: while they are both marked by intensity, in Hassan the mood is pensive while in Kroker and Cook it is one of rapture. Hence, for Hassan, the present is something to be *looked into* for signs of the ahistorical 'verities' which the 'distractions' of 'frenetic' contemporary culture obscure. Culture remains for Hassan, then, in the famous words of the nineteenth-century English cultural critic Matthew Arnold, 'the best that has been thought and said'[14]: one simply has to look long and deep enough into contemporary works of literature to see that the Arnoldian conception of cultural values is timeless. So while Hassan deserves credit for engaging with the new, his reason for doing so is to show that when it comes to evaluating literary truths, nothing ever changes – at least not since the Romantics defined literature as the unpresentable question of itself, which is simply what the new American writers of the 1960s were doing when they reinvented the rules for making literature exciting and challenging again. In a word, for Hassan one must look into the present to find the virtues of the past, knowing that literature's 'experimental' function always plays handmaid to its 'experiential' purpose. But for Kroker and Cook the present is just for *looking at*: one stares with 'idle fascination' at media images, adopting a sentimental 'piety' towards images of politically correct 'victims', perhaps, but otherwise staring coolly out at the 'mediascape', indifferent even to images of death. This is nothing to get melancholic about – on the contrary, one gets ecstatic.

However, a decade before Kroker and Cook's *The Postmodern Scene*, Hassan himself had got rather ecstatic about his own perception of the new quality of mood that could be felt in 'postmodern' America, circa 1975, as a result of all those old rules that the new American writing had broken in the 1960s and of all that new French theory that was now coming through, in translation, to the English-speaking world. Hassan's response was: *Let's go crazy!* In his *Paracriticisms*, then, he decided to experiment with typography and lay-out in ways that had become allowable for fiction writers but not for critics. But with everybody high on ecstasy, what was there to stop a 'critic' from taking full 'creative' licence in and as the expression of his work? If 'creative' texts didn't have to be presented in a standard format, why couldn't 'criticism' be creative too?

In a book that includes a number of previously published essays dating from 1963, it is the later chapters that display the full range of Hassan's 'paracritical' strategies. Nevertheless as an object in its own right the book is visibly different, through and through, from what literary criticism routinely looks like. As its title indicates, *Paracriticisms*, since it does not look like literary criticism, cannot be understood in terms of standard critical moves. Yet this move too is familiar. As we saw in chapters 2 and 3, romantic poetry, because it stresses the performativity of the literary absolute and therefore breaks with the conventions of poetic production (or at any rate it can be said to do so according to an ideal of self-understanding), cannot be understood as poetry at all – ideally it cannot be judged, at least, from the point of view of those rules and standards it claims to have broken. Between 'poetry' and romantic 'auto-poiesis' there is (again ideally) a differend. Now while Hassan is not a romantic poet, it would seem that in moving from the 'critical' to the 'paracritical' he is nonetheless repeating the romantic move from 'literature' to 'literary theory'. As he puts it: 'The subject is frontiers, frontiers of criticism.'[15] Hence the prefix 'para-' (meaning 'beside' or 'beyond') in the title points to a critical approach that takes criticism to be a question – a system in crisis, as it were, if it can be called a system at all – alongside the question of literature and beyond the question of 'itself' as a fixed set of procedures and objectives. In a word, 'paracriticism' is on the threshold of the literary/critical.

In terms of the discussion of *S/Z* in the previous chapter, Hassan's *Paracriticisms* can be seen as an attempt to perform a 'writerly' text, rather than to produce a 'readerly' work, of criticism. Hassan himself seems unfamiliar with these terms, which is strange given that he frequently quotes from French publications in the original and since both *S/Z* and the essay 'From Work to Text' had been available in French for quite some time before *Paracriticisms* appeared in 1975. Even so, Hassan's paracritical project at this time is no less able to be described as an instance of the writerly. Another way of putting this would be to say that 'paracriticism' attempts to displace the traditional distinction between the 'interpretative' role of criticism and the 'inventive' function of literature onto a field of relations characterized by heterogeneity and interdependence. Hence the paracritical occurs in and as the space of the liminal, and because everything gives on to everything else in such a space – frontiers are for playing on. The mood here is one of total ecstasy and the rule is to be unruly (if not perverse): a conventional paragraph gives on to a block of print in the format of a poem, or to words arranged in a circle or laid out in columns or in note form. One font gives on to another as every page takes on its own appearance with its own heterogeneous mix of bold and italic type, various point sizes and different configurations of black on white. And of course this virtuosic display of 'writing' as a technology gives on to the performance of 'writing' as communication: the display of 'stylistic' heterogeneity both expresses and infuses the display of 'thematic' heterogeneity. The self-reflexivity of the paracritical is therefore an effect of seeing and performing the relations of 'invention' to 'interpretation' as productively rather than exclusively different. As paracriticism, then, Hassan's text switches genres as often as it switches typographies. From the conventional essay, whose style defines the authority of a single 'voice', to more openly experimental styles of writing that self-consciously undermine an illusion of critical authority by emphasizing a plurivocal range of opinions, speech-acts and subject positions in relation to critical and cultural objects, moral questions and speculative problems – nothing is rejected as more grist to the paracritical mill. Nor does anything escape the paracritical frame of reference, for there is no historical or contemporary text of literature, philosophy, popular culture and so on that cannot be cited or used to some effect – admiringly, parodically or whatever. Compared to the evaluative (or readerly) function of criticism (the word 'critic' means 'to separate'), the function of paracriticism is *associative* (or writerly). In this it resembles the imaginative function of romantic literature to the extent that rules of association are self-legitimating by comparison to the necessary background of external standards against which evaluative procedures take place. The interdisciplinary associativity of the paracritical (or what might be called a logic of the 'spontaneous overflow' of texts) positions it as a master discourse which is always able to out-manoeuvre (or out-play) other critical discourses. Since it occupies the liminal space of the literary/critical, paracriticism is always ahead of criticism because criticism is always contained within it. The critical inheres in the paracritical, that is to say, since every critical move is always able to be accommodated (and is therefore always already anticipated) by the paracritical. In this sense paracriticism may be seen as an instance of what Lyotard calls the future anteriority of the postmodern.

Now while it was doubtless a good thing for Barthes and Hassan to have opened a space in the 1970s for more rules to count as guidelines in the production of literary criticism – and hence for a wider range of forms of writing to count as literary criticism – that opening might not be quite as radical as they and others have made it out to be. It is one thing to acknowledge that any distinction between fiction and nonfiction is problematic, but another to conclude from this that there are *no* (local, provisional, contextual) distinctions separating them at all. Yet as we have seen it was at a time when the limits dividing the fictional from the nonfictional were being pushed to extremes that Hassan's paracritical project put into question the differences between literature and criticism. The justification for doing so has to be placed in a broader context of the romantic theory of literature as a question, on which basis the literary innovations of the 1960s were able to cross over into criticism. Things changed, of course, as a result of that crossing, so that it was never a simple case of criticism having been turned into literature but rather a more complex one of the interrelations between these terms coming to be seen as much more plural and productive than was either previously thought or allowed. Hence the separatist terms 'literature' and 'criticism' came to be replaced gradually by the more general terms 'text' and 'writing' as applicable to work that would have been seen previously as belonging to one side or the other of the literary/critical divide. Ironically, then, in the name of a certain heterogeneity, a certain homogeneity resulted in shifting the task of criticism from analysis to imitation. Nothing is heterogeneous, in other words, once everything is. So the formation of a kind of writing in general, based on the concept of the literary absolute (and not, as we will see in a moment, on Derrida's quite different conception of a general writing), legitimated the opportunity for criticism to be as 'unpresentable' as literature. In this light it is hardly a surprise that, at the end of *Paracriticisms*, Hassan chooses to illustrate his preferred 'model of change' by quoting from the last page of a book called *Love's Body* (1966) by the American psycho-cultural theorist Norman O. Brown: 'Everything is only metaphor; there is only poetry.' Brown's book is an almost complete pastiche of quotations (a text made self-consciously out of other texts), interspersed with brief narratorial links and comments. Its 'disorganizing' principle is one of association rather than connection, tracing the movements of the unconscious and the liberating effects of Freud's discovery of it: 'Freedom. Freud the great emancipator, from the reality-principle. Free speech; free associations, random thoughts; spontaneous movements'.[16] Hassan's response to such free-floating, wide-ranging associative disorganization is ecstatic:

> Brown demands loss of Self, abolition of the Reality Principle, Resurrection of the Body, knowledge of Nothing. History, philosophy, anthropology, psychoanalysis offer metaphors to his poetry. Let us simply say that in his writings all the sacred and profane thoughts of mankind conspire alchemically to re-create the soul [. . .].[17]

The focus here on the 'knowledge of Nothing' as a radical outcome of the desire for change is surely significant, offering further evidence of the continuation of an always already incomplete romanticism in and as postmodernism. For what can such a 'knowledge' be if not what must never be able to be presented as knowledge in a positive or denotative sense, as defined scientifically? One must therefore aspire to the highest Knowledge – a knowledge of Nothing – by other than 'scientific' means, along the lines of say Lyotard's attention to the ongoing heterogeneity of phrasing or of Brown's to the ongoing heterogeneity of associating this little quotation with that one. In short, by giving in to the 'spontaneous overflow' of one text of history, philosophy, anthropology, psychoanalysis or whatever into another (or of one typeface into another), the unpresentable truth of Unpresentability is able to be shown without ever being known. This is a form of Lyotard's 'justice': the nonviolent – radically uncritical – acceptance of indiscriminate difference as inviolable incommensurability. Touch nothing, in other words. By such a principle the association of 'free speech' with 'random thoughts' is then justified, because associations appear 'alchemically' (or unconsciously) as if by magic. And just as one should never try to demystify alchemy by trying to explain it according to the rules of chemistry, so one should never demystify the associative disorganization of *Paracriticisms* or *Love's Body* by trying to read them logically or critically. Just as liberal humanist theory calls for a wordless 'appreciation' of the truth about literature, then, so too does romantic postmodern theory call for the suspension of a certain will to calculate and measure (a will to know) on behalf of letting free a desire to imagine the unpresentability of truth as the literary absolute. Hence it is not by any coincidence that Hassan finds in Norman O. Brown's work the reaccentuation of one of the strongest voices of English romanticism: 'In a sense, Brown is the major restatement of Blake in our century – and possibly of Calvin!'[18] In a book whose model of critical practice is to make room for everything, it would no doubt be churlish to see it simply as ironic that Brown should, in the end, turn out to be so easily explicable after all – as another (albeit very distinctive) Distinctive Voice. For surely a paracritical project could never end in resolution, even in a resolution as ambiguous and open as irony, and so there must be something more to the association between Brown and Blake (not to mention the Protestant theologian, John Calvin!) that keeps this micro-narrative from being arrested under the rules of an external critical demand for calculable sense.

The problem of such a move, however, is that it opposes the statement 'there must be something more' to 'the critical demand for calculable sense'. In privileging heterogeneity in the form of excess ('there must be something more'), homogeneity is imputed to the statement it opposes. Once again: something presentable is presented on behalf of presenting the unpresentability of the unpresentable, or in other words homogeneous (presentable) 'criticism' is opposed to and negated by heterogeneeous (unpresentable) 'paracriticism'. This is to say that difference occurs only on one side of the opposition, such that the heterogeneity that is affirmed is in fact quite limited – so much so as to be described as homo-heterogeneity. It can be described this way because the multiple forms of heterogeneity that postmodernism affirms are all the same in their dependence on the prior (imagined) existence of completely homogeneous forms of textual production and analysis. Hence the postmodern theory of difference is in fact a theory of mono-difference, or of homo-heterogeneity. Moreover, if it transpired that there *are* no such completely homogeneous forms – and that there never have been, or could be – where would this leave postmodernism?

This is not quite the question Derrida asks in the paper he gave at a conference, on the Sciences of Man, at The Johns Hopkins University in the US in 1966. The paper is called 'Structure, Sign and Play in the Discourse of the Human Sciences', and in it Derrida could be said to put the following question: what if there is no such thing as 'structure'? Where would this leave structuralism? As we have seen, structuralist thinking is part and parcel of postmodern literary theory. The very idea that difference is embedded in the sign, for instance, or that texts are encoded with particular meanings and values arising from sets of rules that correspond to the grammar of a language, cannot be dissociated from postmodern theories of simulation and heterogeneity. It may be true that postmodernism romantically affirms the radical difference of the self-referential sign and the writerly or plural text, but in doing so it is nonetheless committed to a structuralist logic of opposition between such radically 'new' forms of (non)appearance and their 'outmoded' counterparts. So, in one sense, by putting the very notion of structure into question Derrida was undermining the very ground on which postmodernism (as a theory of romanticism) came to be established: that ground continues to be the difference between absolute difference and absolute nondifference. In other words postmodernism, as a theory of absolute difference (or of the literary absolute), relies on attributing absolute nondifference to whatever it opposes. In privileging the hetero-geneity of performative statements, Lyotard depends on constative state-ments being absolutely singular, denotative and rule-bound. Similarly Barthes' theory of the unpresentability of the writerly depends on the presentability of the readerly, and so on. Now if it could be shown that such terms of totalizing negation as the work, the readerly, the Cogito and criticism were no less susceptible to effects of the kind of 'play' that postmodernism ascribes to nonrepresentational orders of textual produc-tivity, then it might be difficult to see postmodernism as anything more than a rediscovery of the romantic affirmation of the will to imagine based on an opposition to the will to reason. In the celebration of what is always 'different', there is always a question to be asked: different from what? This is the question that postmodernism never asks because, in its typically avant-garde avowal of the romantic force of 'radical' ideas and practices, it always already presumes to know not only what 'mainstream' ideas and practices look like, but also that they are oppressive, totalitarian or simply 'safe' and in the service of such non-life-affirming interests as reason, science, power and the liberal individual.

But having said that Derrida's questioning of the concept of structure puts postmodernism at risk, it is something of a great irony that his 'Structure, Sign and Play' paper is often cited as a key influence on the development of postmodern literary theory. Generally, moreover, Derrida's work is often thought to be interwoven with postmodernism, if not one of its principal strands, and this applies also to the many ways in which 'poststructuralism' and 'postmodernism' are used synonymously. The most infamous conflation of Derrida's ideas with those of a thinker such as Lyotard, who is undoubtedly a postmodernist, is associated with the principled position of the German social critic Jürgen Habermas towards what he sees as the unprincipled relativism of postmodern theory.[19] Habermas is simply wrong to liken Derrida to Lyotard (which does not however make his critique of postmodernism 'wrong' also), as I will discuss in chapter 12. Even someone as scrupulous in his critical interpretations of Derrida's work as Christopher Norris, though, while always being careful to situate Derrida outside discussions of the post, nonetheless routinely refers to poststructuralism and postmodernism as if they were interchangeable. Although he is a far better reader than Habermas of Derrida's work, for Norris it is still the case that poststructuralism (despite its strong association with Derrida's name) remains more or less indistinguishable from postmodernism. Now although I disagree with Norris on this point, his reasons for considering these two versions of the post as variations on a theme are understandable. In the first place, 'poststructuralism' and 'postmodernism' *circulate* interchangeably – among students, through the media, at conferences, in journals and books and so on. So these terms have, in very many quarters, a single referent, albeit very often a different one: pejoratively, for example, the referent might be 'anti-enlightenment thinking' or 'apolitical relativism', or more positively it might be 'radical plurality' or 'productive nihilism'. By the same token it is just as likely to be seen as positive that the referent is 'anti-enlightenment thinking' and pejorative that it is 'radical plurality' and so on. In any case, the conflation of poststructuralism with postmodernism is an actual one, even if there are grounds for thinking it is not strictly formal, and I am sure it is to this actual conflation that Norris is responding in his own uses of these terms, approaches or positions. Secondly, nevertheless, this actual conflation (again, even if it is arguably 'wrong' in some sense) is not without reason itself. And the reason that poststructuralism has been conflated – or confused – with postmodernism has a lot to do with interpretations (or misinterpretations) of Derrida's notion of 'play' in his paper to the Sciences of Man conference.

In that paper Derrida offers a critique of the Lévi-Straussian project of structural anthropology. This alone is both interesting and daring, given that the paper was delivered to a conference aimed at establishing a respectable identity for structuralism in the United States at that time. Hence at the very moment of structuralism's intended 'break' in(to) the Anglo-American academy, with so many imposing 'Continental' speakers at the conference to endorse its reputation, Derrida's paper (delivered last) caused rather a jolt to proceedings.[20] For the argument of 'Structure, Sign and Play' is that the structuralist enterprise is based on a misconception or a false opening move that must put into jeopardy what, as a 'discipline', it claims to be able to do and know. That move can be described as what I have been calling totalizing negation, and so we might say that postmodernism inherited the false move in question from structuralism as bequeathed to it originally by romanticism. Indeed Derrida is keen to observe the similarity of Lévi-Strauss's thinking to that of Rousseau, especially in terms of concepts of 'nature' and 'origin'.

For Derrida, structural anthropology is deeply Rousseauian (or in our terms, thoroughly romantic) in the system of oppositions it derives from a particular conception of the nature/culture binary. Lévi-Strauss's mistake can therefore be seen to go as follows: human beings have an original character, a natural state of being. So when culture comes along, we are taken away from ourselves. Hence it follows that the least civilized cultures retain the closest links to nature – by studying their languages, myths and kinship systems we can therefore get a glimpse of human 'institutions' (before they became institutional or historical) in their earliest and least corrupted forms. But 'studying' is not quite the right word, since it implies a kind of enlightenment faith in objectified knowledge acquired by rationalist means. We must be very careful, then, not to impose our own ways of thinking onto the mythological systems of 'primitive' peoples. Or as Lyotard argues much later, we must respect the differends between different language-games. Because it is knowledge that the enlightenment seeks, and since the enlightenment is the very epitome of Western culture and consequently the worst place from which to start looking for an account of mythological thought, the task of the structural anthropologist (or of proto-romantico-postmodernism) is very clear: do not seek knowledge, and do not use reason. So in trying to gain an 'experience' of mythological thought, Lévi-Strauss urges the use of what he calls 'bricolage'. By this he means the ad hoc or unruly assemblage of whatever happens to come to hand in the form of signifying structures (mythemes, for example), with the aim of breaking out of our rule-laden (and rule-leadened) habits of logical and analytical thought. The idea in other words is that mythology is itself rule-producing (a mode of paracritical practice, as it were, or a form of nontotalizing writerliness) and can be understood only in its own terms. Hence the structural anthropologist must learn to think and write 'mythologically', such that the project of structural anthropology can be described as the *imitation* of rule-producing, anti-rationalist mythological or primitive thought. In order to reach an interpretation (in the form of what might be called a heterogeneous combination of little narratives or mythemes), the structural anthropologist – the 'bricoleur' – is required to be *inventive*.

However, as Derrida points out, what actually gets invented is the very idea of 'unruly' bricolage. For Lévi-Strauss, bricolage is defined in opposition to what he imagines are the completely rule-governed principles that determine thinking for someone whom he calls 'the engineer'. In his cartoonish depiction of this figure, the engineer is the one who believes that all knowledge comes from knowledge of machines – and so everything can be understood to work according to strict universal rules that are themselves knowable and have only to be applied correctly to produce correct findings. Like Lyotard's scientist (who surely derives from him), Lévi-Strauss's engineer is conveniently unimaginative and unresourceful, able to think only through predetermined metanarratives and completely gullible in his totalizing acceptance of the 'purity' of Reason. In short the engineer, like the scientist, is a kind of rationalist simpleton who thinks that everything runs like clockwork. Such thinking is then made to typify any theoretical approach to a problem: like engineering discourse, every 'theory' is a metalanguage. What theories try to do, in other words, is to explain phenomena by situating them within sets of rules and procedures that are universalist, uncontextual, totalizing. Now with this as the only model of theory, it is unsurprising that Lévi-Strauss should want to write *against theory* and propose a way of thinking that is at the same time against enlightenment reason. Hence anti-rationalist bricolage is couched in terms of familiar (romantic) oppositions, stressing intuition over analysis, invention over interpretation, opportunity over precedent – or what might be called ways of working 'with' rather than of working 'on'. But as Derrida argues in 'Structure, Sign and Play', the *opposition* of bricolage to engineering discourse is far more troublesome than Lévi-Strauss admits. In the first place it is simply 'a myth' to suppose it is possible for anyone 'to construct the totality of his language, syntax, and lexicon' or to be 'the absolute origin of his own discourse'.[21] But it is precisely such control of theory and method that Lévi-Strauss attributes to the engineer, which would seem a very strange attribution for a structuralist thinker to make. What must motivate the myth, therefore, is its service in the production of the myth of bricolage. In other words the bricoleur would not be nearly as exciting and inventive if the engineer were not so unimaginative and dreary. In this light it is possible to see that 'the engineer is a myth produced by the *bricoleur*',[22] whose own radical innovations can appear completely different only on the basis of an established way of thinking (one that is stupendously dull) to oppose. 'As soon as we cease to believe in such an engineer', however,' and as soon as we admit that every finite discourse is bound by a certain *bricolage* and that the engineer and the scientist are also species of *bricoleurs*, then the very idea of *bricolage* is menaced and the difference in which it took on its meaning breaks down.'[23]

Now this point goes to the very heart of the problem with the romantic tradition. To 'admit that every finite discourse is bound by a certain *bricolage*' is not only to raise trouble for Lévi-Strauss's opposition of the mythological structuralist to the analytical theorist: it also menaces the differences between heterogeneous language-games and metanarratives, writerly and readerly texts, paracriticism and criticism, invention and interpretation, unconscious desire and conscious rationality, imagination and reason – and so on. By a similar move of totalizing negation, in other words, each of these binary oppositions produces the myth of a privileged term by producing the myth of an absolutely opposing term. In every case, the opposing term has absolutely none of the qualities of the privileged one. Insofar as a privileged term such as 'bricolage' actually requires a totalizing negation of its opposite (in this case, 'theory'), however, then the very notion of bricolage cannot be seen as fully independent of what it negates. Bricolage and theory are therefore not in a structure of absolute opposition to one another, since the structure in which they are held (as Derrida puts it) involves some 'play'.

Derrida's argument is that there is indeed no structure that does not involve some play or give (as in the 'play' of a rope or a machine), such that the very concept of a structure that is fixed and organized is a myth.

The myth is a very powerful one, albeit, insofar as the notion of a 'disorganized structure' appears to make no sense, but this is only because the *play* of structure 'has always been neutralized or reduced'.[24] Even such supposedly radical ways of thinking as romanticism, psychoanalysis, structuralism and postmodernism have been unable to think what Derrida calls 'the structurality of structure' as it applies even to the most apparently stable systems – criticism, reason, readerly texts, constative statements and so on. So while the romantic tradition might be said to try to think the unpresentability of a concept of 'disorganized structure', it nonetheless continues to insist that such a concept is exceptional. Hence it continues to think of structure as it applies to an enlightenment tradition of critical, scientific or rational thought in terms of complete closure, organization and stability. This is the ground on which the unpresentability of bricolage, paracriticism, the writerly and so forth comes to appear as a radical challenge to established concepts of criticism, ethics and politics. In other words, without a concept of 'presentable structure', the very idea of the unpresentable (in the form of the differend, unconscious alterity, bricolage, semanalysis, autopoiesis and so on) breaks down.

In the sense that Derrida rethinks the concept of structure in a way that marks it as different from the concept of structure in structuralism, his work can be described legitimately as poststructuralist: not simply because it comes after structuralism, but more importantly because it locates a very different set of relations to concepts, terms and practices that can be seen as similar to those used in structuralist thinking. On the one hand Derrida's 'poststructuralist' rethinking of the concept of structure does bring about a break with(in) structuralism, but on the other hand this breach is not of a kind that is romantically absolute. This is because not even the most radically transgressive attempt to rethink a concept such as 'structure' could hope to do so from *outside* certain limits imposed on thinking within a tradition of what Derrida calls Western metaphysics. Try thinking a 'square triangle', for example. So there *are* some limits to what can be thought, and these cannot be overcome simply by the force of an assertion. It is for this reason that Derrida's poststructuralism (or deconstruction) cannot be seen as absolutely counter to structuralism, as Derrida himself points out:

> There is no sense in doing without the concepts of metaphysics in order to shake metaphysics. We have no language – no syntax and no lexicon – which is foreign to this history; we can pronounce not a single destructive

proposition which has not already had to slip into the form, the logic, and the implicit postulations of precisely what it seeks to contest. To take one example from many: the metaphysics of presence is shaken with the help of the concept of *sign*. But [. . .] as soon as one seeks to demonstrate [. . .] that there is no transcendental or privileged signified and the domain or play of signification henceforth has no limit, one must reject even the concept and word 'sign' itself – which is precisely what cannot be done.[25]

What Derrida refers to as 'the metaphysics of presence' can be seen as equivalent to what I have been calling 'the presentable'. Hence romanticism (and a fortiori postmodernism) can be said to assert the undoing of presence (in the form of stable structures of criticism, theory, rationality, conscious thought and so on) by the move towards a privileging of the unpresentability of such nonpresent forces as have come to be associated with a romantic concept of the imagination. In this way it is the Romantics who should be credited as the first to trouble a concept of stable and presentable 'structure'. However in privileging the unpresentability of the structurality (rather than the structure) of the literary theoretical, romanticism is still able to associate the 'play' of structure only with a domain of 'nonpresence' conceived as radically and absolutely different from the domain of 'presence'. Insofar as nonpresence is *opposed* to presence, and cannot be thought 'outside' this opposition, then it also depends on presence (and vice versa). So the play that is associated with a concept of unpresentable structure turns out to be possible only and always on the basis of its opposition to the 'nonplay' of presentable structure (and vice versa). In a word, neither 'pure' presence nor 'pure' nonpresence is possible.

The structure of the opposition between 'structure' and 'structurality' (presence and nonpresence, criticism and paracriticism and so on) is therefore scandalous. As Derrida argues, the Saussurean concept of the sign as never anything more than an equivalent marker of the real certainly does help to shake 'the metaphysics of presence' – insofar as reality can no longer be thought to be present in or as its signs. There is never any 'transcendental signified' outside semiotic systems, in other words. And because this acknowledgement scandalizes the relation of any sign to the real, the very concept of 'the sign' becomes obsolete. How can 'the sign' continue to have meaning if the relation of the signifier to the signified is not one of structure but of play? If, as Lacan puts it, 'we are forced to accept the notion of an incessant sliding of the signified under the signifier' (see chapter 2), how could we continue to think of the sign's 'structure' in terms of a signifier pointing to a signified? If not, then the sign itself is surely put at risk. But as Derrida argues, what we cannot do is to *stop* thinking of (and through) the sign: because we simply cannot think 'the signifier' on its own. Hence the signifier is never able to be fully present to itself: first because the signified of any signifier is always *another signifier*, and secondly because we cannot think the concept of the signifier in the *absence* of a concept of the signified. It is in this context that Derrida argues that we can never get 'outside' metaphysics in order to undo it.

Nevertheless it is utterly crucial to see that this statement conceives of metaphysics as always already open and dynamic. There is always some play within any metaphysical concept, such that the domain of metaphysics always already includes the possibility of thinking the supposed *outside* of any metaphysical concept. Play in general is the condition of metaphysics, then, and not simply a special condition of so-called unconscious, heterogeneous or writerly forms of 'nonmetaphysical' thinking and practice. This then is the difference between poststructuralist and postmodern thinking: for poststructuralism, the concept of structure always already contains sufficient 'give' (or 'tolerance') to provide a little room for manoeuvre, while for postmodernism a concept of structure as fully closed and present to itself is an essential requirement for the concept of a playfully open and unruly (or 'structureless') structure. For this reason it cannot be said that postmodernism or romanticism causes any great trouble to metaphysics: on the contrary, romantico-postmodern assertions of the unpresentability of the differend, literature, the text and so forth are actually predicated on an *installation* of the metaphysics of presence in the totalizing negation of such allegedly fully presentable concepts as criticism, realism, science and the work.

In arguing the generality of the dynamics of the structure of play, however, Derrida's paper to the conference at Johns Hopkins did not at all bring about an end to postmodernism almost before it had happened. 'In fact', as Norris remarks, 'this text became the principal source for that (mainly American) view of deconstruction which regards it as a kind of hermeneutic free-for-all, a joyous release from all the rules and constraints of normative critical understanding.'[26] What can be seen as Derrida's poststructuralist argument of the impossibility of choosing between concepts of 'structured' and 'structureless' structure, then, was actually read in terms of what can now be called a postmodern rhetoric of the impossibility of 'structure' per se. In other words, Derrida's sense of 'play' as 'give' was transformed ecstatically to mean 'play' as 'playfulness' (or 'unruliness'). In his own words: 'There can be no "completeness" where freeplay is concerned. Greatly overestimated in my texts in the United States, this notion of "freeplay" is an inadequate translation of the lexical network connected to the word *jeu*, which I used in my first texts [including 'Structure, Sign and Play'], but sparingly and in a highly defined manner.'[27] It is this overestimation of the notion of 'play' as 'freeplay', together with the many ways in which Derrida's notion of 'writing' has been read and misread, that is one of the principal grounds on which the postmodern assertion of 'the death of criticism' rests. The following chapter turns, then, to a further elaboration of the structure of play, and to a discussion of Derrida's 'writing', in relation to what might be called the rather greatly exaggerated reports of the death of criticism.

6

The Death of Criticism

If a certain mood arose in America in the 1960s and '70s to do with a felt sense of change in relation to questions of literature, it is expressed most famously perhaps in a short essay called 'The Literature of Exhaustion' by John Barth, whose own fiction was at the forefront of so-called new directions in writing at the time. Published in the *Atlantic Monthly* for August 1967, Barth's essay aimed to restore a sense of calm to the critical reception of works of fiction that are 'about' the *question* of fiction. Citing his own *Giles Goat-Boy* (1966) and *The Sot-Weed Factor*, he describes them as 'novels which imitate the form of the Novel, by an author who imitates the role of Author'.[1] But in this (and the point is made also, to varying degrees, for the work of the Russian-American novelist Vladimir Nabokov, the Argentinian writer Jorge Luis Borges and the Frenchman Alain Robbe-Grillet) they are, in a sense, not so much uncompromising examples of 'experimental' writing as revitalizing instances of a 'tradition'. 'If this sort of thing sounds unpleasantly decadent,' Barth writes, 'nevertheless it's about where the genre began, with *Quixote* imitating *Amadis of Gaul*, Cervantes pretending to be the Cid Hamete Benengeli (and Alonso Quijano pretending to be Don Quixote), or Fielding parodying Richardson.'[2] His point is that the idea that novels ought be 'original' and that novelists ought to be 'individual' breaks faith, in fact, with some of the earliest and best examples of the genre. Hence the self-conscious novel of 'imitation' associated with, but as the references to Borges and Robbe-Grillet indicate, by no means confined to, American writing of the period, can be seen as a revival rather than a rupture. What might be called the novel of 'originality' (or what Zavarzadeh terms the 'totalizing novel' that survived from the early 1800s into the mid-twentieth century), in other words, actually represents a counter-tradition. The novels of Jane Austen, George Eliot,

Charles Dickens, Leo Tolstoy, Henry James and Sinclair Lewis, which are among the foundations of a literary canon based on the preferred style and effectivity of realist fiction, can therefore be said to comprise a brief 'experimental' phase in the history of the novel. From this point of view, metafiction defines the tradition against which realism has to be seen as counter-traditional or unorthodox. Over time, that counter-tradition simply ran out of ideas. So because metafiction was back in vogue in the 1960s, Barth was able to proclaim that the realist *experiment* had arrived at the limits of 'exhaustion'.

It was a canny argument. By repositioning realism as a 'detour' along a path stretching back to Cervantes, Barth was better placed to attribute a seriousness of purpose and a sense of tradition to the nonrealist concerns and practices of his own fiction and that of other writers such as Borges. To this extent he was able to reopen the space of the literary to an appreciation of a much more general notion of *writing*, one that was not restricted to 'pure' generic types. In any case, the novel had started out as a hybrid form – why should there be any fuss about its returning to that form now? More to the point, and adding to the very loose generality of the notion of 'writing' that was then abroad, Barth was prepared even to express his amusement, if not quite his approval, for the new 'intermedia' arts of the time. What he calls a sense of 'the used-upness' of certain possibilities for literature did not result in the exhaustion of literature per se, he argues, but rather in a kind of 'spontaneous overflow' of other, new and revived possibilities, some examples of which he gives in the following anecdote:

> A catalogue I received some time ago in the mail, for example, advertises such items as Robert Filliou's *Ample Food for Stupid Thought*, a box full of postcards on which are inscribed 'apparently meaningless questions', to be mailed to whomever the purchaser judges them suited for; Ray Johnson's *Paper Snake*, a collection of whimsical writings, 'often pointed', once mailed to various friends (what the catalogue describes as The New York Correspondence School of Literature); and Daniel Spoerri's *Anecdoted Typography of Chance*, 'on the surface' a description of all the objects that happen to be on the author's parlour table – 'in fact, however . . . a cosmology of Spoerri's existence'.[3]

Today, thirty years after these words were written, the multimedia possibilities for literature are far greater than Barth could have imagined in 1967. There are two reasons for this: one technological, the other epistemological. It is because of the work of texts such as 'The Literature of Exhaustion', which were making possible a reconceptualization of what

'literature' could mean, that today's hypertextual possibilities for literature are being taken so seriously. A computer-generated text of the
'imagination' is not any different in principle, after all, from an 'imaginative' work presented as 'a box full of postcards'. Presumably, if the
technology had been available to Robert Filliou, his *Ample Food for
Stupid Thought* would have shown up on the internet rather than as an
advertisement in a catalogue in John Barth's mailbox. On this model, of
course, there is no writer of the pre-computer revolution era who would
not have produced and distributed their work by means of the latest
available technology. As they used to say in the 1960s: if Shakespeare
were alive today, he'd be making films. Or as the British metafictionist B.
S. Johnson puts it in his Introduction to *Aren't You Rather Young to be
Writing Your Memoirs?*, a collection of his short stories published in
1973: 'It is a fact of crucial significance in the history of the novel this
century that James Joyce opened the first cinema in Dublin in 1909.'[4]

Now Barth was not quite so ecstatic about new forms of literary
innovation at that time to go so far as to endorse experimentation for its
own sake. But he did at least admit that '[t]hey may very possibly suggest
something usable in the making or understanding of genuine works of
contemporary art.'[5] His own view, however, was that there continues to
be an 'important difference between a proper novel and a deliberate
imitation of a novel, or a novel imitative of other sorts of documents'.[6]
Such a position can be described as cautious radicalism, for Barth's main
concern was to expand the definition of 'a proper novel' to include the
possibility of hybrid forms without sanctioning experimentation in and
of itself. All he wanted was for 'the novel' to be allowed to mean more
than 'the realist novel' – or indeed since it always has, from the beginning, meant more than that, what he wanted was the return to an
acceptance of the novel's heterogeneous possibilities. Just as the Romantics had called for a kind of poetry that could not really be called 'poetry'
in terms of the established forms and meanings of that concept, so Barth
was calling for novels that could no longer be called 'novels' from the
point of view of the very standards whose authority he was calling into
question – an authority moreover that the multiple forms and meanings
of the novel itself (he argued) calls into question. When the term 'novel'
can be applied to so many different canonic and other examples, what is
the point of trying to police a sort of generic purity that has only ever
been purported to exist? What, in other words, is the organizing principle
by which such diversely different texts as *Don Quixote*, *Middlemarch*
and *The Crying of Lot 49* are collected as examples of 'the novel'?

Ironically, then, perhaps it would be more 'proper' to refer to such texts by the general term of 'writing', since this does not discriminate on the grounds of some imagined generic propriety.

At the same time, though, in calling for a freer and more open definition of the novel Barth may be seen as actually reinforcing the mystique in which the novel has been shrouded for so long. In making a case for the literary complexity of Borges's writing, for instance, he praises its ingenuity only to praise Borges, who turns out to be a type of the familiar writer-genius – somebody who combines an 'intellectually profound vision with great human insight, poetic power, and consummate mastery of his means, a definition which would have gone without saying, I suppose, in any century but ours'.[7] So in the end it is in fact the 'originality' of Borges's writing that distinguishes it for Barth, who is 'inclined to prefer the kind of art that not many people can *do*'.[8] The intellectual intricacies and aesthetic borrowings of Borges's writing matter only because there is an 'original' – unpresentable – quality to and as his writing which prevents it from being imitated. Anyone can stand on a street corner in the Haight-Ashbury district of San Francisco handing out flower seeds wrapped in a note that says 'plant a poem', as Richard Brautigan used to do in the 1960s, but of course it takes a genius to think and write like a genius like Borges. And so too, of course, in a sense it might, but that is hardly the point.

What Barth seems to have wanted is a more open space in which to write and to be taken seriously as a writer, and there could be nothing wrong with that. In other words he wanted the 'structure' of literature to become less 'structured', but at the same time he wanted something else – something unpresentable – to go on doing business as usual. He wanted the ground on which the difference between 'proper' and 'improper' forms of unstructuring the structure of literature is made to appear self-evident, to remain the same. He wanted works of literature to be allowed to 'do' imitation and to be taken seriously *as* literature, while wanting also to retain a principle by which it is possible to decide between serious and nonserious forms of what is now called 'intertextuality'. He wanted, in a word, and almost certainly without knowing it, the business of criticism to become that of a kind of 'upside-down' speech-act theory.

As discussed in chapter 3, speech-act theory favours a distinction between normative speech acts in the form of 'constative' utterances, and exceptions called 'performative' utterances. It is true that this distinction is, for Austin, highly problematic, given that he regards language as a fundamentally socio-historical enactment of what constitutes 'reality' for a community; hence his interest in what words *do* as against what they might be said to 'mean' according to a formal or systemic analysis. But the distinction is nonetheless there in Austin, and certainly it is there in the version of speech-act theory developed by his most famous disciple, John R. Searle, who places less emphasis on the Austinian 'community' and more on the Searlean 'individual' as the source of speech acts.[9] Nevertheless a difference between constative and performative utterances can be seen as an analogue of the difference between proper and improper forms of literary imitation for Barth. While Barth approves of literary performativity, then, his approval extends only to what might be called 'constative' performances of literary imitation. The properness of proper instances of performativity, in other words, has all the assurance (which, again, is stronger for Searle than for Austin) of a constative speech act. To this extent Barth's approval of metaliterary performances of rule-production does not undermine the task of literary criticism, which remains that of separating 'good' examples of performative literature from 'bad' ones (or of separating 'felicitious' and 'infelicitious' acts of literature).[10] The only change occurs in the kinds of literary text that should be separated: instead of unfavourably comparing so-called 'imitative' or 'intertextual' works of literature to so-called 'original' works, the critical focus ought to be on the always already intertextual, self-reflexive, performative nature of the literary text in general. In other words, because metafiction is not a literary curiosity but rather the very condition of literature's possibility, the task of criticism should be – as always – to decide between superior and inferior examples of the unpresentable 'essence' of literature. All that seems to change from time to time are critical decisions about what that 'essence' comprises. For Barth it comprises a romantic notion of unpresentability, but this in no way changes the critical imperative to go on making decisions about which literary texts are more essential (or more absolute) than others.

As we saw in the last chapter, though, a seemingly more 'radical' stance is possible in respect of literary/critical relations. Once the 'essence' of literature comes to be associated (or associated again) with a certain 'lack' of structure, the way is opened for such a 'radical' rethinking of the concept of literature itself that results either in its dissemination or its dissolution. If literature's in-principle lack of structure is without limit (and what could be the limits of a 'lack' that is unpresentable?), then the very concept of literature is broadened (disseminated) – either in a positive sense or in one that robs 'literature' of any special meaning. Reconceived in this way, the literary text can no longer be thought of as a structured object (however complex and elusive) waiting to impart its truth and beauty to a properly sympathetic criticism. On the contrary, there is nothing for the critical work of separation to do, nothing for it to separate, if 'literature' itself is inseparable from the lack that may be found both in and as writing in general. If the very concept of a stable structure is an illusion, in other words, then there can be no structure of and as literature as a particular kind of writing. For the very concept of 'a particular kind of writing' implies that a general concept of writing is organized around examples of an orderly set of styles or structures of writing-in-particular. If literature is to be understood as one of these 'structures', then it has to be understood also that 'literature' comprises so many examples of writing-in-particular that it should be understood as closer to a concept of writing-in-general. Even the most conservative understandings of literature are not confined to a particular structure of writing, but allow for that 'structure' to change (albeit not quite willy-nilly) in so many different ways that supposedly conservative concepts of literature are themselves closer to a notion of literature as writing-in-general. However much an institution of literary criticism might want to insist that literature can be defined in terms of the specificities of forms of writing-in-particular, it would still have to confront the question of how it could know those specificities without having always already held a notion of 'writing' in the most general and nonspecific terms. In other words, every example of literature as a particular kind of writing is inseparable from the notion of literature as a general writing. Otherwise literature would never change: it would always comprise a certain number of examples of writing-in-particular, each of which would itself be stable and unchanging.

So at both macro and micro levels, 'literature' (in general and in particular) cannot be regarded as a stable structure. This is a point however that has had to be made over and over since at least the middle of the 1960s by what has come to be known as literary theory. One of its best known expressions is the title essay of Paul de Man's *The Resistance to Theory* (1986). De Man was a leading figure of the so-called Yale school of deconstruction in America in the late 1970s, and I will refer briefly to the influence of that 'school' in chapter 8. However, in 'The Resistance to Theory' de Man argues that the theoretical turn (as it were) in literary studies is the result of having shifted the object of enquiry from 'literature' to 'reading'. As distinct from literary theory, then, literary criticism takes 'reading' as a given and therefore avoids having to engage it as a question:

What is meant when we assert that the study of literary texts is necessarily dependent on an act of reading, or when we claim that this act is being systematically avoided [by literary criticism]? [...] To stress the by no means self-evident necessity of reading implies at least two things. First of all, it implies that literature is not a transparent message in which it can be taken for granted that the distinction between the message and the means of communication is clearly established. Second, and more problemati- cally, it implies that the grammatical decoding of a text leaves a residue of indetermination that has to be, but cannot be, resolved by grammatical means, however extensively conceived.[11]

De Man's first point is that literature (generally or in particular) cannot be understood as a signified ('a transparent message') relayed by a signifier ('a means of communication'). It cannot be understood this way because, on the basis of quite straightforward 'empirical' evidence, there are always already too many different interpretations of what literature 'is' and of what any particular literary text 'means'. This is not something that has been invented by literary theory: it has always been the case that literature and literary texts have been understood differently at different times. This alone is sufficient to claim that neither literature-in-general nor any form of literature-in-particular has 'a transparent message' to 'communicate'. What have the different disciplines of literary history, literary criticism and literary theory been arguing about – within and between themselves – for all these years if in fact literature *is* just 'a transparent message in which it can be taken for granted that the distinction between the message and the means of communication is clearly established'?

Secondly, de Man argues that it follows from this that the meanings or significations of any literary text cannot be exhausted by any act of reading or interpretation. The literary text – no longer conceived as an autonomous object independent of the many possible contexts in which it could be read – cannot be exhausted because on the one hand it is not an 'object' that a critical metalanguage might presume to analyse, and on the other hand there is simply no end to the contexts in which literary/ critical relations can occur. Commonsensically this point is supported by the fact that there is never a single reading of any literary text that has the final word: some readings are always judged more convincing than others, but never so convincing that nothing remains to be said. Hence, on this score alone, literature's defining feature is its 'inexhaustibility': no one has yet exhausted all the possible readings of *Hamlet*, for example. However this is not just a version of the romantic theory of the literary absolute, or of the unpresentability of literature. De Man's point is that even a theory of literature as an 'asystematic' system or a 'structureless' structure still conceives of literature as autonomous and independent. The reason there is no 'last word' on literature or any literary text is not because of some peculiar quality or essence that belongs exclusively to literature, but simply because every word has to have a context. There is no 'outside' to this imperative, which is why there could be no final solution to the question of what literature-in-general 'is' or what any example of literature-in-particular might mean. It is not therefore that literature is always reinventing 'itself', according to a romantic concept of auto-poiesis or of postmodern difference or heterogeneity: the very reason that literature can be (mis)understood as autonomously rule-producing in the first place is precisely that literature is always read in context. Since there is no outside-context, literature is always being read differently. And precisely because there is no outside-context, literature cannot be thought of only in linguistic or grammatical terms. Literature is always more than what can be reduced to a 'pure' linguistics, because there is no context-free zone in which a 'pure' linguistics could be said to function. Take, for example, the reason that John Barth gives for judging the literature of imitation written by Borges to be superior to the other examples he cites: namely that Borges is a genius. But the combination of an 'intellectually profound vision with great human insight, poetic power, and consummate mastery of his means' that Barth somehow 'reads off' from Borges's writing cannot be said to actually be 'in' that writing if 'writing' is understood in 'purely' linguistic terms. 'Vision', 'insight', 'power' and 'mastery' are not linguistic phenomena. Yet these are precisely what Barth judges to be the essence of Borges's *writing*. Moreover insofar as 'genius' is a longstanding benchmark of literary critical judgement, we can say that the very concept of literature has never been confined to a 'pure' linguistics. If, as de Man puts it, 'a residue of indetermination' always remains after every attempt to read a literary text in 'purely' grammatical or stylistic terms, then that 'residue' cannot be regarded as something incidental to or outside concepts of literature. If there must always be something that is left over from every reading of a text, then the structural necessity of this 'remainder' cannot be said to be absent from a notion of the text-in-general or any text-in-particular. There can be no clear-cut division between linguistic presence and nonlinguistic absence, in other words, nor indeed between linguistic and nonlinguistic orders of signification.

This does not mean however that because there is no absolute differ-ence between linguistic and other semiotic systems, therefore there is absolute nondifference between them. It does not mean that because literary structures are unstable (rule-producing, auto-poiesic, a-rational or forever in the act of phrasing), criticism must be dead – or exhausted – since it can no longer act as if it were at some respectable distance from a presentable referent in need of judicious commentary. It is certainly true that the more literature is thought to be heterogeneous, the less faith there can be in the power of criticism to explain and analyse it. But this is to conceive criticism in the terms that Lyotard conceives science: as a metadiscourse that presumes to have knowledge of objects and phenomena that are conceived as prior and denotative. And it is this conception of science that Lyotard associates with the Enlightenment. Hence the romantic solution is simply to think differently about what counts as 'knowledge', by not only allowing for but ecstatically affirming the positive function of 'absence' or 'lack' in the production of signifying effects that science excludes and ridicules.

The affirmation of the importance of 'lack' (or 'excess') to a general literature should lead to the recognition of its importance to a general writing, broadly conceived as a name for textual practices and processes that are irreducible to the structure of the linguistic-versus-nonlinguistic opposition. Hence 'writing' refers not only to linguistic but also, for example, to visual and plastic modes of signification. The concept of a general writing, as Derrida has argued consistently over many publications spanning several decades,[12] extends the notion of difference to the far more troublesome and deconstructive notion of self-difference. For example: instead of thinking that writing stands in opposition to speech because each term is self-enclosed (which is what has to be assumed for that – or any – opposition to be structured *as* an opposition), it is possible to think of speech and writing as being in relation to each other by a process of exchange rather than as being separated by a state of opposition. Derrida has many terms for this relational process, the most notorious of which is 'writing'. Briefly, he uses this term in order to show that the positive values ascribed to speech – honesty, intentionality, truth and (as I will explain) self-presence – cannot be dissociated from their dependence on having to be excluded from the negative values of imitation, ambiguity and lack ascribed to writing and associated with a so-called problem of non-self-presence. Now if this is so, if speech is positive only on the basis of some form of dependence on the equally assured nonpositivity of writing, then speech and writing cannot be said to be opposed to each other as examples of absolute nondifference. Indeed they cannot be 'opposed' at all. And what is at stake in this argument is not only the structure of the speech/writing opposition, of course, but the structure of any opposition. In a word, what is at stake is the very question of the structure of structure.

This is an important point. Derrida's critique of the speech/writing opposition, an opposition he regards as fundamental to the history of Western metaphysics, cannot be understood simply as another 'linguistic' turn in twentieth-century philosophy. That critique, in other words, extends beyond a realm of the 'purely' grammatical to that of 'grammatology' as a kind of critical semiotics of 'writing' in a general sense, such that effects and practices of 'writing' are not contained within 'language' or defined in opposition to 'speech'. Nevertheless the central importance of 'language' to the concerns of twentieth-century philosophy overlaps countless different differences. As de Man points out, 'there is probably no word to be found in the language that is as over-determined, self-evasive, disfigured and disfiguring as "language".'[13] Not everyone, however, has allowed that 'language' could have many meanings. The German philosopher Hans-Georg Gadamer, for example, writing in 1967, argues that the structure of language is universal and fundamental to human cognition:

> The phenomenon of understanding [. . .] shows the universality of human linguisticality as a limitless medium that carries *everything* within it – not only the 'culture' that has been handed down to us through language, but absolutely everything (in the world and out of it) is included in the realm of 'understandings' and understandability in which we move. Plato was right when he asserted that whoever regards things in the mirror of speech becomes aware of them in their full and undiminished truth. And he was profoundly correct when he taught that all cognition is only what it is as re-cognition, for a 'first cognition' is as little possible as a first word. In fact, a cognition in the very recent past, one whose consequences appear as yet unforeseeable, becomes what it truly is for us only when it has unfolded into its consequences and into the medium of intersubjective understanding.[14]

But what Gadamer refers to as 'understandability', Derrida might prefer to call *undecidability*. In this difference we can glimpse a difference also between Gadamer's broadly structuralist view of the 'universality' of language (or 'linguisticality') and Derrida's poststructuralist conception of an a-grammatical 'writing'. For Gadamer, the condition of understandability is not to be found naïvely on the side of speech as opposed to writing. It is not a property of speech, in other words, conceived as a medium through which a speaker's thoughts and words are immediately 'present' to one another (hence the 'self-presence' of speech). For him, significantly, understandability appears as a sort of after-effect, reflected in 'the mirror' of speech. Hence what he calls 'full and undiminished truth' is located on the far side of the speech/writing opposition, an opposition that could be expressed also as prior/post. Gadamer's theory of language, then, is not committed to the priority of speech versus the post hoc nature of writing, at least not in the sense that true understanding is vested in speech. On the contrary it is vested in the post, or in what Derrida calls writing. Understanding comes only after cognition (as 're-cognition'), occurring through and as the 'limitless medium' of 'human linguisticality'. But understanding is nevertheless a positive concept for Gadamer, and in this it differs from Derrida's notion of undecidability. For Derrida, the very argument that allows Gadamer to put understanding on the side of writing (as the name of what is conceived to come after speech in the form of a technology for 'copying' spoken language, allowing it to circulate in the absence, or non-self-presence, of the writer-copyist) ought to convince him that the structure of the prior/post or speech/writing opposition cannot be understood in terms of self-enclosed differences. It is therefore not not case that 'cognition' comes first, followed by 're-cognition'. Hence cognition cannot be 'prior' and equally re-cognition cannot be 'post'.

However Gadamer cannot quite grasp this, or cannot quite grasp its consequences. He allows that the notion of a 'first cognition' is a fallacy, such that cognition is always already re-cognition. So on the one hand he denies that there is anything like a 'first principle' that grounds understandability as a stable structure. But on the other hand he regards the understanding that understandability *lacks* a first principle *as* a kind of de facto first principle for understanding what he understands. In short, and paradoxically, the understanding that there is no first principle of understanding *is* the first principle of understanding. It is for this reason that Gadamer cannot be said to deconstruct the structure of self-presence: he simply relocates it from 'speech' to 'the mirror of speech'. He is canny enough to know that spoken language cannot guarantee the truth, and so he shifts the 'full and undiminished truth' (or self-presence) over to the other side of the speech/writing opposition. But the problem is that the very concept of 'full and undiminished truth' depends on that opposition in the first place: it is not possible to unstructure the opposition in which the concept of truth is held without also unstructuring that concept. The value and meaning of 'truth' cannot be unaffected by arguing that truth does not rest on a first principle, in other words. So in this respect Gadamer can be seen to make a typically postmodern move: he affirms the undervalued or 'secondary' term of the prior/post opposition (the difference between cognition and re-cognition), and therefore thinks to have undone that opposition.

A typically poststructuralist move could come next, though Gadamer does not make it. This move would be to see that the structure of any opposition could never be undone simply by shifting 'presence' across to the far side of any binary, and so what needs to be shown is that the choice between 'presence' and 'absence' is undecidable – not because of any move that could be made by thought or theory, but because it is always already undecidable and has to be so in order for moves to be made at all.[15] It is not sufficient, in other words, to affirm structures of absence, underprivilege or nonpositivity in such a way that they take on a present, privileged and positive appearance. Therefore Gadamer's argument goes only part of the way. It shows that 'cognition' cannot be thought in the absence of 're-cognition', or that concepts such as 'prior' or 'original' cannot be thought in the absence of concepts such as 'post' and 'copy'. In this it shows that 'absence' plays a powerfully indispensable role in the production of 'presence', and therefore it cannot be said that absence is on the 'outside' and presence is on the 'inside' of any concept. But what Gadamer does not show is that the opposite form of this statement cannot be said either. It cannot be said that absence is *not* on the outside and that presence is *not* on the inside of any concept. That would simply be another form of a positive (and therefore self-present) statement. It is just as positive to say what something is 'not' as to say what it 'is'. Moreover it cannot be said positively that either cognition or re-cognition *is* an 'after-effect'. Gadamer certainly unsettles the commonsensical view by which re-cognition would be seen to follow on from the originary term, but this does not lead to an inversion of that succession: it cannot be said that because there is never any 'first' cognition, therefore cognition is an after-effect of re-cognition. Instead the order of the primary–secondary relation remains undecidable, which is quite different from supposing it gets inverted or cancelled.

But for postmodern literary theory, it has to be supposed that binaries *do* get inverted – hence the totalizing negation of terms that were previously positive. For poststructuralism, on the other hand, it is precisely a logic of exclusion or negation that has to be avoided in the critique of binaries. Such avoidance – what might be called an ethics of avoidance – must occur for reasons that are critical, political and ethical all at once.

This is what Norris calls the 'principle of charity' at work in Derrida's arguments,[16] which are never placed in absolute contradistinction to the logics and investments of other arguments and texts. In his detailed engagement with Plato's *Phaedrus* (the source text of Gadamer's theory of re-cognition *as* cognition), for example, Derrida is careful not simply to invert the priority that Plato gives to speech over writing. Indeed Derrida's purpose in the essay 'Platos' Pharmacy' from *Dissemination* (French 1972, English 1981) is to show that this or any priority must function by negating the threat posed by the underprivileged term (in this case 'writing') of any opposition. Hence the reversal of any order of succession or the inversion of any structure of priority could occur only through and as the very logic of negation that enabled that order or structure to be in place from the beginning. In order to assert the priority and self-presence of speech, therefore, Plato is forced to exclude from it everything that is associated with writing. But as Derrida shows, the exclusion is never successfully totalizing – and in fact it never could be. It is precisely because, then, speech and writing are not self-contained opposites that it is possible to think they are.

This is not because of any ambiguity that might sometimes be seen to occur within an opposition or between opposing terms. The very notion of 'opposing terms' is made possible only because of the far more radically problematic structure of undecidability that can be said to structure (as it were) every structure. In his attentive reading of the *Phaedrus*, the famous example that Derrida seizes on to illustrate the always already undecidable structure of any opposition is the Greek word *pharmakon*, whose meanings range from 'poison' to 'cure'. Standard commentaries on Plato's uses of this word routinely make decisions about which of its antinomous senses is intended by Plato in the different contexts of its appearances. Hence the different meanings within the word *pharmakon* are explained as differences between its various senses: difference 'within' is overriden by difference 'between'. Derrida, on the other hand, looks upon *pharmakon* as an example of the structure of *self-difference*, such that (1) there is no possible context in which all the word's different meanings could ever be present at once, and (2) there is no possible context in which only one of its meanings could ever be fully present. *Pharmakon* could never be present to itself because it is always different from itself. Quite simply, *pharmakon* could never mean only 'poison' because in attempting to do so it would at the same time have to mean 'not-cure'. The *pharmakon* is therefore a perfect example of an undecidable since it refuses the self-identity of such oppositions as inside/

outside, essence/excess, truth/error, intention/play and so on. Yet it is precisely on the basis of the self-identity or self-presence of concepts that Plato is able to think of writing as the outside of speech:

> This is the inaugural gesture of 'logic' itself, of good 'sense' insofar as it accords with the self-identity of *that which is*: being is what it is, the outside is outside and the inside inside. Writing must thus return to being what it *should never have ceased to be*: an accessory, an accident, an excess.[17]

In other words it appears logical and to make good sense to think that speech is self-identical with itself and non-self-identical with writing. But Derrida's argument is that the apparent logic of inside-versus-outside (which is the 'inaugural gesture' of Western metaphysics) makes sense only because inside/outside relations are always already undecidable. It is because of this that Plato is able to think two contradictory propositions at once: first that inside and outside are different, and therefore writing is outside speech. However, secondly, because writing takes the place of speech on the one hand and aids it, on the other, by both preserving and disseminating our spoken thoughts and feelings, writing is a kind of *pharmakon*. In this respect it is never decidably inside or outside speech, and so Plato is forced to drive it out – in order to protect not only the self-identity of speech but also the self-identity of the logic of inside-versus-outside, even though that logic has been shown to depend on the undecidability of the inside/outside opposition. If speech were in fact absolutely self-identical, it would not require the exclusion of writing to demonstrate this fact. All the so-called negative or problematic features associated with writing – that the writing subject is always absent from the written word, that written truth can too easily imitate and therefore falsify real or spoken truth and so on – turn out to be the very conditions on which it is possible to derive a concept of self-identical structure. The difference *within* writing, in other words, enables the difference *between* writing and speech. It is writing's self-difference, its very undecidability, that enables decidable differences to occur.

For this reason 'undecidability' is no more on the side of heterogeneity, unconscious alterity or the imagination than it is against common sense, critical thinking or rationality. Undecidability is (n)either in favour of the radical (n)or opposed to the conservative. Once again: the structure of undecidability is what enables the structure of any structure to appear self-present or essential, making it possible for decisions to occur between seemingly opposed alternatives. But those alternatives are always already different in and from themselves, in the way that speech is never fully self-present insofar as it is always in the act of becoming what it ideally should be (independent, self-enclosed, autonomous) by having to define itself against what it supposedly is not. Writing is therefore not the absolute outside of speech, which is not to say that speech and writing are the same. What Derrida calls a 'logic of supplementarity' has to be seen as always in play in the determination of any concept's attempt to appear self-determining – in which case we might say that writing is the 'supplement' of speech. In other words, writing is seen traditionally as an excessive adjunct to speech: the purity and originality of spoken language is aided or complemented by the technology of writing, allowing the self-presence of spoken truth to be recorded and distributed with greater ease and accuracy. Writing performs a convenient supplementary function, then, but one that is strictly unnecessary to or excessive of the truth-telling power of spoken language. Plato makes this point in the *Phaedrus*, but only to warn that we have to be on guard against the possibility of writing going beyond its supplementary role and actually taking over from speech. Writing is able only to imitate self-presence, and therefore only to imitate the 'truth'. But in the absence of the producing subject, how would we be able to tell the truth from a lie? Hence for Plato the *pharmakon* of writing has to, as Derrida puts it, be confined to the status of 'an accessory, an accident, an excess'. It is only if writing is confined to this restricted sense that speech can appear whole and original. Therefore the unitary originality of speech depends on the supplementarity of writing. It is this recurring process of exchange, between writing as necessarily exterior to and a necessary supplement of speech, that defines the essence and presence of speech. So the very concept of the supplement, as Derrida writes in *Of Grammatology*, 'harbors within itself two significations whose cohabitation is as strange as it is necessary': the supplement is both an addition and a substitution. In other words the supplement both complements and replaces what it supplements. 'The supplement adds itself [. . .]. But the supplement supplements. It adds only to replace.'[18] Writing, as seen by Plato, adds to speech but also threatens to replace it. However Derrida's argument is that Plato's conception of speech cannot do without a concept of the writing supplement, even at the cost of the danger it poses.[19] And this argument goes not only to the heart of the speech/writing opposition, but to the very ground of any concept of a self-determining concept or structure. What might be called 'the play' of the logic of supplementarity, then, inheres in the structure of every structure.

So when Plato (as Gadamer observes) holds that things are true when they are regarded in 'the mirror' of speech, we can see now that this conception of the truth depends on the logic of supplementarity. For if 'truth' is what is *reflected* in and as speech, then it is clearly not self-identical with speech. Even for Plato, truth and speech turn out never to be quite fully self-present to themselves or to one another. If truth can be seen only in a mirror, then truth as such can never be seen at all. And if speech is only the medium of truth, then in what sense can it be said to be a more 'proper' medium than writing? How is speech to be self-present if its self-presence has to be self-identical with the truth, with which it can never be self-identical?

Such questions, of course, could be seen as irrelevant to the proper concerns of literary studies. But in that case those so-called proper concerns would be taken to count as the inviolable 'inside' of literary studies, against which Derrida's argument of the undecidability of inside/outside relations would have to belong 'outside' literary studies proper. According to that argument, however, the very 'intrinsicality' of literary studies or indeed of any 'language-game' or 'discourse' depends, like the self-presence of speech, on the exclusion of certain factors that are held to be 'extrinsic' – either absolutely or in the sense of being merely supplementary and nonessential. Yet the very question of what should count as the identifiable and exclusive 'inside' of literary studies is one that has been asked *by* literary studies since at least the time of the Jena Romantics. And there has never been a single answer to that question.

It is only by supposing that there once was a single answer, though, that postmodern literary theory could presume to think of literature now in terms of unpresentability and absolute performativity. The essence or presence of literature lies therefore in the impossibility of defining that essential nature or presence. Literature becomes what is always inexhaustible and hence 'too much' for criticism to cope with. There is no space outside literature from which to judge it critically, since there is no act of commentary on any text of literature-in-particular that is not always already anticipated by the text of literature-in-general. A critical reading of any literary text could never hope to settle or put to rest the inexhaustible performativity of meaning-as-play that defines, without ever quite defining, the very nature of what is sought and always remains out of reach.

While Derrida's argument of the undecidability of inside/outside relations should not be seen as antithetical to the romantic idea of the absolute unpresentability of literature, it should not be confused with it either. Poststructuralism is not 'against' postmodernism, in other words, but it is not reducible to it. The poststructuralist critique of structure is *not opposed to* the postmodern affirmation of 'structureless' structure. However the concept of 'nonstructure' (as it were) still belongs to a metaphysics of presence: the concept of nonstructure can be thought only in opposition to the concept of 'structure'. The poststructuralist *critique* of structure, on the other hand, tries to show that any choice between structured and structureless concepts is always already a choice within those concepts themselves, a choice requiring a decision whose *principle* cannot be decided. Hence the concept of a stable structure depends on the possibility of its opposite, and so a logic of supplementarity can be said to inhabit the structure of any concept or the concept of any structure. In this light – in light of Derrida's argument of the undecidability of the writing supplement or of the structurality of struc-ture – it could not be possible to think of literature as a fixed or shifting domain of different styles of writing that are different in essence from nonliterary styles. By the same token, since we cannot escape the meta-physics of presence, it is not possible to think of literary and nonliterary styles of writing as absolutely nondifferent. But this is not to say that literature is unpresentable: there is a difference, in other words, between the unpresentable and the undecidable.

The difference is that unpresentability is supposed to lie outside meta-physics, whereas undecidability (Derrida insists) is inseparable from metaphysics. In its many different guises – as bricolage, paracriticism, the unconscious, the writerly text, performativity, the differend, semanalysis and so on – the unpresentable is always presented as a mystico-transcen-dental concept (a 'knowledge of Nothing') that cannot be accounted for within a space of the metaphysical determinations of science, theory or criticism. For Derrida, however, it is the very structure of undecidability that enables the appearance of a choice between the unpresentable and the metaphysical. Hence, in principle, the metaphysical is no more deter-mining than the unpresentable is nondetermining or transcendental. This does not deny that there are actual structures of determination; it simply acknowledges that no structure is necessarily determining. Now if it is true that metaphysics is neither determining nor nondetermining in struc-ture, and if it is true also that there can be no possibility of an absolutely nondetermining structure, this may be all the more reason to affirm rather than to negate the importance of criticism. In a word, the principle of undecidability makes it all the more critical to be critical.

From the position of a poststructuralist critique of structure, then, John Barth's assertion of the inexhaustibility of literature's imitative or intertextual function is uncontroversial. The problem is that Barth (and postmodern literary theory) attributes this function only to a particular order of literature, while insisting also that it is a condition of literature-in-general. Hence poststructuralism can be seen to differ from post-modernism in two respects: for poststructuralism (1) the nature of literature-in-general is such that there can never be any hard and fast distinction between orders of literature-in-particular that might be understood in terms of 'closed' and 'open' systems (realism and metafiction, say), and (2) the nature of writing-in-general is such that there can never be any hard and fast distinction between so-called literary and non-literary orders of writing-in-particular. This second point, however, does not have to lead to indecision (and hence the death of criticism) in favour of ecstatic freeplay and performativity. At the same time it may call for closer attention to the rhetorical side of (and as) critical activity – a point I wish to pursue in the next chapter.

7

Rhetorical Reading

In a very broad sense, when I decide to have marmalade rather than jam on my toast for breakfast, I am not making a decision that in its making is fundamentally different from the one a philosopher makes in deciding between concepts when arguing some point or other. This is not to say that philosophical decisions are just a matter of taste. It means that philosophers could no more choose between concepts if they did not regard them as already fundamentally different than I could choose to have marmalade if I thought it were the same as jam. If I thought that jam and marmalade tasted exactly the same as each other, then I might refer to what I had on my toast as 'spread'. In that case I would be using a 'generality' to describe the substance I prefer to have on toast, whereas I would be using a 'particularity' if I decided to spread my toast with orange marmalade or strawberry jam.

This suggests that things (whether as concepts or substances) may not exist innocently or independently of the ways they come to attention as knowledge. Of course their coming to attention as knowledge may be something quite different (certainly on Heidegger's account, as we will see in chapter 10) from their coming into being or, as Heidegger terms it, 'coming to presence'. But the problematic relation of truth to knowledge seems to demand a decision about whether 'truth' is external to truth claims or an effect of them. Very roughly speaking this comes down to a choice, in philosophical terms, between dialectic and rhetoric. For Socrates (470?–399 BC) and his followers, the dialectical method of asking and answering questions was the only guarantee of arriving at a single, universally logical and hence true, answer. Truth, for Socrates, was therefore external and knowable. But this was not how truth was understood by an earlier philosophical tradition, nor by the rival Sophist school in Socrates' own lifetime. For the pre-Socratics and the Sophists (between whom there are important differences which I will overlook here), truth was not constrained by external principles: it was an outcome of pragmatic contingencies. Therefore, in the absence of an absolute truth to which one might appeal (or a single answer to be reached), the teachings of pre-Socratic and Sophistical philosophers were concerned with techniques of persuasion (rhetoric) rather than with methods of argument (dialectic). From Socrates' point of view, however, the rhetorical side of philosophical teaching was a sham, because rhetoric took only itself – and not truth – as its subject. Rhetoric, then, was philosophy's enemy. This was no longer the case a century later when Aristotle (384?–322 BC), for example, included rhetoric as a legitimate part of philosophical training, although it is still the case today that philosophy's proper or defining feature is argument rather than style. In other words, dialectic remains closer to the essence of philosophy – so much so that rhetoric more or less belongs (as it were) to literature, even though philosophy cannot, in a supposedly superficial or supplementary sense, do without it. As George Kennedy observes:

> Modern readers tend to sympathize with philosophy in its dispute with rhetoric. In the former discipline they see devotion to truth, intellectual honesty, depth of perception, consistency, and sincerity; in the latter, verbal dexterity, empty pomposity, triviality, moral ambivalence, and a desire to achieve arbitary ends by any means. The picture is not quite so clear cut. Rhetorical theorists such as Aristotle, Cicero, and Quintilian are not unscrupulous tricksters with words; their recommendation makes the intellectual respectability of rhetoric at least worth considering. Furthermore, rhetoric was at times a greater liberalizing force in ancient intellectual life than was philosophy. It demonstrated that there were two sides to many if not all questions. The basic principle of humane law, that anyone, however clear the proof against him, has a right to present his case in the best light possible is an inheritance from Greek justice imposed by the debates of the sophists. [. . .] At the very least rhetoric imparted vigor to ancient intellectual life; it has long been noted that oratory [rhetoric] flourished most in the democracries and least under tyranny.[1]

Certainly it could not be said that rhetoric has been completely ignored or forgotten by philosophy since Socrates.[2] By and large, though, the distinction drawn by Kennedy between philosophy and rhetoric, such that philosophy is seen to be on the side of truth and rhetoric on the side of play, is uncontroversial, and is perhaps a basis on which a philosopher as 'stylish' as Nietzsche took so long to be taught in university philosophy courses and why he remains at some remove from the discipline's centre.

From the previous chapter, however, the philosophy/rhetoric distinction may be seen as a form of the speech/writing opposition. Hence the self-presence or truth-value of philosophy cannot be separated from philosophy's vested interest in not being confused with writing. If it cannot be separated from that interest, then what philosophy 'is' must include its desire to be what it wants to be. But this desire harbours a lie, since philosophy cannot avoid contamination from and as writing or the rhetorical. Indeed rhetoric is not simply a philosophical 'dimension', as if it could be controlled by the careful administration of general principles and disciplinary procedures. Rhetoric is not something that philosophy can choose to dip in and out of, deciding every once in awhile to sprinkle a plain argument with a few colourful metaphors (see the discussion of Hobbes in chapter 3, for example). But insofar as it is generally understood that what may be called the 'content' of a philosophical argument is separable from the style of its expression, then rhetoric may be seen to act in the role of philosophy's supplement. It is both the post hoc addition to an argument, being spread on top as it were, and also what must stand in for any argument, since it is not possible for arguments to be confined to pure content. In other words every argument is available only inferentially through the style of its expression. Hence it is rhetoric – and not dialectic – that comes first.

This is to follow Derrida's claim (in *Of Grammatology* and elsewhere) that writing comes before speech. It is quite right to suppose that writing may lead to error (misreading, misattribution and so forth) but it is wrong to think that in this capacity it departs from the role of another medium – speech – that guarantees delivery of the truth. Something may be understood as true only to the extent that it is always possible for it to be mistaken, misunderstood or simply missed altogether. And since this possibility is most strongly associated with writing, we may say that writing (as a general structure) must come first.

Now of course the other side of this equation is that writing in the narrow (Socratic or pre-Derridean) sense does have a positive value, which literature has traditionally been allowed to know and perform. Literature is a name bestowed on writing which exploits (rather than resists) the structural potential within writing for suggestion, ambiguity and error – a potential that most other forms of writing-in-particular (an article in a medical journal, say) strive to overcome. What would be the point of a scientific report that emphasized its own performativity to the extent of encouraging readers to misconstrue its constative, referential or dialectical meaning? Or, altering only slightly the terms of Lévi-Strauss's distinction between poetry and myth as cited in chapter 1, we might say that literary writing 'cannot be translated except at the cost of serious distortion', while by contrast the scientific value of scientific writing is 'preserved even through the worst translations'. Literature aside, then, writing is seen as inessential to scientific, medical, philosophical, political and other knowledges, since it plays only a supplementary role of dissemination and not the fundamental one of production. Writing comes into the picture only as a means of recording and distributing a scientific or other nonliterary value, which is to say that writing is added on after the fact of some scientific or philosophical discovery of the truth – the value of that truth remaining independent of how it is written up or written down.

This is clearly not how writing as literature is understood. By the same token, this does not mean that literature is seen to have no 'value' equivalent to those of science and philosophy, as if it were only writing in the purest sense. Literary writing, which is certainly valued as writing for writing's sake, is valued also for equalities that cannot be regarded only as rhetorical or performative. So when John Barth, for example, praises the writing of Borges (see chapter 6), he refers to evidence that is not restricted to a narrow sense of Borges's 'way with words' but which is nonetheless available to be read in (or into) those words, or is available perhaps 'behind' or 'underneath' them. Hence it is not so much the words as the 'way with' that counts in estimations of literary writing. This is to suggest that the speech/writing opposition operates within literature every bit as much as it operates between literature and its outsides in the form of science, philosophy and other discourses. In order to count as literature, that is, any instance of writing has to be seen to display some order of values belonging to speech (originality, truth, sincerity, mastery, courage and so on): it cannot simply 'be' writing in the strict or Platonic sense.

For this reason literature is never only just that. It is always at the same time writing-in-general, such that any instance of literary writing-in-particular could, under certain circumstances, be (mis)taken for an example of philosophical, political, historical, scientific or other writing. This is not simply a point about how the 'contents' of literary texts are often the product of several kinds of knowledge, or about the stylistic diversity that works of literature may display. Although for example *Moby-Dick* (1851) is certainly understood as a whale of a novel in terms of its literary achievements, it is also a book about whales and whaling. Melville's detailed and accurate knowledges of cetology and seafaring cannot be dissociated from his supposed insights into the dark side of human pride. Nor is the novel without an explicit philosophical content (of sorts), since in comparing the heads of two dead whales the narrator decides that one belonged to 'a Stoic' and the other to 'a Platonian, who might have taken up Spinoza in his latter years'.[3] Hence the contents of this and many other great literary works contain examples of knowledges that are not in themselves examples of literature. These knowledges moreover are displayed in *Moby-Dick* in ways that are appropriate to them stylistically: Father Mapple's famous sermon in chapter nine, for instance, is recognizable *as* a sermon not only for its biblical allusions and moral substance but for its sermonizing *style* of delivery, and so on. Similar examples of 'nonliterary' content and stylistic variance within a single text can of course be found in a great many other works of literature.

I am making a very simple point here. The definition of literary writing is so broad as to exclude nothing. There is in fact no single *style* of writing that defines the literary. In a word, literature is irreducible to the purely rhetorical – if rhetoric is understood to be outside something that opposes it (dialectic, say) and which is regarded as more significant. Hence it remains undecidable whether rhetoric is inside or outside the 'real' meaning or value of any text, and this relation cannot be avoided or resolved simply through prioritizing the rhetorical and, by such a move, thinking to have escaped the need for critical engagement with 'content'. This applies also to philosophical texts, where the relation of a dialectical 'inside' and a rhetorical 'outside' is always one of exchange and supplementarity rather than of exclusion.

The move to prioritize rhetoric and to negate or reject its opposites is typically postmodernist. Baudrillard's simulacrum, for example, is emptied of all content and refuses even to play at being a sign of something other than itself (see chapters 2 and 3). To this extent poststructuralism could be said to share with postmodernism a link to the romantic tradition of non-mimetic theories of representation: they are both 'post-Aristotelian', that is to say, insofar as they reject Aristotle's theory of mimesis or the idea that art imitates life.[4] But 'reject' is perhaps too strong a description of the ground on which poststructuralism has developed a critique of mimetic or representational theories: in a word, 'reject' is too romantic.

For poststructuralism, any attitude of rejection risks becoming what it sets out to make impossible – the possibility of being settling. Hence by

rejecting realism, for example, anti-realist theories and practices of literature can easily cohere as a tradition that is no more unsettling, *as* a
tradition, than the one they rejected. Any choice between the traditional
and the radical that is based on a rejection of the traditional, then, cannot
be a radical choice. Such a choice would on the contrary be settling,
because it would reaffirm the very traditional idea that choices are made
on the basis of a structure of self-evident difference between self-present
alternatives. This is not only a commonsensical view but (in Derrida's
terms) a fundamentally metaphysical one also, running through all forms
of the speech/writing opposition to include even philosophical decisions
about the nature of this or that concept.

Certainly decisions do get made, but this is not something that the
Derridean critique of structure (or poststructuralism) is forced to deny.
The structure of undecidability that inhabits every structure, in other
words, does not point to indecision but rather to the ungroundedness on
which decisions are based. For example, the choice between realist and
postmodern literature is not a choice between two absolutely different
forms of writing-in-particular and therefore not quite a straightforward
choice between traditional and radical alternatives. There are some features of realism that postmodernism could never reject, and there are
some features of postmodernism that are not 'outside' realist literature.[5]
This is because both realism and postmodernism are situated within a
tradition of Western metaphysics such that any differences between them
have to be seen as arising from inside that tradition, as part of that
tradition.

If realist and postmodern literature were absolutely different, then it
might be possible to describe the realist text as predominantly referential
in contrast to the predominantly rhetorical postmodern text. If on the
other hand we were to replace the terms 'rhetoric' and 'reference' with
the single term *composition*, which means both the manner or style by
which elements are arranged into a whole and the product or content of
that arrangement, then the differences between texts-in-particular might
seem to be of secondary importance to the difference within the text-in-
general. By focusing on textual composition, in other words, the rhetorical and referential 'aspects' of any text do not have to be understood as
separate from each other, and so any statement about the relative importance of either 'aspect' would have to be seen as the result of a calculated,
contextual *decision*. It could never be seen as an innocent statement 'by'
a text (what it wants to say), but always only as a situated statement
'about' a text (even if it were an assertion of what 'the text' wants to say).

At the same time, any statement about a text could never be made from *outside* the text it was a statement about, so that statements about texts cannot be regarded as absolutely different from statements made by texts themselves. This is simply to refute a naïve distinction between literary 'insides' and critical 'outsides'. A critical reading of any work of literature, that is, cannot be outside the work it reads. But neither can it be inside that work completely, or it would be indistinguishable from it. Yet this is the place of criticism in postmodern literary theory, for the critical is simply a negated category which has been replaced by a romantic concept of the literary absolute.

For a theory of textual composition, however, a concept of the literary absolute (or literariness) could never be allowed to settle into a position of absolute dominance or control. Rhetoric could never be allowed to take over from logic or dialectic, nor from grammar, as a totalizing force. Hence it could not be confined only to a persuasive function, as opposed to the epistemological function of dialectic. As Paul de Man puts it, it is only by accepting 'the epistemological thrust of the rhetorical dimension of discourse' that it becomes possible for rhetoric to be understood as something more than 'a mere ornament within the semantic function'.[6] It is this more compositional understanding of rhetoric that can be seen as a driving force of poststructuralist criticism (or deconstruction, as it can be called in its most slippery and rigorous forms). For deconstruction, then, rhetoric is neither a textual surface concealing the absence of any semantic depth (which is the postmodern view), nor does it function simply as a way to make arguments more attractive. Even literary texts, however, are thought to contain truths that are independent of the means of their expression – and so there is a sense in which even the most appreciationist forms of literary criticism have never quite understood the compositional importance of rhetoric to the production of textual meanings and effects.

It is for this reason that deconstruction has developed a theory of what can be called rhetorical reading, exemplified in the work of Barbara Johnson and Paul de Man. Such readings are characterized by their acceptance of critical differences of opinion over the meanings of different works of literature, an acceptance that sees these differences as necessary rather than as obstacles for criticism to overcome. Criticism's task is not to arrive at the 'correct' reading of a literary text, therefore, but to account for the critical differences between different readings of individual texts which can be said to occur within those texts themselves. The question of whether the governess in Henry James's *The Turn of the*

Screw (1898) is mad or sees ghosts, which is what divides interpretations of that story and produces very different accounts of what must somehow be understood as the *same* text, would be a good example of the necessity of critical difference. Now for a critical approach to literature that saw rhetoric merely as an adjunct to truth, it would be crucial to decide whether the governess is mad or sees ghosts – and there would be no question that decision could be made, based on a careful or faithful reading of the text. However the problem in this case is that there is more than enough textual evidence for deciding either way, or indeed both ways. Hence a third reading is possible: that the question of whether the governess is mad or sees ghosts is undecidable.[7] It is not undecidable because the text is at fault, moreover, as if James had forgotten to include some vital piece of information or had failed at the rhetorical 'level' to find the right turns of phrase for expressing his intentions. On the contrary, it is precisely that the text refuses to come to a decision on the governess that counts as a critical difference within the text itself. It is therefore on the basis of this *textual* difference that critical differences of opinion have emerged, and have done so necessarily.

As this brief example suggests, the aim of a rhetorical reading is not to show that texts do not have meanings. It is to show that the rhetorical 'dimension' of texts is utterly inseparable from the referential 'contents' or dialectical 'positions' that texts are said to contain. This is the view implied by the title of Barbara Johnson's *The Critical Difference: Essays in the Contemporary Rhetoric of Reading* (1980), a book in which the compositional importance of rhetoric is shown to be a key structural element in critical differences of opinion over the meanings of literary texts. For Johnson, the productive (or textual) force of rhetoric is always at work, even when thematic content is seemingly not in question. In other words rhetorical reading is not a critical response to some new order of writing-in-particular, as if it were appropriate only to self-conscious, metafictive or postmodern literature. Although the critical difference *within* every text must always take a particular form, it can do so only on the basis of a general difference that cannot be confined to an example. On this assumption, Johnson approaches literature and, more generally, texts

> by identifying and dismantling differences by means of other differences that cannot be fully identified or dismantled. The starting point is often a binary difference that is subsequently shown to be an illusion created by the workings of differences much harder to pin down. The differences *between* entities (prose and poetry, man and woman, literature and theory,

guilt and innocence) are shown to be based on a repression of differences *within* entities, ways in which an entity differs from itself. But the way in which a text thus differs from itself is never simple: it has a certain rigorous, contradictory logic whose effects can, up to a certain point, be read. The 'deconstruction' of a binary opposition is thus not an annihilation of all values or differences; it is an attempt to follow the subtle, powerful effects of differences already at work within the illusion of a binary opposition. [. . .] Difference is a form of *work* to the extent that it *plays* beyond the control of any subject: it is, in fact, that without which no subject could ever be constituted.[8]

Here the nature of critical difference is argued to be far more troublesome than the impression left by my example of James's governess. In that example, the text itself appears to be in control of the difference within. There is no real difference, in other words, between deciding whether the governess is mad or sees ghosts and deciding that, on the evidence of the text's own authority, this is undecidable. In that case undecidability would function as a *theme* – as the dialectical or thematic substance of *The Turn of the Screw*, which the rhetorical level would be read as containing or expressing. And this would be no different from deciding that the theme is one of the illusory nature of reality, either because the governess is mad (and so reality for her is the direct product of a disordered mind) or because she does see ghosts (and so reality is more than it seems). Whichever choice is made, it must be supposed to be made *by* the text itself: it would be not so much a *reading of* as a *reading off*. As the narrator says at the beginning, 'The story will tell.'[9] So if the governess is read as mad, this will be verified by textual evidence 'read off' from the rhetorical level in support of such a meaning. Hence the text itself will be read as being in control of its own thematic content. But if what the *story* tells is that there is no way of telling whether the governess is mad or sees ghosts, and if this is what is meant by the difference *within* the text, then such an order of difference would not be any different from the difference *between* 'the governess is mad' and 'the governess sees ghosts', because this too is a difference that would have to be understood to occur within the text. Regardless of any decision, it must be acknowledged that the question – is the governess mad or does she see ghosts? – is contained in the text itself. Where else could it come from? If the answer to that question is that there *is* no answer, moreover, then where else could this be said to come from but inside the text?

The order of critical difference that Barbara Johnson refers to, however, is fundamentally different from what can be attributed to a text's own authority or self-control. For her the critical difference is defined as the ways in which a text 'differs from itself'. So it is not self-control but self-difference that is the object of rhetorical reading. The structure of self-difference is common to all texts and not just to particular (metafictive or postmodern) versions of literature, as Johnson shows in her rhetorical reading of a text that may be thought to be the master of its own themes – Melville's short novel *Billy Budd, Sailor*, published posthumously in 1924.

On a standard reading, *Billy Budd* is 'a tale of three men in a boat'.[10] These three are the ship's honourable and erudite British Naval Captain, Edward Vere; the unscrupulous and cultured master-at-arms, John Claggart; and of course young Billy himself, the handsome and unworldly foretopman. Claggart falsely accuses Billy of plotting a mutiny aboard ship, and Billy responds by striking the master-at-arms to his death in front of Captain Vere. In the name of duty, the good Captain calls a trial and Billy is sentenced to hang. While the plot is straightforward, however, interpretations of the story's ultimate meaning have differed markedly, as Johnson notes. But there does seem to be at least one point of critical consensus – that *Billy Budd* is Melville's 'last word'.[11] In this it plays a critically defining role in the organization of Melville's literature, functioning as what one critic (cited by Johnson) calls 'the last will and spiritual testament of a man of genius'.[12] For Johnson, then, there is a question to be asked about the *ends* of *Billy Budd*, since at least one end the story seems to serve is in expressing Melville's 'will' or ultimate intention. Coming at the end of Melville's career, *Billy Budd* 'somehow acquires the metalinguistic authority to confer finality and intelligibility upon all that precedes it'.[13] This particular sense of an ending, therefore, it strictly extra-textual: it lies outside the text of *Billy Budd* itself.

By the same token, there is no definite point *inside* the text at which the story comes to an end. Since in fact the text itself contains four endings, the question of the 'ends' of *Billy Budd* cannot be relegated to a subordinate place 'outside' the text. At first the story ends with Billy's execution. 'But though properly the story ends with his life,' the narrator says, 'something in way of sequel will not be amiss. Three brief chapters will suffice.'[14] The first of these chapters (or the second ending) records the death of Captain Vere, who is shot during a skirmish with the French; the second (or third ending) refers to an 'official' naval account of Billy's execution which paints him as a scurrilous mutineer; and the fourth ending (or last chapter of the novella) commemorates an affection for the

likeable young foretopman that is still felt by his shipmates, one of whom
has composed a ballad recounting Billy's final thoughts on his way to the
gallows that ends with a line delivered from beyond the grave: 'I am
sleepy, and the oozy weeds about me twist.' With these words the
narrator concludes his tale. And so 'like Melville's own', Johnson observes, the last words of Billy Budd are 'spoken posthumously'.[15]

In her rhetorical reading of the 'ends' of *Billy Budd*, then, Johnson
shows up the difficulty of deciding exactly where Melville's text begins
and ends. More generally this raises into a question any concept of 'the
text' (this one or some other) *itself*. For the very end of this text must
remain a question because none of the four internal endings is finally
conclusive; but it remains a question also in relation to Melville's own
ends and ending. And in speculating on the many possible senses of an
ending that the text brings to estimations of the overall nature and
meaning of Melville's literature, the critical differences of opinion over
the years have served to show only that there can be no end to what may
be presented as ultimately conclusive in discussions and debates over
what Melville might have finally intended. For Johnson these disagreements are not unproblematically external to *Billy Budd*: they are a
fundamental part of its composition. The critical difference *of* the text, in
other words, is in a necessary relation to critical differences about it. Or
as Jonathan Culler puts it: the text's own 'articulation of contradictory
modes of signification' corresponds to 'the two modes of reading involved in critical quarrels about the story'.[16]

These quarrels can be seen once more to centre on the question of
ends, inviting a final judgement on the point or telos of the story. In the
text 'itself' it is Captain Vere who has the authority to pass judgement.
For most readers the critical question is whether he judges fairly or
harshly, but for Johnson it is the very structures of authority and judgement that are in question. These structures are not exclusive to their
articulation in *Billy Budd*, and so it cannot be allowed that their articulation is fully determined by the text itself. But insofar as their articulation *does* belong to *Billy Budd*, the text 'itself' cannot be allowed to have
no identity whatsoever. On the assumption that its difference from other
texts constructs an identity for *Billy Budd* that is wholly secure, however,
most readers have supposed that the question of Vere's judgement is
answered *in* the text itself. Hence it is *the text itself* that is the ultimate
authority, always having to have the last word when it comes to questions of judgement. In this way judgements are made by appealing to an
unambiguous authority whose nature, as Johnson remarks, is always to

appear as 'nothing other than the vanishing-point of textuality'.[17] Authority, in other words, is what always seems to be located outside the text – even when it is claimed for the text itself. A presumption of difference *between* textuality and referentiality is what enables authority to appear as its own end and makes 'the function of judgement [. . .] to convert an ambiguous situation into a decidable one'.[18]

This has clearly been criticism's perceived task in commenting or deciding on *Billy Budd*: is the judgement of Captain Vere fair or harsh? But in performing this task criticism has not been acting alone, for it is also the role of law and politics to pass judgement in such a way as 'to convert an ambiguous situation into a decidable one'. Hence 'the function of judgment' is not exclusive to criticism, and therefore criticism can never be fully identical with itself because it can never be completely non-identical with legal, political, ethical, personal or other systems of appraisal. In all such cases, judgements occur as a result of presuming to know the differences between self-present alternatives. 'A difference *within* one of the entities in question', however, 'is precisely what problematizes the very *idea* of an entity in the first place.'[19] Without that idea, judgements lose their authority. Instead of being absolute, they are rendered inconclusive, tentative, contextual. Now for Johnson it is this very structure of inconclusion that can be said to count as one of the ends of *Billy Budd*, since the text itself stages 'the twisted relations between knowing and doing, speaking and killing, reading and judging, which make political understanding and action so problematic'.[20] The political authority that Vere upholds, however, cannot afford to see these relations as problematic in any fundamental sense, but only in the sense of a problem that must and can be resolved on a case-by-case basis. For resolution to occur, such authority is bound to commit a misreading in the name of committing justice: 'the maintenance of political authority requires that the law function as a set of rules for the regular, predictable misreading of the "difference within" as a "difference between".'[21]

In the end, then, for most readers the meaning of *Billy Budd* is decided by a critical difference between opposing interpretations of the story's most significant event – the fatal blow that Billy deals to Claggart. The common assumption here is deeply Aristotelian, based on the idea (or its opposite) that character is revealed through action. On the one hand, for instance, the action of the fatal blow is consistent with Billy's innocent character: he strikes Claggart without giving any thought to the consequences because Billy is both unworldly and morally pure. In a less complicated world, Billy's goodness would vindicate his action, given that the evil Claggart is fully deserving of the retributive end he meets. But a psychoanalytic reading of this event might, on the other hand, argue for a different interpretation, which nonetheless would still be based on a relation of some continuity between action and character. Hence it might be Billy's repressed antagonism and seething violence that the fatal blow reveals. On this reading Billy's goodness is an over-compensation for his unconscious hostility, and so at all other points in the text the relation between Billy's actions and his character is one of radical discontinuity. It is therefore only through the fatal blow that we can see the 'truth' about Billy Budd.

But while it is important to recognize that these interpretations are opposed to one another, it is even more important to acknowledge that each is opposed within itself. 'The crucial point here', as Culler remarks, 'is that in each case the interpretation of the blow is based on premises that undermine the claim the interpretation supports.'[22] In the first in-stance Billy strikes out at Claggart unthinkingly and without any inten-tion of killing him. In this way his action is consistent with his character, inasmuch as Billy reacts (if not appropriately, then at least justifiably) to an offensive 'blow' to his own sense of goodness. Claggart's death is therefore accidental, according to this reading; otherwise Billy's goodness would be compromised. To the extent that Billy does not deliberate before striking Claggart, however, his action must be inconsistent with his good character, since for his goodness to have any value it must be understood as conscious and not simply as intuitive or given. Hence for this reading, Billy is 'out of character' when he delivers the fatal blow. But for a psychoanalytic reading he is only ever 'in' character when he kills Claggart, since this is what Billy unconsciously desires. On the one hand, then, in order to preserve a theory of the continuity between action and character, the fatal blow has to be read *against* such a theory. But equally, on the other hand, in order to preserve a theory of the radical discontinuity between actions and the unconscious motivations of char-acters, the fatal blow has to be read *against* such a theory. In each case the interpretation of the blow is different from itself, because in order to put its case it must advance the interpretation to which it is opposed.

Neither a literalist nor an ironical reading of the blow can sustain its own general theory of the referential or deceptive nature of text–world relations. For a literalist reading, the most significant event of Melville's story has to be read ironically; while for an ironical reading the same event must be read literally. 'The blow destroys each position – Billy's and Claggart's as well as the readings of literalists and ironists. It disrupts any interpretive account because *what* it means is undone by *the way* it means.'[23] There is in other words no transcendental relation of continuity between saying and doing, or between being and action. Even if it were allowed that Billy is by nature good, it could still be said that, in killing Claggart, he performs an action that in itself is bad. In any case whatever moral value might attach to Billy's action, the act itself is certainly, from Captain Vere's point of view, punishable by law. Nor is this to say that, in judging Billy, Vere himself does not perform an action – or that he is not aware of doing so. Vere must weight up not only the consequences of Billy's action, but also of his own judgement. Hence there can be no clemency shown to Billy (on account of his good character), as that would indicate to other sailors that the crime of killing a superior officer is punishable by negotiation. In the position of the judge, Vere is there-fore obliged to act according to historico-legal precedent in making a decision that, as Johnson puts it, 'attempts to eliminate from the future any necessity for its own recurrence'.[24] In this way every judgement is riven by a constative/performative split between unambiguous truth and undecidable effectivity:

> every judge is in the impossible position of having to include the effects of his own act of judging within the cognitive context of his decision. The question of the nature of the type of historical causality that would govern such effects can neither be decided nor ignored. Because of his official position, Vere cannot choose to read in such a way that his reading would not be an act of political authority. But Melville shows in *Billy Budd* that authority consists precisely in the impossibility of containing the effects of its own application.[25]

This is not to suggest, however, that it is only Vere who is forced to read politically, as if it were possible for any act of reading to be politically neutral. Simply because Vere has no choice but to make a decision about an ambiguous event, this does not mean it is possible otherwise to read ambiguity purely in and as 'itself'. It is not only political readers who read politically. Even a literary critical reading, for example, cannot avoid being a political act simply by claiming to read ambiguity (or unpresentability) as the very essence of the literary absolute.

For Johnson this point is made (once again) in *Billy Budd* itself, through the character of the old Dansker. Since he 'never interferes in aught and never gives advice',[26] the Dansker appears as an ideal type of the neutral commentator. He speaks only rarely and always in riddles, his few words weighted for maximum ambiguity. Leaving the work of

interpretation to others, the Dansker shuns responsibility for the meanings of his utterances and any effects that might attend them. When he
tells Billy that Claggart is '*down* on you',[27] for example, he refuses to
provide any further information and to say exactly what he means,
preferring to remain detached from the ship's politics. Hence he 'drama-
tizes a reading that attempts to be as cognitively accurate and as
performatively neutral as possible'.[28] Yet it is by way of this remark that
events lead to the fatal blow. In seeking to avoid politics, then, the
Dansker cannot get outside the space of the political. No matter how
much he tries to convey a statement that is purely constative, he could
never be unaccountable for the performative effects of his attempt to
present knowledge as disinterested truth. The idea that knowledge and
politics are separable, in other words, is not an innocent one, 'for it is
through the impossiblity of finding a spot from which knowledge could
be all-encompassing that the plays of political power proceed.'[29]

What is perhaps most striking about Johnson's approach to *Billy
Budd* is its attention to the necessarily political status of every event of
reading, which does not overlook the so-called literary status of what is
being read. Johnson does not deny that *Billy Budd* is a work of literature,
but for her this is precisely what is unsettling about it. And it is precisely
for this reason that she refuses to engage with *Billy Budd* in terms set
down by a notion of literary critical 'standards'. Hence a distinctive
feature of her approach is the lack of privilege accorded to idealized
forms of aesthetic and moral truth, as if these were locatable as anything
other than a consequence of decisions (such as those made about literature) that try to conceal their own work of decision *making*. What kind
of a decision must be made, for example, in order to read *Billy Budd* (or
any text) at all? While the answer to this could take many different
forms, from the bio-cultural to the historico-institutional, the point is
that a decision of some sort does have to be made, even if it does not have
to be acknowledged. So one might decide to read *Billy Budd* because
(say) it is a work of literature, as mountaineers are supposed to climb
mountains because they are there. This would not necessarily be to
suppose that literature is as sedimentary as solid rock, since literary and
geological formations are not the same, but it would be to leave unacknowledged the many orders of decision making and the many kinds of
decision that shape the contours of literature at different times and in
different places. On the assumption, then, that at its deepest or most
residual level literature is fundamentally constative or dialectical, it has
to be supposed that there are certain principles, which are equally as

permanent, for getting down or through to its core. But one of the problems with this assumption, which is really a decision, is that it never questions how these so-called principles came to be. It never asks the question of the rules of judgement that are meant to apply in any reading of a literary text. How did they get to be rules and on what basis are they applicable to *my* reading of *this* text, here and now? Will they still be applicable tomorrow, or to another text, or to someone else's reading of the text that I happen to be reading today? To the extent that they are principles at all, of course, they must be able to be applied generally, and the problem here is that every single instance of a general type differs from what it is supposed to be an example of. In applying principles, therefore, one is always having to confront or ignore whatever it is those principles are inapplicable to. To take an obvious case: one could isolate a set of principles governing 'the novel' from a sample confined to nineteenth-century works of realism, only to find that those principles would be conspicuously absent from many novels written in the twentieth century. This might cause one to adapt the first set of principles, taking into account the evidence of the new sample, but this would simply be to set in chain a neverending process of reappraisal. After a time, the defining principles of the novel may look nothing like the original set. And this would be to place that original set in a very awkward state indeed, for it would now have to become the *former* set of principles of the novel. At that point the question of how a set of principles could be made obsolete – of how *principles* could ever be *contingent* – might begin to make some trouble for the very of idea of principles as such, since every set of principles (even the latest) risks being made 'former' by the possibility of another set being extrapolated from some new case or series. If it is possible for principles to become obsolete, then we might have to accept that what are called principles are really just at best educated guesses, imperfect indicators, or pragmatic yardsticks. They are not deterministic rules, and they are certainly not permanent.

If so-called principles are no more than expedient guidelines, however, then the question of how one is to arrive at a decision of any kind looms suddenly very large and threatening. Unable to defer to the ultimate authority of some law or principle, how is one to judge the truth of *Billy Budd*, say? In one sense, this is to describe a very old problematic: either the ontic realm (the realm of things as they are) is discovered by the epistemic realm (the realm of knowledge of things as they are), or the ontic is produced by the epistemic. The latter alternative, broadly conceived, is very much the position taken up by structuralism and psycho-analysis, for example. There is also a third possibility: the ontic is inaccessible to the epistemic, in which case it could always exist but would always lie outside claims to know it.

The ontic-versus-epistemic debate posits degrees of absoluteness for each realm such that there appears to be a demand to choose between them. This is the demand of post-Socratic philosophy: choose between universals and particularities, between spread and marmalade-or-jam, between a structuralist and a psychoanalytic approach to literary texts. However in its *appearance* as a demand, what might be called the post-Socratic imperative to decide has had to suppress an earlier, pre-Socratic, philosophical tradition. In this tradition there simply was no ontic-versus-epistemic debate. For the pre-Socratics, truths and knowledges were the inseparable outcomes of rhetorical thought and practice. They were concerned with the metaphoricity of truth, with its rhetorical or figural nature.

Nevertheless, in making this point I have had to generalize. I went from asking how one might judge the truth of *Billy Budd* in the absence of a principle of judgement to taking this question for an example of a more general type of the ontic-versus-epistemic debate. In doing so, the singularity of the question I asked had to be overlooked. This is not to say however that there is an easy answer to that question, but simply that it is impossible not to generalize because it is impossible to see things as they are completely, in all their singular specificities. And to say it is impossible not to generalize is to say that it is impossible not to make decisions. Decisions have to be made. But this does not mean that they are made according to firm principles that guarantee the 'right' decision will always be made. Even more radically: if decisions, which have to be made, are always made in the absence of determining principles, then it follows there could never *be* a right decision, since there are no rules for distinguishing 'right' from 'wrong'. There are just decisions, and they have to be made.

This is the view of John D. Caputo in his *Against Ethics* (1993). Caputo's concern is not the question of literature specifically but the question of decision: how do we decide, about anything whatsoever, if there are no hard and fast rules for deciding? How do we decide the truth about *Billy Budd*, for instance, or to help someone in pain? For Caputo, we could answer these questions with confidence only if there were some absolute distinction between texts and referents. But if, as he argues, all the candidates for such a distinction are *textual* themselves, then what has to be faced is the textuality of the so-called referential. And without any clear-cut distinction between referential (or dialectical) truth and textual (or rhetorical) expression, we are left to make decisions, which have to be made, entirely on our own:

> Textuality is a quasi-transcendental condition, the impossible condition, the condition of possibility of referential operations, the condition that makes it possible for reference to be effected and the condition that makes it impossible to do so without a differential-textual event. The existing individual, the referent, is in this sense 'im/possible,' 'in/effable,' effable and ineffable, or, to cite the admirably precise language of a great poet, who thinks poetically and poeticizes thoughtfully (not about Being or the Holy, but about cats), 'effanineffable.' We are always inside/outside textuality, for textuality makes it possible to say everything we have to say about the individual, including that the individual is ineffable, which is the most striking thing we say about individuals. But textuality makes it impossible that we would ever reach a pure, unmediated, naked, pre-textual, un-textual, de-contextualized fact of the matter. Textuality is the condition of im/possibility, the condition that makes it possible to address the individual or to be addressed by individuals, and the condition that also makes it impossible that we would have to do with some sort of pure, naked, virginal individual. Textuality marks the individual up, leaves marks and traces all over it, leaves tracks in its polar snow, sends a camera crew down into the bottomless depths. All this eloquence about ineffability [. . .] all these striking representations of the unpresentable, bring home to us hyperbolically the individuality of the individual. Textuality makes it possible to say that it is not possible to say anything about what is absolutely individual. Unsayability is a modification of sayability.[30]

The kind of judgement that Captain Vere is called on to make is of course precisely of the order of 'a pure, unmediated, naked, pre-textual, un-textual, de-contextualized fact of the matter'. Taking everything into account, Vere is called on to decide the facts of the case and to judge accordingly in such a way that, as Johnson puts it, his verdict appears at 'the vanishing-point of textuality'. However, to paraphrase Caputo, it is textuality that makes it possible to say everything there is to say about textuality, including that there is a 'vanishing-point' of textuality. Hence it is textuality that enables the possibility of saying whatever can be said about the 'opposite' of textuality, or whatever is said to lie 'outside' it, past the point at which textuality ends and referentiality begins. It is textuality (rhetoric), in other words, that makes it possible to say whatever can be said about referentiality (dialectic).

While it is obvious that literature is textual, it cannot be allowed that textuality is confined to the literary or that self-difference is a feature only of literary texts. 'Literature' is not an explanation; it is what must be explained. This is so precisely because literature *is* textual, and so it cannot settle anything. To say there is no vanishing-point of textuality is to say there is no vanishing-point of literature, no point at which it comes to rest or to settle on a referential meaning. But this is to say too that literature has no fundamental identity and therefore that it cannot be opposed to something fundamentally other than itself. In saying this, moreover, I am saying something not only about literature but also about what are said to be its 'opposites' or 'outsides'. I am saying something about, for example, politics and justice. This implies (as shown also by Johnson's reading of *Billy Budd*) that it is impossible to make statements (which is to make texts) that are exclusively literary. And it implies something which is even perhaps more troubling: that it is impossible to make statements that are exclusively nonliterary, such as political state-ments. If so, however, this need not pose a threat to the identity and future of literary studies, let alone politics. Rather it might be seen that the very impossibility of a non-textual distinction between the literary and the nonliterary has politically democratic implications, in contrast to the sorts of political tyranny that are well served by a lack of doubt pertaining to the difference between rhetoric and dialectic. But, ironi-cally, what might be called the democratic potential of literary studies is precisely what threatens literary studies' identity. It is this irony that I wish to discuss in the following chapter with respect to what I see as its complex articulations in Derrida's *Specters of Marx* (French 1993, Eng-lish 1994), a book which has much to say on questions of 'the post' concerning politics and literature.

8

Performing Politics

Some ideas are difficult to shake, such as the idea that literature has an essence. But to be so sceptical of this idea as to refuse literature any constraints at all, so that 'literature' can mean whatever anybody likes to call it, can lead to a kind of relativism which has nothing to say about events in the world that might otherwise be said to call for a decision. Now this is not what literary critics usually mean, of course, when they claim that works of literature express understandings and truths about 'the world', for the kind of world invoked by such a claim is so indistinct as to be ludicrously inadequate to the sorts of decision that have to be made in other contexts – scientific, political, sociological or whatever – upholding, or underpinned by, very different accounts of the world. This is not to argue that truths about the world are *merely* discursive, rhetorical, ideological or positional declarations about which we are all free to make up our own minds concerning their 'relevance' to where each of us is 'coming from'. Nor is it to assert a single order of truth about the world that would press all forms of difference (cultural, personal, historical, discursive and so on) to deny their singular identities and manifold valencies.

But insofar as literary criticism is concerned with questions of literature rather than with literature as a question, which is what concerns literary theory, it may be said that literary criticism does its most effective work in continually re-applying the rules and procedures by which 'literature' is marked off from its outsides, or defined against external limits. Such work is effective in making it very clear that literature has an identity of its own, even if it is not very clear what that identity is. So long as there is agreement on the principle that literature *has* an identity, however, literary criticism remains unsettled by the fact of considerable disagreement over what should stand in for it. Hence the availability of literary critical 'perspectives' is legion: feminist, Marxist, Leavisite, New Critical, new historicist, structuralist, psychoanalytic, postcolonial, reception, myth and other critics vie for determining the truth about literature. Each of these perspectives sees the world in different ways, or sees a different world, in terms of say a fundamentally gendered or classed system (as in the case of feminism and Marxism) which infuses every aspect of that system, including works of literature; or in terms of a world that, in its very disorder, cannot impinge on the sovereign unity that organizes literary works as understood by New Criticism; and so on.[1] It is clearly possible for postmodernism to be added to this list, as another way of looking at literature, in which form it would pose the least threat to literary criticism. This may explain why many literature departments nowadays are putting 'postmodernism' into the titles of some of their courses. Deconstruction too is able to be accommodated on this model, as yet another 'approach' to literature, especially since, because of its famous association in the United States with the work of a few staff in the English faculty at Yale in the 1970s (most notably de Man, Geoffrey Hartman and J. Hillis Miller),[2] it tends to circulate in that country as a form of obsessive close-reading whose origin is closer institutionally to New Criticism than poststructuralism. All the same there is certainly a resolute desire among some literary critics for a less concessional approach to teaching literature that would consign the current 'perspectives' to an order of politically motivated (if not politically impaired) outlooks and identity-based sectional interests.[3] Such nostalgia for a 'disinterested' literary studies, of course, may not itself be disinterested, though that is not quite the issue here.

Like it or not, literary studies has had to engage with questions of *the politics of reading*, for even what had previously seemed so fundamental and unquestionable – the very notion of a literary canon – has gone from an anatomical tenet to a bone of contention today. Judged politically, then, postmodern literary theory can appear to offer nothing in the way of strategic opposition to forms of violence and injustice enacted on the bodies of real historical subjects who are variously oppressed, victimized or silenced by monolithic forces of institutionalized power throughout the world. This is an overwhelming charge, and it appears to demand a response along the lines of choosing between literature and politics, or more generally between 'textualism' and politics. The problem (if there is one) with this, however, may be that it is 'politics' which remains the stable term in such calls for literary studies or aesthetic interests and practices generally to become accountable to the interests of those who have been made to suffer in a manifestly unjust world. While standing on the solid rock of 'politics', one is in a position to cast a great many stones. But all this might mean is that it is possible to do so, even if sometimes it may also be necessary. And if it is possible to hurl stones of abuse at an enemy (and much else besides), perhaps it is necessary to be absolutely certain, or as certain as one can be, about who the enemy is.

Every decision to act politically, then, has to conceal that it rests on a decision about what counts as certain. How could one decide to act politically in the belief that nothing is certain? Such a belief may be allowable in the contexts of speculative philosophy, imaginative literature or radical mathematics,[4] where the 'game' is to press beyond certain limits of knowledge, thought, experience and so on, but it cannot be allowed to divert political action from having to decide on what needs to be done about actual events in the lives of actual people. For a decision to count as 'political' (regardless of being seen as radical or conservative), its referent must (on this view) be understood as 'actual'. So in order to make political decisions, certain questions must be discounted – especially any question that might call 'actuality' into doubt. It may not be only political decisions, however, that have to mark themselves off against an outside in the form of questions seen as appropriate, say, only to certain types of literature and philosophy (where it is allowed that fictional and speculative texts may doubt the nature of actuality). For how could it be possible to make literary or philosophical decisions in the absence of any certainty that anything is certain?[5] How could one decide whether Captain Vere judges fairly or harshly, for example, or when *pharmakon* was intended by Plato to mean 'poison' and when to mean 'cure'? Therefore not only politics but also scholarship requires an 'outside' to the actual, taking the appearance of 'silly relativism', 'perverse scepticism', 'irrationality', 'intuitionism,' 'anti-intellectualism', 'apoliticism' or whatever. As a *requirement*, though, actuality's outsides do nothing to threaten the structures of either politics or scholarship, insofar as these are merely confirmed in their *difference from* silly relativism and the like. The challenge to political and scholarly thinking comes only in the form of whatever menaces the structured opposition between the actual and the non-actual (being and non-being, the living and the dead, presence and absence and so on), such that something might be said to lie within and between those limits. In *Specters of Marx*, Derrida performs this challenge as arriving in the figure of the ghost, a figure that traditionally has seemed unthinkable not only in political terms but also from the point of view of every scholar:

There has never been a scholar who really, and as scholar, deals with ghosts. A traditional scholar does not believe in ghosts – nor in all that could be called the virtual space of spectrality. There has never been a scholar who, as such, does not believe in the sharp distinction between the real and the unreal, the actual and the inactual, the living and the non-living, being and non-being ('to be or not to be,' in the conventional reading), in the opposition between what is present and what is not, for example in the form of objectivity. Beyond this opposition, there is, for the scholar, only the hypothesis of a school of thought, theatrical fiction, literature, and speculation.[6]

From previous chapters, it may be seen that one name for this 'beyond' is *the literary absolute*. But what Derrida is marking here is not a conflict between an orthodox belief in opposition ('the actual and the inactual' and so on) and a heterodox belief in its opposite (the reconciliation or transcendence of opposition via romantic 'literature' or the postmodern 'text'). Instead, *Specters of Marx* is an attempt at thinking what might be called the neglected third term *within* any such opposition as 'the actual and the inactual'. That term is the word 'and' in the present instance, conjoining the other terms ('the actual', 'the inactual') in a relationship of exchange and supplementarity. It is this 'third' term, which is in fact internal to the structure of the actual/inactual opposition, that always (as Derrida implies) remains unread in 'the conventional reading' of Hamlet's dilemma: 'To be, or not to be, that is the question.'[7] Conventionally, that is, Hamlet is seen to question whether he should live *or* die, or whether he should avenge his father's death and so jeopardize the well-being of the Danish body politic *or* do nothing and allow the status quo to go unchallenged. For Derrida, however, what is most interesting about this question is what precedes it – and what precedes it is precisely what makes the 'to be or not to be' opposition undecidable: namely, the ghost of Hamlet's father, the dead King Hamlet.

But this is not quite the right way of expressing it. For it is precisely the question of its *identity* that 'it' or the 'thing' (as it is most often called at the beginning of the play) poses to those who would confront it, and this question cannot be said to be resolved once Hamlet and the others agree to call 'it' after the name of Hamlet's dead father, to whom, clad from head to foot in the king's armour, it bears a powerful resemblance. What would it mean, in other words, to say that you had had a conversation with your dead father? In the first place, your 'dead' father could no longer be opposed to your father when he was 'living' – and so the identity of the thing you called your father or your father's ghost could not be reduced to the status of the non-living. Secondly, though, since the ghost (as distinct from a speculative fantasy) appears, at least in Hamlet's case, in the very likeness of a corporeal being, it troubles the identity of the living as well. Such a figure, as Derrida remarks, resides somewhere in 'the tangible intangibility of a body proper without flesh, but still the body of some*one* as some*one other* [. . .] that we will not hasten to determine as self, subject, person, consciousness, spirit and so on'.[8]

Thinking the ghost, then, may be seen to challenge 'conventional' ways of thinking. For not only does the ghost put paid to the assurance of the opposition between living and non-living, it also troubles the self-identity of such concepts as time and place. What would it mean to say that you had seen a ghost yesterday, for example, or to say there is a ghost in your house? How could the concept 'yesterday' include ghosts? The ghost is what is 'out of joint' with time as understood conventionally in terms of past, present and future 'dimensions',[9] and yet it cannot be said that the disjointed time of the ghost is outside of time in every conceivable (or still to be conceived) sense. But neither could it be said, exactly, that there 'is' a ghost in your house, for houses are where the living reside – and ghosts could hardly be thought to live in *houses*. The moment then that one first sees – or countenances – the ghost at all, the 'where' and the 'when' of the ghost always remain undecidable.

Despite such undecidability, nevertheless, the ghost always remains 'some*one* as some*one other*'. What might be called the *singularity* of the ghost is what causes all the trouble: what is 'it', what is its 'time', where does it 'abide'? Hence the ghost vexes the very metaphysics of presence on which political and literary critical decisions rely. For it would be no good politically to ask after the nature of an oppressed class of citizen in the way one might question the ghost, and in which the ghost puts into question any grounds for deciding between the actual and its outsides. Neither is it of any literary critical advantage to question 'literature' in such a way that one might ask 'what is it?', 'what is its time?' and 'where does it abide?'. These are 'spectral' questions, as it were, having to do with spectres rather than with literature or politics. But Derrida's point is that politics and literature are no less spectral than the ghost in *Hamlet*, whose appearances result in all kinds of unexpected (and therefore in a sense 'literary') events whose consequences are manifestly 'political'. And these quite certain (although unpredictable) consequences are no less political for having been brought about by a 'thing' of whom nothing certain may be said.[10] Yet still it cannot be allowed, politically or from the standpoint of literary criticism, that decisions might be based on the undecidability of the actual versus the non-actual. In a sense, therefore, if the opposition between the living and the non-living were not understood as absolutely certain, there would be no basis for making either political or literary decisions.

Yet it is this very opposition that the ghost calls into doubt. One cannot say that the ghost of Hamlet's father, or whatever it might be, is dead, inactual or non-present. On the other hand, as Derrida notes, it cannot be called a 'person' or a 'subject', or be imputed with a 'consciousness' and so on. In this way the ghost in *Hamlet* (or Derrida's reading of the ghost) does not work its unsettling effects as the consequence of an act of totalizing negation. Indeed, any attempt to totalize the ghost by deciding its identity in terms of the opposition between living and non-living, being and non-being and so on, would in fact be a denial of its identity, or a denial of what always remains the undecidable singularity of 'some*one* as some*one other*'. And so in responding to the ghost – or to the 'thing' – Hamlet responds to *the very least* that may count as certain: the fact that, whatever 'it' is, it cannot be said that 'it' *is not*. Whatever the time and place of its coming, there can be no denying that – look! – *somewhere it is*, in all its undecidable singularity:

> *Hamlet.* Angels and ministers of grace defend us!
> Be thou a spirit of health, or goblin damned,
> Bring with thee airs from heaven, or blasts from hell,
> Be thy intents wicked, or charitable,
> Thou com'st in such a questionable shape,
> That I will speak to thee. I'll call thee Hamlet,
> King, father, royal Dane. O, answer me!
> Let me not burst in ignorance, but tell
> Why thy canonized bones hearsèd in death
> Have burst their cerements? why the sepulchre,
> Wherein we saw thee quietly inurned,
> Hath oped his ponderous and marble jaws
> To cast thee up again? what may this mean
> That thou, dead corse, again in complete steel
> Revisits thus the glimpses of the moon,
> Making night hideous, and we fools of nature
> So horridly to shake our disposition
> With thoughts beyond the reaches of our souls?
> Say why is this? wherefore? what should we do?
>   [*the Ghost 'beckons'*][11]

Hamlet is certain of only one thing here: that whatever the thing in front of him might be, it 'com'st in such a questionable shape' that he will speak to it. In other words, the figure is of such a guise ('shape') that it appears able to be questioned.[12] But everything else about the figure is 'questionable' in the standard sense of being uncertain and in doubt, to the point even that we might all be 'fools' for ever having believed in life's illusion of the difference between nature and the supernatural. Hamlet responds, therefore, not to what is *most certain* about the figure (since there is nothing that qualifies in this regard), but rather to what is the very least that must *count* as certain in order to recognize that a response, other than one of aggression or flight, is called for: simply that the figure is of 'a questionable shape'. Although Hamlet clearly wants the figure to be his father's ghost (perhaps in order that his mother's 'untimely' marriage to the uncle he so despises might be explained), he nevertheless responds not to what the figure 'is' but only to the *fact* that there 'is' a figure. In a word, he responds to the ghost as an *event*.

Now of course it could be objected that the structure of Hamlet's response has to be seen in context, the context of a theatrical fiction. But for Derrida this context is not able to be confined to the limitations of a book or a performance, or a text (in the usual sense), but extends rather to what he calls 'the space of spectrality'. Such a space is irreducible to the opposition of the actual (referring to something which either *is* or *is not* present, immediate, objective and so on) and the ideal (referring to what is *never* present, manifest, declarative – or realized). As Derrida puts it, the space of spectrality is what exceeds 'the logic that distinguishes or opposes *effectivity or actuality* (either present, empirical, living – or not) and *ideality* (regulating or absolute non-presence)'.[13] This is his reason for 'insisting so much [. . .] on the logic of the ghost'.[14] The spectral figure of the ghost, in other words, stands outside the opposition of 'effect' and 'ideal'.

In *Hamlet*, when the ghost appears (or when Hamlet's father is thought to 'return'), this raises unsettling questions about what it means to remember or mourn the dead, and about the nature of inheritance, succession and history. For the dead to go on living (in however difficult a sense), the very structure of historical periodization has to seem out of joint. It is this disjointure that describes the space of spectrality, which is the condition (Derrida argues) of actual or 'effective' history in which it appears possible to decide the opposition of 'to be or not to be'.[15] The spectralizing force of the ghost, however, makes this opposition *undecidable*, such that Derrida's reading of *Hamlet* is radically unconventional in not attributing Hamlet's indecision to the 'fatal flaw' of his so-called procrastination. In disregarding the centrality of Hamlet's 'character' to an understanding of the play, Derrida might be said even *not* to read the play as a work of literature and therefore not to have produced a 'literary critical' reading of it. But this does not mean that his reading is an example of 'postmodern literary theory'. Derrida's theory of spectrality, in other words, is not quite equivalent to romantico-postmodern concepts of the imagination, the differend, simulation, heterogeneity and so forth, because it is not an attempt at breaking 'free' from binary or oppositional thought. A spectral logic, as it were, does not *transcend* the opposition of actual and ideal occurrences or structures; still less does it cause the difference between them to appear insignificant. On the contrary, the difference between actuality and ideality is *produced* by the logic of the ghost, although it is also prevented by it from ever becoming absolute.

Since the space of spectrality or what might be called ghost logic is irreducible, moreover, to a concept of the literary absolute, then Derrida's reading of *Hamlet* may be seen as neither literary critical nor postmodern. Indeed, one of its functions is to undo such a concept as the literary absolute or any ontological certainty of an underlying fundamental identity that might be thought to ground being in opposition to non-being. For even the concept of a literary absolute holds to the essential self-presence of 'literature' in (and as) 'literary theory'. Rather than an ontological ground of identity, then, Derrida refers instead to its 'hauntological' origins and movements:

> This logic of haunting would not be merely larger and more powerful than an ontology or a thinking of Being (of the 'to be,' assuming that it is a matter of Being in the 'to be or not to be,' but nothing is less certain). It would harbor within itself, but like circumscribed places or particular effects, eschatology and teleology themselves. It would *comprehend* them, but incomprehensibly. How to *comprehend* in fact the discourse of the end or the discourse about the end? Can the extremity of the extreme ever be comprehended? And the opposition between 'to be' and 'not to be'?[16]

The interest here in death (eschatology) and ends (teleology) is reminiscent of the discussion in chapter 7 on Melville's ends concerning *Billy Budd*, which was published after his death. If it may be said that the posthumous status of *Billy Budd* and the question of Melville's final intentions exceed the domain of 'purely' literary speculation per se, then it is even more the case that, in *Specters of Marx*, Derrida shows the space of literature to be always insecurely at risk of contamination from any of its 'outsides' – such as politics – and vice versa. For the logic of hauntology is not reducible to a reading of *Hamlet*, but opens up the possibility of a re-reading of Marx.

Since the twin events of the 'collapse' of the Berlin Wall and the 'collapse' of the Soviet Union, it has become conventional to say that Marx is 'dead' and the time of Marxism is 'over'. One effect of this apocalyptic response to what are seen as two conjoined 'historical' events has been the emergence of an ecstatic, triumphalist affirmation of a so-called New World Order in which a certain ideal of liberal democracy or the capitalist system has now been 'realized'. In terms of such a discourse, history – conceived as the struggle between democracy and totalitarianism – is understood to have come to an 'end'. Freed from the ideological ('Marxist') conception of human beings as the product of class-historical conflict, 'man' therefore arrives at the end of history as his 'true self', which is to say that he in fact returns to his original self in the form of the universal, trans-historical individual.

This is the situation as outlined famously by Francis Fukuyama in his bestselling book, *The End of History and the Last Man* (1992), which Derrida discusses at some length in *Specters of Marx*. For Derrida, the logic of Fukuyama's triumphalism represents a problem for any counter-discourse (such as one that might want to hold on to a certain 'ideal' of Marxism, or to a certain 'spirit' of democracy that is not bound to the absolute priority of a 'free market') insofar as that logic is not exclusive to the end-of-history thesis or the affirmation of a new global order of political concurrence. In fact, as Derrida points out, another reading of recent trends would regard 'globalization' as cause only for alarm, not celebration, given that the 'new world order' may be seen as comprising such *events* as homelessness, 'virtual' unemployment, the arms trade, foreign debt, inter-ethnic wars and 'the growing and undelimitable [. . .] worldwide power of those super-efficient and properly capitalist phantom-States that are the mafia and the drug cartels on every continent'.[17] These examples cannot be understood as 'events', however, according to a logic based on the opposition of the actual and the inactual, living and non-living, 'to be or not to be', through which a certain concept of history constructs 'the collapse of the Berlin Wall' as an event, but cannot see the event-ness in what Derrida calls the absence of a word for describing the new experience and structure of 'unemployment' which exceeds the opposition of 'being in work' or 'not being in work'. International finance, for example, is well served by many forms of what is classified as 'non-work' – such as 'invisible' domestic labour – and so the very concept of 'labour', based on the opposition of (paid) work and (unpaid) non-work, is inadequate to the calculation of any type of labour that remains 'uncosted' according to economic reckoning. Moreover the concept is inadequate to the many forms of work (carried out through the media, the stock market and the wired, 'postmodern' home) that appear not to result in the production of 'commodities' but only in the circulation of image and information 'flows'.[18]

Hence one might say it is 'the ghost factor' that has gone uncosted in a certain theory of history grounded in the ontology of an opposition of the living and non-living, being and non-being, effectivity and ideality, *actual* event and *non-actual* thought, speculation, image or text. In this way – and for reasons that must be regarded as never less than political – it is crucial not to think that 'metanarratives' (whether Fukuyama's 'Marxism' or Lyotard's 'Enlightenment') can be conveniently laid to rest or consigned to history, without coming back to haunt the living. For it is only by thinking of 'history' on the assumption of a radical separation between being and non-being, presence and non-presence, before and after, effect and ideal and so on, that it is possible to think (1) that 'micro-narratives' such as Marxism are dead, which means we are all joined together by the homogeneous force of a single metanarrative (the 'new world order') and (2) that metanarratives such as the Enlightenment are dead, and so we are all disjoined by the heterogeneous forces of countless micro-narratives (the 'postmodern condition'). Neither view can take account of its opposite except to dismiss it out of hand, such that between them there is a gaping differend. Yet this gap is effected on the basis of a common ground: the opposition of 'to be or not to be'. In other words the differend – any differend – is a consequence of not thinking through 'the ghost', of re-ontologizing 'difference' instead of seeing its hauntological movements and effects. For a theory of history *as spectrality*, however, it could not be possible to think of Marx being dead and buried (as a historical event), since this would be to ignore the incalculable but not inactual effects of his ideas and ideals on the actual formations of parliamentary democracies in the present and in any present to come. To say that Marx's 'revolutionary spirit' has not been realized in the form of communist governments, is not to say that its spectralizing force has been ineffective in establishing such democratic principles and institutions as a social welfare system, a free press and unionized labour (regardless of whether these are presently under threat). Similarly, for a theory of history as spectrality it could not be possible to think of the historical event of the Enlightenment as a thing of the past. The Enlightenment is what opens the space of its own critique, as I indicate in the following chapter, and so may be said to have anticipated romanticism to the extent that it has never been in opposition to it. In this way the 'critical spirit' of the Enlightenment (regardless of whether it is presently under threat) is no less a condition of today's democracies, and of democracry as an ideal, than Marx's revolutionary spirit. Nor are these spirits separated by a differend.

What Derrida's reading of *Hamlet* – which we may now say is also a reading of Marx, and vice versa – points to is the great difficulty in thinking of effects and ideals as not opposed to one another, while also thinking of them as remaining apart and being conjoined at the same time. This is to re-think 'time' outside the opposition of presence and non-presence. Hence it can be said that *Specters of Marx* tries to think a different concept of history, such that it is possible to see how the conventional concept of history (grounded in the oppositional ontology of 'to be or not to be') can lead both Fukuyama and Lyotard, who might otherwise have nothing in common, to support an end-of-history thesis. According to a conventional reading of historical events (and of the concept of 'event') both a radical conservatism and a radical post-modernism conceive history as dead. Yet in all other respects each side is turned against the other as its enemy, suggesting that neither side sees any necessity to re-think its position as the consequence of a *decision* – a decision to see, in the other, the actualization of a theory or a dogmatics to which it is opposed on principled grounds (either on the principle of liberal democracy or on the principle of the literary absolute). As scholars, then, Fukuyama and Lyotard, who have never actually confronted one another (and so the confrontation here is 'purely' spectral, though not merely fanciful), do not believe in ghosts. And so it can appear that conservative and postmodern scholars are always separated by a differend, albeit by many different differends or even by several differends at once. As labels, 'conservatism' and 'postmodernism' attach to many different scholars and to many different disciplines and intra-disciplinary positions, and they do so very often in the name of 'politics' *or* in the denial of that name. But while there are many differences within Western democratic academic communities, they may not always be as important as the differences between those communities and others, inside and outside the West.

All the same, it is the case that academic disagreements are expressed sometimes in such a way that the difference between academic knowledge and political responsibility appears never to be a problem. Hence there are critics on the 'right' who have no problem in separating their 'disinterested' literary appreciationism from the sorts of decision they might make at the ballot box, and critics on the 'left' who have no problem in 'politicizing' their whole relationship to professional teaching and research. For the former, academic knowledge (especially of the truth and beauty variety) is far superior to politics; while in the case of 'leftist' critics, politics is every subject's overriding concern. From both points of view, postmodern literary theory is seen as an enemy and often as the enemy in the guise of the other side. So for conservative critics it is seen to *politicize* truth, and therefore to deny the possibility of universal values on which conservative discourses depend for their authority. But for radical critics on the left, postmodern literary theory is seen to *textualize* truth and therefore to deny any effectivity to political actions on which radical discourses depend for their authority.

Postmodernism comes as a *blow*, in other words, to both sides of politics. In having to defend itself against this blow, each side is forced to contradict its own assumptions. Critics on the side of a progressive left are forced to betray a revolutionary ideal in speaking against postmodernism's claim to represent anything new. Hence for these critics the 'new' must be what is always already known in advance, such that 'progress' and 'revolution' are defined programatically (against themselves) and in opposition to any notion of the radical. Perhaps, though, for any radical politics the most radical possibility of all is a complete indifference to politics; and so if postmodernism is indeed 'apolitical', this may be cause for regarding it as ultra-progressive. For conservative critics, on the other hand, the sort of liberal tolerance that they derive as a value from appreciating great works of literature is precisely what they have to break faith with in their rejection of postmodern literary theory. In contrast to the left, critics on the conservative side condemn postmodernism as a political attack on timeless truths and values. But if in fact there *were* such an order of timeless verities, one might wonder why it would ever have to be defended since it could surely never come under threat. If it is true that truths and values are unchanging, why should there be any need to say so? If, however, the statement that truths and values never change offered only a *perspective* on the question of truth, then it would certainly be necessary to put this statement over and over again – and to do so from a motive that could legitimately be called political – up against competing statements from various other perspectives. And so, on the question of postmodern literary theory, conservative critics are compelled to act politically in their radical defence of a position that is meant to stand for civilizing tolerance and goodwill, while radical critics are compelled to act conservatively in preventing an ideal of revolutionary force from leading to unexpected change.

This is not to say that we should all accede to the perspective of postmodern literary theory, but simply that the choice between literature and politics is not obviously straightforward. Barbara Johnson's reading of a work of literature, *Billy Budd*, in terms of the political lesson it stages (see chapter 7) is a case in point. More recently, Derrida's reading of Marx and *Hamlet* suggests it is all the more critical that the question of literature be seen as opening a passage to the question of politics, and vice versa. Following the Jena Romantics, the question of literature is able to be taken as shorthand for a revolutionary opening up of established orders of self-identical thought and meaning to the very question of identity as such. In this way it is wrong to think of literature as something to which one may choose to adopt a theoretical 'approach', since literature is always already theoretical through and through. Its identity (or its composition), then, is itself as *the question of itself*. And insofar as the question of literature destabilizes – or spectralizes – the separation of a field of questions about literature (literary criticism) from questions about what literature is (literary theory), then it follows that 'literature' is just another name for 'literary theory'. The fact that 'literature' happened historically to come first is merely an accident, although it is precisely in mistaking this contingency for an essential condition that literary criticism continues to put itself *behind* literature as a simple adjunct or supplement to the self-identical truth and priority *of* literature. On a romantic model, however, literature is the name of what refuses the designation of simple inside–outside relations, in the form of say text–commentary or creative–critical orders of truth and practice. This does not mean, as we have seen repeatedly, that everything must become 'creative text', as this would in fact be to limit the question of literature to an affirmation of qualities comprising its *identity*, such that all texts were understood indiscriminately as open, heterogeneous and other – in a word, as literary. On the one hand, then, the romantic move of putting literary theory *before* literature is revolutionary in its effect of radically throwing open the question of literature's identity to the question of literature itself. But such effect is able to be contained by a counter-revolutionary force of re-appropriation. On the other hand, that is, by *only* moving to put literary theory before literature, romanticism can go only so far towards unsettling 'literature' and hence the system of inside–

outside relations in which its identity is assured. For if all it means to regard literature as a question is to see the unpresentable power of indeterminacy (the heterogeneous, the irrational, the sublime, the open text and so on) as a totalizing force, then this would not be to unsettle inside–outside relations but on the contrary to displace them altogether through the repetition of a single recurring term: instead of inside–outside relations, there would be only those belonging to an apparently new order of an inside–inside or outside–outside repetition and hence no difference between 'inside' and 'outside' at all. Nor would it make any difference to this configuration whether the recurring term were 'literature' or 'politics', given that arch generalizations actually incline towards a very old order of thinking. So, for example, with 'literature' as the arch term it is possible to claim that everything is metaphorical, such that even 'politics' cannot assert direct and immediate access to a referent of social or other inequality in whose name it avows to speak and act. For any such referent – the real-historical effects of patriarchal, class, rationalist, Anglo-centric or whatever oppression – would have to be, at some level, a transposition from one kind of thing (brute, non-signifying 'stuff') to another kind of thing ('stuff' that signifies) and therefore in this base sense would be metaphorical. Hence the arch claim that everything is literature (in the sense of being metaphorical) can appear to anticipate every seeming counter-claim. To insist that some or other socio-historical phenomenon constituted a political fact, for example, would not destroy the claim that everything is metaphorical but rather, from the point of view of the claim itself, only reinforce it. There is therefore no outside to an arch generalization; but neither is there any inside. For this reason it is just as banal, or just as important, to claim that everything is political (dialectic, constative, calculable or presentable) as to claim it is literary (rhetorical, performative, incalculable or unpresentable).

Now of course one does not often encounter statements which declare, in so many words, that everything is political or literary – no doubt because such statements are totalizing and to that extent too easily opposed by antithetical forms. But even in their 'non-appearances' they may provide a firm basis for decision making, in the semblance of a ground understood as given. Hence it is possible for literary critics to reproach what they see as 'political' readings of literary texts on the assumption that literature transcends the gross imagination of politics. The counter-assumption – that politics is inescapable – is equally possible, however, and so other critics may censure what they see as 'disinterested' readings of literary texts on the ground that all texts and readings are political, including (if not especially) any reading that might want to maintain that some texts are unpresentable and therefore beyond scope of political comprehension. From this latter perspective it becomes all too easy (if not imperative) to regard whatever appears not to conform unconditionally to its baseline assumption as conjoined in mutual opposition to it, which may account for why postmodernism and poststructuralism are often conflated by critics on the left. But these terms are conflated just as often by critics on the right, for whom 'the post' is synonymous with 'the left'.

In this contradiction it is possible to detect what might be called a pharmakon effect, in the manner of the following propositions which appear not to share a common referent or to allude to the same world: (1) apples and oranges are identical; (2) they cure cancer; (3) they cause cancer. Although from a political perspective postmodernism is seen usually as a 'poison', in other words, conservative critics nonetheless suppose that postmodernism is understood by the left as a political 'cure' or corrective, even while the left might see it as malignant precisely for pretending to seem politically disinterested or benign. Hence the pharmakon effect shows up in the self-contradictory meanings that these viewpoints mark out for 'postmodernism'. From the left it is seen as coming from the right, while from the right it is seen to come from the left. For each side, then, it marks the negation of a first principle: postmodernism is 'apolitical' according to the principle that political responsibility calls for intervention, not indifference; and it is excessively 'political' according to the principle that art and literature express a higher order of truth about the world than politics could ever dream of. In this way postmodernism is seen to threaten both the radical assumption that culture is political and the conservative view that culture safeguards human identity from political rot. Consequently it has come to function as a collecting term for whatever is regarded as a danger to these first principles: on the ground that culture and politics are separate, for instance, postmodernism is often taken to include literary theory, feminism, postcolonialism, queer theory, semiotics, cultural studies and the like; while on the view that culture is political, it is often seen to cover literary criticism, textualism, aestheticism, continental philosophy, rhetoric and so on (and sometimes also literary theory, cultural studies, semiotics and psycho-feminism). When considered dangerous to either of these first principles (that culture is political or that culture is above politics), poststructuralism – or deconstruction – too is subsumed under 'postmodernism' or placed in its stead.

If this shows that postmodernism is an unstable term, it does not do so by showing that the political and literary-cultural perspectives, each of which blames postmodernism (and deconstruction) on the other, are stable by comparison. If politics and literature did have secure identities, then in a sense there would be nothing of a 'political' or 'literary' nature to be decided. This is not to suggest that political and literary decisions are always indistinguishable, but simply that if they were always able to be distinguished – they would never qualify as *decisions*. A decision (and not only in an etymological sense) is what calls for something to be 'cut off' or arrested. If the cut-off point were not always a question, if it were not always possible in other words for a decision to risk being *wrong*, to cut in mistakenly at an inappropriate time or place, it simply would not *be* a decision. Again however it is important to stress that this risk which is essential to the structure of every decision should not be taken to mean that all decisions are strictly erratic, in the sense of being either capricious or imperious. It means only that every decision *risks* becoming fickle or dogmatic, however much it might be made in all due consciousness under mature consideration of every last circumstantial detail. Ideally, of course, decisions are made in the hope of achieving absolute certainty and precision: they aspire, in the words of John Caputo, to become 'a pure, unmediated, naked, pre-textual, un-textual, de-contextualized fact of the matter' (see chapter 7). So whenever we make a decision, this – the actualization of an ideal – is what we are aiming for. Whether it is a decision about what movie to go see or which political candidate to vote for, we hope to make a decision that will not result in us saying the movie was 'a dog' or the candidate 'broke her promises'. We hope instead that our decisions, which have to be made and which have to be made under all kinds of occasional demands, will always be the 'right' ones insofar as they are always of the order of a pure, unmediated and so on *fact of the matter*. We want this ideal – that a decision could ever be uncontextual while always having to be made in a context – to be actual. Sometimes, of course, what we want is what we get. But this doesn't prove that we got it *because* we wanted it. It may suggest instead that we got what we wanted accidentally, and so in that particular case the risk of not getting what we wanted did not eventuate. All the same, the risk was undertaken. We risked going to a dog of a movie, but it happens that we really enjoyed the film and so we congratulate ourselves on having made the right choice. Or we risked voting for an unprincipled candidate who espoused empty promises, but as it happens he or she honoured their election commitments and so we feel vindicated in our decision. But the movie could have turned out to be unwatchable and the candidate to be dishonourable, which is precisely the condition of possibility on which – retrospectively – we are able to judge our decisions as 'correct'.

It is in this space between ideality and actuality that decisions have to be made, and so it is here that decisions of a political nature must occur. One makes political decisions about actual events in the name of upholding a political ideal. This would seem to make good sense. On behalf of an ideal of democracy, for example, political decisions are made about events which are understood as actual. But the same simple opposition between ideals and actualities enables very different kinds of political decision to be made – and so the opposition conceals (or carries) an overwhelming risk. On behalf of an ideal of fascism, for example, political decisions are made about events which are understood as actual. For a fascist ideal, what may count as an actual event could be that a nation's immigration policy puts the racial identity of its dominant citizen group at serious risk of 'contamination' and therefore ultimate extinction. A decision on this event, according to a fascist ideal, might be to call for a ban on further immigrants while at the same time expressing hostility and resentment towards 'foreign' citizens already living in the country. For a democratic ideal, however, what may count as an actual event could be that a nation's economic policy puts the social well-being of all its citizens at serious risk, because the nation's economy is linked to the fate of international finance. A decision on this event, according to a democratic ideal, might be to call for immediate protectionist measures on behalf of local industry while at the same time demanding an extensive programme of state-funded public works to solve the domestic unemployment problem caused by the flux of international capital's opportune investments in third-world labour markets. Different ideals see different events as actual, in other words. But this is not by any stretch where the matter rests. For it is possible for a single political ideal – and one that might announce itself as democratic *or* fascist – to regard both these events as actual. It is possible to identify oneself as a democrat while calling for a halt to 'multiculturalism', as it is possible to vote left and be racist. Indeed this is not only possible: it actually happens. It is also possible to align oneself with the right (if not as a fascist) and to be in favour of a state-regulated economy, and this happens too.

Such conflict is sought to be resolved usually through an appeal to what might be called the actual nature of the ideal in question. Hence one might argue that the actual ideal of democracy or the actual ideal of left politics contains no room for racism, or that the actual ideal of conservative or liberal politics holds no place for nationalist economies run along either fascist or socialist lines. In such an appeal to the actuality of an ideal, what might be said to be invoked is a concept of *the political absolute* – the absolute of democracy, the left, conservatism or liberalism and so on. In this way it is possible to speak out against racism, say, as a violation of the democratic absolute. Yet it remains the case that there is no actual democracy in the world today, nor has there ever been, devoid of actual instances of racism, where nothing might actually count as race-based intolerance or discrimination.[19] In response to this, one might uphold the democratic absolute as *remaining to come*. This would amount to saying that all the world's actual democracies are, in a sense, actually undemocratic or not fully democratic in the *ideal* sense of 'absolute democracy'. But this ignores the contradiction which every ideal contains – the impossibility of actualizing an ideal, for to do so would be to use up its force of aspiration and so deny its purpose. Hence 'the democratic absolute' describes the *always to come* of actual democracy.[20] Every actual democracy falls short of the ideal of democracy, because that ideal remains open to all kinds of differences concerning its actual nature and future possibilities. As an ideal, in other words, 'democracy' must always remain open to the future, to whatever is 'to come'. The limit of this ideal is precisely what might come in the form of an opposition to democracy, which is precisely what democracy cannot decide to close off in advance. It is for this reason that the democratic ideal is perpetually at risk of turning into its opposite, and it is this risk which maintains the inexhaustible openness of that ideal. Hence it is democracy, alone among all forms of the political absolute, that carries the force of its own critique. In the name of democracy, for example, political opposition may sometimes be oppressed. But what happens then to the *ideal* of democracy? Or what happens to that ideal when, in democracy's name, legislation is enacted making it an offence to be, in effect, 'undemocratic' – by being fascist or racist, say?

This discussion of the political absolute is clearly indebted to the romantic concept of the literary absolute, as discussed in previous chapters. Such a link, however, is no cause for arguing that politics is romantic or that the political is literary. But neither should it be accepted that because 'politics' has emerged as a key term in the present chapter, therefore this is no longer a book about postmodern literary theory. On the contrary, a certain form of resistance to postmodernism would see it simply as grist to the mill that someone writing about postmodern literary theory should stray into an airy, disingenous and thoroughly noncommittal discussion of 'politics' – in order, of course, to empty the political of any force. Hence a discussion of politics which treats the political as a kind of literary text, over which one is invited to press its romantically unruly instability to extreme if not preposterous limits, is in full accord with a certain critique of the postmodern. The postmodern flattening-out of all forms of cultural practice and commitment to a level playing field (where the single purpose is to make room for a pun on 'play') is only to be expected. It is therefore all too predictable what must come next – a humdrum correlation between the literary and political 'absolutes'. The comparison might run as follows: people who vote left can also hold very conservative views on a wide range of issues, and vice versa. This shows that politics has no grounds; it is unstable. As everyone knows, positive instability is a condition of the romantic conception of literature. Literature, for the romantics, is the name of what must always remain open to the unexpected, since it is always only retrospectively that its principles of rule-formation may be discovered. Such a conception of literature in terms of the literary absolute collapses the literary/critical divide, turning literature into literary theory. Hence the absolute of literature is the unpresentable, or what must always remain out of reach of any 'critical' approach to an object whose self-theorizing nature preempts all approaches to it. In this way literature becomes the figure of figuration itself, the primal condition of revolutionary force and positive destabilization. Over time it lends itself as a model for Freud's 'unconscious', Lacan's 'language', Lévi-Strauss's 'bricolage', Barthes' 'text' and so on, to arrive finally as 'the postmodern condition' where we find ourselves today in the presence of absent rules for exchanging even the most minimally stable senses, let alone large-scale truths and values. There is nothing left for us to do, then, except resort to parody. As everyone knows as well, however, the romantic literary absolute is still a contested concept. In the mainstream literary tradition, literary criticism continues to flourish on the basis of a quite different conception of literature. For this tradition the absolute of literature is presentable truth and value, such that great literary works read the world back to us. What distinguishes the romantic absolute of literature, then, is its thoroughgoing openness to what might come, to what has not yet been thought of as literature – even to what might be considered today as the very antithesis of literary forms and affects. After all, the romantics themselves wrote poetry *against* a canonical sense of poetic composition, which is simply how literature has proceeded from its inception. The more that literature appears to be unlike itself, in short, the more it reveals its self-identity.

Hence the literary absolute is closer to the edges (or the traces) of the canon, where a text such as Truman Capote's *In Cold Blood* blurs the distinction between fiction and nonfiction and therefore challenges the rules by which 'literature' comes to be settled. In this way literature is reinvigorated through being kept open to the always nonclosural limits of an abolute unpresentability, in the form of new rules to come. But insofar as literature's reinvention of itself is *perpetual*, insofar as every literary text is in this sense always 'new', it is possible to regard such a process not as endless rejuvenation but as endless *repetition* – to the point where every literary text is always the same. Once the literary absolute is seen to have no *value*, then, its revolutionary force is emptied, and hence there is no room for any response to literature – or to a general condition of permanent flux and instability – except *radical indifference*. This is the characteristic response of the postmodern condition, whose favoured mode of expression is listless parody.[21] When the possibility of the newly made is reduced to the inevitability of the recently made-over, when the new becomes the neo, then there is nothing for it but to parody the sort of faith that once believed in revolutionary change – either as the next 'new' poem or the next politically 'progressive' intervention (or move). When change is precisely what never changes, nothing can be extreme: instead of indignity and inspiration, there is perpetual in-difference.

Postmodern literary theory empties, then, the revolutionary force of romantic literary theory's openness to what always remains to come. For romanticism, it is this openness that defines literature in its undefinability and raises it to the order of the sublime. But if literature is what must always remain so open as to exclude nothing, not even the possiblity of its own undoing, then it cannot be said that literature excludes even what might *not* be considered as literature. Hence 'literature' is either a misnomer or the very name of *difference* itself. And of course it is in the name of difference that postmodern literary theory sees the operations of literature – as instability, ambiguity, heterogeneity, a-rationality, unpresentability, contextuality and so on – everywhere. Since not even politics may escape such operations, what is the point of trying to change anything?

But such hyper-indifference (as it were) to political and other metanarratives may itself be an order of political response, on the assumption that the political absolute is no less susceptible to effects of instability and impermanence than romantic literature. On this assumption both the mainstream literary tradition and the mainstream political order would be seen as fitting hand in glove with a false totalizing belief in the universal subject of history and knowledge. The disjoined, schizo-phrenic postmodern subject, however, has no faith at all in a literary system whose whole identity is fixed on the absolute priority of 'Shake-speare' or in a political revolution inspired by the absolute authority of 'Marx'. But what might be seen as postmodern literary theory's deliber-ate neglect of these figures – Marx and Shakespeare – can be seen also as a political move. The appreciation of Shakespeare, in which a certain ideal of literature is so deeply invested,[22] has not led to the actual emergence of a universal ethical subject who is both tolerant of difference and shuns violence. On the contrary, violence and intolerance arise most often from a belief in some absolute truth (national interest, gender or class position, racial identity, political or religious conviction and so on) – and such belief, it may be said, is reinforced by an assemblage of literary values based on its own ideal of the absolute truth of Shake-speare. In this way it can be seen as 'political' *not* to read Shakespeare. Similarly, the study of Marx has failed to actually produce a universal socialist or democratic revolution, whereas it is in Marx's name that many kinds of political terror (purges, gulags, wars) have in fact been waged. In light of the so-called failure of communism, then, it may be seen as a 'political' move not to engage with totalizing *programmes* of social revolution that are always only one step from becoming totalitar-ian in their insistence on the absolute truth or revolutionary force of those programmes.

But silence too, as Lyotard argues, is a phrase, and so the neglect of Marx and Shakespeare by postmodern literary theory cannot hope to avoid taking part in a political game. What might be called the postmodern politics of silence that surrounds these figures may then be justified as an affirmative move on behalf of all kinds of difference which are themselves kept silent under political and aesthetic regimes that have no tolerance for whatever cannot speak 'itself' in the idiom of a metanarrative. Any move away from a dominant discourse, however, risks appearing to become what it opposes – a last phrase, or a ground on which to settle a dispute and so to close off a difference. The silence surrounding Shakespeare and Marx, in other words, has developed into a kind of postmodern orthodoxy, and one that is no more necessarily liberating than the 'dominant' aesthetic discourse on Shakespeare and the 'dominant' political discourse on Marx are necessarily oppressive. Nor indeed is this silence or neglect exclusively postmodern, since what it may be well to regard as a global discourse of economic rationalism is equally dismissive of the *value* of culture and politics except as defined by its own financial needs. And this is of course precisely the basis of the left's critique of postmodernism: that it plays into the hands of 'late-capitalism' or the economic interests of multinational finance.

From this point of view, postmodernism comes to be seen as a kind of 'politics of exhaustion'. Like the literary work and the literary tradition, political 'action' and 'organization' are, for postmodernism, utterly depleted possibilities that continue to exist only insofar as they continue to be imitated or performed. The rules and procedures of political action and organization have exhausted all possibility for change, having become (as metanarratives) part of the problem to which they once promised a solution. Hence postmodern 'politics' may be seen to focus on microscopic events, but without organizing itself into a general, decontextualized programme of action. In this way postmodern politics (as indistinguishable from postmodern literary theory) may be based not only on an end-of-history thesis but also on a thesis of the 'death' of *theory*, as I will now go on to discuss in the following chapter.

9

The Death of Theory

In what is sure to become, for different reasons, a famous essay (vener-
ated for its admirable strength and clarity or vilified for the heroic bathos
of its 'male' highbrow tone), Harold Bloom writes as follows in the
'Elegiac Conclusion' to *The Western Canon*:

> I began my teaching career nearly forty years ago in an academic context
> dominated by the ideas of T. S. Eliot; ideas that roused me to fury, and
> against which I fought as vigorously as I could. Finding myself now
> surrounded by professors of hip-hop; by clones of Gallic-Germanic theory;
> by ideologues of gender and of various sexual persuasions; by multi-
> culturalists unlimited, I realize that the Balkanization of literary studies
> is irreversible. All of these Resenters of the aesthetic value of literature are
> not going to go away, and they will raise up institutional resenters after
> them. As an aged institutional Romantic, I still decline the Eliotic nostalgia
> for Theocratic ideology, but I see no reason for arguing with anyone about
> literary preferences. This book is not directed to academics, because only a
> small remnant of them still read for the love of reading. What [Samuel]
> Johnson and [Virginia] Woolf after him called the Common Reader still
> exists and possibly goes on welcoming suggestions of what might be read.[1]

The key phrase in this passage is 'the love of reading', whose key term is
'love'. This would be all that is needed to de-Balkanize literary studies in
the re-unifying name of 'the aesthetic value of literature', if the process
were not unstoppable; and for the common reader who does not know
the meaning of 'Balkanization', he or she may look it up in a dictionary.
But no one could understand the meaning of 'love' that way.

For common readers who, moreover, may not know that 'the Common Reader' was developed as a powerful concept in the writings of Dr
Johnson (or more generally through the literature of the Augustan age),
they need consult only such a passage as the following, from Johnson's

literary periodical *The Rambler*, No. 60, dated Saturday, 13 October, 1750:

> there is such an Uniformity in the state of Man, considered apart from adventitious and separable Decorations and Disguises, that there is scare any Possibility of Good or Ill, but is common to Humankind. A great Part of the Time of those who are placed at the greatest Distance by Fortune, or by Temper, must unavoidably pass in the same Manner[. . . .] We are all prompted by the same Motives, all deceived by the same Fallacies, all animated by Hope, obstructed by Danger, entangled by Desire, and seduced by Pleasure.[2]

For all this, Johnson still insisted on the importance of human difference as well as on the invariance of human nature: hence 'Instruction', as he puts it in the same issue of *The Rambler*, must consider 'every Diversity of Condition'. The duty of the Common Reader, whose nature was universal but whose condition was a direct consequence of moral and intellectual tutelage, was to cultivate, therefore, his or her 'good sense' as the measure of all things reasonable and felicitous.[3] Above all this involved an ethics of public responsibility and care, such that, as the character Imlac remarks in Johnson's *Rasselas* (1759), a marvellous didactic tale that was immediately popular in its day, one must guard against the dangers of an excessive imagination and too much solitude:

> 'To indulge the power of fiction, and send imagination out upon the wing, is often the sport of those who delight too much in silent speculation. When we are alone we are not always busy; the labour of excogitation is too violent to last long; the ardour of enquiry will sometimes give way to idleness or satiety. He who has nothing external that can divert him, must find pleasure in his own thoughts, and must convince himself what he is not; for who is pleased with what he is? He then expiates in boundless futurity, and culls from all imaginable conditions that which for the present moment he should most desire, amuses his desires with impossible enjoyments, and confers upon his pride unattainable dominion. The mind dances from scene to scene, unites all pleasures in all combinations, and riots in delights which nature and fortune, with all their bounty, cannot bestow.'[4]

The situation is summed up by Imlac only a few lines earlier: ' "All power of fancy over reason is a degree of insanity".' And of course it is precisely the absolute authority of good sense (the cultivated power of reason over fancy, as it were) that stirred the Romantics to rebellion. But this all too truistic version of events elides several problems. In the first place, returning to *Rasselas* as a text that typifies the Age of Reason, one may be surprised that it points finally to a moral that is not so much an instruction as a riddle, for the last chapter is entitled 'The conclusion, in which nothing is concluded'. Hence a postmodern text such as Pynchon's *The Crying of Lot 49*, as discussed in chapter 1, might be said to resemble *Rasselas* in the inconclusiveness of its last words, which repeat but don't resolve the riddle of the title. At any rate, according to the opposition of Enlightenment Reason and Romantic Imagination, riddles, which are an offence to plain thoughts and sensible habits, should not be what moral instructions are couched in. Riddles are posed by Grecian urns (see chapter 2), as one may begin to understand only through romantic poems. In this way the Common Reader of the Age of Johnson is everything that the Romantic Reader is not.

This raises yet another problem, though. For if it confounds the opposition of reason and imagination that a reasonable text such as *Rasselas* poses an imaginative question (what is a conclusion that does not conclude?), the opposition is further blurred by the fact that at the same time as Johnson was writing for the Common Reader, exhorting him and her to take an active role in public discourse, the Frenchman Jean-Jacques Rousseau was extolling the virtues of solitude to a Romantic Reader as a mode of averting some of the evils of modern society. As discussed in chapter 3, Rousseau is a major figure of the romantic tradition, yet his lifespan (1712–78) coincides almost exactly with that of Johnson (1709–84). The lesson here is simply that the Enlightenment is not quite as forbiddingly monolithic as sometimes thought, and of course also that if romanticism may be seen to stretch forward into today (as postmodern literary theory) it must be seen as stretching back, as well, to before the time of the Jena 'school'. But no less than romanticism, the Enlightenment exceeds periodicity and may even, at least according to Kant (1714–1804), exceed actualization: 'If it is now asked whether we at present live in an *enlightened* age, the answer is: No, but we do live in an age of *enlightenment*.'[5] For Kant, in other words, 'enlightenment' was of the order of spectrality (to use Derrida's term from the previous chapter), and so it must always remain to come. But for Rousseau it was precisely the ideas of the *philosophes* (proponents of the Enlightenment) that needed to be quelled. From as early as 1750, in his *Discourse on the Sciences and Arts* (the *First Discourse*), for which Rousseau won the Prize at the Academy of Dijon, he clearly saw the Enlightenment not as something – like Fukuyama's New World Order (see chapter 8) – to get triumphalist about, but rather as an unfortunate turn for the worse:

Before art had moulded our manners and taught our passions to speak an affected language, our customs were rustic but natural, and differences of conduct announced at first glance those of character. Human nature, basically, was no better, but men found their security in the ease of seeing through each other, and that advantage, which we no longer appreciate, spared them many vices.

Today, when subtler researches and a more refined taste have reduced the art of pleasing to set rules, a base and deceptive uniformity prevails in our customs, and all minds seem to have been cast in the same mould. Incessantly politeness requires, propriety demands; incessantly usage is followed, never one's own inclinations. One no longer dares to appear as he is; and in this perpetual constraint, the men who form this herd called society, placed in the same circumstances, will all do the same things unless stronger motives deter them. Therefore one will never know well those with whom he deals, for to know one's friend thoroughly, it would be necessary to wait for emergencies – that is, to wait until it is too late, as it is for these very emergencies that it would have been essential to know him.[6]

So more or less precisely at the same time as Johnson was entreating a concept of the Common Reader, Rousseau was appealing to an opposing concept of the reader who could see through the 'perpetual constraint' on our naturally unruly 'inclinations' exacted by imperatives of 'politeness' and 'propriety' that could result only in moral weakness. For Rousseau, being modern meant being moderate – and moderation had nothing to do with being true to oneself, as distinct from being part of 'this herd called society'.[7] But this doesn't mean that Rousseau was an advocate of absolute heterogeneity, as might be associated now with a postmodern theory of difference (as the differend, the literary absolute, the paracritical and so forth). For him it was simply that the democratic project of the Enlightenment *philosophes* was, in a sense, doomed to failure: for if the purpose of philosophy was to call ideas into question, then it must be philosophically antithetical to want to spread ideas democratically among all citizens. Since philosophical truth is a result of continuing struggle, how could the point of that struggle ever hope to arrive at a kind of 'settlement' in the form of common sense? If it did arrive at such a settlement – and if the *philosophes* were the driving force behind it – then surely they would have betrayed the first of all philosophical principles: to ask the next question. Instead, for Rousseau, the only way forward lay behind, in classical antiquity. Ancient philosophers held to an ideal of disinterested knowledge, and so did not see themselves in the role of popular educators. Socrates, Plato and Aristotle were not in the least concerned to disseminate their ideas among the citizens of antiquity, though it is certainly true that they were deeply worried over the question of how to live a good life. Their 'disinterested' probings after an answer to this question, then, should not be seen as unconnected to political quests for the best means of organizing a society in such a way that all its members might enjoy individual freedom without compromising the principle of collective well-being. Nevertheless, rather than trying to inculcate the masses with their 'difficult' responses to the question of what well-being or good living means, the philosophers of antiquity, insofar as they sought to influence 'history' at all, lent their advice to the aristocratic ruling class of the ancient world, albeit in the hope, perhaps, that their advice would lead to a better world.

In the *First Discourse*, then, Rousseau's view is that knowledge is inherently dangerous because it appeals to our natural vices and so corrupts our otherwise strong inclination to be virtuous. There is no reason to think, moreover, that great scientific discoveries have led to any increase in human virtue. On the contrary, great truths (let alone insignificant ones) have proven by and large to be pretty useless to society, and certainly to ethics:

> Answer me then, illustrious philosophers – you who taught us in what proportions bodies attract each other in a vacuum; what are, in the orbits of planets, the ratios of areas covered in equal time intervals; what curves have conjugate points, points of inflexion, and cusps; how man sees everything in God; how soul and body could be in harmony, like two clocks, without communicating; which stars could be inhabited; what insects breed in an extraordinary manner – answer me, I say, you from whom we have received so much sublime knowledge: had you taught us none of these things, would we consequently be fewer in number, less well governed, less formidable, less flourishing or more perverse? Reconsider, then, the importance of your products; and if the works of the most enlightened of our learned men and our best citizens provide us with so little that is useful, tell us what we must think of that crowd of obscure writers and idle men of letters who uselessly consume the substance of the State.[8]

Turning to antiquity, Rousseau finds that the strongest societies were in fact those that vigilantly controlled the spread of arts and sciences, in stark contrast to the modern principle of enlightenment. In Sparta and republican Rome, he saw that the basis of political unity rested on the shared conviction of the importance of virtue and patriotism. In Athens and late-classical Roman society, however, more and more time was spent in the pursuit of aesthetic and scientific knowledge, to the detriment of social harmony and of the fundamental ethical concern 'to commune with oneself and listen to the voice of one's conscience in the silence of the passions', which for Rousseau is 'true philosophy'.[9]

On such evidence, readers today might too easily mistake Rousseau for a 'fascist'. While this would be grossly unfair, it would certainly not be inconsistent with the rancour he incurred from many of his contemporaries. Yet Rousseau, who was an unremitting defender of the principle of human freedom, was no friend at all of brutal or despotic governments, as may be seen in the following passage from one of his later political works, *Considerations on the Government of Poland and on its Proposed Reformation* (1772):

> the state of weakness to which so great a nation now finds itself reduced is the fruit of that feudal barbarism which serves to cut off from the body of the state that part of the nation which is the most numerous, and oftentimes the most wholesome.
>
> God forbid that I should think it necessary at this point to prove something that a little good sense and compassion will suffice to make everyone feel! And whence does Poland expect to recruit the strength and force that she arbitrarily stifles in her bosom? Noblemen of Poland, be something more: be men. Then only will you be happy and free. But never flatter yourselves that you will be so, as long as you hold your brothers in chains.[10]

The appeal here to basic justice and goodwill is clearly not out of joint with similar calls today. In this then Rousseau may be seen as an advocate of the fundamental democratic principle of freedom, while on other grounds he could be regarded (unfairly, I repeat) as leaning towards a defence of totalitarianism.

The point however is that Rousseau's critique of enlightenment thought occurred from within the Enlightenment itself. The Academicians at Dijon, after all, honoured him with the Prize in 1750 for the best submission on the question, 'Has the restoration of the sciences & arts tended to purify morals?'. They did so again, in 1755, for his *Discourse on the Origins and Foundations of Inequality* (the *Second Discourse*), which was even more resoundingly critical of the times in its response to the question, 'What is the origin of inequality among men; and is it authorized by natural law?'. While it is true that Rousseau was later persecuted for *Émile* (the Parisian parliament ordered that the book be burned and its author arrested, causing him to remain in exile from France for several years), this was in reaction to what the authorities saw as the book's anti-Christian teachings and open hostility to the Catholic

Church. The *philosophes* were certainly critical of Rousseau (his one-time friend Denis Diderot called him 'a deserter from our camp')[11] but it was Church Law – the nemesis of enlightenment thinking – that was behind the move to censure him.

Moreover, Rousseau was not at all opposed to his contemporaries' faith in the basic soundness of men's natural good sense. It is just that, for him, that very soundness stood at risk of being lost, not enriched, by interference from popular educators. This was similarly the view of Dr Johnson, who was roundly dismissive of the fanciful abstractions of the *philosophes* whose only effect could be to get in the way of clear and practical thinking. But the irony is that Johnson saw Rousseau himself as a fanciful abstractor, chiefly because of the Frenchman's nostalgia for what Johnson regarded, in Hobbesian terms, as a 'state of nature' that men are well rid of. For the Englishman it was a good thing that people should aspire to social improvement, and nothing could be more ridiculous than to glorify a lack of riches as a mark of moral distinction and contentment. 'When I was running about this town a very poor fellow', Johnson's biographer, James Boswell, records him as saying in the *Life of Johnson* (1791), 'I was a great arguer for the advantages of poverty; but I was, at the same time, very sorry to be poor.'[12]

What can be said after all this is that the 'Common Reader' to whom Harold Bloom addresses *The Western Canon*, and whose conceptualization (if not idealization) goes back to the eighteenth century, cannot be taken for a simple fact. For if Johnson may have wanted his readers to have enough good sense to know that Rousseau was 'one of the worst of men; a rascal who ought to be hunted out of society',[13] and therefore not to read him, the fact is that both writers were hugely popular with the reading public of their day. Now of course this might simply prove Bloom's point: that outside all efforts to tell people what they should read, the incomparable good sense of ordinary folk will always convince them of what is actually worth reading. All that's needed is a simple 'love' of literature to see the 'value', then, in works that might otherwise, from the 'theoretical' perspective of some 'ideologue' or 'multiculturalist', be condemned in bad faith or resentment, or separated out from one another according to a passing fad. But if such a love is indeed the single requirement for appreciating literature, and if Dr Johnson surely had it, then how could he not see the value of Rousseau's writing? Or are we to believe that Harold Bloom alone is so full of the milk of literary kindness as to be the one reliable 'Common Reader' in the history of this concept?

By raising the love of reading to the order of the unpresentable, nevertheless, Bloom's effort is in one sense truly unexceptional: in seeking to de-contextualize 'reading' from the flux of historical, social and critical facts, ideas and practices, Bloom repeats a by now familiar romantic move. In this way it is similarly unremarkable that he opposes what might be called the indifference of sentimentalism to the interested sectarianism of theory. For him, theoretical approaches to literature are simply oxymoronic; they have nothing to do with literature as such, but only with the misguided opinions of 'amateur political scientists, uniformed sociologists, incompetent anthropologists, mediocre philosophers, and overdetermined cultural historians'.[14] The attempts to theorize or re-define literature, which are always based on some whim or a fanciful relevance deriving from some 'identity' or 'context', miss the crucial point that literature is unpresentable: 'if you can't recognize it when you read it, then no one can ever help you to know it or love it better.'[15] This was also very much Rousseau's opinion, so that he too was unforgiving in his reproach to those whom he saw as the enemies of honest judgement and common sense; and he was likewise sure of his own unaided ability to recognize the truth: 'I always come back to my first principle and it supplies the solution of all my difficulties. I study what is, I seek its cause, and I discover in the end that what is, is good.'[16] However, as we have seen, Samuel Johnson was no less confident of *his* innate capacity to know what's what, without help from the distracting complications of abstract philosophy, and yet he objected strongly to the 'sense' of Rousseau's account of things.

This simply shows that 'good sense' has about as much substance as a ghost, which does not therefore show it is a fiction. And it shows too that a certain strain of anti-theoreticism runs right through the Enlightenment. Johnson was not alone, in other words, in disapproving of what he saw as a form of fanciful speculation which even then was associated with the French. His fellow countryman Horace Walpole, for example, shortly after arriving in Paris in 1765, wrote to the English poet Thomas Gray that '[t]he *philosophes* are insupportable, superficial, overbearing, and fanatic; they preach incessantly.'[17] Walpole is a fine example too of an emergent romanticism within the Age of Reason, for not only did he try to re-capture the spirit of a valorous medieval past in his writing, but he converted the small cottage he owned a few miles from London ('Strawberry Hill') into an imposing Gothic castle, whose ramparts enclosed all the accoutrements of the real thing – an armoury, a great hall, a chapel and so forth. It might indeed be said that Strawberry Hill was more 'real' than any actual medieval fortress, at least to a majority of the visitors who flocked to see it (so many came, in fact, that admission was by ticket only) since there were very few in the way of 'authentic' medieval castles to compare it with. As incongruous as a Gothic castle on the Thames must have seemed at the time, it was clearly not out of joint with public taste. Nevertheless, Walpole's simulations, in his writing and in his life, do not make him the Baudrillard of the late eighteenth century (see chapters 2 and 3), and neither should we be so glib as to think of Strawberry Hill as an Augustan 'Disneyland'.[18]

Once again, the point is that there was no single metanarrative of the eighteenth century that conjoined the whole Enlightenment in terms of cultural, metaphysical and historical unison. Yet it is fair to say that Rousseau's and Walpole's yearnings for different earlier times were untypical of most writers and thinkers of the period, who were not at all disenamoured of the modern world (although they could be highly critical of it) but who were still at once steeped in admiration for the ideas and history of the Classical age. It is fair to say too that the Enlightenment *philosophes* did share a commitment to the value of reason (and to reasonableness), though they may not have been always diligent in practising that commitment (in either or both domains) but it should not be supposed that 'reason' was a monolithic concept among them. Neither should we think that their belief in reason (or perhaps their 'love' of reason) blinded them to the value of what the romantics would call imagination, or what Bloom calls the love of reading. What Bloom sets up, in other words, as a confrontation between 'love' (reading) and 'resentment' (theory) is just that – a set-up – for there is really no reason to have to choose. At the same time there may be some very good reasons for making a distinction between such terms as 'love' and 'theory', if only because they are used most often to refer to quite different faculties of understanding or orders of relation. This is why, for example, we are not in the habit of saying 'I theory you' to someone we care deeply about.

But it is perfectly grammatical to 'love' books. It would be highly idiomatic, nevertheless, to suppose that in saying (for example) 'I love my wife', one in fact meant the same as when saying 'I love this book.' So when we say we love books, that is patently not quite what we mean. What then do we mean? For Kant, who indeed set out to answer this question in his *Critique of Judgement*, what is meant by expressing a 'love' for literature, or for reading, cannot be codified scientifically. Quite simply, scientific judgements can take no account of the quality of 'beauty' and so cannot involve judgements of 'taste'. But responses to literature, although not scientific, are not therefore immune to inspection. 'There is no science of the beautiful, but only a Critique',[19] and the basis of such critique has to do with the nature of the beautiful, of which literature is a prime example (although for Kant the beautiful refers to what may be found in nature as well as in art). Hence for Kant the question becomes that of 'what kind of rule' is the principle by which art can be understood as art?

> For every art presupposes rules which are laid down as the foundation which first enables a product, if it is to be called one of art, to be represented as possible. The concept of fine art [involving but not restricted to cognitive understanding, as distinct from the sensations aroused by 'agreeable art'], however, does not permit of the judgement upon the beauty of its product being derived from any rule that has a *concept* for its determining ground, and that depends, consequently, on a concept of the way in which the product is possible. Consequently fine art cannot of its own self excogitate the rule according to which it is to effectuate its product.[20]

Art, then, is what calls on us to judge it in the absence of a rule of judgement. Hence aesthetic (or 'reflective') judgement involves finding a principle by which to judge, since the rules of reflective judgement (as against 'determining' judgement) are not given a priori. In this way art calls us to the limits of our understanding, because it gives us nothing to go on (by way of concepts) and yet at the same time it proposes the difficulty of finding a principle by which to understand it *as the primary task* of understanding it.

From this brief summary of the Third *Critique* it should be clear that the question of reflective judgement holds an important place in the work of Lyotard (see chapters 3 and 4), and therefore in postmodern literary theory in general. The question is important also to Derrida, especially in *The Truth in Painting* (French 1978, English 1987) where he may be said explicitly to critique the Third *Critique*. I will return to its importance to Derrida later in this chapter, wishing to focus for now on the significance that Lyotard sees in the faculty of understanding that Kant calls aesthetic or reflective judgement.

By Lyotard's own account, the considerable Kantian influence on his work derives not from 'the Kant of the concept or the moral law but the Kant of the imagination, when he cures himself of the illness of knowledge and rules'.[21] On this account Kant was 'poisoned' from too much rational thinking when he wrote the First and Second *Critiques* (dealing

with 'pure reason' and 'practical reason' respectively), and so gave thera-
peutic vent to his 'imagination' – which Lyotard opposes to 'knowledge
and rules' – in writing *The Critique of Judgement.*[22] Once again, as
we found in chapters 3 and 4, Lyotard's positive reading of the
unpresentable (the healthy or creative Kant 'of the imagination') is set
against a starkly determined negative (the sick Kant 'of knowledge and
rules'). So for Lyotard there are two Kants: one who is on the side of
reason and the Enlightenment, and who is therefore poisoned; and another who is on the side of the imagination and romanticism, who is
therefore cured. It is this principle of opposition – another version of the
opposition of 'to be or not to be', discussed in chapter 8 – that determines
Lyotard's reading of Kant's Third *Critique*, which Lyotard privileges for
throwing into question the very notion of determining principles. In
other words Lyotard may be said to use determining judgement to
support his theory of the transcendent nature of reflective judgement. In
this way, too, he may be said to follow Kant himself, for after all it was
on the basis of 'presentable' forms of understanding (pure and practical
reasons) that Kant could see that some other form of understanding
remained in excess ('unpresentable' to reason) with respect to questions
of aesthetic judgement. Derrida's version of this succession – *from* determining *to* reflective judgement – is quite different, and we will come to it
in a moment.

However, for Lyotard the succession is crucial and allows him to think
of Kant as having been sick before he got well. And for him the Kant who
is healthy is the one who sees, in the Third *Critique*, that cognition is no
basis for deciding aesthetic, political and ethical events. Hence for
Lyotard the realms of ethics and politics (or the realm of the ethico-
political) are illuminated as it were by the transcendental operations
of reflective judgement on the aesthetic. Or, as we might say, literature
gives on to politics. The distinguishing feature of reflective judgement is
simply that it does not know the rules by which the object it judges is
constituted *as* an object. For Lyotard, this situation is not confined to
aesthetic objects but describes the nature of political and ethical objects
as well – and so in this sense our political and ethical judgements are
reflective, or 'aesthetic'.[23] Ethico-political events, then, call for aesthetic
decisions.

This amounts to saying that, in Lyotard's terms, 'linkages' must be
found between 'phrases in dispute' for which there is no prescriptive
principle able to be deduced on whose authority the link could be
legitimated. It is true that law courts have to decide, on the basis of

deducing 'the facts', which party in a dispute is in 'the right'. But the process of litigation leaves open the question of *obligation*:

> How does a prescription in general (of which a plea put before a tribunal by a party is a case) have the authority to obligate its addressee? To answer this question would be to deduce prescription. But how can the prescriptive phrase be deduced without making it lose its specificity?[24]

Lyotard's 'obligation' is therefore of the order of Kant's 'aesthetic'. In a word, there is a differend between 'the descriptive metalanguage of deduction' associated with theoretical reason and 'its supposed object-language which is the prescriptive phrase'.[25] This differend is what makes it impossible for there ever to be a *theory* of ethics. Insofar as Lyotard is on the side of obligation (or in favour of ethics), then, he is therefore in a sense 'against' theory. This is where he positions Kant, too, for whom, according to Lyotard, obligation is received 'in an ideal nature by the faculty of desire, and not in the real world by sensibility'.[26]

Now, without arguing that Lyotard is wrong about obligation, or that he is wrong to read the Kant of the Third *Critique* as a proponent of desire and imagination, it is important to see that he arrives on the side of ethics (that is, against theory) through a series of oppositions, some of which he derives from Kant and some of which he imposes on him. Hence the rational Kant who was sick is opposed to the Kant who cures himself by discovering his imagination and 'the faculty of desire'; the Kant who was the friend of laws and definitions is opposed to the Kant who becomes the friend of the differend; the Kant who spent too long in the grip of theoretical reason is opposed to the Kant who frees himself in a 'spontaneous overflow' of desire and imagination exceeding the limits of 'knowledge'. As we saw in chapter 5, postmodern literary theory is committed to a certain 'knowledge of Nothing' as a sort of repressed absolute within thought as limited to presentable concepts or to understandings arrived at by determining judgement. In a sense, then, Lyotard's reading of the Kant whose desire and imagination exceed 'knowledge' places Kant on the side of the 'knowledge of Nothing'. Given that it is theoretical reason that sides with knowledge and that desire and imagination side with the knowledge of Nothing, then it must be possible (according to Lyotard) for desire and imagination to express themselves 'untheoretically'. But of course, if so, then such 'expression' would be inexpressible to (and as) the operations of presentable concepts delimiting the field of historical knowledge. Nevertheless there would remain a 'feeling' that something remained to be expressed, and this feeling would disclose a differend:

> The differend is the unstable state and instant of language wherein something which must be able to be put into phrases cannot yet be. This state includes silence, which is a negative phrase, but it also calls upon phrases which are in principle possible. This state is signaled [sic] by what one ordinarily calls a feeling: 'One cannot find the words,' etc. A lot of searching must be done to find new rules for forming and linking phrases that are able to express the differend disclosed by the feeling, unless one wants this differend to be smothered right away in a litigation and for the alarm sounded by the feeling to have been useless. What is at stake in a literature, in a philosophy, in a politics perhaps, is to bear witness to differends by finding idioms for them.[27]

For Lyotard the exemplary instance of the differend, which is underpinned by 'Nothing', by a sort of abyss, but for which there is a feeling nevertheless that 'something which must be put into phrases cannot yet be', is the sign 'Auschwitz'. Following Kant, Lyotard maintains that signs are 'not referents to which are attached significations validatable under the cognitive regimen'; instead 'they indicate that something which should be able to be put into phrases cannot be phrased in the accepted idioms.' Within a phrase universe where all referents are signs in this Kantian sense, it follows that 'the addressee is situated like someone who is affected, and that the sense is situated like an unresolved problem, an enigma perhaps, a mystery, or a paradox'. But the feeling that so arises is not locatable in the experience or mental state of a subject; it is rather 'the sign that something remains to be phrased which is not, something which is not determined'. And such remaining silence is the immeasurable measure of the horror of 'Auschwitz', the full extent of which can neither be proven by the presentation of historical facts nor redressed through litigation. Indeed, along with those who were exterminated in the camps, '[m]any of the means to prove the crime or its quantity were also exterminated'; and so the historical record contains the unpresentable absence of many historical 'facts'. This absence cannot be accounted for by the historian, however, since the cognitive regimen in which the historian functions makes it imperative that signs must have referents. But this is only all the more reason why the feeling that arises from the silence surrounding 'Auschwitz' is felt not by the theoretician, but by 'the common person':

Suppose that an earthquake destroys not only lives, buildings, and objects
but also the instruments used to measure earthquakes directly and indirectly. The impossibility of quantitatively measuring it does not prohibit,
but rather inspires in the minds of the survivors the idea of a very
great seismic force. The scholar claims to know nothing about it, but the
common person has a complex feeling, the one aroused by the negative
presentation of the indeterminate. *Mutatis mutandis*, the silence that the
crime of Auschwitz imposes upon the historian is a sign for the common
person.[28]

Hence it may be said that, for Lyotard, the crime of Auschwitz stages the
death of theory. Auschwitz is an offence to theoretical reason and to the
enlightenment concept of universal good sense, and cannot be accounted
for within the cognitive regimen of a historico-political idiom: 'with
Auschwitz, something new has happened in history (which can only be a
sign and not a fact)'. This 'something new' is not only the singularity of
Auschwitz as a sign, but also the feeling that history is impossible except
on the basis of signs rather than facts. Or as Lyotard succinctly puts it:
'there would be no history without a differend.' The 'signs of history',
then, call for an aesthetic rather than a theoretical response, and to this
extent they call the historian away from the cognitive idiom and towards
the phrase regimen of 'the common person':

> the historian must break with the monopoly over history granted to the
> cognitive regimen of phrases, and he or she must venture forth by lending
> his or her ear to what is not presentable under the rules of knowledge.
> Every reality entails this exigency insofar as it entails possible unknown
> sense. Auschwitz is the most real of realities in this respect. Its name marks
> the confines wherein historical knowledge sees its competence impugned. It
> does not follow from that that one falls into non-sense. The alternative is
> not: either the signification that learning establishes, or absurdity, be it of
> the mystical kind.[29]

The opposition of sense and non-sense, in other words, occurs only
within the order of what is 'presentable under the rules of knowledge'. In
Lyotard's efforts to get beyond this opposition, or to rethink the concept
of 'historical event', we may see a strong resemblance to Derrida's notion
of a 'spectral history' as discussed in the previous chapter. But if Lyotard
may be linked to Derrida, the problem is that he may also be linked to
Harold Bloom. For, according to Lyotard, historical signs are 'felt' by
'the common person', who knows that there is always something more to
be said about any historical event than it is possible to say in words: that
is, the common person's 'feeling' is closer than theoretical discourse can

ever hope to get to the truth (or the singularity) of historico-political events. But this is also what Bloom argues in relation to the 'love' of reading that belongs only to 'the Common Reader', by which he or she knows that the truth (or singularity) of literature is that literature expresses itself untheoretically. And so Lyotard's 'feeling' is haunted as it were by the ghost of Bloom's 'love' – and vice versa.

Lyotard's reading of *The Critique of Judgement* may not then be as radical as might seem, and this may have to do with his acceptance of a quite orthodox opposition of sign and referent. For the Third *Critique* is well known to literary criticism – via the New Critics – and precisely on the basis of a reading that locates it as a justification of the autonomy of the aesthetic work or 'object'.[30] The New Critical poem as verbal icon, in other words, is a version of the Kantian sign without referent. For New Criticism, then, poems may be thought of as 'the signs of literature'. In this they remain inexpressible (like the signs of history) in terms of any cognitive phrase regimen or theoretical discourse.

Now all theories of the sign, regardless of whether they use the name 'semiotics', have tended to begin from an assumption of the sign's difference from something outside it. The candidate 'outsides' have included ideology, human nature, factical life, socio-political history, sensorial experience, psychic interiority and so on. But in practice, as Alec McHoul argues, the various forms of what are supposed to be outside the sign (which he collects under what he very neatly calls 'the not-sign') have functioned by and large as *objects*.[31] So the classical sign/referent distinction relies on a conception of referents as objects. Simply, the sign 'chair' refers to an object for sitting on, and this object is the not-sign. Hence we can see that the possibility of thinking 'the signs of history' or 'the signs of literature' seems to depend on a prior notion of history or literature as a mass of objects (or at least of object-like 'things' such as facts, events, names, dates, manuscripts and so on) to which history and literature are irreducible. 'Feeling' and 'love', then, are in the sign, while 'facts' are in the not-sign. Clearly this means that not-signs are fairly unimportant for making any kind of aesthetic judgement (which, following Lyotard on Kant, must include ethico-political judgements). For New Criticism the not-signs of a poem (something like a literary-historical context or tradition, for example) are radically cancelled in an exclusive attention to the poem as pure sign or verbal icon. Using Lyotard's example, the not-signs of Auschwitz (so many actual deaths and death camps, and other cognitive phrases) are insufficient to explain the *crime* of Auschwitz, which remains (in)expressible only as its signs.

While the New Critical cancellation of the not-sign results in an affirmation of the sign as 'self-referential', however, Lyotard's cancellation has a different effect. For him the sign (following Kant) is without referent, and so the question arises as to what it refers to or to what it may perhaps link onto. The answer must be that it links onto an 'other-sign', as McHoul calls it, albeit in regards to the work of the early American semiotician, Charles Sanders Peirce.[32] This view of the not-sign as an other-sign risks, of course, some 'highly relativistic consequences', including that 'sign-to-sign reference goes on endlessly beyond any not-sign.'[33] This is certainly so for Lyotard concerning the case of Auschwitz: 'The indetermination of meanings left in abeyance, the extermination of what would allow them to be determined, the shadow of negation hollowing out reality to the point of making it dissipate, in a word, the wrong done to the victims that condemns them to silence – it is this, and not a state of mind, which calls upon unknown phrases to link onto the name of Auschwitz.'[34] That is, Auschwitz, as a sign of history, exceeds the mind's capacity to absorb the reality of that sign, which is always 'beyond' the not-sign of any cognitive phrase.

Hence, for Lyotard, the not-sign is whatever is presentable, which has to be cancelled or bracketed off in making an ethico-political (or aesthetic) judgement. The problem here is Lyotard's over-estimation of a difference between the signs *of* history and the not-signs *in* history. By a curious twist, this looks like a reversal of the Kantian distinction between noumena (things-in-themselves, which might otherwise be considered 'not-signs') and phenomena (the appearances or 'signs' of things-in-themselves).[35] For Lyotard, though, it seems that signs are more or less noumenal and that not-signs are the phenomena we need to get beyond if we are to have any understanding of the reality of something like Auschwitz. But what I have just termed a problem may actually be closer to what should be called a mistake. For, as Horst Ruthrof argues:

> This is not what Kant says at all. For Kant the phenomenal is what it is as a result of both noumenal constraints (which we cannot know) and our cognitive faculties (not sentences). [. . .] To attribute to the noumenal any kind of signification, however vague, is a misrepresentation of *das Ding an sich* [the thing-in-itself]. Moreover, to separate two kinds of sentences, linguistic ones and their non-linguistic cousins, or 'quasi-sentences,' along the lines of the Kantian phenomenal and noumenal deprives us of the possibility of conceiving of reality in other than linguistic terms.[36]

Ruthrof is especially severe on what he calls Lyotard's 'entirely linguistic presentation of reality' such that, as Ruthrof puts it, in Lyotard 'the semiotics of gestural, proxemic, kinetic, tactile, olfactory, visual, and aural sign systems are collapsed at one stroke onto the plane of language.'[37] Although Lyotard does admit that '[a] wink, a shrugging of the shoulders, a taping [sic] of the foot, a fleeting blush' or even an excessively rapid heart rate 'can be phrases',[38] his concession to a nonlinguistic semiotics of the body is merely momentary and quite incidental to the linguistic dominance of his account of the differend. Nor, it should be added, does his notion of the linguistic seem to include any consideration of nonlinguistic elements *within* language, as for example Derrida attempts in his notion of 'grammatology' and which I touched on briefly in chapter 6.

For Ruthrof, 'Lyotard's emphasis on the "phrase" at the expense of other signifying systems' leads to another consequence: 'our inability to distinguish between the fictional real and the actual real'. As we have seen, this remains a persistent problem for postmodern literary theory. In collapsing actuality into textuality (or as we may say now, in its cancellation of the not-sign), postmodern literary theory levels heterogeneity to the order of mono-difference (see chapter 5). This, in Baudrillard's terms, turns reality into 'hyperreality' and signs into 'simulacra', while for Lyotard the consequence is that the micro-political arena of unpresentable signs calls for a response on the basis of 'feeling' at the expense of critical judgement. As a corrective, then, what may be needed is an attention to what Jack Gladney, the narrator of Don DeLillo's canonically postmodern novel, *White Noise* (1985), refers to as 'a philosophical argument rendered in terms of the things of the world':

> I watched the coffee bubble up through the center tube and perforated basket into the small pale globe. A marvellous and sad invention, so roundabout, ingenious, human. It was like a philosophical argument rendered in terms of the things of the world – water, metal, brown beans. I had never looked at coffee before.[39]

But of course this could be only a corrective, insofar as it would be an attempt to restore the not-sign to the order of the noumenal while leaving the opposition of the noumenal and the phenomenal ('to be or not to be') securely in place. Alec McHoul, however, proposes a more interesting move:

> All I would suggest is this: We can keep the not-sign (to continue with the shorthand) but we must think of it radically, as something other than an

object. In short, it's the idea of the object that blocks the path to a dynamic, historical, and complex idea of the sign.[40]

McHoul's suggestion is to see that 'a sign has both internal and external relations, relations that seem never to arise alone in their purity but that instead [. . .] infect one another in the space of the frame or parergon.'[41] In this he is following Derrida's reading of Kant, though his own interest is in the specific *constructions* of not-signs through particular community practices such that an 'effective semiotics' would be able to describe instances not only of the orthodox idea of a sign-using community but also the radical one of a not-sign-using community. Nevertheless, in *The Truth in Painting*, Derrida argues that Kant's seeming distinction between aesthetic and theoretical orders of knowledge in the Third *Critique*, or simply between art and theory, is considerably more troublesome than it looks. The trouble, as Derrida sees it, arises from Kant's inattention to the work that is carried out on and by the frame or border that is supposed to separate art and theory.

In Greek, *ergon* means 'work'; *parergon* therefore means that which runs 'alongside' the work – its frame or border. Hence the parergonal is neither inside nor outside the work, although it is crucial in the very designation of works themselves insofar as they must be cut off from all external relations in order to have any self-identity as works. In this way the parergon must be seen as *doing work*, as working on and in the work/ non-work opposition as the very possibility of that opposition. When we look at a painting, for example, we are inclined not to attribute any intrinsicality to its frame: insofar as we think about the frame at all, we might be said to regard it as a not-sign. The painting is the work, and it is *as* the painting that the work 'works'. But of course without frames, without some way of limiting a work, paintings would in principle be indistinguishable from the walls they hung on – and we would be forced to say either that nothing 'works' or that walls do as much 'work' as paintings. In other words, either nothing *or* everything works. Frames then may be said to do the very important work *of framing*, and so the parergonal borders of a work are irreducible to an absolute not-sign (the immaterially material or the insignificantly actual) as opposed to the pure sign-value or significatory effects of the work 'itself'.

In arguing this, however, Derrida is not claiming that the parergonal is a sign. His point is to show that the separation of art and theory (text and commentary, the aesthetic and the extra-aesthetic) is enabled by a certain *passage* that parerga open up between and within the opposition

of art and theory. Hence it is in this passage that art and theory both ·
work. Kant's order of the sublime, however, especially in the form of
what he calls 'the colossal', is supposed to resolve the problem of the
frame as that which both encloses art and opens it to theoretical inspection. But Derrida's argument is that by thinking of the sublime in terms
of transcendent unpresentability, Kant has to overlook the unpresentable
force of the parergon's *work* at the margins of the art/theory opposition.
So what might be called parergonal effectivity is always at work *within* art and theory, making it impossible to separate completely aesthetic heterogeneity from theoretical, or simply 'extra-aesthetic', factors
and forces. The sublime, then, may not be what transcends 'the work
of the frame', reaching a kind of absolute formlessness beyond
parergonality, but rather what *draws attention* to framing work or to the
passage within which the aesthetic and the extra-aesthetic (in such forms
as theory, society, history, politics and so on) are forever situated and
forever being re-situated. It is in this way, Derrida argues, that Kant's
'colossal' works:

> The colossal seems to belong to the presentation of raw, rough, crude
> nature. But we know that the sublime takes only its presentations from
> nature. The sublime quality of the colossal, although it does not derive
> from art or culture, nevertheless has nothing natural about it. The cise [cut,
> shape] of the colossus is neither culture nor nature, both culture and
> nature. It is perhaps, between the presentable and the unpresentable, the
> passage from the one to the other as much as the irreducibility of the one
> to the other. Cise, edging, cut edges, that which passes and happens,
> without passing, from one to the other.[42]

On this account the Kantian sublime is not quite the very figure of
absolute heterogeneity that postmodern literary theory makes it out
to be. For although the sublime seems to be what must 'exclude the
parergon [...] because the infinite is presented in it and the infinite
cannot be bordered',[43] Derrida's point is that it is precisely the parergonal
work of the passage from nature to culture, culture to nature, that allows
the sublime to present the 'unpresentable'. So there is no hope, on
Derrida's view, of getting to an aesthetic or heterogenous 'inside' (the
sign) by supposing it is able to be cut off from all relations with a
theoretical or socio-political 'outside' (the not-sign). Yet Lyotard's argument commits him to precisely this cut-off point, such that in his blindness to parergonality he cannot see the frames around the three *Critiques*
as anything but occlusions, rather than as openings or passages within
Kant's overall critique of reason.

Despite the many apparent differences between them, then, it is possible to see both Harold Bloom and Jean-François Lyotard as being on the side of 'art against theory'. This is in one sense unsurprising, given Bloom's declared romanticism and a certain fidelity to a concept of the literary absolute in Lyotard's work. But while Lyotard's allegiance derives from his reading of *The Critique of Judgement*, Bloom is smugly dismissive of Kant's importance to anyone searching for the truth about literature: ' "Aesthetic value" is sometimes regarded as a suggestion of Immanuel Kant's rather than an actuality, but that has not been my experience during a lifetime of reading.'[44] They both seem to agree nevertheless that 'theory' obstructs the passage to a 'love' of or a 'feeling' for the aesthetic, whether in the form of Auschwitz or Shakespeare, and in this they are conjoined with a certain strain of anti-theoreticism going back to Rousseau but which is observable also in the work of a figure such as Dr Johnson. In such light it is starkly ironic that Bloom should worry over the immortality of theory, when Lyotard is all for seeing Auschwitz as having brought about its death. Hence they both share something like a common aestheticism, which ought to allay the 'very little confidence' Bloom has that 'literary education will survive its current malaise.'[45] What they have in common is a belief in the idea of a 'higher' order of understanding that is fundamentally non-cognitive (the 'knowledge of Nothing'), and although on Lyotard's account it may look as if it is Kant's Third *Critique* which is the source of this conviction, Bloom is much closer to the mark in denying that 'aesthetic value' starts with Kant. It starts in fact with the Jena Romantics (especially Friedrich Schiller), who saw in *The Critique of Judgement* a romantic validation of the sovereignty of the aesthetic faculty (imagination) over cognitive faculties of understanding (reason).[46] Kant, however, insisted on the separation of the faculties, rather than on the elevation of one above all others. And so, among what might be called the many spectres of Kant, it is the Jena Romantics' reading of the Third *Critique* to which aestheticism ever since has had to swear. By handing over to cognition the work of inspecting the not-sign, romanticism set loose the unruly energies of the imagination in a search for the perpetually elusive sign. One effect of this for what is called postmodern literary theory has been to deny, paradoxically, that 'theory' has anything to contribute to an understanding of the question of literature. This effect is quite strongly reinforced, as we will see in the following chapter, through a certain reading of Nietzsche and Heidegger. However, another effect of raising aesthetic judgement to supreme importance has been to revitalize the philosophical concept (or the concept of theoretical reason) in terms of aesthetic freeplay. This effect too is associated with a certain reading of Nietzsche and Heidegger, though it is perhaps observable more directly in Deleuze and Guattari's work – especially in the form of what might be called concept creation – as I will now go on to discuss.

10

Concept Creation

'We're tired of trees', Deleuze and Guattari sigh in *A Thousand Plateaus*. 'We should stop believing in trees, roots, and radicles. They've made us suffer too much.'[1] This is not a timber industry pitch, but part of an attempt (both wildly celebrated and fiercely contested) to rethink thinking; or as Brian Massumi puts it in his 'Translator's Foreword', *A Thousand Plateaus* is 'an effort to construct a smooth space of thought'.[2] Ever since Plato, in Deleuze and Guattari's view, human thought has been dominated by what they call the 'arborescent model' (the tree of knowledge) and the time has come to hack it down. For them, 'thought is not arboresent'; it is rhizomatic, a term I will explain in a moment. 'Many people have a tree growing in their heads,' they write, 'but the brain itself is much more a grass than a tree.'[3]

From this tiny fragment of a huge book, which is itself part of a larger project of 'capitalism and schizophrenia' that starts with *Anti-Oedipus* in 1972, something may be glimpsed of the immense attraction and immense frustration that surrounds their work. If Deleuze and Guattari were pop stars, they'd be the sort of which press reports would always begin, 'Love them or hate them . . .'. Indeed, at least in Deleuze's case, one could say his academic reputation is exceeded only by his pop celebrity, judging from the two compilation-CDs of rave music that were released recently in honour of his death (by suicide) in 1995. One of these, a double-CD called *In Memoriam Gilles Deleuze*, is issued by a German independent company that takes its name from *A Thousand Plateaus* (the Mille Plateau label), while the other compilation, released under a Belgian label and called *Folds and Rhizomes for Gilles Deleuze*, pays tribute in its title to two of Deleuze's typically exotic or outlandish terms. Deleuze is not the first French philosopher of recent times to arouse the interest of the music industry (there is now a UK dance label called Deconstruction, for example, while the British 'post-pop' band, Scritti Politti, recorded a song called 'Jacques Derrida' in the early-1980s),[4] but perhaps it is his philosophy that is most open to being reworked (or 'reterritorialized', to use a term from A Thousand Plateaus) as music. 'In fact', Massumi writes, 'Deleuze and Guattari would probably be more inclined to call philosophy music with content than music a rarefied form of philosophy.'[5]

Hence Massumi prefers to think of 'playing' A Thousand Plateaus instead of reading it. 'When you buy a record [he is writing just before the compact disc revolution] there are always cuts that leave you cold. You skip them. You don't approach a record as a closed book that you have to take or leave. Other cuts you may listen to over and over again. They follow you. You find yourself humming them under your breath as you go about your daily business.'[6] This then is the (anti-arborescent) model for approaching Deleuze and Guattari. But the problem is that the 'anti-ness' of the model depends on a totalizing negation of what it counters: in short, no less than Harold Bloom, Brian Massumi knows what 'reading' is. Unlike Bloom, however, for Massumi reading is a kind of undemanding, dispassionate, impersonal activity that forces us to follow a predetermined sequence of events. Our playing of a record or a CD, on the other hand, is driven by desire and pleasure; and so we do not have to follow any determining principle in selecting the order of songs we wish to play.[7] By now this should be recognizable as a more or less prescriptive postmodern statement of the positive force of nonprescriptive desire and heterogeneity. So 'playing', as Massumi calls it, involves what Lyotard calls 'feeling' (see chapter 9) and to this extent it carries over unexpectedly into mundane areas of our lives as we hum our favourite tunes: we are always playing (in the double sense of 'playing' music and 'playing with' music, being playful with it), because we are never lost for feelings (though of course on Lyotard's account we are often lost for words). But reading is cut off from our 'daily business'; it occurs only under strict conditions and according to austere rules by which we have no choice but to always turn the next page rather than flicking to the page we might want to turn to. Reading, then, rules out playing (in both senses).

The trouble with this is that a reader such as Harold Bloom, a canonical reader as it were, already does what Massumi thinks that Deleuze and Guattari are calling for. There can be no doubt that the author of The Western Canon is always reading, and in the sense that Massumi means by 'playing'. No one could mistrust that, in the course of his daily business, Bloom doesn't often find occasion to quote Shakespeare, for example, or that he isn't often reminded of some favourite bit of writing from the canon. Bloom's canon morever is massively eclectic and complex, a vast network of texts that is full of surprises in its historically far-reaching and culturally diverse extensions. In this sense too then he may be said to 'play' with texts, to see connections within and between them on the basis of his nonprescriptive 'love' of reading. In a word, Bloom's canon – 'the' Western Canon – is rhizomatic.

A rhizome is any plant (like ivy or grass) whose root-system is coextensive with the plant itself, as the plant grows ever outwards and across. It is possible to identify the different parts of a tree (leaves, branches, trunk, roots) but not so with a rhizome; in principle, a single grass seed could grow rhizomatically to cover the whole land mass of the planet, but of course a tree is always rooted to the spot. 'There are no points or positions in a rhizome, such as those found in a structure, tree, or root. There are only lines.'[8] Hence for Deleuze and Guattari the rhizome becomes the figure of what they call 'acentered systems', and in this it may appear as yet another example of a postmodern notion of 'structureless' structure (see chapter 5). Trees, then, are structured and hierarchical, whereas the rhizome is nonhierarchical, structureless, open, perambulatory, consisting only of 'multiple entryways and exits and its own lines of flight'.[9] Such lines of flight (as against fixed points of origin) are typical of acentred or 'nomadic' thought, in contrast to 'tree logic' which has dominated Western thinking since Plato. Nomadic thought, or 'nomadology', uproots itself from the strictures of theoretical reason and follows only the nondetermining decrees of impulse and desire. But for Deleuze and Guattari, as Edith Wyschogrod astutely points out, desire is not at all the romantic or psychoanalytic concept associated with the subject's unconscious or hidden drives. For them, desire is 'transformed into an economic resource like hydroelectric or nuclear power, and its modus operandi decided by those who possess sufficient force to control its circulation.'[10] For this reason it would be wrong to see Deleuze and Guattari as calling for the complete abandonment of critical thinking (tree logic) to a sort of absolute of desire in the usual sense, allowing 'freeplay' to mean 'anything goes'. Indeed they themselves warn against mistaking nomadic or 'multiple' assemblages of thought for effects simply of a subject's creative rapture:

> To attain the multiple, one must have a method that effectively constructs it; no typographical cleverness, no lexical agility, no blending or creation of

words, no syntactical boldness, can substitute for it. In fact, these are more often than not merely mimetic procedures used to disseminate or disperse a unity that is retained in a different dimension for an image-book. Technonarcissism. Typographical, lexical, or syntactic creations are necessary only when they no longer belong to the form of expression of a hidden unity, becoming themselves dimensions of the multiplicity under consideration [. . .].[11]

While this caution is not always heeded by their aficionados, it serves to indicate here that Deleuze and Guattari are perhaps not quite as 'hallucinatory' in their thinking and writing as admirers and critics of their work often suppose. For the crucial statement above is that 'one must have a method' (thought of course the question remains open as to what should define this method); it is therefore not enough to write self-consciously in a 'transgressive' or 'experimental' style, because a certain notion of creative transgression and experimentation is itself a product of the fact that 'the tree has dominated Western reality and all of Western thought.'[12] In short, lexical creativity is part and parcel of any arborescent system, and in this way a text such as Ihab Hassan's *Paracriticisms*, as discussed in chapter 5, may be more mimetic than rhizomatic (more radicle than radical). Deleuze and Guattari are certainly in favour of creativity, but it is clear from the passage above that the sorts of creation they are calling for are not those of a lexical or 'literary' type. Instead, as we will see shortly, they advocate a radical creativity at the level of *concepts*. In this way nomadology is a philosophical, not a literary, practice; its concern is not to create new metaphors, but to rethink concepts.

By 'philosophy', nevertheless, Deleuze and Guattari do not mean simply what is on the side of 'dialectic' as opposed to 'rhetoric' (see chapter 7) since philosophical concepts are at work within and *as* literature, for example, especially in the form of the concept of 'the book'. So for them it is possible to see that different forms of this concept result – theoretically and effectively – in quite different types of book.[13] First there is the 'root-book' (or sometimes, as above, the 'image-book') which is grounded (rooted) in the assumption that art's function is to reflect or 'image' external reality: 'art imitates nature', in short. 'This is the classical book, as noble, signifying, and subjective organic interiority' – or, recalling McHoul's terms from the previous chapter, the root-book may be seen as a 'sign' that purports to adequate the 'not-sign' of objectified nature, or just simply 'the world'. We might see a connection here to Baudrillard's first- and second-order signs of 'reflection' and 'malefice' (see chapter 3). The second type of book, however, 'to which our modernity pays willing allegiance', takes the not-sign as a problem, since the world is seen to be fragmented, unstable and chaotic. In the absence of any stable not-sign to reflect or imitate, mimesis is uprooted and its role is assumed by the figure of the 'radicle-system, or the fascicular root'. Based on a strict sign/not-sign distinction, that is, the root-book's function as a point of origin (the root of all knowledge about the world) is dispersed across a far less stable field of not-signs, turning the radicle or fascicular book into the figure of a chain-like series of sign-to-sign relations (corresponding perhaps to Baudrillard's third-order sign which masks 'the *absence* of a basic reality'). As Deleuze and Guattari put it, each text of this second type needs to be seen in terms of 'the folding of one text onto another'.

Recalling the discussion in chapter 5, the distinction between the classical root-book and the modern radicle-text may be seen as a version of the difference between the totalizing novel and metafictive writing. In a sense, then, the distinction is already well known to literary criticism. But Deleuze and Guattari's point is that the radicle-text (or, possibly, metafiction) remains in a one-to-one relation with the world of not-signs, and is therefore not opposed to tree logic but rather supplements it. In reflecting the not-sign's shattered unity, that is, the radicle-text simply affirms the higher unity of the sign. Such a relation is exemplified in the texts of James Joyce and Friedrich Nietzsche:

> Joyce's words, accurately described as having 'multiple roots,' shatter the unity of the word, even of language, only to posit a cyclic unity of the sentence, text, or knowledge. Nietzsche's aphorisms shatter the linear unity of knowledge, only to invoke the cyclic unity of the eternal return, present as the nonknown in thought. This is as much to say that the fascicular system does not really break with dualism, with the complimentarity between a subject and an object, a natural reality and a spiritual reality: unity is consistently thwarted and obstructed in the object, while a new type of unity triumphs in the subject. The world has lost its pivot; the subject can no longer even dichotomize, but accedes to a higher unity, of ambivalence or overdetermination, in an always supplementary dimension to that of its object. The world has become chaos, but the book remains the image of the world [. . .].[14]

The examples of Joyce and Nietzsche serve to show that the radicle-text is not quite equivalent to metafiction as that term was used in literary criticism in the 1960s and '70s. As a concept, however, metafiction refers to the textual reflection of what Mas'ud Zavarzadeh, for example, calls 'a total communal fear, estrangement, and paranoia' outside the text (see chapter 5). Hence there is a conceptual equivalence between metafiction and what Deleuze and Guattari call the radicle-text, which signifies a concept of the book as 'the image' of a world that has 'become chaos'. Whereas 'metafiction' is in one sense a historical term, referring to the period of 'new' writing in post-War America, the concept of the radicle-text is more concerned with describing (or performing) a particular mode of sign/not-sign relations. This is true also of the concept of the root-book as distinct from that of the totalizing novel, since although the latter term does refer to an order of sign/non-sign relations, it tends to mark that order as periodic or historical.

The point here is that Deleuze and Guattari are seeking to describe not a succession of literary phases, but a series of text–world relations encapsulated in concepts of 'the book'. Hence, as a series, these concepts may (or may not) co-exist historically, so that there is no reason to suppose that say the root-book is no longer being written – and this applies also to the radicle-text. In this way too the attention to concepts rather than histories of 'the book' corresponds to Baudrillard's interest in certain orders of 'the sign'. In both cases what is being affirmed is the most 'open' or heterogeneous instance of its type: for Baudrillard this is the simulacrum, while for Deleuze and Guattari it is of course the rhizome:

> The tree is filiation, but the rhizome is alliance, uniquely alliance. The tree imposes the verb 'to be,' but the fabric of the rhizome is the conjunction, 'and . . . and . . . and . . .' This conjunction carries enough force to shake and uproot the verb 'to be.' Where are you going? Where are you coming from? What are you heading for? These are totally useless questions. Making a clean slate, starting or beginning again from ground zero, seeking a beginning or a foundation – all imply a false conception of voyage and movement [. . .]. But [. . .] American literature, and already English literature [. . .] know how to move between things, establish a logic of the AND, overthrow ontology, do away with foundations, nullify endings and beginnings. They know how to practice pragmatics.[15]

The contemporary New York writer Paul Auster's work may be a good example of what Deleuze and Guattari mean by 'a logic of the AND' which defines the concept of the rhizomatic book, and it is from the viewpoint of this concept that I will consider Auster's writing in the following chapter. But first I want to discuss briefly how this concept relates to a certain order of difference that is characteristic of post-modern literary theory (and which is therefore different from poststructuralism) as derived from the romantic concept of the literary absolute.

For Christopher Norris, Deleuze and Guattari typify 'the truth about postmodernism', especially in *A Thousand Plateaus*. This for Norris is 'by far the most sustained postmodernist assault on all the concepts and categories of Western intellectual tradition' – an 'out-and-out polemical crusade against "enlightenment" reason in every shape or form'.[16] The judgement is perhaps a little harsh if one takes account of what Deleuze and Guattari say in the passage above: that 'a logic of the AND' should be affirmed for making it possible 'to practice pragmatics'. In other words their interest in a rhizomatic or nomadic logic is not quite for the sake of an 'anything goes' approach to truth: their anti-foundationalist stance is taken, they claim, not in the name of what might be called 'aesthetic' or 'creative' truth, but in the name of an underprivileged (or perhaps unthought) *pragmatics* of truth. 'Pragmatics', they write in *A Thousand Plateaus*, 'is a politics of language.'[17] For them 'language is a political affair before it is an affair for linguistics'[18] (and here we might recall the discussion, in chapter 3, of the question of 'proper grammar'), because linguistics is not in itself a purely symmetrical system of rules and propositions cut off from a socio-historical world of asymmetrical facts and events:

> *If the external pragmatics of nonlinguistic factors must be taken into consideration, it is because linguistics itself is inseparable from an internal pragmatics involving its own factors.* It is not enough to take into account the signified, or even the referent, because the very notions of signification and reference are bound up with a supposedly autonomous and constant structure. There is no use constructing a semantics, or even recognizing a certain validity to pragmatics, if they are still pretreated by a phonological or syntactical machine.[19]

From this it may be said that Deleuze and Guattari are trying to move away from a linguistic emphasis on signs towards a pragmatic consideration of not-signs – or from a theoretics to an empirics, as it were. 'Empiricism' is of course a most unfashionable term within humanities scholarship in general nowadays, but especially from the standpoint of literary studies. Yet it is precisely to the question of empiricity that *A Thousand Plateaus* directs us.

In philosophy, empiricism refers to the view (associated with John Locke, George Berkeley and David Hume, for example) that private sense-experience is the only ground of knowledge. Following the breakthrough of Newtonian physics in the seventeenth century, however, scientists were convinced that knowledge was independent of sensorial experience, and so within science 'empiricism' came to mean a form of proof by observation or experiment. But in both cases the empirical has to do with the pragmatic rather than the theoretical: it belongs on the side of practical experience rather than systematic enquiry. In Deleuze and Guattari's terms, the empirical is rhizomatic: as what is always outside theory, the empirical is every theory's not-sign.

However, and this point is crucial, Deleuze and Guattari's objection to theory (or system) is not that it is abstract, as opposed to say the concrete materiality of the empirical. Rather it is that theory 'is not abstract enough.'[20] Every theory is therefore 'linear', in Deleuze and Guattari's view, because it relies on the separation of factors that are internal to it from those that are outside the theory and which are therefore 'untheoretical'. Hence it looks as if theoretical abstraction (generality) is bracketed off from empirical contingency (singularity), on which view every theory is a kind of abstract machine that runs over the top of empirical raw material. But for this split to occur, Deleuze and Guattari maintain, there must be a level of abstraction which is prior to the theoretical/empirical divide. Theoretical abstraction, then, is only a weak form of abstraction compared to the greater abstraction that precedes it. This greater abstraction is what Deleuze and Guattari refer to as 'a true abstract machine' since it 'pertains to an assemblage in its entirety'[21] – and by an assemblage they mean, as I will discuss shortly, something close to Nietzsche's concept of 'will to power'. Taking the example of language as an abstraction, they argue it is not enough to think only of abstract linguistic elements (grammatical, lexical, syntactical signs and units) versus concrete nonlinguistic elements (the not-signs of social history and so forth), because

> as soon as pragmatic values or internal variables are taken into account, in particular with respect to indirect discourse, one is obliged to bring 'hypersentences' into play or to construct 'abstract objects' (incorporeal transformations). This implies superlinearity, in other words, a plane whose elements no longer have a fixed linear order: the rhizome model. From this standpoint, the interpenetration of language and the social field and political problems lies at the deepest level of the abstract machine, not at the surface.[22]

In order to approach empiricity, then, Deleuze and Guattari are forced to think ever more abstractly. In this, it could be said, they are concerned

not so much with empirics as *ethics*. This is after all Foucault's view in
the Preface to *Anti-Oedipus*: 'I would say that *Anti-Oedipus* (may its
authors forgive me) is a book of ethics, the first book of ethics to be
written in France in quite a long time (perhaps that explains why its
success was not limited to a particular "readership": being anti-oedipal
has become a life style, a way of thinking and living).' And this way of
thinking-living concerns the task of 'keep[ing] from being fascist, even
(especially) when one believes oneself to be a revolutionary militant'.[23] In
apologizing to the authors, Foucault recognizes that any attempt to
define Deleuze and Guattari's work is already to misunderstand and
misrepresent it. This perhaps explains Norris's claim that *A Thousand
Plateaus* launches a full-scale attack on reason. Nevertheless, for
Foucault at least (if not also for other admirers), Deleuze and Guattari's
refusal to work 'within reason' has to be seen as the expression of an
ethical desire to 'keep from being fascist'. To oppose reason, in short, is
to oppose fascism.

So what Foucault means by an 'ethics' here is also what Norris calls
'by far the most sustained postmodernist assault on all the concepts and
categories of Western intellectual tradition'. Hence it would appear that
to be on the side of ethics is to be against the philosophical tradition, or
against what might be called the concepts and categories of theoretical
reason in general. Once again: to affirm, we must negate! To keep from
being fascist (that is, to be ethical), we must stop thinking as we have
been taught to think and learn to think anew – just as the romantic poets
had to (as it were) unthink poetry in order to be able to write poems. And
in order to write poetry anew, of course, the romantics had to create a
new *concept* of 'the poem': the concept of the literary absolute, as
Lacoue-Labarthe and Nancy call it. For Deleuze and Guattari, then, the
great achievement of romanticism might be said to be its concepts rather
than its poems – a philosophical rather than a literary achievement, in
other words.

Yet it must be repeated that, by philosophy, Deleuze and Guattari do
not mean 'the concepts and categories of Western intellectual tradition'.
This is in fact what they call 'State philosophy', referring to what they
see as a determined link (a 'linear' connection), which functions in the
interests of power and government, between the well-trained philosopher
and the well-trained citizen. Nevertheless Deleuze himself was certainly
trained within the State philosophical system, although it would appear
that he did not quite *read* the 'great philosophers' as his teachers might
have wanted: 'What got me through that period was conceiving of the

history of philosophy as a kind of ass-fuck, or, what amounts to the same thing, an immaculate conception. I imagined myself approaching an author from behind and giving him a child that would indeed be his but would nonetheless be monstrous.'[24] In light of this remark it is unsurprising that Deleuze should be on the side of anti-State philosophers who denounce power and affirm joy, among whom of course Nietzsche looms largest of all. From Nietzsche, Deleuze may be said to derive a philosophy of outright affirmation based on Nietzsche's concept of the will to power as the will (or the willing) that obeys no force, no law, no God or no authority but itself.[25] The force of affirming-willing (which Deleuze and Guattari will call an assemblage or a 'desiring-machine') is crucial to Deleuze's whole project, including his collaborations with Guattari, and something of its significance can be seen in the following summary by John D. Caputo:

> Deleuze defends a philosophy of pure affirmation, the affirmation of affirmation, a pure and undiluted affirmation of affirmation itself rather than of something else. This unencumbered willing and affirming means the free creation and the invention of new values. The essence of willing and of the free spirit is to steer clear of dead weights and heavy burdens. The free spirit is no beast of burden, no ass braying 'yes, yes' when confronted with something onerous. Beware the spirit of bearing, which is the spirit of gravity and taking on heavy weights. Beware the unbearable heaviness of Being.
>
> The will of the free spirit guards against all 'responsibility,' which is nothing but the weight of Being, an ontological weight brought to bear upon a will made for serving. The heaviness of Being is the center of gravity in classical metaphysics [. . .]. In such a metaphysics, affirmation means 'acceptance' (of weighty responsibilities). True affirmation can never be a 'function' of Being, i.e., of something other than itself, which would reduce the will to a 'functionary' – not only of the party, the church, or the state but of Being or truth, of anything that in any way impinges on the will, anything that would bind the will or tie it up.[26]

There are two points to note from this. First, affirmation (or affirming-willing) involves 'free creation' and 'invention'; second, it is unaccountable both to institutional and metaphysical interests. Taking the second point first: for Deleuze, and for Deleuze and Guattari, affirming-willing is fundamentally *irresponsible* – and this is what Foucault calls an 'ethics'. But in extending his ethical approval to the concept of a desiring-machine, Foucault is registering his disapproval not simply of institutions and metaphysics in general but especially his frustration with what

Caputo refers to above as 'the party': namely the French Communist
Party to which, in the 1960s, a great many French intellectuals belonged.
At that time (and from about the 1920s) the goal of French political
thinkers was to synthesize Freud and Marx: to open up Marxism to
an understanding of human desire, and to open up Freudianism to
an understanding of economic desire. Louis Althusser, for example,
the leading Marxist intellectual of the day, borrowed the term
'overdetermination' from Freud to better account for the complex ways
in which subject positions are an effect of not one but many determining factors working together. More generally, Freud's influence on
Althusser's Marxism shows up in Althusser's rethinking of ideology as a
force that works by subtle deception rather than blatant coercion. The
key term here is 'interpellation', referring to the way that subjects are
called or hailed by an ideological system into positions that allow them
to think of themselves as free agents, whereas their agency is in fact fully
circumscribed by external interests that interpellate them (or 'us') as
'independent'. The capitalist 'trick', in other words, is to constrain our
array of choices (among cultural, political and other options) while
making us believe in our absolute freedom to choose.[27] But while
Althusserian 'ideology' emerges from a general background of Freud's
ideas concerning the unconscious, it is linked even more directly to
Lacan's concept of the 'imaginary'. At the same time as Althusser was
working towards a kind of 'Freudianization' of Marx, that is, Lacan
might be said to have been working in the other direction by opening a
passage to the 'Marxification' of Freud. As we saw in chapter 2, Lacan's
work relies on a notion of disunified subjectivity (such that our
positionings within the symbolic order are constituted by lack, both
blocking and opening a passage to the imaginary) and this is broadly
consistent with Marx's views concerning the illusionary but effective
relationship between meanings and social forms, as indicated for example in the following passage from *Capital*, Volume I, first published in
German in 1867 and translated into English in 1886:

> The name of a thing is something distinct from the qualities of that thing.
> I know nothing of a man, by knowing that his name is Jacob. In the same
> way with regard to money, every trace of a value-relation disappears in the
> names pound, dollar, franc, ducat, etc. The confusion caused by attributing
> a hidden meaning to these cabalistic signs is all the greater, because these
> money-names express both the values of commodities, and, at the same
> time, aliquot parts of the weight of the metal that is the standard of money.
> On the other hand, it is absolutely necessary that value, in order that it may

be distinguished from the varied bodily forms of commodities, should assume this material and unmeaning, but, at the same time, purely social form.[28]

For Deleuze and Guattari, however, the dominating 'deterritorialization' of Marxism via Freudianism had led to a kind of ethico-intellectual sickness throughout France in the 1960s that could be cured only through a process of 'reterritorialization'. Through the Oedipus complex, Freud's intellectual territory was confined largely to the family; hence the increasing influence of psychoanalysis over Marxist thought in France at that time was undermining the broader socio-political terrain of Marxism by reducing all social phenomena to familial effects. In Deleuze and Guattari's view, then, the Freudian Oedipalization of history was at odds with the Marxist politicization of history – in short, psychoanalysis was unhealthy. What was needed was an account of the flows of capital and the flows of desire that could not be territorialized (or colonized) by any single theory or method, or by any one figure or party. And since capital and desire are always in flux and should not be seen as belonging to strictly different territories or domains (of economics and sex, for example), what was needed was an analysis not of fixed territories but of nomadic movements or processes of ongoing re- and de-territorialization.

Such an analysis, of course, could never be allowed to take root as a kind of disciplinary system or knowledge-tree. Like the nomad, it could have no natural homeland (hence no disciplinary base or centre, such as sociology or political science or whatever); and like the rhizome, it could have no single root as the source of its profusion (hence its roots would be in every discipline – politics, history, literature, philosophy and so on). By the same token the effort to rethink desire outside the limits of psychoanalysis must, insofar as it concerns thought, be understood as a philosophical necessity. This is to say that the project of capitalism and schizophrenia is 'philosophical'. But the rethinking of desire is also a rethinking of thought, since it is concerned to uproot such concepts as desire from the various zones in which they are traditionally thought to be located. In this way Deleuze and Guattari's philosophical project must also be seen as a reterritorialization of 'philosophy', so that philosophy is allowed to extend rhizomatically to cover such fields as history, politics, literature and popular knowledge. For Deleuze and Guattari, then, the roots of philosophy are rhizomatic; while they may be said to have to do with questions concerning the limits of thought or the scope of knowledges, such questions are also asked by poets, painters, film-makers and others who dare to venture into 'new' (aesthetico-philosophical) territories. So Deleuze and Guattari's philosophical analysis of desire is at the same time a political analysis, a literary analysis, a sociological analysis and so on.

In this way it is a kind of pragmatics, since its interest lies in wanting to describe an 'object' (the force of desire, or the flows of desiring) without relying on an overall system of description. Here we might notice a resemblance not only to Kant's reflective judgement, and especially to Lyotard's reading of Kant (see chapter 9), but also to Levi-Strauss's concept of bricolage as discussed in chapter 5. At its most basic level, the resemblance has to do with an in-difference between production and product. In producing a rule for explaining an art object, for example, one also produces that object as art; and in producing mythological assemblages from whatever is 'to hand', the assembled product (myth) is inseparable from the assembling production (bricolage). For Deleuze and Guattari, then, bricolage is a more useful concept-practice (or 'method') than anything to be found in psychoanalysis, where the fixation on familial effects is too restrictive even to begin to describe the sorts of desire they're interested in. Hence it comes as no surprise that a preference for 'bricolage' (and precisely on the basis of opposing it to psychoanalysis) is announced almost at the very beginning of *Anti-Oedipus*:

> When Claude Lévi-Strauss defines *bricolage*, he does so in terms of a set of closely related characteristics: the possession of a stock of materials or of rules of thumb that are fairly extensive, though more or less a hodgepodge – multiple and at the same time limited; the ability to rearrange fragments continually in new and different patterns or configurations; and as a consequence, an indifference toward the act of producing and toward the product, toward the set of instruments to be used and toward the over-all result to be achieved. The satisfaction the handyman experiences when he plugs something into an electric socket or diverts a stream of water can scarcely be explained in terms of 'playing mommy and daddy,' or by the pleasure of violating a taboo. The rule of continually producing production, of grafting producing onto the product, is a characteristic of desiring-machines or of primary production: the production of production.[29]

Like 'the affirmation of affirmation', 'the production of production' is a form of Nietzschean will to power. And perhaps as Nietzsche's joyous affirmation of living can be seen as a reaction against the abstemious, life-denying morality of the nineteenth century, Deleuze and Guattari's joyous affirmation of producing might be seen as a deliberate counter-force to a certain Marxist pessimism of their own times concerning an over-determined lack of access among cultural and political citizens to the means of cultural and political production. If power lies in the hands of. producers, one way of redistributing that power might simply be to rethink the *concept* of 'production' through Lévi-Strauss's 'bricolage'. In that way too it might be seen that psychoanalysts, no less than industrial capitalists, are in control of a certain means of production: the production or commodification, as it were, of psychic disorders and of psychoanalytic subjects. And just as the capitalist production-line must always promise, but never fulfil, total satisfaction for all, so the psychoanalytic production-line can never afford to find a 'cure' for the Oedipus complex but must instead go on producing ever new varieties of anxiety for the unconscious to fall victim to.

Since both psychoanalysis and capitalism are involved in the production of anxiety (for the latter this occurs in the deliberate 'failure' to satisfy consumers' desires by always promising another 'better' commodity), then for Deleuze and Guattari the figure who troubles the psychoanalytic and capitalist 'product' – a product that might be called anxiety-production – is the schizophrenic. 'The schizophrenic is the universal producer', because schizophrenics inhabit only worlds of their own making.[30] In this way schizophrenics produce their own concepts, and so in a sense schizophrenia may be seen as the ultimate model of the affirmation of affirmation or the production of production. Hence the affirming-willing of the schizophrenic is a kind of bricolage, making do with whatever is to hand in the free expression of desire. It is only the Oedipalized subject of psychoanalysis and capitalism who represses his or her desire to act 'inappropriately', to behave 'out of order', while the schizophrenic knows nothing of propriety but only appropriation (re- and de-territorialization). In a word, the schizophrenic knows nothing of anxiety but only affirmation. So the schizophrenic might fart in public, eat dessert before the main course, speak and write ungrammatically – all the while producing new concepts according to 'a logic of the AND'. For Deleuze and Guattari, it is only the fascist resistance to affirming-willing that would seek to re-unify the schizophrenic by returning him or her to the binary logic of the either–or: 'There are those who will maintain that the schizo is incapable of uttering the word *I*, and that we must restore his ability to pronounce this hallowed word. All of which the schizo sums up by saying: they're fucking me over again.'[31]

In the schizophrenic production of multiplicity, then, we have the figure of what was referred to earlier as 'the method' that 'effectively constructs' what Deleuze and Guattari call 'the multiple'. Their name for this method is 'schizoanalysis', where the emphasis is not on cleverness (and so mere neologisms or lexical ingenuity cannot pass for it) but rather on the egoless production of what is irreducible to the structure of a resemblance or an identity, for which Deleuze and Guattari use the term 'becoming'. For them 'becoming' is anti-fascist (anti-arborescent) since it refuses the opposition of being and non-being and cannot be understood as an evolution. Indeed, they prefer the term *involution*, 'on the condition that involution is in no way confused with regression. Becoming is involutionary, involution is creative.'[32] The creative force of becoming is enacted on the 'plane of consistency' (also called the plane of 'immanence' or 'composition'), a dimension of radical heterogeneity in which many different differences are loosely held together. We might think of this plane as a kind of tool-kit, as schizophrenics might be thought to have a took-kit that enables them to 'scramble all the codes' of tree-logic and State philosophy.[33] In this tool-kit might be found, as Ronald Boyne suggests, 'equally and indifferently fluxes of words, plants, ideas, minerals, dreams, and animals, shifting configurations of particles and alignments of force', so that it is on the plane of consistency or immanence that 'a non-organic life emerges, the life of the abstract, immanent, virtual lines of variation of all experimentation, creation, and becoming'.[34]

Those who are most in touch with this life-force are schizophrenics and philosophers, both of whom are treated with suspicion by psychoanalysis:

> For we must not delude ourselves: Freud doesn't like schizophrenics. He doesn't like their resistance to being oedipalized, and tends to treat them more or less as animals. They mistake words for things, he says. They are apathetic, narcissistic, cut off from reality, incapable of transference; they resemble philosophers – 'an undesirable resemblance.'[35]

For Deleuze and Guattari, then, schizophrenia is already a type of philosophy and philosophy a form of schizophrenia. In this they come close to identifying philosophy with literature, insofar as schizophrenia may be characterized by a certain will to de- and re-codify (language, values, ideas and so on) associated with literature and especially with the romantic concept of the literary absolute. The writer and the schizophrenic are fellow nomads on the plane of consistency, happy to follow the lines of flight suggested not by signs but by forces, fluxes and intensities that pulsate within and between any system of signs (or system of not-signs) and which effectively (or perhaps only ideally) scramble the very notion of system. The point is never to leave the in-between (to work 'from the middle'), affirming the importance of 'coming and going rather than starting and finishing'.[36] Of course, from the perspective of State philosophy (governed by tree-logic or determining reason), such a 'method' appears closer to intuition than philosophy, or appears at best counter- or a-philosophical. Once again, however, Deleuze and Guattari's understanding of philosophy (as schizoanalysis or nomadology) is precisely in terms of the affirmation of what State philosophy excludes or marginalizes. So Nietzsche is more philosophical for them than Hegel, say.

The problem with Hegel, as Deleuze and Guattari see it, is that he insists on defining philosophy as a *system*. The goal of speculation (or absolute reflection), as Hegel termed it, is to achieve a totalizing synthesis of knowledge and knowing, subject and object, abstract thought and concrete substance or content, without cancelling the oppositions between these pairs. For Hegel, then, part of what has to be synthesized by the work of speculation is the very structure of opposition itself, so that the Hegelian totality includes both the identity and the non-identity of opposites. In the romantic philosophy of his contemporaries at Jena, however, Hegel saw only 'mystic rapture' based on a kind of subjectivism that grants a privilege to contingent acts of the imagination rather than to systematic (or 'scientific') speculation.[37] But for Deleuze and Guattari, of course, contingency is precisely all that matters and therefore philosophy cannot afford to ignore or suppress it. Hence they see the asystematic desiring-machine of Nietzsche's philosophy as a far more productive (or producing) line of flight for schizoanalysis to pursue.

What is perhaps most admirable in Nietzsche, from their point of view, is his affirmation of difference for its own sake. This, as Caputo remarks, is in contrast to Hegel, whom Nietzsche saw as significant for acknowledging difference in terms of opposition but whose mistake was to regard it as a stage in the production of a totality:

> Nietzsche advocates a kind of reverse Hegelianism, a perverse totalization, an affirmation of the *whole* of life, of the position and the opposition, of creation and destruction, of joy and suffering, of pleasure and pain, precisely in the face of the cold fact [. . .] that the flux is the endless destruction of whatever it produces, that the whole has no *telos* and makes no sense, that the whole is a sheer a-telic becoming. Nietzsche is not opposed to a certain totalizing thought – everything is interwoven, a circle, and everything is to be affirmed – but his totality is a negative one, a totality with-

out goal or origin, without a finger of God, without unity or a divine
sensorium, without a guiding star.[38]

In his rejection of telos and the affirmation of difference, Nietzsche opens
a space for Deleuze and Guattaris's schizoanalysis to 'free' itself from the
confinements of systematic (or State) philosophy. And just as Nietzsche's
own version of the will to power affirms a kind of aesthetic absolute as
the only hope for triumphing over the sway of mass opinion or enforced
rule (hence a democracy is a kind of fascist regime, for Nietzsche), so for
Deleuze and Guattari the only true form of nomadology (or, for them,
philosophy) is closer in fact to what is understood more often as literature. Traditionally, that is, literature is allowed to work associatively
(according to a logic of the 'and'), while philosophy is supposed to work
by careful separation and distinction (the logic of the 'either-or'). Literature 'spreads'; philosophy 'sifts'. And in its sifting, philosophy is meant to
establish certain grounds as the unshakable foundations of what is true;
whereas literature, in its disseminatory (rhizomatic) extensions, is
allowed to go on imagining ever more (im)possible worlds that defy
philosophical truth, and of course that defy scientific truth as well.
Alternatively, the (im)possible worlds that literature imagines turn out to
be what science and philosophy catch up with at a later date: so for
example the early, nontotalizing form of the novel (see chapters 5 and 6)
might be said to express the 'fractured' or 'perspectival' nature of truth
long before philosophy and science started coming around to this view at
the beginning of the twentieth century.

In their reconceptualization (or perhaps their reaffirmation) of philosophy as schizoid, rhizomatic and nomadological, therefore, Deleuze
and Guattari may be seen as belonging to a romantic tradition of the
aestheticization of thought. A more recent influence on their approach
to philosophy, however, is the work of Martin Heidegger, though
Heidegger is rarely mentioned by them – and nor does Brian Massumi, in
a book that is supposedly a 'guide' to Deleuze and Guattari's thinking,
find space to refer to him.[39] Nevertheless, as Calvin O. Schrag argues, an
important aspect of Heidegger's thinking concerns 'the transvaluation of
aesthetics', especially in terms of repositioning the 'inquiry standpoint'
from which traditional aesthetics has tended to look at art. The key text
here is 'The Origin of the Work of Art' (published in German in 1935–
6), in which Heidegger may be said to ask different questions about art
or to ask questions of the sort of questions that are usually put to it. The
traditional aesthetic approach to art has been to regard it in terms of

objects that lend themselves to an 'experience' of 'appreciation'. For Heidegger, though, '[a]rt is truth setting itself to work.'[40] In other words, art is not simply a category of truth (sensuous experience); rather it is what 'unconceals' the truth of truth or brings truth to light. But this is not to say that the bringing to light or the unconcealment of truth is of the order of a definition. Instead, truth is such that, in setting itself to work in art, one may say that it also sets to work *as* art. In questioning art, then, one is led to question truth: 'What is truth itself, that it sometimes comes to pass as art?'.[41] Now insofar as art opens onto questions concerning the nature of truth, then it may be said that this very *opening* is what is 'essential' to art (and as art) – and therefore also that this openness must be essential to truth. As Schrag puts it:

> Truth as openness and unconcealment is neither a property which attaches to the work of art nor is it the contribution of an appending and appreciating aesthetic consciousness. It is resident within the work itself. The happening of truth is a 'letting come to pass' whereby the work opens itself up. The work of art provides, if you will, its own self-disclosure.[42]

It is this essential openness of truth that leads Heidegger to regard what he calls 'poetic thinking' as the most fundamental aspect of thought, and therefore in a sense to be the essence of philosophy. Such poetic thinking, however, must also be seen as a way of living – a way of 'bringing to presence' that our place is on this earth, in this world of 'things' that are not simply 'objects'. Once again, the openness of art can show us this: for not only does the art work have a 'workly-character'; it also has a 'thingly-character'. Briefly: all art works must be said *to do work* (that is their workly-character), but not in such a way that an art work stops being a 'thing'. There cannot be a world in which there are things (the 'raw materials' of art) and another world in which there are art works (or in which art 'works'). Hence the openness of art shows us, or reminds us, that art is both 'thingly' and 'workly'. To see this, however, we must think poetically, in the sense that poetry allows a non-utilitarian and non-objective truth about things to be unconcealed. Such unconcealment has always been the primary task of language, but today it is only through poetic language that this task continues to be carried out. While 'language alone brings what is, as something that is, into the Open for the first time',[43] this has been forgotten by the specialized languages of science and philosophy whose task has become that of 'communicating' information on the basis of 'objectifying' things.

Now, for Deleuze and Guattari, we might see that Heidegger's poetic thinking is an important component of their own approach to the aestheticization of thought in the form of schizoanalysis. Indeed poetic thinking could, in their terms, be said to occur on the plane of immanence, where things remain thingly in their non-objectified pulsations, intensities and configurations. It may also be that, by thinking poetically, one can see the essential openness of philosophical concepts, such that philosophy may be conceived as doing the work of art. For Deleuze and Guattari, that is, 'the concept is real without being actual, ideal without being abstract.'[44] In this way, like works of art, philosophical concepts are non-objectifiable and must be understood in terms of what Deleuze and Guattari call 'becoming' or what Heidegger calls unconcealment or openness. 'A concept is a heterogenesis', they write, since for them it is made up of several components (hence a type of bricolage or an assemblage) rather than being a pure and single entity in itself.[45] Among these components must be counted what they call 'a nonconceptual understanding', which is 'perhaps close to Heidegger's notion of unconcealment as the primary task of language. This nonconceptual or 'intuitive' understanding is 'prephilosophical', just as for Heidegger the unconcealment of poetry and poetic thinking comes before the 'functionalization' of philosophy as a particular form of language use and mode of thought. By 'prephilosophical', though, Deleuze and Guattari do not mean 'something preexistent but rather something *that does not exist outside philosophy*, although philosophy presupposes it'.[46] In this way too unconcealment is 'prelinguistic', though in a sense it does not exist outside language. But for Deleuze and Guattari, at any rate, the point is to posit (or revive) for philosophy ways of thinking that are not strictly rational, and therefore in a sense not strictly philosophical while also being (in their view) the very possibility of philosophy. Such ways involve 'a sort of groping experimentation' which 'belong[s] to the order of dreams, of pathological processes, esoteric experiences, drunkenness, and excess'.[47] It might therefore be supposed that one thinks most philosophically (in the sense of thinking poetically) when one is in a most 'unphilosophical' state – such as being drunk or pathological. In any case, what cannot be supposed is that 'unphilosophical' states are *outside* philosophy.

This is the sense in which poetic thinking is also a kind of poetic living, a heightened sense of being alive while one is thinking poetically (drinking, dreaming, hallucinating – experimenting). Since the time of romanticism, of course, it is the lives of writers and artists that have been seen as inseparable from their work, especially when they are thought to live self-destructively or close to the edge. So a writer who also drinks to excess or takes a lot of drugs can be understood as a writer *because* he or she drinks or takes drugs, inasmuch as the desire to be experimental or to push oneself to a limit may be an essential component of one's writing rather than simply a reason to write. Nowadays the life–work connection is more evident perhaps among pop stars, for whom the distinction between drug-taking and music-making is deliberately blurred. If so, then perhaps it is popular culture rather than State philosophy that is the more philosophical today: more philosophical because all the more connected to flows of capital as well as desire – and so all the more vital, mobile and dispensable. Hence one might find that today the best concepts are created by filmmakers and DJs and users of the internet, rather than in works of philosophy, which is not to say that these concepts are unphilosophical. Indeed, following a line of flight from romanticism to Nietzsche and Heidegger, one might say that such concepts are all the more philosophical for being all the more 'poetic' or 'literary' in an absolute sense. In not belonging to any disciplinary 'system', they better affirm the fragmentary, contextualist, rule-producing, *experimental* essence of literature as a mode of responding to life – a way of thinking-living poetically. This then is postmodern literary theory in its most rhizomatic form: the 'asystemic' production of concepts. As I have argued throughout, however, such production deserves it earlier name of romanticism. As Philippe Lacoue-Labarthe puts it, the romantic artist has always been concerned with 'the transformation, the shaping, the figuration, or even the fictioning [. . .] of his life into a work of art'[48] – and such romantic fictioning should not be overlooked as an important feature of Deleuze and Guattari's schizophrenic desiring. What remains to be seen now is whether, as Foucault seems to think, this desiring-fictioning can be thought of as an ethics. This is what I will look at in the following chapter, where I will try to apply some principles of schizoanalysis (and the fact that there are, or that there may be, such principles is already to anticipate a certain critique of Deleuze and Guattari) to some of Paul Auster's writing. My aim in this is twofold: first to consider whether there are any critical advantages for literary studies in turning to a method of schizoanalysis, and secondly to see where such advantages (if there are any) might sit in relation to any ethical evaluation of them.

11

Ethical Evaluations

From the previous chapter, we can say that fascism and ethics are opposed. This at any rate is the opposition that Foucault sees as an organizing principle of Deleuze and Guattari's capitalism and schizophrenia project. Fascism seeps into every corner of a society, demanding and receiving obedience to a system of moral absolutes at every turn – from the level of official state politics to the micro-levels of everyday thought and practice. Sealed off from doubt and surprise, fascism closes itself to ethical (in)decisions. On such a reading, ethics is the space of openness, whether in a Heideggerian sense or in terms of Deleuze and Guattari's concept of becoming.

But there is a potential danger in opposing ethical openness to fascist absolutism. The danger lies in confusing ethics with relativism, such that 'ethics' comes to mean 'anything goes.' In an absolute form, that is, 'anything goes' permits nothing whatsoever to be excluded; and so the principle of an absolute relativism, having forsaken all normative critical standards and values of judgement, cannot be opposed to fascism. Hence even fascism can lay claim to relativism, as the Italian Fascist Benito Mussolini argued in 1921:

> Everything I have said and done in these last years is relativism by intuition. [. . .] If relativism signifies contempt for fixed categories and men who claim to be the bearers of an objective, immortal truth [. . .] then there is nothing more relativistic than Fascist attitudes and activity. [. . .] From the fact that all ideologies are of equal value, that all ideologies are mere fictions, the modern relativist infers that everybody has the right to create for himself his own ideology and to attempt to enforce it with all the energy of which he is capable.[1]

The right to create an ideology for oneself could be seen as an analogue of Nietzsche's will to power, so that perhaps Mussolini (no less than

Deleuze and Guattari) might be seen as 'Nietzschean' in his thinking. Hence the genealogy of postmodern literary theory may run from the Jena Romantics to Nietzsche, Freud – and Mussolini! In this way the essential anti-foundationalism of postmodern literary theory would belong to a lineage extending from romanticism to fascism, with Nietzsche as its central figure or key turning point.

Now this is not to condemn Nietzsche as a proto-Nazi, though it is very often on this basis that one is warned away from reading him. At the same time, it should not be supposed that the Third Reich's enlistment of Nietzsche's work in support of its ideology of racial strength represents a complete misreading of Nietzsche's intentions or a perverse interpretation of his ideas. It is not quite as easy as saying that the Nazis' reading of Nietzsche is vulgar or over-simplified, which is a point that both Deleuze and Derrida have made. I will come back to Derrida later. For Deleuze, however, it is Nietzsche's aphoristic style of writing and philosophy (and of writing *as* philosophy) that allows his texts to be appropriated by external forces, since the aphoristic style is linked to an authorial subject only in the most minimal of senses and cannot be taken for an expression of Nietzsche's interiority; nor can it be taken for the essence or interiority of some object outside the style, as if Nietzsche were a traditional metaphysician who believed in the revelation of truth via the mediation of philosophical concepts and rational discourse. So for Deleuze the Nazis were not 'wrong' to read Nietzsche as a prophet of the Third Reich, just as many present-day feminists are not wrong in reading him as a misogynist. But this does not make either party 'right'. The point is that, for Deleuze, Nietzsche's ethico-textual nomadism is so radically shifting and heterogeneous as to make it, in effect, impossible to get Nietzsche wrong. Nietzsche is important therefore not because he manages to convince us of an absolute or positivistic truth, but because his writings serve to show that truth is what emerges only through relationships to texts. Hence it is not so much a question of deciding between 'true' and 'false' readings of Nietzsche, but of accounting for the different *effective* readings of his work. Such a notion of an 'effective' reading would deny that truth is internal to texts (or for that matter to historical events and subjects), considering it rather in terms of what Foucault calls 'the exteriority of accidents'.[2]

Foucault uses this phrase in discussing Nietzsche's idea of 'effective history' or 'genealogy', which I cannot develop fully here. Briefly, though, Foucault argues that effective history, which for him is closer to a practice than a concept, offers an alternative to the study of history in its usual sense (although it is not opposed to history), because it rejects ideas of system, origin, continuity and telos. If the task of the historian is to subsume historical events under an over-arching *theory* of history, the genealogist's task is to 'record the singularity of events outside of any monotonous finality'. In doing so the genealogist looks for history in things and places that are thought to be ahistorical – 'in sentiments, love, conscience, instincts'.[3] Through painstaking analysis of a complex archive, then, the genealogist can construct an effective history of a concept such as 'love', showing that the concept has no founding origin, no determined telos, and no cultural or metaphysical continuity. In a word, 'love' has no essence. Instead it is a heterogeneous assemblage of relationships to external forces (sexual practices and institutions, moral codes, regimes of health and so on) that have at different times resulted in different operations of the concept (or, for Foucault, the discourse) of love. 'Love' then has a history – and at all times the operation of this history 'attaches itself to the body'.[4]

It should be clear from this short summary that the practice of effective history resembles what Deleuze and Guattari call schizoanalysis. In identifying *Anti-Oedipus* as a book of ethics, therefore, Foucault may have been responding to what he saw as the genealogical method of the capitalism and schizophrenia project. This is all the more likely given that Foucault's 'Genealogy' paper (1971) was published only a year before the Preface to his friends' book. In this light it is no surprise that Foucault describes that book in terms of an art, albeit in a special sense:

> I think that *Anti-Oedipus* can best be read as an 'art,' in the sense that is conveyed by the term 'erotic art,' for example. Informed by the seemingly abstract notions of multiplicities, flows, arrangements, and connections, the analysis of the relationship of desire to reality and to the capitalist 'machine' yields answers to concrete questions. Questions that are less concerned with *why* this or that than with *how* to proceed. How does one introduce desire into thought, into discourse, into action? How can and must desire deploy its forces within the political domain and grow more intense in the process of overturning the established order? *Ars erotica, ars theoretica, ars politica.*[5]

By 'art', then, Foucault means something like a pragmatics here: the 'art of living'. In this he is anticipating what 'ethics' will come to mean in his own *History of Sexuality* project, spanning three volumes from 1976 to 1984. But the point for now is that, in the Preface to Deleuze and Guattari's *Anti-Oedipus*, 'art' refers to a kind of skill that involves both learning and intuition; as a knowledge, it is a kind of know-how. So by 'intuition' is meant not something universally innate to the human species, but rather something that is learned informally or even unconsciously within a nonetheless strictly measurable set of historico-communal constraints. An example might be the face one pulls to signify that one has registered an intended irony on the part of another speaker: we do not, in any direct or official sense, learn how to make that face, in the way we might learn to conjugate verbs or to perform the role of best man at a wedding, and so it is easily categorized as intuitive. Nevertheless, such a face might signify something altogether different at another time or in some other place: hence it cannot be regarded as ahistorical or independent of certain community trainings. And although it may be difficult to describe the exact muscular movements required to make that face, we need to exercise complete precision in making it so that it isn't confused with another face – one that might signify disapproval or surprise, for example. So what is thought of as an intuitive response actually requires the perfection of certain skills peculiar to some community; in other words, intuition is an art.

And of course, for Foucault, ethics too is an art. It is clear from the passage above, moreover, that theory and politics are arts as well, according to Foucault. But again it needs to be stressed that such arts are not to be confused with forms of creative self-expression, though they do involve an aesthetic dimension. They are arts in the sense of being skills, the perfection of which requires a certain knack or know-how. Above all they are arts concerned with questions of living, which have to do with pragmatic considerations – 'with *how* to proceed'. And knowing how to proceed requires a certain judgement, one which is neither fully determining nor fully reflective. Hence, for Foucault, pragmatics – which is also an ethics, which is also an art – describes a space opened, as it were, by the opposition of determining laws and aesthetic reflection. It is therefore not opposed to creativity, and certainly not reducible to natural intuition or to mundane rationality. 'Pragmatics' refers to a space that is always in excess of the opposition of the calculable and the incalculable.

From this we can see that effective history is a pragmatics, which is also an ethics. Its concern is to record 'the history of morals, ideals, and metaphysical concepts', but to do so in such a way that their singularities are exposed rather than subsumed.[6] Hence the artful genealogist is interested primarily in self-difference rather than self-identity, such that the genealogist's history differs from 'the historian's history [which] finds its support outside of time and pretends to base its judgments on an apocalyptic objectivity'.[7] The crucial difference between genealogy and history is that the former 'refuses the certainty of absolutes' on which understandings of 'human nature' depend. This refusal extends to whatever is regarded as immortal or immutable – feelings and sentiments, for example, or the 'natural' laws governing our bodies:

> We believe [. . .] that the body obeys the exclusive laws of physiology and that it escapes the influence of history, but this too is false. The body is molded by a great many distinct regimes; it is broken down by the rhythms of work, rest, and holidays; it is poisoned by food or values, through eating habits or moral laws; it constructs resistances. 'Effective' history differs from traditional history in being without constants. Nothing in man – not even his body – is sufficiently stable to serve as the basis for self-recognition or for understanding other men.[8]

Remembering that Foucault wrote these words at about the same time he wrote the Preface to *Anti-Oedipus*, in which he describes that book as 'an art' and an 'ethics', it is likely that Foucault saw the capitalism and schizophrenia project as something like an instance of effective history. Certainly there are several analogues between Foucault's descriptions of the principles of genealogy and of the principles pertaining to Deleuze and Guattari's work. Those of genealogy, for example, may be put as follows: (1) the notion of historical 'origin' must be thought as self-difference (Foucault calls it 'dissension' and 'disparity') rather than self-identity; (2) the notion of historical 'descent' (*Herkunft*, in Nietzsche) must be thought as discontinuity, whether in relation to a self, a race, a culture, an idea or a sentiment; (3) the notion of historical 'emergence' (*Entstehung*) must be thought as 'series' rather than 'succession', such that no historical event can be understood as final but simply as a stage (marked by 'eruption' and 'conflict') in the unfolding of a discourse. On the basis of these principles it is then possible to see history as 'a complex system of distinct and multiple elements, unable to be mastered by the powers of synthesis'.[9] Any attempt at mastery, therefore, must be seen as a lie – aimed at maintaining false ideas of cultural 'destiny', individual 'identity' and primordial 'truth'. To put it simply: the belief in synthesis is fascist; the affirmation of dispersion is ethical.

The fascism/ethics distinction, based on the difference between 'unities' and 'multiplicities', becomes all the clearer in Foucault's Preface to *Anti-Oedipus*. There he proposes an alternative title for Deleuze and Guattari's book – *Introduction to the Non-Fascist Life* – and lists among its principles the need to '[d]evelop action, thought, and desires by proliferation, juxtaposition, and disjunction, and not by subdivision and pyramidal hierarchization'; and the importance of affirming 'what is positive and multiple, difference over uniformity, flows over unities, mobile arrangements over systems'.[10] In this we might say that Foucault asserts the ethical superiority of dispersion (difference, multiplicity, heterogeneity) over synthesis (unity, coherence, identity); and this in turn might be seen as an analogue of Lyotard's affirmation of the ethical superiority of 'little' to 'big' (see chapter 4). Hence Foucault's 'ethics' of difference is opposed to what he sees as the 'fascism' of coherence. But in that case how is it that Mussolini – 'everybody has the right to create for himself his own ideology' – was on the side of difference too?

There are several points we need to be clear on here. The fact that Foucault and Mussolini were both in favour of an absolute difference does not make Foucault a post-fascist, any more than Nietzsche was a proto-Nazi because the Third Reich approved of him. What it may suggest, however, is a certain complicity with a metaphysical tradition, in which it is not only possible but also desirable to think the opposition of self-creation and systemic oppression, which Foucault and Mussolini both express. Through the totalizing negation of 'system' and 'coherence' (for Foucault) and 'fixed categories' and 'objective, immortal truth' (for Mussolini), then, the task of self-creation or of self-proliferation is raised to the order of an absolute, analogous to the romantic notion of literature. Hence Foucault's affirmation of absolute difference, which for him is the ground of ethics, cannot exclude what Mussolini regards as the ground of fascism: namely everybody's absolute 'right to create'. But for Mussolini, of course, that right includes everyone's right to 'enforce' his or her ideology on everyone else; and so perhaps it is on this point that Foucault's reading of the ethics of Deleuze and Guattari must be seen as fundamentally different from the fascism of Mussolini. For Foucault, after all, the very notion of 'the "rights" of the individual' is what must be overcome, since '[t]he individual is the product of power.' Politically, therefore, '[w]hat is needed is to "de-individualize" by means of multiplication and displacement [. . .]. The group must not be the organic bond uniting hierarchized individuals, but a constant generator of de-individualization.'[11] Yet there is nothing in Mussolini's affirmation of the right to create that could be said to preclude the creative process of de-individualization, if that happened to be how an individual or a group chose to express – and then to enforce – that right. Nor does Foucault's affirmation of 'multiplication and displacement' preclude that process from being understood as a 'right', the right (as it were) to de-individualize. Hence an underlying romanticism may be seen to produce a certain, if surprising, similarity between the affirmation of the force of difference (ethics) and what might be called the affirmation of the force of force (fascism).

The question now is whether this similarity is a mere coincidence, or a familiar episode in the history of thought. It is here also that another question might arise: why choose? Or perhaps even – *how* to choose, assuming one might want to? For such a question has often been asked too of Nietzsche's affirmation by the Nazis – was it a perversion or a fulfilment of his philosophy? – and there is no simple answer to it. In Derrida's view, it is not enough to say that Nietzsche's 'intentions' were utterly and wilfully misconstrued by the Third Reich, for this would be to identify authorial intentions with self-present truth.[12] In Nietzsche's case especially, such identification is difficult given that his very style of writing (the aphoristic style, as Deleuze calls it) encourages interpretative speculation and conflict; hence his 'writing' is indissociable from his 'philosophy' and cannot be looked on as a transparent medium through which his intentions are revealed. In defending Nietzsche by claiming that the Nazis 'misread' him, then, one has to commit another misreading of Nietzsche by neglecting the philosophical importance of his *style*. To mount this defence, it has to be maintained that truth and rhetoric are separable in Nietzsche. But if this way of thinking exaggerates the importance of Nietzsche's 'intentions', the problem is that the counter claim – based on the centrality of Nietzsche's style – risks ignoring his intentions altogether. Hence to read Nietzsche only in terms of 'pure style' is to deny any hierarchy among the many different readings of that style. If Nietzsche's 'philosophy' is *reduced* to his 'writing', in other words, then there can be no 'right' and 'wrong' readings of Nietzsche, but only a *multiplicity* of readings.

There is no question for Derrida that there are indeed many different readings of Nietzsche, and that no single reading is 'right' above all others. But it is not enough to say there is only a multiplicity of readings of Nietzsche, since there is also a hierarchy of readings. Hence there is not only horizontal difference (multiplicity); there is also vertical difference (hierarchy). The cancellation of either axis must result in a certain perversion of Nietzsche's philosophy: in this way the Nazis might be said to have read Nietzsche only 'vertically' (in terms of an underlying affirmation of Aryan supremacy) and to have disregarded a 'horizontal' reading in which his affirmation of the will to power is associated with a diverse range of possibilities (or desires) and not confined to the destiny of the German people. On the other hand, to read Nietzsche only 'horizontally' would be to deny that there is any 'depth' at all to his philosophy, as if the rhetorical surface of his writing remains uncut by a vertical axis of intention. Crucially, however, although a reading of Nietzsche confined to one or the other axis must be skewed, it cannot be seen as completely 'wrong' either. It is not that there is no evidence in Nietzsche's texts for the Nazi interpretation or for its opposite, a kind of interpretative free-play. The case is rather that the singularity of Nietzsche's writing is characterized by the interpretative multiplicity to which it gives rise: the extreme differences between interpretations of Nietzsche, then, are an effect of the difference within Nietzsche's writing. Without suggesting there is an underlying truth or authorial intention embedded in that writing, it should not be supposed that it is open to absolutely any interpretation whatsoever. So *how* Nietzsche is read cannot be dissociated from *what* Nietzsche wrote, but neither is it reducible to it. Hence we might say that, in reading Nietzsche, we are obliged to pay attention to his writing in the most literal sense – to the words on the page, as he wrote them – but not in order to find a unitary or coherent meaning 'behind' those words. Instead it is a question of considering how certain interests 'outside' Nietzsche's texts can attach themselves to certain rhetorical devices 'in' his texts, bringing them under the sway of those interests. The aim of all such interests is to determine the meaning of Nietzsche's philosophy – to have power over it. Yet given Nietzsche's affirmation of the will to power, this aim can scarcely be seen as 'external' to his philosophy. It is therefore not the case that 'interested readings' are outside and 'disinterested truth' is inside Nietzsche's texts, but rather that those texts themselves play out the very problem of inside/outside relations in such a way that the difference between what Nietzsche wrote and what Nietzsche meant must remain undecidable. In must remain undecidable since that difference is already within the texts in which it appears as a question, and so we might say that, in Nietzsche, 'difference' operates both horizontally and vertically.

This does not mean that Nietzsche was always conscious of the difference 'within' difference. Once again: Nietzsche's texts are not grounded in his intentions or some notion of authorial consciousness. Nevertheless it is the difference within difference – such that difference is never absolutely internal or external, never absolutely horizontal (associative) or vertical (selective) – which distinguishes those texts, even if sometimes in a way that appears to work 'against' them. In his writings on 'the question of woman', for example, Nietzsche is often accused of misogyny. Perhaps, by intention, Nietzsche was a 'misogynist'. Perhaps also a certain misogyny lies 'behind' his writings on woman. But this vertical account of Nietzsche's intentions ignores the fact that, in Nietzsche, 'woman' is *associated* with 'truth'. On the horizontal plane, then, the question of woman leads onto the question of truth. For Heidegger, as we saw in chapter 10, it is art that opens (unconceals) truth, though this does not mean that Nietzsche's 'woman' is the equivalent of Heidegger's 'art'. Indeed, for Heidegger, Nietzsche's conception of truth is in the end too 'metaphysical' to think the truth of Being in terms of what Heidegger calls the ontological difference: namely, the difference that is 'prior' to or 'within' the difference between Being and beings. Despite his radicalism, in other words, Nietzsche remains for Heidegger part of the metaphysical tradition since Plato which cannot think of Being in itself or as such, without recourse to thinking of beings in their various difference.[13] In Derrida's view, however, Heidegger is amiss in consigning Nietzsche to the metaphysical tradition, which he is able to do only by imposing a kind of hermeneutic order on the otherwise disturbing force of Nietzsche's texts.[14] Such disturbance, for Derrida, must be seen in terms of Nietzsche's 'style', but also in relation to the unsettling question of 'sexual difference' in Nietzsche.

Here we are led back to the question of 'woman'. In Nietzsche's writing, 'woman' may be taken as the figure that troubles the very difference between 'concept' and 'metaphor' – or more generally between philosophy and literature. Now for Heidegger, philosophy as we know it today begins with a 'wrong turn' taken by Plato, which we may call the specialization of philosophical thought.[15] According to Heidegger, that is, the Platonic tradition (which he terms 'metaphysics') mistakenly separated philosophical thought from thought in general, and hence opened the way to further specialisms in the form of science, literature and so on. As a consequence, 'thought' came to be associated with a particular way of thinking known as 'philosophy', such that other ways of thinking were downgraded and put under philosophy's sway. Philosophy was installed, therefore, or installed itself, as the master discourse, able to know and translate the thinking of other discourses. In this way, for example, what may be called literary thought remains open to philosophical inspection and control, and so philosophy continues to have power over literature because, in a sense, it knows what literature does not: it 'knows' what literature is 'thinking'. Hence it may be said that philosophy converts metaphors into concepts, or that it grasps the meaning of 'metaphor' by understanding the ground of metaphoric (literary) thought. But if it could be shown that the concept/metaphor distinction is another swerve away from the ontological difference, and therefore a distinction that philosophy guards and polices only in the interest of maintaining its privileged hold over thought, then surely this would show too that philosophy (as metaphysics) is doomed never to know truth as such, or to know the truth of Being. And this, Derrida argues, is precisely what the figure of 'woman' in Nietzsche shows. Although in his writing Nietzsche is infamously virulent towards women, yet it is 'woman' that represents for him, through his writing, everything that philosophy tries to exclude – passion, contradiction, style, metaphor and even writing itself. On Derrida's reading, then, Heidegger's mistake is not to have seen that Nietzsche's 'writing' (as both practice and philosophy) is an attempt to think the difference within difference – or, in Heidegger's terms, an attempt to think 'nonmetaphysically'.

But if, on Derrida's account, Heidegger's 'Nietzsche' is too narrow (or vertical), this does not mean that we should read Nietzsche only in terms of an ideal of pure or horizontal difference. If it is possible to read Nietzsche too 'narrowly', it is also possible to read him too 'broadly'. And it may be that this is how Deleuze and Guattari read Nietzsche (too broadly, or too laterally), in a way that is both against Heidegger's reading and at the same time faithfully Heideggerian. Their reading differs from Heidegger's in its acceptance of Nietzsche's affirmation of a very broad notion of difference as the energizing force of disequilibrium, disparity and general multiplicity that always disrupts and overturns the orderly concepts of State philosophical discourse. But in attributing this force to a kind of prephilosophical or pre-ontological drive as the beginning without origin of metaphysics, Deleuze and Guattari may be said to keep faith with Heidegger. In this too it may be said that the capitalism and schizophrenia project is as much Heideggerian in its commitment to finding a way 'back' to the ontological difference (or, for Deleuze and Guattari, to the level of abstraction that must precede the abstractions of philosophical thought) as it is Nietzschean in its affirmation of the force of difference as the force of force.

Here, though, we may recall an earlier distinction between 'ethics' as the force of difference and 'fascism' as the force of force. Are we to suppose now that this distinction is simply another deviation from the ontological difference, such that 'nonmetaphysical' or 'prephilosophical' thinking sees no difference between ethics and fascism? If so, then what Deleuze and Guattari call schizoanalysis (which they offer as a form of prephilosophical thought in practice) may express a desire to be 'unethical' as much as a desire to be 'anti-fascist'. This is not to accuse Deleuze and Guattari themselves of wanting to abrogate all responsibility in their attempt to loosen the concept/metaphor distinction by which the separate identities of philosophy and literature are maintained. But it leaves very little room for 'ethics' to have any meaning or force once the concept/metaphor distinction is seen as inherently and insuperably 'fascist'. In this way the desire to be 'anti-fascist' may in fact be a desire that lies within fascism itself, as the remarks by Mussolini quoted at the beginning of this chapter might indicate. In wanting 'fascism' to mean 'relativism', that is, Mussolini may have been expressing a desire analogous to that of Deleuze and Guattari's urge to become 'schizoid', since for them the relative instability of schizophrenic 'thought' (which is in fact the antithesis of thought, from the viewpoint of State philosophy) is aphilosophical and therefore anti-fascist – and therefore also closer to thought in Heidegger's sense of 'poetic thinking' (see chapter 10).

So if Mussolini wanted 'fascism' to mean 'relativism', we might say that Deleuze and Guattari want 'fascism' to mean 'metaphysics'. The anti-fascist opposition to political oppression, then, must be seen as indistinguishable from the ethical opposition to philosophical oppression. Hence the political (fascist) control of desire and the philosophical (metaphysical) control of thought are as one. In this way the metaphysical desire to preserve the separation of concepts and metaphors is entwined with the fascist desire to maintain political hierarchy and division within the State. One defeats fascism, therefore, by defeating metaphysics (and of course vice versa). And the way to defeat metaphysics (which is fascism) is through the affirmation (which is ethics) of everything it denies. In its commitment to logic, metaphysics is serious and rigorous; and so one must be playful and loose in following the flows of desire. In its commitment to impersonal truth, metaphysics denies any force to context and contingency; and so one must corporealize, metaphorize and politicize the truth. In a word, one must affirm the exterior, the superficial, the accidental and the a-rational over the metaphysical commitment to the deep internal force of reason.

Now on this model it is clear that literary studies too is metaphysical (or fascist) in its desire to enforce the 'arborescent' logic of hierarchy and division between texts (in the form of a canon) as well as within them (in terms of levels of meaning). Hence we might say that a first principle of the ethical, nonmetaphysical, anti-fascist, schizoanalytic approach to literature would be to refuse literature's status as a 'branch' of knowledge, and therefore to refuse its subsumption under philosophy. Laid out across a smooth surface, thought could no longer be hierarchically divided into metaphorical and conceptual territories policed by literary and philosophical regimes. Nor indeed could thought be seen as a lifeless abstraction separated out from the flux of desires, intuitions, experiences, politics, histories and cultural contexts into which thought flows and which flow into thought. Stretched over such a plane, literature could no longer be analysed in terms of individual works but only in terms of *the work of* literature – or the work of multiplicity. Such work (in a sense that is indebted to Heidegger) could then be seen in terms of openings and openness, in contrast to the traditional aesthetic understanding of the finality and self-identity of works of art. It could also (in a sense that is indebted to Nietzsche and Foucault) be seen as work that is effective in its discontinuous, conflictual, asystematic eruptions across a series of historical unfoldings and becomings. And what the work calls for in its openness is not an explanation of its origin and finality, but rather a description of its heterogeneous effects – effects which cannot be confined to a notion of the work as an autonomous entity or to the notion of an autonomous system or regime (such as literature, philosophy, politics or whatever) in which works are understood by metaphysics to belong. In not being confined to concepts of autonomy, system and identity, however, the work does not recede; rather its very singularity is affirmed in its irreducibility to those concepts. The work's singular identity is its *multiple identities* (or simply its multiplicity), on the model of the multiple personas of the schizophrenic. Hence the object of schizoanalysis is not so much 'works' as *workings*, not what 'has become' but what 'is becoming'. In this way a schizoanalytical approach to any literary text would operate from certain principles: (1) texts are assemblages, not entities; (2) assemblages are multiplicities, not compounds; (3) multiplicities are problem-responsive pragmaticalities, not rule-bound abstractions. The emphasis then is on difference as an active process that sets up an assemblage of possible relations between the production and consumption of literature, such that 'literature' is always inseparable from so-called exteriorities such as history, politics, desire and so forth. This is to deny literature an identity based on notions of interiority and tradition, and therefore to deny that literature constitutes a 'system' of unified objects or texts. The point of such denial, however, is not to rarify or idealize literature (in terms of say the romantic concept of the literary absolute), but rather to show that its workings are as much an effect of breakdowns, like those of everyday factical life, as of breakthroughs. So by thinking of literature as an asystematic assemblage,

Deleuze and Guattari are attempting to think of it pragmatically. For them, the desire to see literature in terms of a systematic succession (a 'tradition') of breakthroughs and innovations (of 'canonical' texts) is fascist, serving an ideal of social order and oppression; hence to see literature in terms of schizophrenic breakdown – or as a pragmatics of living – is ethical, if not revolutionary, since its purpose is to show the liberating dysfunctionality of structures of power.

As a discipline or an institution, for example, literary studies must preserve an ideal of literature as a self-identical system, an ideal which is compliant with the interests of social power and order. To preserve this ideal, the system of literature must be defended against invasion (territorialization) from other disciplines (philosophy, sociology, economics and so on) and 'external' forces such as history, politics, technology, the publishing industry and popular culture. Ironically, perhaps, this ideal is thoroughly 'theoretical', inasmuch as it conceives the essence or identity of literature in terms that must be understood as impersonal, ahistorical, apolitical, aphilosophical and so on. Therefore we might say that Harold Bloom is more of a 'theorist' than Deleuze and Guattari for insisting on a notion of literature as a unified (if complex) system or tradition of canonical texts, a system which is currently breaking down under the weight of external appropriation by popular, political, philosophical and other 'vested' interests. In Deleuze and Guattari's view, though, a theory of literature such as Bloom advocates is itself vested in the interests of a theory of social order based on hierarchy and division. But of course 'social order' is not just a theory; it is also a practice, one that is most effective when it is most covert. Hence the theory of the Western canon should not be seen merely as an idle abstraction, but rather as an effective social practice of control: the theory works at producing 'literature' as an autonomous domain of universal truth and value, independent of the circumstantial forces of power and pragmatics. In this way truth and value appear as ends in themselves, separated out from history and politics but also always available to these interests to appeal to in order to disguise their interestedness. It is precisely the pragmatics of power, therefore, which is served in the production of literature as a bastion of 'disinterest'. For if no one believed in the possibility of un-corrupted 'truth' and 'value', then for example political power would never be able to appeal to that possibility as its primary motivation: instead it would have to expose its own pragmatic aims and self-seeking ambitions and prejudices as the sum of its identity and the full extent of its desire.

On Deleuze and Guattari's account, then, truth and beauty could never be hermetically sealed off from power and pragmatics. Sociohistorical phenomena and contexts intrude on every operation of thought in all its forms. Even the creation of philosophical concepts, they argue, should not be seen as thought in its absolute purity, for concepts arise in relation only to exteriorities: 'even in philosophy, concepts are only created as a function of problems which are thought to be badly understood or badly posed.'[16] Hence they look upon philosophy not as a metaphysical system to bow down to, but as an experimental *practice* to be taken up: 'What is the best way to follow the great philosophers? Is it to repeat what they said or *to do what they did*, that is, create concepts for problems that necessarily change?'[17] But in this reconceptualization of philosophy as a kind of radical empiricism, there may lurk a potential danger: in conceiving empiricism in terms of fundamental abstraction, Deleuze and Guattari's 'pragmatics' risks becoming relativist in its anti-foundationalist, anti-rationalist, anti-metaphysical, anti-'fascist' defiance. In this it risks becoming no less militant and dictatorial in its affirmation of horizontal (rhizomatic, nomadic) difference than the systematic or vertical (hierarchical and divisive) difference it opposes. It might even be said that in Deleuze and Guattari's radical, indeed revolutionary, rethinking of the empirical, the romantic concept of the literary absolute is taken full circle: having in a sense been created as a counterforce against the deadening empiricity of modern life, the concept of the literary absolute becomes, for Deleuze and Guattari, the very basis of rethinking the empirical in the postmodern present. Their affirmation of a schizophrenic process of the de-and re-territorializations of objects, forces and concepts may be seen as an analogue of the romantic affirmation of dynamic unruliness as the condition and the very absolute of literature itself. Hence a concept that was never named as such by the Romantics but which was invented by them nonetheless as a way of responding to a certain problem – a problem that might be called the problem of modernity, seen as the rationalization of thought and the urbanization of life – has been taken over by Deleuze and Guattari as a response to a different but related problem: namely, how to 'fit in' with the ideas and expectations of a regulating system of thought, when the problem is precisely that of 'fitting in'? Nothing ever quite fits because, in their view, thought is characterized by dynamic irregularity, and so there is no basis for grounding even the difference between concepts and objects. The desire to find a fit between any series of events such that the series is made over into a sequence is, for them, paranoid.

However it is not conformity (the fit between, as it were) but convulsion (the fit within) which for Deleuze and Guattari is the true nature of desire: the paranoid is therefore really a repressed schizophrenic. And no one could suppose that schizophrenics will conform to ways of thinking and behaviour understood as 'proper' by those in power – the politicians, metaphysicians and other fascist 'Oedipalizers'. But the anti-Oedipal, anti-fascist schizophrenic thinks differently, of course, which is to say convulsively, nomadically, asystematically. In this way the schizophrenic is unfit for thought as defined by metaphysics or State philosophy, although for Deleuze and Guattari thought is not fitted: it is fitful. The anti-Oedipal schizophrenic then is, on their account, the true philosopher, precisely because schizophrenic thinking proceeds not theoretically, but pragmatically, from one problem to the next. It is therefore in its pragmatic a-theoreticism that schizophrenic thinking may be seen as an empiricism, but an empiricism which is 'literary' in the romantic sense.

As a practice rather than a theory, schizoanalysis is empirical rather than metaphysical. This does not mean it is opposed to theory, however. The stress on practice is instead an affirmation of the impossibility of detaching theory from socio-historical phenomena and contexts, from pragmatic contingencies and problems, from political events and processes. In the constant in-folding of theory and society, as it were, what counts as 'empirical' cannot be opposed to what is understood as 'conceptual' or even 'cultural'. There cannot be a world of ideas and another world of matter, a world of signs and another world of not-signs. Metaphysics though is dedicated to maintaining a lack of fit between differences (concepts and objects, for example), just as capitalism may be said, in Marx's terms, to be dedicated to maintaining a difference between exchange and surplus values. On this view, 'difference' as conceived metaphysically and economically is the same. Hence, Deleuze and Guattari argue, difference is controlled by metaphysics and economics as the regulating structure of desire: vertical difference drives a wedge between desiring subject and desired object. But the schizophrenic converts (de- and re-territorializes) this wedge into a plane, thereby creating a new concept of difference through which 'subject' and 'object' can be seen as related horizontally rather than divided hierarchically. And on this horizontal (rhizomatic) plane of difference there are no longer separations but only positive associations between literature, philosophy, politics and so on. These associations moreover are not abstract, but empirical; they cannot be formulated theoretically but only experienced pragmatically. Hence there are no rules for governing the flows of experience across the plane of difference – no theory of where or why to proceed, but only a pragmatics of *how* to proceed. Pragmatics is the absolute of living, then, where living is without origin or telos but is nonetheless effective. In terms of such an absolute, or in terms of what might be called effective living, there could be no set of ethical precepts to emulate but only a series of ethical relations to be invented or experimented with according to different pragmatic eventualities. On the plane of absolute, effective, schizophrenic living, ethics is a practice – not a theory.

Deleuze and Guattari's affirmation of radical empiricism, then, is also an affirmation of radical scepticism.[18] For them, empirics is not opposed to theory and so it cannot be seen as the ground of nonmetaphysical truth. The empirical is not 'solid' in contrast to the insubstantiality of thought; but for Deleuze and Guattari, rather, thought – and everything else understood as insubstantial, abstract, theoretical or imaginary – has to be seen as empirical. Whatever 'is', including thought, is empirical; just as for Foucault, whatever seems to escape historical effects – the body, intuition, conscience and so on – must be seen as all the more historical for appearing to be outside history. This does not mean of course that the 'empirical' in Deleuze and Guattari's sense should be understood as ahistorical; on the contrary, the point of repositioning the empirical outside the opposition of theory and empirics is to show that the empirical is always utterly historicized and politicized, and therefore always within culture and the space of desire. As I have suggested, however, the danger in this approach may lie in a certain aestheticization of the empirical on the model of the romantic concept of the literary absolute. In wanting to stress the political (actual) rather than psychic (virtual) economy of desire, for example, as well as the historical rather than abstract economy of theory and so on, Deleuze and Guattari are forced to subsume everything under the 'empirical'. By opening up the empirical – so that it becomes positively unstable and dynamic, like romantic 'literature' – they are in a sense forced to close off difference. Empirical *plenitude*, as it were, is a form of full-blown presence and therefore subject to the terms of Derrida's critique of presence as discussed in chapters 5 and 6. The affirmation of the empiricity of difference (as horizontal difference) forces Deleuze and Guattari to construe differentiation (vertical difference) only in negative terms – as lack, privation, suffering, oppression and so on. In such a way their ecstatic affirmation of empirical plenitude depends on a certain negation or cancellation of 'absence', suggesting that their version of the empirical is also a kind of theology: what might be called their theological faith in empirical plenitude could be seen as an expression of their fear of voided non-being.[19] But in any case the ecstatic tone of their affirmation of the empirical should be seen as constituting a certain ontology of presence, in which the aestheticization of the empirical appears as the fullness of living. In terms of this ontology, ethics must be on the side of plenitude, present in the overflowing of desiring-producing affirmation, so that the ethical being is the one whose will to power is rich. For such a being, ethics cannot be construed as a 'demand' – a demand to take responsibility for others or to hear their calls for justice, perhaps – but only as an act of 'generosity' which the willing being chooses to bestow. It is in this way that hierarchy and division, despite the attempt to eradicate vertical difference from their ontology of affirmation, can be seen as crucial to Deleuze and Guattari's conception of ethics. If ethics is not a demand but only a choice, in other words, then beings must be seen in terms of rank: the higher being, whose will to power is overflowing, generously chooses to be ethical towards (as John D. Caputo puts it) 'everything that is less than it [. . .] whatever is lower'. It does so because 'giving proceeds from a being capable of making promises only to itself, of being endebted only to itself, and it promises itself it will be generous to everything else.'[20]

In a certain sense, then, the poor are on this account condemned to be 'unethical', thought of course 'poverty' here means the lack of affirmation. Nevertheless a certain elitism attaches to the association of schizophrenic thought with ethical practice, which may be recognizable as a version of the romantic contempt for what was seen as the lack of *imagination* on the part of the Enlightenment *philosophes* (see chapter 9). In defining ethics *as* the practice of concept creation, nomadology, schizoanalysis, rhizomatic thinking and so on, Deleuze and Guattari may be seen to continue a romantic tradition of privileging the imaginative or avant-garde artist above all other modes of being. Other beings, trapped in the repression of their desires and enslaved by reason, are beneath the artist (or the schizophrenic, for Deleuze and Guattari) who nonetheless chooses to be ethical towards them. Hence, like art, ethics comes from within, as a consequence of the affirmation of being in terms of the negation of non-being. In this 'literary absolutist' conception of ethics, however, all hope is lost of understanding ethics as a demand: one is simply ethical from choice, not from necessity. And for this reason ethics, as a function of will, is a practice to which not only the anti-arborescent schizophrenic can lay claim: it can also be claimed by the supposedly tree-loving, unethical, State philosophical 'fascist'.

While there may be problems however with Deleuze and Guattari's 'theory' of ethics as a practice of the affirmation of being (or no doubt, for them, of beings in their multiplicities), this does not mean their work has nothing to contribute to literary studies. Their insistence on seeing writing as a pragmatics, for example, can help to demystify notions of authorial consciousness, literary appreciationism, literary absolutism, sensuous truth, and the idea that literature is a special kind of writing whose essence is unpresentable. The pragmaticization of literature might then lead on to the task of writing effective histories of those concepts (authorial consciousness and so on) which have seemed so innate to understandings of literature, but which could be revealed as having done the work of limiting the ways that literature might otherwise have developed as a set of more open or perhaps more democratic practices. In approaching literature as a pragmatics, then, literary studies could 're-skill' itself as the discipline of 'practical criticism', a term first used by the British critic I. A. Richards in the 1920s and which became central to the development of New Criticism.[21] However, there would need to be a radical shift away from the New Critical doctrine of the self-identity of the literary text towards an understanding of literature's self-difference, an understanding that would regard self-difference as a pragmatics and not simply as a conceptual abstraction revered by some 'Continental' philosophers. In this way Deleuze and Guattari's concept of the rhizome may help to unsettle the metaphysical idea that literary texts are autonomous entities full of underlying meanings. Instead of our seeing meaning as 'layered' and 'hidden', the concept of the rhizome may help us to see that meanings extend in manifold ways across manifold surfaces (though of course this should not be allowed to occlude the work of the vertical dimension).

It is precisely in terms of the pragmatics of self-difference that Paul Auster's writing, for instance, might be approached. Auster's writing forms a kind of radicle-system or rhizome of interconnecting links and filaments to his own and other writers' texts. In this way none of his titles may be seen to stand alone (as a root-book), but each text carries traces of the others and of a kind of writing-in-general – though of course the tracing itself constitutes a writing-in-particular. There are many examples that might be given here, but one will have to suffice. In *The New York Trilogy* (1987) – the title of a single volume that includes three previously published but strongly interlinked stories: *City of Glass*

(1985), *Ghosts* (1986) and *The Locked Room* (1986) – a writer of detective novels, Daniel Quinn, turns detective himself in tracing the daily movements of the mysterious Peter Stillman as he rambles across the streets of Manhattan's Upper West Side. After a while, Quinn begins to think that Stillman's perambulations are not haphazard but intentional and that when he is walking he is actually writing, spelling out a letter a day by carefully crossing a deliberate combination of streets. Once this idea occurs to him, Quinn cannot help but believe that Stillman has written out a cryptic message – THE TOWER OF BABEL – although at the same time Quinn knows that Stillman 'had not left his message anywhere. [. . .] It was like drawing a picture in the air with your finger'.[22] Quinn's *desire* to solve the case, in other words, or to find a solution to the question of whether or not Peter Stillman is plotting to murder his own son, has pragmatic effects, necessarily framing everything *as* case. We might say his desire is parergonal (see chapter 9), then, such that even the most seemingly insignifcant detail is encrypted with the signifying power of a clue. Henceforth there is no longer the possibility of an outside-case or the not-sign, but only the world as space of inscription and plot. And this is of course the 'Oedipal' space of Pynchon's heroine in *The Crying of Lot 49* (see chapter 1).

But it is not the space of the classical or root-book form of the detective novel. Philip Marlowe, for instance, despite his cynicism never fails to close the book on every case: he knows he is 'part of the nastiness', but still there is no mystery he undertakes to solve which doesn't end in resolution.[23] Through Quinn's paranoia, then, *The New York Trilogy* appears to imitate the classical form of the detective novel at the same time as it subverts its most rooted assumption. Quinn is simply too entangled in the in-difference of sign and not-sign to play the root-book detective's role of separating clues from red herrings, and so all he can do is to mirror the surface effects of that role, to go through the motions of being 'in' character.

Moreover the very question of what it means to be in character, as opposed say to being true to a 'self', arises frequently across the rhizomatic surface of Auster's writing. When Quinn performs his detective work, for instance, he is in a sense literally performing his own detective, Max Work, the hero of the private-eye novels that Quinn writes under the pseudonym of William Wilson, which happens also to be a pseudonym used by the narrator of a short story published in 1839 by Edgar Allan Poe.[24] Before he can carry out his detective work, however, Quinn has to impersonate the private-eye whose telephone number is mistaken for Quinn's at the start of the story, and whose name is 'Paul Auster'. This is also, of course, the name of the writer who creates Daniel Quinn as a character who writes under the name of William Wilson about a character he himself has created who is a private detective. But it is not necessarily the same Paul Auster, and so it is perhaps only by chance that when Quinn finally meets 'Paul Auster' he should turn out to be a writer, not a detective (and so not perhaps the 'Paul Auster' mentioned in the beginning), with a son whose name is Daniel. One way of solving the riddle might be to play the role of detective ourselves and to follow a possible line of flight to another text by Paul Auster, *The Invention of Solitude* (1982), which is divided between Auster's reflections on the death of his father and on his meditations over the fear that one day his son – whose name is Daniel – will die too. Yet the repetition of a Paul Auster who is the father of a child called Daniel doesn't constitute a unity, but functions rather as a link in a complex chain of associations and coincidences involving the name 'Paul Auster' within the radicle-system of Paul Auster's writing.

Although the Auster whom Quinn meets, that is, does link up with the Auster of the earlier memoirs, he can be linked also to other characters in other texts written by the Paul Auster whose name appears on the cover of *The New York Trilogy*. Fanshawe, for example, is a character who is a writer and for the most part a ghostly absence from *The Locked Room*, and he shares a number of similarities with the Auster of *The New York Trilogy*: each once earned money by ghostwriting a book for the wife of a Russian film producer, crewed as an ordinary seaman on an oil tanker in the Gulf of Mexico, lived in a one-room apartment in Paris for two years in his early twenties and has a sister who suffered a nervous breakdown as a teenager.[25] It also happens that the parents of Fanshawe's 'widow' are Norwegian, that the Auster whom Quinn meets is married to a woman of Norwegian descent and that in a dream from *The Invention of Solitude* the narrator A. (who 'speaks of himself as [. . .] A., even as he means to say I') imagines knocking on the door of his ex-wife's house to tell her that she is about to become a widow because he is about to die. Of course A. doesn't die and his wife does not become a widow, despite the inevitability of her becoming so according to the logic of the dream. Neither is Fanshawe dead, despite the inevitability of his being so according to the facts presented to his 'widow'. Are A. and Fanshawe the same character, then? Each 'widow' (the same woman?) after all is named executrix of her husband's literary estate. But then how is it that A. and Auster each have an only son called Daniel, while the name of Fanshawe's only son is Ben? So if A. is Auster, it would seem he cannot at the same time be Fanshawe. But if A. is indeed Paul Auster (in whose name are written the books in which A. and Fanshawe appear), is the Paul Auster who appears (or reappears) in *The New York Trilogy* the same Paul Auster who is A.? If A. is also 'I', moreover, the first-person narrator of part of *The Invention of Solitude*, then is A. who is 'I' who is Auster also Daniel Quinn?:

> The detective is the one who looks, who listens, who moves through this morass of objects and events in search of the thought, the idea that will pull all these things together and make sense of them. In effect, the writer and the detective are interchangeable. The reader sees the world through the detective's eye, experiencing the proliferation of its details as if for the first time. [. . .] Private eye. The term held a triple meaning for Quinn. Not only was it the letter 'i,' standing for 'investigator,' it was 'I' in the upper case, the tiny life-bud buried in the body of the breathing self. At the same time, it was also the physical eye of the writer, the eye of the man who looks out from himself into the world and demands that the world reveal itself to him.[26]

'I' is also the letter that literally inhabits the centre of Daniel Quinn's surname, a centre that is at the same everywhere at once since there is no name that 'I' cannot stand in for. If A. is I is Quinn, in other words, the name 'Paul Auster' must be legion.

Hence the traces of that name are left behind whenever – or where ever – Paul Auster writes. Marco Stanley Fogg, for example, the narrator of *Moon Palace* (1989), is a graduate of Columbia University, while A. holds two degrees from Columbia and Daniel Quinn uses his alumni card to borrow a book from the Columbia University Library.[27] Moreover Marco Fogg's best friend is called Zimmer, who saves his life and takes care of him during convalescence by letting him stay in his 'tiny hogan' of an apartment 'on the second floor of an ancient West Village tenement building'.[28] Zimmer is the name also of the carpenter, A. tells us, who built the tower in which the German poet Hölderlin, supposedly suffering from chronic bouts of schizophrenia, lived alone for thirty-six years. 'If not for Zimmer's generosity and kindness, it is possible that Hölderlin's life would have ended prematurely.'[29] Hence, each having at one time or another retired to the solitude of a locked room in order to write, A. is I is Auster is Quinn is Fanshawe is Fogg is Hölderlin.

From this brief discussion it can be seen that a 'rhizomatic' approach to the practice of literary criticism would ask more questions than it answered. Having forsaken certain assurances (the self-identity of the text, the determining consciousness of the author, the sensuousness of literary meaning and so on), rhizomatic criticism is left to carry out the pragmatic task of speculation on its own, or at least without the back-up of a fully developed theory or method. In the absence of any particular frame of reference, the structure of the literary text appears much more open than traditional literary criticism allows. In the case of Auster's writing (although not confined to it), this openness may appear as a sort of multiplicity – not only in terms of the identities of characters but also as the undecidably coincidental or deliberate repetitions within and between his texts and those of other writers (Poe, for example). Such openness suggests that Auster's writing should be approached not through a notion of his texts as different or separate entities, but in terms of the in-difference of the multiplicity of the text of writing – a text whose surface incorporates literary, autobiographical, popular and many other sources or traces of influence. Such openness, moreover, calls for a certain loosening up on the part of criticism (possibly in the form of a type of schizophrenia, though this is clearly not the only model), which must allow its findings to emerge pragmatically rather than be predetermined theoretically. But this does not preclude pragmatics from being 'creative' or inventive; indeed, since pragmatics is concerned with finding solutions to problems, it must also be 'imaginative' in its recognition of those problems as well as in its attempts to resolve them. Above all, though, a rhizomatic approach to the pragmatic self-difference of literature would involve a commitment to becoming 'nonmetaphysical'; and in this commitment, as I have suggested, there is a certain risk of becoming 'unethical'. For if metaphysics *cannot* be avoided (as Derrida argues), then the association of ethics with the avoidance of metaphysics (through the affirmation of affirmation) must result in an ethics which is less effective than desired. Deleuze and Guattari's restriction of difference to an associative or horizontal plane of operations is an attempt to counteract what they see as the oppressive force of reason (separationism or differentialism, as it were), but in this they are compelled to construe reason only in negative terms and hence to romanticize ethics and pragmatics in terms of a notion of *imaginative* self-difference. Their work may not after all, then, herald the return of practical criticism (based on the recognition of literature as the pragmatics of self-difference) as the most open or asystematic 'disciplinary' method of literary analysis. On their account the openness of such a method is in fact restricted to the exclusion of what are seen as rational methodological practices, in the name of affirming what reason is supposed to oppress. But if the operations of reason are not simply oppressive, then perhaps it is the return and not the exclusion of reason – as I argue in the final chapter – that warrants more attention.

12

The Return of Reason

The previous discussion of Paul Auster's writing raises an important question, which perhaps has been nagging our discussion all along: what, for postmodern literary theory, counts as a text?[1] Now, in the past, this question would have seemed either trivial or absurd; and of course it still seems that way to many literary critics today. Literary critics believe they have no more need of asking what a text 'is' than a car mechanic needs to ask, 'What is an engine?'. Mechanics are more interested in differentials than in differends, and so too probably, for that matter, are most literary critics. The reason that mechanics are uninterested professionally (though not necessarily privately) in Lyotard's theory of the differend is of course that it has nothing practical to do with mechanical repairs. Fixing the engine of a car and theorizing about the differend are different language-games. Or as a car mechanic who wasn't up on Wittgenstein might put it, 'Fixing and theorizing are two very different things.'

On Lyotard's account, however, the differend is not a theoretical abstraction but an empirical obstruction. In this way it presents the pragmatic problem of how to fix it. While there is still no doubt a world of difference between fixing a differend and fixing a leaky petrol filter, the problem of how to link onto a differend remains, for Lyotard, a pragmatic and not a theoretical one. There are rules for fixing petrol filters, but no rules for linking phrases in dispute. So the pragmatic problem of linkage posed by a differend calls for a creative or intuitive response. The differend must be felt or imagined, so that the problem of fixing it bids an act of judgement which is in a word reflective rather than determining. We are called on to be at our most creative, then, when confronted with problems of justice, not only with problems of art.

This suggests that an ethical decision is an aesthetic or textual practice (and vice versa), which could be an inducement for literary studies to consider the possible links between 'appreciation' and 'obligation'. In this way literary texts may be seen as a part of – not apart from – the factical, political, pragmatic, social and historical environments in which they are produced and read. This is perhaps the most challenging aspect of postmodern literary theory: its call for the discipline of literary studies to, in a sense, undiscipline itself. For the 'autonomy' of literature supposes the 'autonomy' of culture, conceived as a domain which is independent of society. In calling for literary studies to loosen up or undiscipline itself, then, postmodern literary theory refuses the division between 'culture' and 'society'. By teaching students to appreciate the cultural values of literature, literary studies is engaged in a social practice. For the most part it has been concerned with the lofty question of *what* to judge rather than the lowly pragmatics of *how* to judge. So perhaps it is in shifting attention away from the 'what' and onto the 'how' that the significance of postmodern literary theory should be measured.

Yet it needs to be measured cautiously. Postmodern literary theory's romantic inheritance of the radical affirmation of imaginative becoming is vested in the opposition to what it sees as the oppressive force of rational being. But the opposition of dynamic imagination and despotic rationality is based on a misreading of Kant, such that the performance of reflective judgement is both opposed to and raised above the use of practical reason. On this misreading, the Third *Critique* is taken as a 'proof' of the groundlessness of thought, which 'proves' in turn that the socio-historical valuation of practical reason is an elaborate hoax designed to repress the 'truth' that truth is always unpresentable, relative, multiple, textual, rhetorical, metaphorical, contingent, gendered, situational, cultural, perspectival, heterogeneous, rhizomatic, discontinuous and in every conceivable sense open to interpretation and dispute. Broadly speaking, this is a literary understanding of truth, especially in terms of 'literature' understood as the 'literary absolute', and this is why I have used the general term 'postmodern literary theory' throughout to refer to the more commonly used terms, 'postmodernism' or 'postmodern theory'. For it is *the literary text* which is the analogue, for postmodernism, of the dynamic interpretability of truth and being, thought and desire, power and culture. In its openness to being read in different ways, moreover, the literary text provides an analogue of the unconscious and of the structuralist theory of language, so that both psychoanalysis and structuralism are also part of the romantic heritage of postmodern literary theory.

Why not, then, see postmodernism simply as the return of romanticism? One answer to this is given in a famous essay, 'Postmodernism, or The Cultural Logic of Late Capitalism' (1984), by Fredric Jameson, who argues that the *social* position of postmodernism is very different from that of romanticism in the past. The romantic sensibility, once seen as scandalous and anti-social, has undergone 'a mutation in the sphere of culture' that renders it unthreatening today. This mutation is the result of the 'canonization and academic institutionalization' of romantic texts, defusing the earlier shock-value of their radical extravagance and immorality. The romantic will to experimentation as expressed through modernist art and letters, for example, may also be seen to have exhausted itself in modernism, and so Joyce and Picasso are, for us, 'no longer ugly'. 'This is indeed surely one of the most plausible explanations for the emergence of postmodernism itself, since the younger generation of the 1960s will now confront the formerly oppositional modern movement as a set of dead classics', condemning the earlier notion of oppositional or scandalous art to a future in which 'opposition' and 'scandal' are available only as commodities.[2] So for example a television programme such as *The X-Files* might be said to 'market' an attitude of cynicism in regards to the actual workings of democracy, or perhaps simply to quote back to the audience a sense of its own political alienation as evidenced within everyday culture by the rising popularity and credence of conspiracy-theories and alternative knowledges. The show therefore incorporates – and therein commodifies – so-called oppositional or resistant readings of public institutions (law enforcement agencies) and public values (rational consensus). On prime-time network television, 'alternative' truth is made over into popular reality, such that events become more credible only as they become more bizarre. And of course the extraordinary must be made over into the ordinary when it is believed that all kinds of reality-expanding information (especially concerning aliens) is kept 'secret' from the public by order of successive governments acting in league with shady consortia of corrupt old men who will stop at nothing to protect their anonymity and the value of their clandestine power. Hence the body politic is riddled with cancer, a trope which *The X-Files* loves to pun on by always showing the bad guy with a cigarette in his hand.

Now on this reading it may look as if *The X-Files* is a rewriting of *The Crying of Lot 49*, which I discussed briefly in chapter 1. But in the gap between these texts – a gap which is not only historical – paranoia has been normalized and made over into cynicism. It seems to support

Jameson's argument, then, that the emergent postmodernism of Pynchon's novel reaches full-blown proportions in *The X-Files*, where a paranoic approach to political culture and history is no longer a potential sign of delusional thinking but a mark instead of the postmodern art of thinking differently. As a signifier of an over-active imagination, paranoia has shifted its social position within postmodernism to be seen now as the citizen's only defence against a system vested in rationality but bent on total mind-control. Reason is not an instrument of human enlightenment on this view, but a technology of subjugation that keeps us from daring to desire more than to serve the interests of a totalitarian political economy disguised as the 'free market' or 'democratic government'. Jameson's point, of course, is that if such paranoia might once have seemed shocking or revolutionary, and therefore only marginally effective in its romantic excess, the economic regime of 'late-capitalism' actually sells back revolutionary paranoia (and why not also revolutionary schizophrenia?) to a public whose political imagination is so thoroughly romanticized that nothing shocks it. In one sense, then, paranoia has been de-specialized and returned to the order of a popular form of the ontological difference (such that perhaps a relation appears between 'different' and 'poetic' thinking). In another sense, and contrary to Lacoue-Labarthe and Nancy's argument, romanticism is far from 'unfinished': in fact it ends (according to Jameson's argument) with the canonization of the 'radical transgression' of the modernist text, which loses the power to scandalize through being institutionalized. Similarly, on Lyotard's view, romanticism might be seen to end with Auschwitz as the limit of the scandalous within history, thereby exhausting the historical imagination's capacity to experience and express outrage. Before its socialization as a general position, then, brought about either by the canonization of Joyce or the silencing effect of Auschwitz, it might be said that 'cultural' romanticism believed in the idea that truth must be made up; it is therefore literary. But 'social' romanticism believes that truth is made over; it is therefore textual. Once it comes to be believed that truth extends (rhizomatically, perhaps) across the whole textual surface of social, historical, political and cultural space, how could one be other than cynical about the possibility of aesthetic 'innovation', political 'solution', historical 'finality' and so on? For although 'literature' may have been flattened out into 'text', it is still no less the case that textual operations are understood in terms of the romantic theory of literature as the neverending theory of itself. So every 'innovation' or 'solution' is just another text or gambit, open to multiple readings or to many possible successive moves. And since there is nothing new under the sun after Joyce and Auschwitz, every text is just a mish-mash of other textual concepts and contours, images and ideas, philosophies and feelings that have been tried out before.

According to Jameson's argument, then, postmodernism should be seen as both returning to and breaking away from romanticism. This would be to attribute a certain self-identity to postmodernism and so lend support to Lyotard's assertion that 'now' is the time of the postmodern 'condition'. It would also help to verify any version of an anti-foundationalist philosophy or politics, such as Deleuze and Guattari's, which equated reason with fascism (or some other form of imposition) and therefore as a structure to be opposed. In this light the cyberpunk novels of William Gibson or Pat Cadigan may appear as textual 'eruptions' in response to a radically new world order of self-dissociating information flows and economic lines of flight, rather than as recent examples of a gothic sci-fi tradition whose origins go back to the Romantic era and Mary Shelley's *Frankenstein* (1823). In Cadigan's *Fools* (1992), for instance, characters buy memories made over into micro-chips, and so can 'experience' tiny fragments of the lives of others. Technology turns the category of 'mistaken identity' into a tautology, making cases of 'characterization amnesia' a common risk in a world where persons are just so many multiple computerized personas and in which there is a nomadic underclass of desperate 'memory-junkies' hooked on their insatiable desire for the next new 'virtual' feeling. The old romantic idea that nothing is what it seems is now so stock that it's perfectly natural to wonder if a present emotion might not be a 'leak through' from some previous persona; while indeed the sheer banality of the fantastic is so much a fact of daily life that, out on the street, the only way to tell the difference between people and holograms is that you can't pass through people. 'It was all too preposterous', the narrator says, 'but those were the times we lived in.'[3]

The times most certainly are preposterous when 'reality' is turned so inside out that it stretches to encompass the virtual dimensions of 'cyberspace', an environment conceived originally in Gibson's *Neuromancer* (1984) and which is now a standard feature of the cyberpunk genre (having also, as a concept, leaked through to popular science).[4] Given the right technology, one may simply 'jack in' to cyberspace, a shadowless matrix through which it is possible to travel to and enter different places, meet and talk with other people, and above all to steal information. It is also possible to die in there, although as a character in Gibson's *Mona Lisa Overdrive* (1988) explains: '*There's no there, there.*'[5] Similarly, one might say the same about Deleuze and Guattari's concept or space of the plane of consistency, which is never 'there' as an actual space although neither is it not 'there' simply as a consequence of being virtual. As a concept, moreover, 'cyberspace' may be a good example of Deleuze and Guattari's claim that radical philosophy today is more likely to be practised as popular culture, within which one is not obliged to think according to strict or formal rules and so can think more creatively in addressing each problem (the next possible narrative move, the next possible bar of a song, or the next possible film shot) as a pragmatic demand to meet it – or perhaps to meet up with it, by connecting or aligning oneself to it in some undetermined way. On their view, of course, such thinking is disallowed within philosophy, where the imperative to think 'logically' is an injunction against the element of surprise.

But to see postmodernism simply as the socialization or normalization of romanticism is to risk confining it to an attitude of disrespect for traditional values. On this view the postmodern represents the popularization of a certain privileged stance within romanticism towards what might be called the allure of the abject, or of whatever society forbids us to think or desire and therefore tries to repress. So if romanticism worked at giving offence to the notion of a 'tradition' of higher taste and learning, it might be said to have done so in the name of what a 'cultivated' moral and aesthetic sensibility was supposed to guard against: the turmoil of human desire, and the vulgar emotional life of everyday political society. Through the romantic affirmation of the forbidden, then, the repressive force of high culture was demystified. Desire and politics could be seen thereafter as both inseparable from one another and inseparable from notions of 'culture', helping to turn 'elite' and 'popular' orders of representation into mutually informing rather than mutually exclusive spheres of production. On this view, postmodern literature might be seen less in terms of a high/low distinction than in terms of a certain fascination with the abject, expressed both in 'dime store' novels and in those of 'serious' writers whose work is supported by government arts grants and acclaimed by literary awards committees. The bestselling American author James Ellroy's *Silent Terror* (1986), for example, is a grossly violent first-person narrative of a serial killer's life and crimes. Perhaps the mark of its postmodernism is the text's refusal to excuse or explain Martin Plunkett's *desire* for killing and the abject pleasure he gets from it. As Plunkett warns us from the start, he will remain 'silent' on the question of why he chooses to create 'terror':

> above all, I have my mind; my silence. There is a dynamic to the marketing of horror: serve it up with a hyperbolic flourish that distances even as it terrifies, then turn on the literal or figurative lights, inducing gratitude for the cessation of a nightmare that was too awful to be true in the first place. I will not observe that dynamic. I will not let you pity me. Charles Manson, babbling in *his* cell, deserves pity [. . .]. I deserve awe for standing inviolate at the end of the journey I am about to describe [. . .].[6]

In refusing to sound the 'depth' of Plunkett's desire to kill, the novel may be seen as tracing the nomadic or rhizomatic movements of 'desire' as a force which operates only across surfaces. Hence it could be considered a 'fictional' instance of Deleuze and Guattari's account of the absence of any psychic or moral interiority 'within' the force of desiring-willing as the driving force of being. Like *Anti-Oedipus* and *A Thousand Plateaus*, then, *Silent Terror* approaches the abject not as the repressed 'underbelly' of society or the dark 'core' of human nature, but as what appears empirically *on the surface of* everyday factical living. Nor is this approach confined to Ellroy's novel as a work of 'popular' fiction, since it is taken up by 'serious' literature too. In *Child of God* (1973), for example, written by the award-winning American novelist Cormac McCarthy (who is often compared with Melville and Faulkner), the abject is everywhere inscribed on the surface of the text. But it is nowhere more visible perhaps than in this description of what happens to the corpse of Lester Ballard, the serial-killing backwoodsman who terrorizes a small hills community in East Tennessee, gets caught and sent to prison, and then one morning 'was found dead in the floor of his cage':

> His body was shipped to the state medical school at Memphis. There in a basement room he was preserved with formalin and wheeled forth to take his place with other deceased persons newly arrived. He was laid out on a slab and flayed, eviscerated, dissected. His head was sawed open and the brains removed. His muscles were stripped from his bones. His heart was taken out. His entrails were hauled forth and delineated and the four young students who bent over him like those haruspices of old perhaps saw monsters worse to come in their configurations. At the end of three months when the class was closed Ballard was scraped from the table into a plastic bag and taken with others of his kind to a cemetery outside the city and there interned. A minister from the school read a simple service.[7]

From these examples it could be said that the 'postmodern' describes a space in which the allure of abjection is affirmed or given in to. To see this as a very weak or loose signifier of a general 'condition', moreover, would also be to see it as the measure of its strength. In other words, what might be called the organizing principle of freely succumbing to or affirming 'the allure of abjection' allows for radically different configurations of cultural production to appear than can be seen by a more traditional approach to culture as an internally divided field of separate activities (literature, philosophy, history and so forth) concerned with the protection of different objects or practices (literature as the custodian of the figure; philosophy as the custodian of the concept; history as the custodian of the event; and so on). In Deleuze and Guattari's terms, this would be to see the allure of the abject as a force extending across divisions within culture, as well as across the division between 'culture' as the space of aesthetic production and 'society' as the space of political and economic production. Culture would no longer be seen then as a tree with distinct branches of knowledge or activity, rooted in but towering over the shifting sands of politico-economic social history. It would be seen instead as a rhizomatic assemblage in which the cultural and the social were indivisibly and heterogeneously conjoined. Hence in their affirmation of the allure of the abject, such novels as *Silent Terror* and *Child of God* might be seen as forming a kind of loose alignment not only with themselves but also (among other examples) with *The Crying of Lot 49*, where abjection figures as the impossibility of a rational solution to Oedipa's dilemma; Kathy Acker's *Empire of the Senseless* (see chapters 2 and 3), in which the violence of abjection operates both sexually and linguistically; and Auster's *New York Trilogy*, where events are undecidably outside or inside the space of interpretation and so cannot be understood by rational thought but only witnessed out of a desiring curiosity – abject in its lack of purpose or meaning – to be involved in their unfoldings. Nor is this assemblage confined to works of literature. On television, for example, *The X-Files* not only displays corporeal abjection (autopsies and monstrous bodies) but also delights in the allure of abject irrationalism as the explanation of a truth which is always in excess of historical sense and social belief. Nor indeed does the rhizomatic allure of the abject extend only to aesthetic or creative texts. What might be called the affirmation of abjection in the work of Deleuze and Guattari (in the form of insults and expletives, say, or in their robust disrespect for cultural icons and values based on the supremacy of rational thought) suggests that 'theory' too is connected to this assemblage. Hence in her recent work the Australian corporeal feminist Elizabeth Grosz argues for an urgent attention to abject bodily seepages as a means of overcoming the 'problem' of Cartesian dualism.[8] For Grosz, the social repression of desire and historical injunctions against the allure of the abject are 'patriarchal' in their efforts to subsume the a-rational, bio-political forces of the body under a totalizing regime of mind-control: cultural forms of representation, in a word, are seen as occurring in oppostion to or with complete disregard for the body as a desiring-producing source of social meaning (rather than simply as a given). Such repression is articulated most famously in Descartes' so-called mind/body split. As a counter to the common charge, however, that thinking and corporeality are separated in Descartes, Edith Wyschogrod suggests a very different reading:

> In fact, the Cartesian cogito may be interpreted in a less damaging way than the standard objections would indicate. Consider Descartes' actual language about the self as a *thing* that thinks. To the contrary, thought has a locus; it is here, where my body is. It can be argued that the body excluded by Cartesian doubt is not the body as subject but the body as object. Far from barring experienced corporeality from the cogito, Descartes has instead cordoned off the body as thing.[9]

In a related manner, Abigail Bray and Claire Colebrook argue that orthodox condemnations of Descartes can only repeat what they hope to overcome: any appeal to 'the body' as a source of production (for example in such a way that 'women's images would no longer by given from outside but generated from within') could therefore not afford to ignore its own inscription within 'the very interior/exterior model of Cartesian dualism which it sought to critique'.[10]

The point here is that while the concept or figure of assemblage may open up the possibility of new forms of cultural theory and analysis, this does not cause older forms to become instantly redundant. In its greater extensions, the concept of assemblage may indeed ease the restraints of such traditional concepts as genre, consciousness and work, making it possible to trace connections between texts which are otherwise seen only in terms of their different identities and values. In this way the assemblage or multiplicity I described above forms a loose and heterogeneous *text* comprising instances of 'popular' fiction and television, 'high' theory, and 'serious' literature. Such a text presents as a problem not the psychological or theological question of its authorship, but the pragmatic question of how to approach it or of how perhaps to account for the effective history of its formation? Hence the question *of* the text's assemblage cannot be ignored in approaching the assemblage *as* a text. But this is not to say that any notion of 'critical distance' has to be discarded by virtue of seeing this assemblage as something which is both produced and producing. While clearly the assemblage is not simply a 'found object' or a 'given', this does not mean that all approaches to it are already fully inscribed within it, turning every 'sense of perspective' into an 'angle of distortion'.

The opposition of 'perspective' and 'distortion' is a false one, like many other oppositions we have encountered. To suppose that every perspective is distorted, such that all angles of coincidence within text–commentary relations must be skewed, is to suppose that a certain ideal concept of 'perspective' gives the impression that texts can be read and interpreted from an unmediating space outside them, making it possible to see a text in all its self-identical plenitude. There is no doubt that such an ideal of perspective does still linger within literary studies: the whole edifice of Bloom's Western canon, for example, depends on it. But to critique an ideal is not necessarily to cause it to disappear. As we saw in chapter 5, Derrida'a critique of 'structure', while showing that concepts of structure are always divided internally by the play or force of structurality, does not pretend to reveal a space which is *outside* structures – a pure space of the 'prior' or the 'post' – in which it would be possible to think an absolutely different concept of structure. What is called 'post'-structuralism should not be regarded as a practice of thinking which is different, in an absolute sense, from structuralism, or as a philosophy which thinks 'beyond' concepts of structure as understood by metaphysics. For poststructuralism, metaphysical concepts of structure are not 'fascist', by comparison say to an 'ethical' concept – or pragmatics – of a 'structurelesss' structure. The opposition between 'structure' and 'play', in other words, is no more absolute than the opposition between fascism and ethics. Fascism *is* an ethics,[11] though it may not be one that many of us would choose to affirm. Similarly, the play or 'performativity' which is always internal to any structure means that the structure-versus-nonstructure opposition must be seen as a problem to be worked through rather than as a given starting point to work from. And of course it must always be seen in terms of its singularities, according to the particular conditions and contexts of its manifold pragmatic occurrences and effects. If any version of the structure-versus-nonstructure opposition (say in the form of reason-versus-imagination, or fascism-versus-ethics) were *not* to be approached as a pragmatic singularity – a singularity that would also always be an assemblage – then it would have to be supposed that the opposition existed outside the factical, empirical or effective forces of social and political histories. In a word, any general, decontextualized, ahistorical form of the structure-versus-nonstructure opposition would be metaphysical.

So instead of seeing an ideal of critical perspective as a fascist or oppressive structure to be opposed, through say the ethical affirmation of structureless distortion, what needs to be acknowledged is that text–commentary relations constitute an unavoidable pragmatics. But the affirmation of pragmatic singularities does not have to occur in the name of opposing nonmetaphysical practice to metaphysical theory, any more than it need occur in the name of opposing reflective judgement to practical reason, ethics to fascism, or desire to thought. Yet these terms should not be deemed absolutely un-opposed either. While reason and imagination, for example, are not the same, they are not therefore completely different. It remains the case however that, at different times and in different contexts, a sort of all-or-nothing distinction does appear to operate between the value accorded to rational thought on the one hand and to imaginative desire or intuition on the other. But what needs to be seen as the problem here is not the question of choosing between thought and intuition: it is rather the very ground on which the question of choosing is made to seem inescapable which is problematic. That ground is the all-or-nothingness of the opposition.

If the ground or structure of all-or-nothingness is not seen as a problem, then of course it becomes easy to affirm the 'ethics' of any anti-foundationalist pragmatics. The affirmation is made easy by the presumption that ethics and pragmatics are opposed to fascism and theory, as play is opposed to structure. As we saw in chapter 8, however, the apparent all-or-nothingness of the opposition between the political left and the political right is no prevention against pragmatic 'leak throughs' from one side to the other. More to the point, the fact that such leakage is unpreventable means that neither side's 'self-identity' is completely watertight or pure. So it is possible to vote left and to be a racist, or to vote right and be against racism. But of course in one sense there *is* no 'left' or 'right' to vote for: votes are cast directly for political parties, and only indirectly for ideals. One does not go into a polling booth and vote for 'the' left or 'the' right, or at any rate one's vote is not *tallied* in that way. It is tallied for a political party within a political system; and there has never been a party or a system which has not been an assemblage, and which – as an assemblage – has not been made up of an inconsistent or discontinuous mix of policies and practices, covenants and compromises, alignments and antagonisms, and so on. There has never been a party or a system which has not been a multiplicity, in other words. Yet this does not mean that political ideals are irrelevant. Since political theory is not opposed, however, to political pragmatics, it could be only a metaphysical dream to hope for an 'untheoretical' pragmatics of the political, or of any other assemblage or multiplicity.

Ideals, then, are not easily abandoned. There can be no hope of turning to a pragmatics of the political – or the literary – and supposing that such a turn avoids having to engage with questions in any general form, or that somehow it escapes theory and is therefore non-metaphysical and nonidealistic. There is no such thing as an absolute singularity, beyond all recognition except in terms of its own self-presence or outside all historico-communal concepts of structure and identity. Even in the radical sense of a multiplicity or an assemblage, singularities cannot be regarded as unrelated to general conditions of formation and interpretability, or to general norms of judgement and critique. This does not mean that such conditions and norms can guarantee the truth of any singularity. It does not mean that what may be called the generality of the general suffuses the singularity of the singular, systematically putting into place everything that might otherwise have appeared disruptive or anomolous. It simply means that nothing can be absolutely and uniquely singular, a pure 'itself' cut off in every sense from all possible (virtual and actual) relations to an outside.

Now there is no doubt that, in the form of a general concept or an ideal, the purpose of every system is to put things in their rightful place. But it is in the nature of things – in their singularities – often to be stubbornly erratic and hence to resist being systematized. This neither means that systems are 'fascist', however, nor that singularities want to be 'free'. Neither does it mean that ethics is on the side of freedom-loving singularities in some struggle against the rule-enforcing generalities of systems whose real aim is to put everyone in concentration camps. As we have seen repeatedly, though, postmodern literary theory requires just such a notion of goose-stepping 'structure' to function as the enemy of desire and imagination, thereby raising a notion of 'structureless difference' to the order of an ethical absolute. In a sense, then, having taken its concept of structureless difference from the romantic theory of literature, postmodern ethics permits – indeed requires – the confusion of the high aesthetic ground with the high moral ground. Such an ethics is superior to any *system* of ethics, since it is based on the knowledge that every system is dysfunctional. Every system must fall short of its own ideal;

hence the real purpose of every system is to hide the knowledge of its inevitable failure. It can do this only by suppressing its internal self-difference in the name of asserting its ideal self-identity. The whole system of culture is therefore based on a lie: culture has no foundational origin, no underlying meaning, and no immanent purpose. Perversely, then, the 'purpose' of every cultural system or institution is to conceal the fact that it has no purpose other than to conceal its futility. So the point of State philosophy and of what might also be called State literature, as well as the purpose of the party political system, is to keep us from seeing that philosophy, literature and politics are ungovernably asystematic and radically discontinuous both in terms of their relations to themselves and with each other.

Once again: it is unnecessary to go from a critique of structure to the totalizing negation of it. To acknowledge that some systems are oppressive is not to have to say that all systems are therefore indistinguishable from Nazi Germany. Some systems are indeed oppressive, but all systems are not therefore 'unethical'. By acknowledging the different differences within ethics, then, it is possible to avoid having to oppose the 'unethical' practices of the German Nazi Party (or any system) to an 'ethics' conceived only as the affirmation of pure difference, absolute singularity and the radically untheoretical. For literary studies, this would mean that to see a text such as *Silent Terror* in terms of an assemblage of relations to other texts (not all of which need be literary) does not mean having to see it as 'liberated' from the metaphysical constraints of such concepts as genre and tradition. All that needs to be acknowledged is that, while *Silent Terror* is a work of crime fiction, its textual operations and effects are not confined to its generic identity. This may enable both the individual text to be seen as rhizomatic (multiple, heterogeneous – even schizophrenic) in the waywardness of its inside/outside extensions, and so to be seen less in terms of self-identity than self-difference, and also the structure of genre to be seen as nondetermining without having to be disregarded altogether. Not only texts but genres too are assemblages. In this way the concept of assemblage allows for a more pragmatic approach to texts, enabling both the 'structure' of genre and the 'system' of literature themselves to be understood as textual. As an assemblage, literature does not pose the metaphysical question of its 'essence' but rather the pragmatic one of its effects. All the same, the notion of what might be called an effective literature should not be mistaken for a nonmetaphysical refuge from the question of literature's identity. To see that identity in terms of a problem, or in terms of a multiplicity, does not mean having to see it as a fascist structure of oppression that must be destroyed at all costs!

This – the view that structures are problematic, but not necessarily oppressively so – is a position attributable to poststructuralism. Hence while poststructuralism may be seen to affirm difference, it cannot be seen to oppose identity. The nonoppositional affirmation of difference distinguishes poststructuralism from postmodern literary theory; but again in such a way that poststructuralism is 'against' postmodernism only in the sense of being in a relation to it which is neither incommensurate nor inclusive. By comparison, the postmodern affirmation of difference as the totalizing negation of identity prevents ethical decisions from being seen as critical decisions. But for ethics to be seen as a pragmatics, the role of practical reason has to be seen as crucial – not as what needs to be overcome. As Drucilla Cornell, the American feminist legal theorist, writes: ethics is 'a way of being in the world that spans divergent value systems and allows us to criticize the repressive aspects of competing moral systems'.[12] On this account, moral systems are not by definition 'repressive', although they may comprise repressive 'aspects'. How then are we to make decisions about which aspects to see as 'repressive'? This is not a question for postmodern literary theory, which regards all systems as repressive through and through. So there is no need, on this account, to maintain a critical stance towards any system – or metanarrative – because all systems are unethical, concerned only with the repression of desire, imagination and difference. But this would scarcely be an effective strategy to adopt in a court of law, for example, where there would seem very little point in saying, 'Between the defence and the prosecution, your Honour, there is a differend.' Imagine a legal system based on the idea that a crime must always remain incalculable, on the model of Lyotard's claim that the crime of Auschwitz is incalculable, despite all evidence of its calculation. Now of course no legal system is perfect: as a system, it is always going to be dysfunctional to some extent. It will never be able to calculate crimes beyond all possible objection or dispute; and so in a sense it will never be able to fully calculate any crime, or at least it will not be able to do so except by a sort of accident and then only insofar as it will never be able to know it has fully calculated a particular crime despite believing that it has. But to say that a legal system is always going to be dysfunctional (if only in the sense that, as a practice, it is always going to be different from the general or ideal form of its self-identity) is not quite the same as saying that every legal system *is* dysfunctional, and so therefore, as a line in a Bob Dylan song goes, 'To live outside the law you must be honest'!

No less than legal practitioners, literary critics cannot afford to forsake the use of practical reason. If justice and literature are seen only in terms of the incalculable or the unpresentable, then one is left to speak out on their behalf only from a sense of empathy or intuition. There is no doubt that lawyers make arguments and that juries make decisions on the basis of feelings as well as rational calculations, but it does not follow from this that arguments and decisions cannot be made rationally. The fact that justice exceeds the use of practical reason, or that practical reason is insufficient to determine what is just, does not make practical reason redundant on the ground that justice is 'a feeling thing'. As Carolyn D'Cruz puts it: 'in coming through the form of singular idioms, the demand of justice comes with no definitive criteria that can merely calculate whether a decision within law is just', but this is no excuse for thinking that law and justice are opposed.[13] Similarly, even on the view that literature is 'asystematic', it does not follow that literature is beyond all reach of rational calculation. The idea – or theory – of literature as incalculable or unpresentable is indeed a profoundly conservative one, expressed most recently in Bloom's theory of 'love' as the condition of 'literature'. In order to critique that theory, it is in fact necessary to assert the role of practical reason as an important component of thought. For to suppose that thought is more originary or more radical in the form of reflective judgement, or as a type of schizophrenia on its own, is to risk reducing it to the order of creative or imaginative expression. But if thought is allowed to mean only 'creative thought' – or worse, if it is subsumed under 'sensuous feeling' – then we can give up any hope of a critical ethics. The ethical would be only what creative thinkers or desiring bodies chose to dispense – not a demand to criticize whatever might be seen as repressive about a particular system, or as an aspect of that system in practice.

In this way perhaps what may appear as the postmodern challenge to literary studies to 'undiscipline' itself is at the same time a familiar call, one which is deeply immanent to literary studies as a result of its romantic inheritance. A certain notion of undisciplinarity, in other words, or at least of a-disciplinarity, is a proud feature of literary studies' self-identity. 'English,' for example, as Geoffrey Hartman writes, 'when it gets beyond spelling and grammar, is not a technique but a cultural acquisition of great complexity: a literature as well as a basic literacy.'[14] Now of course the distinction between 'technique' and 'cultural acquisition' may not be nearly as plain as Hartman's statement makes it seem, but the point is that the notion of 'a cultural acquisition' conveys a very different sense from that of 'a discipline'. And while such a notion is clearly an attempt to think beyond the concept of 'love' or 'appreciation' as the foundation of literary studies, it is also clearly resistant to the idea that literature is an effect of disciplinary training: instead it is something which is culturally acquired. This is not at all to say that Hartman is wrong, but simply to acknowledge that there is nothing terribly controversial about the idea that literary studies is (or that it sees itself as) a discipline in only a very loose sense. So any call for literary studies to undiscipline itself, or to reaffirm its a-disciplinarity, really ought to come as music to the ears of a critic such as Harold Bloom. That he receives it, however, only as dreadful interference is a sign that he regards his own theory of literature as completely untheoretical, while seeing the 'postmodern' approach to literature as the ideological driving force behind an invading army of disciplinary theorists, if not a rabble of spiritualless barbarians.

Bloom is not wrong to regard literature as something more than can be known through rational thinking. But in this, literature is not especially unique. There are many things which rational thinking alone cannot give us to know, which is why Kant wrote three accounts of reason and did not stop at the account of practical reason. But neither did Kant argue that we should just forget about the uses of reason altogether, simply because sometimes we have to use reflective judgement to try to figure out the rules by which something might be able to be judged. Kant's affirmation of reflective judgement is not based on the totalizing negation of practical reason, despite the fact that such a move seems to have become a requirement of postmodern literary theory. Indeed we might refer to this *as* the postmodern requirement: the totalizing negation of whatever seems not to present itself as the unpresentable, or of whatever appears as fully inscribed within a set of rules by which to judge it. It is clear that, on behalf of ethics as a practice (in contrast to a moral system), it is necessary to be critical of rules; but it may not be necessary to defy them. Defiance, indeed, is an oppositional attitude towards something which is required to be seen as oppressive; and in this way defiance and oppression may be seen as linked metaphysically. And in their metaphysical conjoinings, defiance and oppression are at constant risk of turning into each other's opposite because each is committed to the cancellation of the other and to the cancellation of 'otherness'.

We might say too that the task of cancelling, reducing or controlling otherness belongs also to philosophy as metaphysics. Any attempt to think the possibility of a 'nonmetaphysics', then, would have to involve a rethinking of the philosophical cancellation of the other. Insofar as a poststructuralist or deconstructive project can be seen as an instance of the attempt 'to attain a point of exteriority', as Simon Critchley puts it, to metaphysics, then perhaps such a project may be described in the following terms:

> as the desire to keep open a dimension of alterity which can neither be reduced, comprehended, nor, strictly speaking, even *thought* by philosophy. To say that the goal of Derridean deconstruction is not simply the *unthought* of the tradition, but rather that-which-cannot-be-thought, is to engage in neither sophistical rhetoric nor negative theology. It is rather to point towards that which philosophy is unable to say.[15]

In a sense, what philosophy cannot say *is* able to be said by literature, or by a certain notion of the literary as that which always causes trouble for philosophy and which philosophy therefore tries to cancel or exclude, defining it as 'other' than philosophy. In this way, then, postmodern literary theory might be understood as a radical intervention in the history of metaphysical thought. Through its affirmation of the literary absolute, postmodern literary theory might be seen as a revolutionary attempt to think nonmetaphysically, and hence as an attempt to think outside the structure of oppositions in which 'the other' is always reduced or cancelled. But by the same token its affirmation of the literary absolute requires the totalizing negation of philosophy as metaphysics, and in this sense postmodern literary theory represents only the return of the romantic opposition to reason. As a return, it comes not so much as a challenge to literary studies but as a familiar fold within it, since literary studies is already quite comfortable with the idea that something unpresentable presents itself as literature. To think differently, however, it is not enough to acknowledge that literature says what philosophy is unable to say; it has to be acknowledged also that philosophy is able to say what *literature* cannot say.

Without this double acknowledgement, either philosophy or literature must stand as a master discourse. Now it is not that a master discourse is destined to function as a fascist dictatorship, always on the lookout for an opportunity to crush dissent; but certainly any discourse or system which installs itself as the model for decision-making is clearly going to produce more sameness than difference. If one way of thinking came to dominate all others, you wouldn't stand much chance of being listened to if you didn't think – and therefore express yourself – in that dominant way. And of course it is often supposed that there *is* a dominant way of thinking (in the West at any rate), known variously as patriarchy, eurocentrism, colonialism, rationalism and so forth. The usual response to any form of dominance is to oppose it, such that feminism, ethno-multiplicity, postcolonialism and anti-rationalism are sometimes advocated as 'alternative' ways of thinking. But if thought is understood only in terms of comprising so many different ways of thinking, then thought cannot be understood – or thought – differently. The unthought within thought, as it were, cannot be thought if it is simply a matter of choosing between this way or that way of thinking. If thought were understood as a choice between thinking philosophically or thinking in a way considered to be literary, or between thinking as a patriarch or thinking as a feminist, 'thought' as such would remain quite unaffected. Of course, how one views this claim will depend on what kind of force one attributes to – or as – metaphysics.

If one takes the view that metaphysics is just a projection of philosophy's self-importance, then it could be that one might assert the higher importance of a political justification for trying to propose alternative ways of thinking as a counter-measure to the dominance of patriarchy, eurocentrism or whatever. But in that case the desire or motivation of the counter-measure would not be simply to oppose whatever was perceived as the dominant way of thinking: it would be to usurp it. Hence the structure of domination and oppression would not be unsettled, but rather reaffirmed.[16] Instead of a politics of the right, a politics of the left would dominate; or instead of thinking philosophically, the dominant way of thinking would be literary; and so on. But to suppose there is a clear-cut choice between different politics or between different ways of thinking, a choice that could overcome the difference *within* politics and thought, would still be to think metaphysically. And this would be to maintain the risk of the usurper becoming the usurped – the unavoidable risk of a previously oppositional but now dominant force turning into what it once opposed.

There are countless historical (and not merely 'abstract') examples of the unavoidability of such a risk. The risk, then, is empirical, and cannot simply be dismissed as a philosophical concept or a literary figure. It is because the risk is empirical – such that its effects are never less than political, historical and actual – that the critique of metaphysics cannot be seen as other than connected to political and historical actualities. It does not follow necessarily, however, that the critique of metaphysics sounds the death of all ideals or of a certain notion of idealism. In *Specters of Marx*, for example, as we saw in chapter 8, Derrida's critique of the metaphysical concepts of 'history' and 'revolution' could even be said to be inspired by his commitment to a certain ideal of democracy and an ideal of revolutionary spirit derived from Marx. The attempt to think the ghost, then, as an instance of the attempt to think the unthought within thought, is at the same time an affirmation of the struggle for – and as – democracy. Similarly, Deleuze and Guattari's attempt to rethink philosophy as the practice of schizoanalysis (see chapters 10 and 11) is at the same time a political intervention in the process of what they see as the 'fascist' separation of thought and desire. Hence their project might be put as the attempt to return thought to its vital connections with history, politics and the pragmatics of living. If, as I have suggested, their affirmation of thought as a pragmatics requires too strong a rebuke of thought as a system, frustrating the possibility of what I would call a critical ethics, this is not to dismiss as 'apolitical' or 'postmodern' their attempt at thinking differently or to think the differ-ence within difference.

To a certain extent, too, the romantic concept of the literary absolute may be seen as an attempt to think difference differently. But the effects of this attempt are limited to a notion of self-theorizing literature as an instance of the sublime, as that-which-cannot-be-thought by practical reason. Hence the affirmation of the unpresentable absolute of literature is not so much an attempt to rethink thought as to transcend or get outside it. For romanticism, then, literature is an ethics because it says what thought (defined as reason) cannot say. And what it 'says' is that there are some things that are unsayable. The truth and beauty of being, for example, cannot be said; it has to be lived. 'To live' is not to succumb to the demands of a system – whether as a social system of moral norms or a philosophical system of conceptual norms – but to live as one imagines and desires to live. To live is to imagine, which is also not to think (at least not in the sense accorded to thinking by the system of philosophy). All of this is 'said' by literature as the 'unsayability' of what cannot be thought by thought conceived as practical reason.

It should be clear from this that there is nothing necessarily apolitical or unethical about literary theory in any of its forms. To ask the question of literature is not necessarily to avoid questions of politics and ethics. Indeed, one might well say that the romantic understanding of the system of literature as the *question* of literature provides a very open concept of 'system' which could be put to many useful political effects. Moreover, in the recognition that there are some aspects of human experience which philosophy cannot know, romanticism at least raises a suspicion that a certain order of thinking (which it perhaps defines unfairly as rationality) will never know the truth of being. Since it is that order of thinking which underlies the formation of social and political institutions, whose purpose is perhaps to discipline us to live according to the interests of those institutions, then clearly a critique of such thinking could open onto the possibility of socio-political critique.

For the most part, however, the romantic opposition to reason has not led to very much in the way of political pragmatics. This, I have suggested, is because its opposition to reason is also an opposition to society, or at any rate to concepts of system. So in opposing reason and society, romanticism affirms a certain ideal of the 'asystematic' as a space outside the regulatory force of rational thought. It is this ideal which postmodernism has inherited, via the psychoanalytic concept of the asystematic unconscious and the structuralist concept of the asystematic or arbitrary sign. But the locus of this ideal remains the romantic conception of the literary text as what must always remain unpresentable to rationality. Hence it is as a work of literature that the unconscious may be understood to say what reason is unable to say, or that the structure of language comprises more than is merely sayable. While there is no doubt that 'being' does exceed whatever is understood as reasonable or whatever can be put into words, this does not mean that what is understood as reasonable and what is able to be said are therefore external to being. The truth of being cannot be found only within 'culture' as a space of textual operations analogous to the work of the literary absolute. For if being is confined to 'cultural being', then the lives of social beings must be seen as less than human. On this model the purpose of being would be to escape the oppressive force of social structures by entering the transcendent realm of culture, where one is allowed 'to be' in ways which are undetermined by the rules and procedures of social institutions, political ideals, moral norms and rational beliefs. If postmodernism, however, has given up on the possibility of such 'escape', so that the romantic stance of rebellious disrespect has been made over into an attitude of cynicism, this may simply be because postmodernism regards all structures in terms of the operations of the literary text.[17] As a 'structure', every literary text is without origin and telos; its operations are undetermined by an authorial consciousness, or by the rules of a genre or the contours of a tradition. Every literary text is open to be read in multiple ways, according to the different contexts in which it is read and to the different identities and interests of its readers. Hence the 'structure' of the literary text is 'structureless'. But while the concept of 'nonstructure' was once confined to the romantic theory of literature, and therefore seen as the exemplary possibility of self-affirmation via the escape from social production into the transcendent realm of cultural producing, it is seen now by postmodernism as the condition of all structures. So the concept of nonstructure no longer functions as a special case, but has been taken back (as it were) into the world of the social. All structures – in the form of an ideal, a metanarrative, a social institution, a political system, a method of analysis and so on – are regarded by postmodernism as 'oppressive' because they are forced to conceal the fact that they are 'structureless'. What was once seen as special to literature is now seen as absolutely routine and inseparable from society. And once society is seen to function as a work of literature, why should anyone believe that there is any rational basis on which to judge one 'reading' as better than another? There is no right reading of any text, but only a multiplicity of readings.

One of the most famous alternatives to postmodern multiplicity is Habermas's notion of 'communicative rationality', as discussed in the essay 'Modernity – An Incomplete Project' that he first gave as a talk in 1980 and which was published the following year. For Habermas, the enlightenment project of developing a consensual public sphere, based on the values of reasoned debate and reasonable comportment, cannot be given up simply because of postmodernism's cynical disbelief in the possibility of communal understanding. Far from being radical, moreover, such cynicism is actually 'neoconservative'. On Habermas's view, the truth about postmodernism is that it falsely attributes a contemporary incredulity towards grand narratives of social organization, historical progress and political will, to changes in the field of culture. 'In fact, however, culture is intervening in the creation of all these problems in only a very indirect and mediated fashion.'[18] The real problem, as Habermas sees it, is that an increasing sense of discontent and powerlessness is felt today because 'the dynamics of economic growth and the organizational accomplishments of the state' are pressing 'deeper and deeper into previous forms of human existence', sending shock-waves through 'the communicative infrastructure of everyday life'.[19] Like Deleuze and Guattari, then, Habermas is no friend of 'the State'. But unlike them he refuses to let go of rational conduct as the foundation of ethical life. It is in this refusal, however, that his arguments against postmodernism can be seen to run along the single purpose of accom-

plishing a totalizing negation of the postmodern, which is why I have not
spent much time calling on Habermas as a witness in my critique of
postmodernism here. The point, really, is that Habermas does not want
to debate postmodernism; he wants to silence it. To do this he must deny
any credibility to it whatsoever, all in the name of a defence of what
Habermas calls 'reason'. His method of debating-by-negating, as it were,
turns into a kind of theological diatribe – rather than anything which
might be called a reasoned defence of reason – in his treatment of
Derrida, whom he regards wrongly as the very pith and psyche of the
postmodern and to whom he attributes all manner of ridiculous ideas
and statements without actually quoting a single word that Derrida has
written.[20]

I have tried to argue something different, though. In my view,
Habermas's relation to postmodernism is quite uninteresting and very
ineffective. Indeed, I think it is ineffective because it is uninteresting; and
what makes it uninteresting is Habermas's repetition of the tiresome
prejudice that society is a matter of life and death, but culture is a game.
Society has got economics and politics; culture has got aesthetics and
privilege. Faced with that opposition, who – when push came to shove –
would be prepared to stand up for culture? Yet if it were argued that it
is the *structure* of that opposition which *effects* the support for 'society',
then surely that argument would count as an example of reason in
practice. Surely, too, the structure of that opposition could therefore be
seen as oppressive. Now it may well be that postmodernism exaggerates
the 'argument' against structure, and it could be that in doing so it
undervalues the importance of practical reason; but that doesn't mean it
has nothing to say about concepts of 'structure' which should not be
listened to, or that one should try to counter the postmodern concept of
'nonstructure' simply by reaffirming the unimpeachable authority and
stability of reason. The defence of reason should not have to exclude the
critique of reason; indeed without the possibility of critique, any defence
of reason could never be anything other than an expression of faith or
superstition. This is the lesson, it could be said, which poststructuralism
gives us to contemplate; a lesson, or a challenge, which is inseparable
from a certain ideal of the Enlightenment and of the promise of democracy to come. The poststructuralist critique of structure, in other words,
is neither unreasonable nor undemocratic. Moreover, in its critical approach to structure, poststructuralism – or deconstruction – stands in a
far more interesting relation to postmodernism than is the case with a
position such as Habermas's, which is simply one of unenlightened

refusal and belligerent opposition. There are, I think, good reasons for critiquing postmodernism; but unless the critique is enacted in the *name* of reason, it has no choice but to be *against* ethics.

This leads to a very simple point. The romantico-postmodern opposition to reason should, on behalf of reason, be welcomed. While its desire to find a space outside metaphysics may delude postmodern literary theory into thinking the possibility of a 'nonmetaphysics', the delusion itself cannot be seen as nonmetaphysical. The 'delusion' is actual; it belongs to metaphysics. In other words we cannot separate rational thought and actuality from their opposites; and in this way the postmodern 'delusion' may tell us something about the nature of reason. What it may tell us is that desire and reason are not opposed, even if postmodern literary theory comes close to saying that they are. In the nonoppositional relations of desire and reason, then, concepts of structure can be seen as open and indeterminate. This does not mean that structures are in fact structureless, but simply that their operations cannot be understood by theory alone. If the concept of structure and the structure of the concept are not pure abstractions or products of pure thought, separated out from the pragmatics of everyday socio-political and historical living, then there can be no point in trying to oppose 'theory' and 'pragmatics', culture and society, ideals and actualities, and so on. For literary studies, this may indicate a need to reconsider the concept and structure of the literary text in terms of a nonoppositional relationship between theory and pragmatics. Such a reconsideration would be concerned to see literature in terms of its 'external' relations to history, politics and society – as well as to theory. This would involve having to consider the question of *how* to approach literary texts, on the understanding that the structure of the literary text is not a sublime ideal but a pragmatic problem. Literature would no longer be seen in terms of an essence, then, but as an assemblage; and so literary texts could be approached not as part of a system of values, but *as* the problem of how to approach them. Hence the question of 'the text' would be seen as indissociable from the question of ethics, calling for a pragmatic response. If – against its own intentions, as it were – postmodern literary theory helps to show this to literary studies, then perhaps it is not the death of literature (and with it, the collapse of civilization) but the return of reason that postmodern literary theory may yet help to bring about.

Notes

Chapter 1   Mind and Myth

1   See the poem 'An Essay on Criticism', in Pope, *Selected Poetry and Prose*.
2   Manley, *Convention*, p. 2.
3   Freud, *Introductory Lectures*, pp. 243–5, 372–82.
4   See Mickler, *Gambling*.
5   Strachey, 'Some Unconscious Factors', p. 329.
6   Ibid.
7   Ibid., p. 331. But don't 'daughters' read?
8   See Klein, *Psycho-Analysis of Children*.
9   Strachey, 'Some Unconscious Factors', p. 330.
10   Freud, *Introductory Lectures*, p. 373.
11   Lévi-Strauss, *Structural Anthropology*, pp. 68–9.
12   See Saussure, *Course*.
13   Lévi-Strauss, *Structural Anthropology*, p. 69.
14   Ibid., p. 210.
15   Ibid.
16   Ibid., p. 215.
17   Ibid., p. 214.
18   Ibid., p. 216.
19   Ibid.
20   Ibid., p. 217.
21   Ibid.
22   Pynchon, *Crying of Lot 49*, p. 118.
23   Thwaites, 'Miracles', p. 86.
24   Ibid., p. 87.
25   Mendelson, 'Sacred', p. 118.
26   The idea that presence and absence form a set of complex relations is one of
      the key ideas of poststructuralism, as I will discuss more fully in chapter 5,
      though the postmodern view is rather different. For a reading of Pynchon in

terms of this and many other poststructuralist ideas, see McHoul and Wills, *Writing Pynchon*.

27 On this reasoning there would be nothing to prevent the 'tradition' being seen to emerge far earlier still, say with Laurence Sterne's *Tristram Shandy* published over the years 1759–67. Indeed such reasoning is crucial, as I discuss in chapter 6, to a certain idea of 'metafiction' which both precedes and is contained in the idea of 'postmodern' literature.

28 The exact term is the 'dissociation of sensibility', which roughly refers to the separation of ideas and feelings that occurred, according to Eliot, in the seventeenth century (locating the Enlightenment as the birth of modern society) and 'from which we have never recovered'. Since that time, European civilization (though Eliot's focus was on English poetry) has suffered from being either too rational or too sentimental and so there has been this 'dissociation of sensibility'. See the essay 'Metaphysical Poets', in Eliot, *Selected Prose*, first published in 1921.

29 See the poem 'The Hollow Men' (1925), in Eliot, *Selected Poems*.

30 See especially Foucault, *Order of Things* and *Archaeology of Knowledge*.

31 'Exhaustion', though, is an important concept to John Barth on metafiction (see chapter 6) and to Fredric Jameson on postmodernism (see chapter 12).

32 This does not mean – far from it, as we will see later – that the 'sound and fury' of postmodernism must be heeded. As John Frow puts it: 'Pseudo-totalities generate pseudo-histories; the epochal concept of the postmodern depends for its existence on such historico-spiritual fictions' (*What Was Postmodernism?*, p. 35).

33 A general disbelief in all such explanations is what characterizes the 'postmodern condition', according to Jean-François Lyotard, whose views I begin to discuss in chapter 3. See chapter 8 for a discussion of the supposed loss of faith in a Marxist explanation of culture as a necessary feature of the very idea of that 'condition'.

Chapter 2   Simulation and the Sublime

1 Braidotti, *Patterns of Dissonance*, p. 17.
2 Lacan, 'Insistence of the Letter', p. 97.
3 See *Meditations on First Philosophy*, published originally in Latin in 1641, in Descartes, *Philosophical Writings*.
4 Lacan, 'Insistence of the Letter', p. 87.
5 Saussure's theory of 'reality' need not be inconsistent, therefore, with Freud's theory of the 'reality-principle' discussed in the previous chapter. For Saussure, reality may not be positive but this does not make it ineffective.
6 Eagleton, *Literary Theory*, p. 168.
7 Felman, *Jacques Lacan*, p. 156.

8 Lacoue-Labarthe and Nancy, *Literary Absolute* (French 1978), p. 2.

9 'Parapraxis' is the word coined by James Strachey for the German word *Fehlleistungen* ('faulty acts') and refers to such phenomena as a slip of the tongue, a misreading or a mishearing. Freud devotes *Psychopathology of Everyday Life* to the analysis of such phenomena, and see also the section 'Parapraxes' in *Introductory Lectures*, pp. 50–108.

10 Kristeva, *Desire in Language*, p. viii.

11 Kristeva, *Nations Without Nationalism*, pp. 92–3.

12 See McHoul and Lucy, 'That Film'.

13 Coleridge, *Biographia Literaria*, p. 152.

14 Cited in Lacoue-Labarthe and Nancy, *Literary Absolute*, p. 6.

15 Shelley, *Selected Poetry and Prose*, pp. 447–8. The 'last national struggle' is a reference to the English Civil Wars of the 1640s resulting in the execution of Charles I in 1649 and the inauguration of Oliver Cromwell as 'Protector' of England in 1653.

16 Ibid., p. 445. The embedded quotation (which is actually a slight misquotation) is from Milton, *Paradise Lost*, I. 254–5: see Milton, *Poetical Works*.

17 Kant, *Critique of Judgement*, p. 93 (§ 24). For further discussion of Kant's philosophy, see chapters 9–12.

18 Lacoue-Labarthe and Nancy, *Literary Absolute*, p. 11.

19 Barthes, *Image Music Text*, pp. 156–7. The essay is called 'From Work to Test', published originally in French in 1971. For a somewhat different notion of 'work' (closer perhaps to what Barthes means by 'text'), see the discussion of Heidegger beginning in chapter 10.

20 Keats, 'Ode on a Grecian Urn', in *Poems*.

21 Baudrillard, *Simulations*, p. 11.

22 Ibid., p. 25.

23 Ibid., pp. 25–6.

24 Acker, *Empire of the Senseless*, p. 12.

Chapter 3   The Death of History

1 Wordsworth, *Selected Poems and Prefaces*, pp. 449–50.

2 Ibid., p. 448.

3 Ibid., p. 447.

4 Ibid., p. 449.

5 See Virilio, *War and Cinema*.

6 Rousseau, *Émile*, p. 26.

7 Ibid., p. 18.

8 Ibid., p. 414.

9 Ibid., p. 131.

10 Ibid., p. 46.

11 Hobbes, *Leviathan*, p. 186.

12 Acker, *Empire of the Senseless*, p. 29.

13 Blake, *Selected Poems*. From the evidence of Blake's notebook, known as the Rossetti MS., 'London' is thought to have been written around 1791–2.

14 Berlin, *Crooked Timber*, p. 232. The quotation is from 'The Apotheosis of the Romantic Will: The Revolt Against the Myth of an Ideal World' (published originally in Italian, 1975).

15 It is geometry, rather than philosophy, that provides the best method of social analysis and the model of social order: 'And the reason is manifest. For there is not one of them [the philosophers] that begins his ratiocination from the Definitions, or Explications of the names they are to use; which is a method that hath been used onely in Geometry; whose Conclusions have thereby been made indisputable' (Hobbes, *Leviathan*, pp. 113–14).

16 Ibid., pp. 116–17.

17 Acker, *Empire of the Senseless*, p. 17.

18 Hobbes, *Leviathan*, p. 185.

19 Acker, *Empire of the Senseless*, p. 95.

20 Baudrillard, *Simulations*, pp. 11–12.

21 On the terms *langue* and *parole*, see Saussure, *Course*, pp. 17–20, where these are translated as 'language' and 'speech' respectively.

22 Baudrillard, *Simulations*, p. 146.

23 Ibid.

24 Ibid., p. 125.

25 Ibid., pp. 147–8.

26 Acker, *Empire of the Senseless*, p. 28.

27 Ibid., p. 38.

28 Baudrillard, *Simulations*, p. 12.

29 Acker, *Empire of the Senseless*, p. 227.

30 This is not to deny, as I note in chapter 12, the legitimacy and popularity of what is now called the 'graphic' novel, which both extends and challenges an idea of 'the novel' as such.

31 Acker, *Empire of the Senseless*, p. 55.

32 Ibid., p. 69.

33 Ibid., pp. 133–4.

34 See Wittgenstein, *Blue and Brown Books* (which he wrote separately in the 1930s although they did not appear until 1958, published as a single volume) and *Philosophical Investigations* (1953).

35 Wittgenstein, *Blue Book*, p. 17.

36 Lyotard, *Postmodern Condition*, p. xxiii.

37 See, for example, Harding, *Whose Science?*

38 See Austin, *How To Do Things*.

39 Lyotard, *Postmodern Condition*, p. 9.

Chapter 4   Literature and the Liminal

1 McHale, *Postmodernist Fictions*, p. 3. Notice that McHale starts out by putting postmodernism as a question and into question. This too may be a typical move. See, among other examples, the start of American art critic Hal Foster's editorial introduction to *Postmodern Culture* (published originally in 1983 as *The Anti-Aesthetic*): 'Postmodernism: does it exist at all and, if so, what does it mean?' (p. ix), and the start of Canadian cultural theorists Arthur Kroker and David Cook's first chapter in *Postmodern Scene*: 'What is the postmodern scene?' (p. 7).
2 Lyotard, *Postmodern Condition*, p. 10.
3 Ibid., p. 81.
4 Lacoue-Labarthe and Nancy, *Literary Absolute*, pp. 11–12. Heidegger (see especially chapter 10) is a crucial source of their argument here.
5 Shelley, *Selected Poetry and Prose*, p. 443. The quotation is from 'A Defence of Poetry'.
6 Ibid.
7 Lyotard, *Postmodern Condition*, p. 27.
8 Ibid., p. 25.
9 Ibid.
10 Ibid., p. 27.
11 Ibid.
12 Ibid., p. 26.
13 Ibid., p. 46.
14 Connor, *Postmodernist Culture*, p. 32.
15 Jameson, 'Foreword', p. viii.
16 Carroll, *Paraesthetics*, p. 158.
17 Lyotard, *Differend*, p. xii.
18 Ibid., p. xi.
19 Ibid., p. 66.
20 Ibid., p. xii.
21 Carroll, *Paraesthetics*, p. 166.
22 It is of course possible to defend a notion of academic standards, or to justify the logic of argumentation and proof, without holding to a 'progressivist' theory of history.
23 Barthes, *S/Z*, p. 5.
24 Ibid., p. 10.
25 Ibid., p. 5.
26 See Rorty, *Contingency, Irony, Solidarity*.
27 Norris, *Truth and the Ethics of Criticism*, p. 12.
28 This is the refrain of the eponymous scrivener, 'Bartleby', in Melville, *Billy Budd, Sailor and Other Stories*.
29 Norris, *Truth and the Ethics of Criticism*, p. 13.

Chapter 5   Interpretation as Invention

1   In this respect the term was used more or less descriptively, as distinct from the term 'metanarrative' in Lyotard, where the prefix 'meta-' carries a pejorative sense of 'higher', 'transcendental' or 'grand'.

2   Hassan, *Radical Innocence*, pp. 115–18.

3   Ibid., pp. 102–3. Hassan turned out to be wrong about the obsolescence of 'longer novels'. Throughout the 1960s, American fiction was indeed characterized by the popularity of shorter forms, but this has to be set against the many novels of extreme length that were also published in the period and which were no less favoured critically.

4   Tanner, *City of Words*, p. 29.

5   Ibid., p. 404 (Barthelme) and p. 410 (Brautigan).

6   Roth, 'Writing American Fiction', p. 224.

7   Podhoretz, 'Article as Art', pp. 77–8.

8   Zavarzadeh, *Mythopoeic Reality*, p. 115.

9   Ibid., p. 117.

10 Ibid., pp. 35–6.

11 See especially Kuhn, *Structure of Scientific Revolutions*.

12 Kroker and Cook, *Postmodern Scene*, pp. 12–13. The term *ressentiment* is Nietzschean and refers to a kind of moral sickness by which one is required to regard others unfavourably in order to think better of oneself: see Tapper, '*Ressentiment* and Power'.

13 In France, at least, the popularity of *Anti-Oedipus* was not restricted to an academic readership, and in this its influence is comparable to Frazer's *The Golden Bough*, for which the author wrote an abridged version in 1922. I discuss Deleuze and Guattari's work, and Nietzsche's influence on it, in chapters 10–12.

14 The sentiment is formalized in *Culture and Anarchy* (1867–9), where Arnold defines culture as 'the *best* knowledge and thought of the time, and a true source, therefore, of sweetness and light' (p. 79).

15 Hassan, *Paracriticisms*, p. 3.

16 Brown, *Love's Body*, p. 243.

17 Hassan, *Paracriticisms*, p. 174.

18 Ibid., p. 175.

19 See especially Habermas, *Philosophical Discourse*.

20 See Macksey and Donato (eds), *Structuralist Controversy*, for the conference proceedings, including 'Structure, Sign and Play'. However, I will be quoting from the Alan Bass translation of Derrida's paper in *Writing and Difference*.

21 Derrida, *Writing and Difference*, p. 285. For the account of bricolage and its difference from engineering discourse, see Lévi-Strauss, *Savage Mind*.

22 Derrida, *Writing and Difference*, p. 285.

23 Ibid.

24   Ibid., p. 278.
25   Ibid., pp. 280–1.
26   Norris, *Derrida*, p. 139.
27   Derrida, *Limited Inc*, pp. 115–16. The quotation is from 'Afterword: Toward an Ethic of Discussion'.

Chapter 6   The Death of Criticism

1   Barth, 'Literature of Exhaustion', p. 79.
2   Ibid. The references are to Cervantes' *Don Quixote* (1605–15), Henry Fielding's *Tom Jones* (1749) and Samuel Richardson's *Clarissa* (1747–8).
3   Ibid., pp. 70–1.
4   B. S. Johnson, 'Introduction to *Aren't You Rather Young?*', p. 151.
5   Barth, 'Literature of Exhaustion', p. 72.
6   Ibid., p. 79.
7   Ibid., p. 77.
8   Ibid., p. 71.
9   See especially Searle, *Speech Acts* and *Intentionality*. For a discussion of Searle's rather odd but extremely influential version of speech-act theory, see the chapter 'Austin and Searle Together and Apart', in Petrey, *Speech Acts and Literary Theory*. For further discussion of Searle's ideas in relation to literary theory, see Lucy and McHoul, 'Logical Status'.
10 A speech act is 'felicitous', for Austin, if its outcome is successful or valid according to social rules. A marriage ceremony would be felicitous if performed by an official celebrant and if both bride and groom were not married to someone else at the time of the ceremony. But if any of those conditions did not apply, the ceremony would be infelicitous; that is, it would be invalid or unsuccessful. While this looks like a very nice distinction, though, Austin himself is never quite able to maintain it, except as an ideal. As Norris rather wryly puts it in *Deconstructive Turn*, speech-act theory 'begins to look less like a philosophy of "how to do things with words", and more like a case of how words do unexpected things with what philosophers want to say' (p. 74): see the chapter ' "That the Truest Philosophy is the Most Feigning": Austin on the Margins of Literature'.
11 De Man, *Resistance to Theory*, p. 15. The essay 'The Resistance to Theory' was published originally in *Yale French Studies* in 1982.
12 There are many references that might be given here. But the main one I have in mind for now is *Of Grammatology*, especially the section entitled ' "… That Dangerous Supplement…" ' to which I will be referring in a moment.
13 De Man, *Resistance to Theory*, p. 13.
14 Gadamer, *Philosophical Hermeneutics*, p. 25. The quotation is from 'On the Scope and Function of Hermeneutical Reflection'.

15 Derrida borrows the term 'undecidable' from an essay published in 1931, 'On Formally Undecidable Propositions of Principia Mathematica and Related Systems', by the German mathematician Kurt Gödel. As Derrida explains in *Dissemination*, an undecidable proposition is one 'which, given a system of axioms governing a multiplicity, is neither an analytical nor deductive consequence of those axioms, nor in contradiction with them, neither true nor false with respect to those axioms' (p. 219).

16 Norris, *Derrida*, p. 29.

17 Derrida, *Dissemination*, p. 128.

18 Derrida, *Of Grammatology*, pp. 144–5. For an excellent and more extensive discussion of Derrida's reading of the *pharmakon*, see the chapter 'Derrida on Plato: Writing as Poison and Cure', in Norris, *Derrida*.

19 The 'dangerousness' of writing is actually a reference to Rousseau, whose concept of Nature is the explicit object of Derrida's critique here. But the 'threat' of supplementarity extends to every concept of presence, and so it can be seen as active in the formation of Plato's notion of speech.

Chapter 7   Rhetorical Reading

1 Kennedy, *Art of Persuasion*, p. 23.

2 Nietzsche and Heidegger were both influenced by the pre-Socratics, while, more recently, Lucé Irigaray's project of the possibility of thinking the feminine as something other than simply 'the other' of the masculine may be a return to a broadly-conceived pre-Socratic mode of thought. For Irigaray, the most pressing question of our time is that of 'sexual difference' and the challenge is to think such difference in ways that do not rely on a notion of 'sexual opposition': see, for example, *Ethics of Sexual Difference*, published originally in French in 1984.

3 Melville, *Moby-Dick*, p. 443.

4 See Aristotle, *Poetics*. By 'imitation' or 'mimesis', however, Aristotle does not mean that art should resemble nature according to mere appearances. It is not the products but the productive forces of nature that art imitates, and so on this view realism could be only one form (and by no means necessarily the highest one) of such imitation.

5 How could a work of literature be made up entirely of something other than words, for example? And no matter how 'transgressively' the words were used, how could they not refer to something other than just themselves (without becoming a 'private language')? Postmodern literature may try to overcome text–world relations by collapsing everything onto the plane of 'text', but that does not mean that realist literature is therefore 'unaware' of itself *as text*, as if it could be understood to function somehow as pure 'world'.

6 De Man, *Resistance to Theory*, p. 14.

7 For a concise discussion of the critical differences at stake in commentaries on the story, see Anderson, ' "Fury of Intention" '.
8 Johnson, *Critical Difference*, pp. x–xi.
9 James, *Turn of the Screw*, p. 147.
10 Johnson, *Critical Difference*, p. 79.
11 Ibid., p. 80.
12 Ibid.
13 Ibid.
14 Melville, *Billy Budd*, p. 405.
15 Johnson, *Critical Difference*, p. 80.
16 Culler, *On Deconstruction*, p. 237. Culler includes a discussion of Johnson's reading of *Billy Budd* in his chapter 'Deconstructive Criticism'.
17 Johnson, *Critical Difference*, p. 104.
18 Ibid., p. 105.
19 Ibid., p. 106.
20 Ibid., p. 108.
21 Ibid., p. 106.
22 Culler, *On Deconstruction*, p. 237.
23 Ibid., p. 238.
24 Johnson, *Critical Difference*, p. 108.
25 Ibid.
26 Melville, *Billy Budd*, p. 363.
27 Ibid.
28 Johnson, *Critical Difference*, p. 107.
29 Ibid.
30 Caputo, *Against Ethics*, p. 78. The 'great poet' is T. S. Eliot, and the poem referred to is 'The Ad-dressing of Cats' from *Old Possum's Book of Practical Cats* (1939).

Chapter 8   Performing Politics

1 For the New Critics, whose dominance was felt especially in the United States from the 1930s through to the late 1950s, works of literature (but principally poems) were understood as sensuous entities in their own right which needed to be studied in isolation from the social and other contexts in which they were written. For contrasting accounts of the purpose and effects of such a project, see both the chapter 'The New Criticism', in Wellek, *History of Modern Criticism*; and the chapter 'The Rise of English', in Eagleton, *Literary Theory*.
2 See de Man, *Blindness and Insight* and *Allegories of Reading*; Hartman, *Fate of Reading* and *Saving the Text*; and Miller, *Fiction and Repetition*. Harold Bloom is another figure associated with deconstruction at Yale, despite his allegiance to a steadfast notion of literary value which has tended to mark

him as controversial or, from a different point of view, as the very confirma-
tion of deconstruction's real agenda: see Bloom, *Anxiety of Influence* and
Map of Misreading. For a volume containing essays by all members of the
Yale 'school', including Derrida, see Bloom et al. (eds), *Deconstruction and
Criticism*.

3 This is very much the view expressed recently by Harold Bloom, in equal
parts elegy and polemic, across almost 600 pages of *The Western Canon*. I
will have more to say about Bloom in chapter 9.

4 See Gleick, *Chaos*, for a survey of mathematical and scientific investigations
of the uncertain, irregular and erratic aspects of many natural laws.

5 The nature of 'certainty' has been a question also for twentieth-century
scientists, who have by no means abandoned themselves to the mathematical
equivalent of hermeneutic 'freeplay' simply because of developments in the
field of chaos theory. As the physicist Mitchell J. Fiegenbaum, speaking of
the revolution caused by quantum mechanics in the 1920s, put it in a
conversation with James Gleick: 'If you start asking more and more subtle
questions – what does this theory tell you the world looks like? – in the end
it's so far out of your normal way of picturing things that you run into all
sorts of conflicts. Now maybe that's the way the world really is. But you
don't really know that there isn't another way of assembling all this information that doesn't demand so radical a departure from the way in which
you intuit things' (Gleick, *Chaos*, p. 185).

6 Derrida, *Specters*, p. 11.

7 Shakespeare, *Hamlet*, 3.1.56.

8 Derrida, *Specters*, p. 7.

9 The ghost is also, of course, what disjoins or unhinges (the concept of) time
itself. 'The time', as Hamelt says after his encounter with the spectre, 'is out
of joint' (1.5.188).

10 On the question of Derrida's relations to 'politics', see my *Debating Derrida*.

11 Shakespeare, *Hamlet*, 1.4.39–57.

12 John Dover Wilson glosses 'questionable' as 'that may be interrogated or
spoken to' (see Shakespeare, *Hamlet*, p. 282).

13 Derrida, *Specters*, p. 63.

14 Ibid.

15 The term 'effective history' derives from Nietzsche (see *Genealogy of Morals*, first published in German in 1887) and is crucial to Foucault's approach
to historical events (see the essay 'Nietzsche, Genealogy, History', in
Foucault Reader), as I discuss in chapter 11.

16 Derrida, *Specters*, p. 10. 'Being' (with a capital 'B') is a reference to
Heidegger, *Being and Time*, first published in German in 1927.

17 Derrida, *Specters*, pp. 81–4.

18 The point here is that events should not be confined to what is calculable
according to conventional logic, as this would allow (for example) the

'phantom-States' of the mafia and drug cartels to remain invisible – because they do not look like nation-states. For a ghost logic, however, the apparent virtuality of international crime syndicates and other such 'non-present' events would not allow them to go unnoticed simply because they seem incalculable according to a demand for events to appear as manifest actualities.

19 Indeed, it is worth being reminded that today, in the moment of the so-called triumph of democracy, 'never have violence, inequality, exclusion, famine, and thus economic oppression affected as many human beings in the history of the earth and of humanity' (Derrida, *Specters*, p. 85).

20 Whatever is supposed 'to come' (the absolute of history, literature, democracy, truth and so on) must, according to Derrida's argument in *Specters*, *remain* as coming, and this is consistent with his critique of structure and presence in earlier works. Hence the absolute of history and so forth (or the essence of Marx's revolutionary spirit) remains a kind of secret, whose manifestation is always deferred or always 'remains to come'.

21 This is not to deny the force of an 'ecstatic' mode (as seen in Hassan, for example), but simply to acknowledge the higher 'chic' value of the postmodern parodic as seen in the likes of Baudrillard and Acker.

22 The second chapter of Bloom's *Western Canon*, for instance, is entitled 'Shakespeare, Center of the Canon'. Hence Shakespeare is 'the largest writer we will ever know' (p. 3).

Chapter 9   The Death of Theory

1 Bloom, *Western Canon*, pp. 517–18.

2 Johnson, *Rambler*, p. 986.

3 It should not be overlooked that the many periodicals in circulation from the mid to late eighteenth century were addressed to both sexes. Women readers formed an important constituency, and the periodicals (although written and published predominantly by men) contributed greatly to raising the status and education of women.

4 Johnson, *Rasselas*, p. 1059.

5 Kant, 'Answer to the Question: What is Enlightenment?', p. 58.

6 Rousseau, *Discourses*, pp. 37–8.

7 For a discussion of that other reviler of 'the herd' – Nietzsche – see chapters 10 and 11.

8 Rousseau, *Discourses*, pp. 49–50.

9 Ibid., p. 64. In his later work, Foucault also argues for a return to the ancient ethical practice of the relation of a self *to* itself: see Foucault, *Care of the Self*.

10 Rousseau, *Considerations*, pp. 185–6.

11 Cited in Gay, *Enlightenment*, p. 7.

12 Boswell, *Life*, p. 310. The entry is dated Wednesday, 20 July, 1763 (that is, following the publication of *Émile*).

13 Ibid., p. 359 (Saturday, 15 February, 1766). Boswell took a different view, however, and kept company with Rousseau during the year he spent in England while still in self-imposed exile from France.

14 Bloom, *Western Canon*, p. 521.

15 Ibid., p. 520.

16 Rousseau, *Émile*, p. 346.

17 Cited in Gay, *Enlightenment*, pp. 6–7.

18 The temptation to glibness, rather, might point the other way.

19 Kant, *Critique of Judgement*, p. 165 (§ 44).

20 Ibid., p. 168 (§ 46).

21 Cited in Carroll, *Paraesthetics*, p. 173. This is Carroll's translation from Lyotard's *Instructions païennes* (*Pagan Lessons*, perhaps), a work which appeared in French in 1977 but has yet to appear in English.

22 The *Critique of Pure Reason* first appeared in 1781 and, with a revised preface, again in 1787, followed by The *Critique of Practical Reason* in 1788.

23 Lyotard is following Kant here: 'it is not man's cognitive faculty, that is, theoretical reason, that forms the point of reference which alone gives its worth to the existence of all else in the world [. . .]', Kant writes. 'On the contrary, it is the worth which he alone can give to himself, and which consists in what he does – in the manner in which and the principles upon which he acts in the *freedom* of his faculty of desire, and not as a link in the chain of nature' (*Critique of Judgement*, pp. 108–9 [§ 86]). See also Kant, 'Renewed Attempt', where he considers the importance of a certain 'disinterestedness' in relation to the ethico-political (he uses the example of the spectators to the French Revolution).

24 Lyotard, *Differend*, p. 118.

25 Ibid., p. 119.

26 Ibid., p. 120.

27 Ibid., p. 13.

28 Ibid., pp. 56–7.

29 Ibid., pp. 57–8.

30 The American critic John Crowe Ransom, for instance, whose book *The New Criticism* (1941) gave the New Criticism its name, was a great admirer of the Third *Critique*, which he saw as a radical justification of the non-objective reality and truth of poetry. This is not to say the New Critics were especially good or 'close' readers of Kant, but they were at least aware of his *Critique of Judgement*, which they took for a philosophical justification of the ineffable nature of aesthetic truth.

31 McHoul, *Semiotic Investigations*, pp. 55–6.

32 See Peirce, *Collected Papers*.

33 Ibid., p. 56.
34 Lyotard, *Differend*, p. 57.
35 See for example, Kant, *Critique of Pure Reason*, pp. 210–15.
36 Ruthrof, *Pandora and Occam*, p. 126.
37 Ibid., p. 122.
38 Lyotard, *Differend*, p. 70.
39 DeLillo, *White Noise*, p. 103.
40 McHoul, *Semiotic Investigations*, p. 57.
41 Ibid., p. 58.
42 Derrida, *Truth in Painting*, p. 143.
43 Ibid., p. 128.
44 Bloom *Western Canon*, p. 1. Thereafter Kant is mentioned only once again: 'we must remind ourselves that Shakespeare, who scarcely relies upon philosophy, is more central to Western culture than are Plato and Aristotle, Kant and Hegel, Heidegger and Wittgenstein' (ibid., p. 10).
45 Ibid., p. 517.
46 See Schiller, *Aesthetic Education*, published in German in 1795.

Chapter 10   Concept Creation

1 Deleuze and Guattari, *Thousand Plateaus*, p. 15.
2 Massumi, 'Translator's Foreword', p. xiii.
3 Deleuze and Guattari, *Thousand Plateaus*, p. 15.
4 Even their name (Italian for 'political writings') nods to Derrida.
5 Massumi, 'Translator's Foreword', p. xiii.
6 Ibid., pp. xiii–xiv.
7 The shuffle function on CD-players builds in this capacity to 're-arrange' musical texts, though the capacity is extremely minimal and no great cause for thinking that consumers have been 'liberated' or that they are naturally 'creative' or 'transgressive' in their interactions with the textual products of corporate culture.
8 Deleuze and Guattari, *Thousand Plateaus*, p. 8.
9 Ibid., p. 21.
10 Wyschogrod, *Saints and Postmodernism*, p. 192.
11 Deleuze and Guattari, *Thousand Plateaus*, p. 22.
12 Ibid., p. 18.
13 Ibid., pp. 5–7.
14 Ibid., p. 6.
15 Ibid., p. 25.
16 Norris, *Truth About Postmodernism*, p. 231.
17 Deleuze and Guattari, *Thousand Plateaus*, p. 82.
18 Ibid., pp. 139–40.
19 Ibid., p. 91.

20 Ibid., p. 90.
21 Ibid., p. 91.
22 Ibid.
23 Foucault, 'Preface', p. xiii. Within a few years Foucault's understanding of 'ethics' would change quite radically: see ch. 9, n. 9.
24 Cited in Massumi, *User's Guide*, p. 2.
25 See Deleuze, *Nietzsche and Philosophy*; and Nietzsche, *Will to Power*.
26 Caputo, *Against Ethics*, pp. 44–5.
27 See especially Althusser, *For Marx* (French 1965) and *Essays on Ideology*, containing several of his important essays from the period; see also Kaplan and Sprinker (eds), *Althusserian Legacy*. For Freud's discussion of over-determination, see Breur and Freud, *Studies on Hysteria* (German 1893–5).
28 Marx, *Capital*, p. 324.
29 Deleuze and Guattari, *Anti-Oedipus*, p. 7.
30 Ibid.
31 Ibid., p. 23.
32 Deleuze and Guattari, *Thousand Plateaus*, p. 238.
33 Deleuze and Guattari, *Anti-Oedipus*, p. 15.
34 Boyne, *Deleuze and Guattari*, p. 149.
35 Deleuze and Guattari, *Anti-Oedipus*, p. 23.
36 Deleuze and Guattari, *Thousand Plateaus*, p. 25.
37 See especially Hegel, *Phenomenology of Spirit* (German 1807); see also Gasché, *Tain of the Mirror*, pp. 23–65.
38 Caputo, *Against Ethics*, p. 51.
39 See Massumi, *User's Guide*, which is more an imitation than an explanation of the 'capitalism and schizophrenia' project. In a sense, of course, Deleuze and Guattari call for such imitation (as a form of dissemination) as the only way of 'explaining' them.
40 Heidegger, *Poetry, Language, Thought*, p. 39.
41 Ibid.
42 Schrag, 'Transvaluation of Aesthetics', p. 116.
43 Heidegger, *Poetry, Language, Thought*, p. 73.
44 Deleuze and Guattari, *What is Philosophy?*, p. 22.
45 Ibid., p. 20.
46 Ibid., p. 41.
47 Ibid.
48 Lacoue-Labarthe, *Subject of Philosophy*, p. 128.

Chapter 11 Ethical Evaluations

1 Cited in Veatch, *Rational Man*, p. 41.
2 Foucault, 'Nietzsche, Genealogy, History', in *Foucault Reader*, p. 81.
3 Ibid., p. 76.

4 Ibid., p. 84.
5 Foucault, 'Preface', p. xii.
6 Foucault, 'Nietzsche, Genealogy, History', p. 86.
7 Ibid., p. 87.
8 Ibid., pp. 87–8.
9 Ibid., p. 94.
10 Foucault, 'Preface', p. xiii.
11 Ibid., p. xiv.
12 See the essay 'Otobiography', in Derrida, *Ear of the Other*.
13 See Heidegger, *Nietzsche*.
14 See Derrida, *Spurs*.
15 It should be noted that Heidegger does not intend a kind of prephilosophical origin to have existed prior to Plato's mistake. In a sense, the 'prephilosophical' is not, for Heidegger, 'prehistorical' but rather a beginning without origin – a beginning that never 'was' (in a historical sense) but always 'is' (in a philosophical sense): see Heidegger, *Identity and Difference*.
16 Deleuze and Guattari, *What is Philosophy?*, p. 16.
17 Ibid., p. 28.
18 In this they may be seen as inheritors of Hume's sceptical approach to ideas of uniformity and causality, which made him something of a scandalous figure in Britain in the eighteenth century although he was revered as a genius in France. See Hume, *Enquiry Concerning Human Understanding*, first published in 1758; and see also Deleuze, *Empiricism and Subjectivity*, for an account of Deleuze's interest in Hume and the sceptical tradition.
19 A similar point is made in Wyschogrod, *Saints and Postmodernism*, pp. 212–14. For a remarkable reading of Deleuze and Guattari, see the chapter 'Depravity, Sanctity, and Desire' in which this point is made.
20 Caputo, *Against Ethics*, p. 58.
21 See Richards, *Practical Criticism*. This is the source of the New Critical method of 'close reading' which defined the discipline of literary studies, especially in the US, from about the mid-1930s until the advent of structuralism in the 1970s occasioned a so-called disciplinary 'crisis'.
22 Auster, *New York Trilogy*, p. 71.
23 Chandler, *Big Sleep*, p. 220. The novel was first published in 1939.
24 'Let me call myself, for the present, William Wilson. The fair page now lying before me need not be sullied with my real appellation' ('William Wilson', in Poe, *Fall of the House of Usher and Other Writings*, p. 158).
25 Auster, *New York Trilogy*, pp. 288, 270–8 and 263; and *Invention*, pp. 60–4 and 25–7.
26 Auster, *New York Trilogy*, pp. 8–9.
27 Auster, *Moon Palace*, p. 97; *Invention*, p. 60; *New York Trilogy*, p. 41.
28 Auster, *Moon Palace*, p. 72.
29 Auster, *Invention*, p. 100.

Chapter 12 The Return of Reason

1 To further complicate this question, Auster's 'writing' is now available in comic book (or 'graphic novel') format: see Karasik and Mazzucchelli, *Paul Auster's City of Glass*, the first title in a series called 'Neon Lit: Noir Illustrated', specializing in 'picture fiction' adaptations – drawn in the moody light of the film noir tradition – of contemporary American crime novels which both recreate and warp the conventions of the genre developed by Dashiell Hammett and Chandler. Moreover, Auster's 'writing' extends now also to film: his novel *The Music of Chance* (1990) has been made into a film of the same title (1994); he wrote the screenplay for director Wayne Wang's *Smoke* (1995); and more recently Auster himself wrote and directed the film *Blue in the Face* (1996).

2 Jameson, 'Postmodernism', p. 16.

3 Cadigan, *Fools*, p. 117.

4 See Gibson, *Neuromancer*. This novel too has been given the graphic adaptation treatment: see de Haveu and Jensen, *William Gibson's Neuromancer*.

5 Gibson, *Mona Lisa Overdrive*, p. 45.

6 Ellroy, *Silent Terror*, p. 8.

7 McCarthy, *Child of God*, p. 194.

8 See Grosz, *Volatile Bodies*.

9 Wyschogrod, *Saints and Postmodernism*, p. 77.

10 Bray and Colebrook, 'Haunted Flesh'.

11 I own this point to Alec McHoul.

12 Cornell, *Philosophy of the Limit*, p. 13.

13 D'Cruz, 'Responding to a Heritage', p. 167.

14 Hartman, *Criticism in the Wilderness*, p. 290.

15 Critchley, *Ethics of Deconstruction*, p. 29.

16 See Tapper, '*Ressentiment* and Power', for a discussion of this point in relation to the requirement of a certain form of feminism to regard thought as patriarchal and therefore as oppressive, especially in its operations on 'the' body.

17 Hence the postmodern may be seen as little more than a game *within* (literary) theory, as Frow argues in *What Was Postmodernism?*

18 Habermas, 'Modernity', p. 7.

19 Ibid., p. 8.

20 See the chapter 'Excursus on Leveling the Genre Distinction between Philosophy and Literature', in Habermas, *Philosophical Discourse*. For a critique of this chapter, which measures Habermas's assertions against an informed discussion of some of Derrida's writing, see the chapter 'Deconstruction, Postmodernism and Philosophy: Habermas on Derrida', in Norris, *What's Wrong with Postmodernism*.

Bibliography

Acker, Kathy. *Empire of the Senseless*. London: Pan, 1988.

Althusser, Louis. *Essays on Ideology*. London and New York: Verso, 1984.

Althusser, Louis. *For Marx*, trans. Ben Brewster. London and New York: Verso, 1979.

Anderson, Don. ' "A Fury of Intention": The Scandal of Henry James' *The Turn of the Screw*'. *Sydney Studies in English*, 15 (1989–90), pp. 140–52.

Aristotle. *Poetics: Aristotle XXIII*, trans. and ed. Stephen Halliwell. Cambridge, MA: Harvard University Press, 1995.

Arnold, Matthew. *Culture and Anarchy*, ed. J. Dover Wilson. Cambridge: Cambridge University Press, 1960.

Auster, Paul. *The Invention of Solitude*. London and Boston: Faber and Faber, 1988.

Auster, Paul. *Moon Palace*. New York: Viking, 1989.

Auster, Paul. *The New York Trilogy*. London and Boston: Faber and Faber, 1987.

Austin, J. L. *How To Do Things With Words*. London: Oxford University Press, 1962.

Barth, John. 'The Literature of Exhaustion', in *The Novel Today: Contemporary Writers on Modern Fiction*, ed. Malcolm Bradbury. London: Fontana, 1977, pp. 70–83.

Barthes, Roland. *Image Music Text*, trans. Stephen Heath. London: Fontana, 1977.

Barthes, Roland. *S/Z*, trans. Richard Miller. New York: Hill and Wang, 1974.

Baudrillard, Jean. *Simulations*, trans. Paul Foss, Paul Patton and Philip Beitchman. New York: Semiotext(e), 1983.

Berlin, Isaiah. *The Crooked Timber of Humanity: Chapters in the History of Ideas*, ed. Henry Hardy. London: John Murray, 1990.

Blake, William. *Selected Poems of William Blake*, ed. F. W. Bateson. London: Heinemann, 1957.

Bloom, Harold. *The Anxiety of Influence: A Theory of Poetry*. New York: Oxford University Press, 1973.

Bloom, Harold. *A Map of Misreading*. New York: Oxford University Press, 1975.

Bloom, Harold. *The Western Canon: The Books and School of the Ages*. London: Macmillan, 1995.

Bloom, Harold, Paul de Man, Jacques Derrida, Geoffrey Hartman and J. Hillis Miller, eds. *Deconstruction and Criticism*. London and Henley: Routledge and Kegan Paul, 1979.

Boswell, James. *Life of Johnson*. Oxford: Oxford University Press, 1970.

Boyne, Ronald. *Deleuze and Guattari*. London and New York: Routledge, 1989.

Braidotti, Rosi. *Patterns of Dissonance: A Study of Women in Contemporary Philosophy*, trans. Elizabeth Guild. New York: Routledge, 1991.

Bray, Abigail and Claire Colebrook. 'The Haunted Flesh: Corporeal Feminism and the Poetics of (dis)Embodiment'. *Signs* (1997, in press).

Breur, Josef and Sigmund Freud. *Studies on Hysteria: The Standard Edition of the Complete Psychological Works of Sigmund Freud*, vol. II, trans. and ed. James Strachey. London: Hogarth, 1955.

Brown, Norman O. *Love's Body*. New York: Vintage, 1966.

Cadigan, Pat. *Fools*. London: HarperCollins, 1994.

Caputo, John D. *Against Ethics: Contributions to a Poetics of Obligation with Constant Reference to Deconstruction*. Bloomington: Indiana University Press, 1993.

Carroll, David. *Paraesthetics: Foucault Lyotard Derrida*. New York and London: Methuen, 1987.

Chandler, Raymond. *The Big Sleep*. Harmondsworth: Penguin, 1988.

Coleridge, Samuel Taylor. *Biographia Literaria, or Biographical Sketches of My Literary Life and Opinions*, ed. George Watson. London: J. M. Dent, 1975.

Connor, Steven. *Postmodernist Culture: An Introduction to Theories of the Contemporary*. Oxford: Blackwell, 1989.

Cornell, Drucilla. *The Philosophy of the Limit*. New York and London: Routledge, 1992.

Critchley, Simon. *The Ethics of Deconstruction: Derrida and Levinas*. Oxford: Blackwell, 1992.

Culler, Jonathan. *On Deconstruction: Theory and Criticism After Structuralism*. London: Routledge and Kegan Paul, 1983.

D'Cruz, Carolyn. 'Responding to a Heritage: Justice, Deconstruction and Injunctions of Marx'. *Social Semiotics*, 6, 2 (1996), pp. 159–78.

de Haveu, Tom and Bruce Jensen. *William Gibson's Neuromancer: The Graphic Novel*. New York: Berkley, 1989.

de Man, Paul. *Allegories of Reading: Figural Language in Rousseau, Nietzsche, Rilke, and Proust*. New Haven: Yale University Press, 1979.

de Man, Paul. *Blindness and Insight: Essays in the Rhetoric of Contemporary Criticism*. New York: Oxford University Press, 1971.

de Man, Paul. *The Resistance to Theory. Theory and History of Literature*, 33. Manchester: Manchester University Press, 1986.

de Saussure, Ferdinand. *Course in General Linguistics*, trans. Wade Baskin, ed. Charles Bally and Albert Sechehaye, with Albert Reidlinger. London: Fontana, 1974.

Deleuze, Gilles. *Empiricism and Subjectivity: An Essay on Hume's Theory of Human Nature*, trans. Constantin V. Boundas. New York: Columbia University Press, 1991.

Deleuze, Gilles. *Nietzsche and Philosophy*, trans. Hugh Tomlinson. New York: Columbia University Press, 1983.

Deleuze, Gilles and Félix Guattari. *Anti-Oedipus: Capitalism and Schizophrenia*, trans. Robert Hurley, Mark Seem and Helen R. Lane. Minneapolis: University of Minnesota Press, 1983.

Deleuze, Gilles and Félix Guattari. *A Thousand Plateaus: Capitalism and Schizo phrenia*, trans. Brian Massumi. Minneapolis: University of Minnesota Press, 1987.

Deleuze, Gilles and Félix Guattari. *What is Philosophy?*, trans. Graham Burchall and Hugh Tomlinson. London: Verso, 1994.

DeLillo, Don. *White Noise*. New York: Penguin, 1986.

Derrida, Jacques. *Dissemination*, trans. Barbara Johnson. Chicago, IL: University of Chicago Press, 1981.

Derrida, Jacques. *The Ear of the Other: Otobiography, Transference, Translations: Texts and Discussions with Jacques Derrida*, trans. Peggy Kamuf. New York: Schocken, 1986.

Derrida, Jacques. *Of Grammatology*, trans. Gayatri Chakravorty Spivak. Baltimore, MD and London: The Johns Hopkins University Press, 1976.

Derrida, Jacques. *Limited Inc*, ed. Gerald Graff. Evanston, IL: Northwestern University Press, 1988.

Derrida, Jacques. *Specters of Marx: The State of the Debt, the Work of Mourning, and the New International*, trans. Peggy Kamuf. New York and London: Routledge, 1994.

Derrida, Jacques. *Spurs: Nietzsche's Styles*, trans. Barbara Harlow. Chicago, IL: University of Chicago Press, 1979.

Derrida, Jacques. *The Truth in Painting*, trans. Geoff Bennington and Ian McLeod. Chicago, IL and London: University of Chicago Press, 1987.

Derrida, Jacques. *Writing and Difference*, trans. Alan Bass. London: Routledge and Kegan Paul, 1978.

Descartes, René. *Philosophical Writings*, trans. and ed. Elizabeth Anscombe and Peter Thomas Geach. London: Thomas Nelson, 1970.

Eagleton, Terry. *Literary Theory: An Introduction*. Oxford: Blackwell, 1983.

Eliot, T. S. *Selected Poems*. London: Faber and Faber, 1954.

Eliot, T. S. *Selected Prose*, ed. Frank Kermode. London: Faber and Faber, 1975.

Ellroy, James. *Silent Terror*. London: Arrow Books, 1990.

Felman, Shoshana. *Jacques Lacan and the Adventure of Insight: Psychoanalysis in Contemporary Culture*. Cambridge, MA: Harvard University Press, 1987.

Foster, Hal. 'Postmodernism: A Preface', in *Postmodern Culture*, ed. Hal Foster. London and Sydney: Pluto, 1985, pp. ix–xvi.

Foucault, Michel. *The Archaeology of Knowledge*, trans. A. M. Sheridan Smith. London: Routledge, 1972.

Foucault, Michel. *The Care of the Self: The History of Sexuality 3*, trans. Robert Hurley. New York: Vintage Books, 1988.

Foucault, Michel. *The Foucault Reader*, ed. Paul Rabinow. Harmondsworth: Penguin, 1986.

Foucault, Michel. *The Order of Things: An Archaeology of the Human Sciences*, no trans. specified. London: Routledge, 1970.

Foucault, Michel. 'Preface' to Gilles Deleuze and Félix Guattari, *Anti-Oedipus: Capitalism and Schizophrenia*, trans. Robert Hurley, Mark Seem and Helen R. Lane. Minneapolis: University of Minnesota Press, 1983.

Freud, Sigmund. *Introductory Lectures on Psychoanalysis*, trans. James Strachey, ed. James Strachey and Angela Richards. Harmondsworth: Penguin, 1973.

Freud, Sigmund. *The Psychopathology of Everyday Life*, trans. Alan Tyson, ed. James Strachey with Angela Richards and Alan Tyson. Harmondsworth: Penguin, 1960.

Frow, John. *What Was Postmodernism?* Sydney: Local Consumption (Occasional Paper No. 11), 1991.

Fukuyama, Francis. *The End of History and the Last Man*. New York: The Free Press, 1992.

Gadamer, Hans-Georg. *Philosophical Hermeneutics*, trans. and ed. David E. Linge. Berkeley: University of California Press, 1977.

Gasché, Rodolphe. *The Tain of the Mirror: Derrida and the Philosophy of Reflection*. Cambridge, MA: Harvard University Press, 1986.

Gay, Peter. *The Enlightenment: An Interpretation: The Rise of Modern Paganism*. New York and London: W. W. Norton, 1977.

Gibson, William. *Mona Lisa Overdrive*. London: Victor Gollancz, 1988.

Gibson, William. *Neuromancer*. London: Grafton, 1986.

Gleick, James. *Chaos: Making a New Science*. London: Cardinal, 1988.

Grosz, Elizabeth. *Volatile Bodies: Toward a Corporeal Feminism*. Sydney: Allen and Unwin, 1994.

Habermas, Jürgen. 'Modernity – An Incomplete Project', trans. Seyla Ben-Habib, in *Postmodern Culture*, ed. Hal Foster. London and Sydney: Pluto, 1985, pp. 3–15.

Habermas, Jürgen. *The Philosophical Discourse of Modernity: Twelve Lectures*, trans. Frederick Lawrence. Cambridge: Polity Press, 1987.

Harding, Sandra G. *Whose Science? Whose Knowledge?: Thinking From Women's Lives*. Ithaca, NY: Cornell University Press, 1991.

Hartman, Geoffrey H. *Criticism in the Wilderness: The Study of Literature Today*. New Haven, CT and London: Yale University Press, 1980.

Hartman, Geoffrey. *The Fate of Reading and Other Essays*. Chicago, IL: University of Chicago Press, 1975.

Hartman, Geoffrey. *Saving the Text: Literature/Derrida/Philosophy*. Baltimore, MD: The Johns Hopkins University Press, 1981.

Hassan, Ihab. *Paracriticisms: Seven Speculations of the Times*. Urbana: University of Illinois Press, 1975.

Hassan, Ihab. *Radical Innocence: The Contemporary American Novel*. New York: Harper and Row, 1961.

Hegel, G. W. F. *Phenomenology of Spirit*, trans. A. V. Miller. Oxford: Clarendon Press, 1977.

Heidegger, Martin. *Being and Time*, trans. John Macquarie and Edward Robinson. Oxford: Blackwell, 1962.

Heidegger, Martin. *Identity and Difference*, trans. Joan Stanbaugh. New York: Harper and Row, 1969.

Heidegger, Martin. *Nietzsche*, Vol. 1, *The Will to Power as Art*, trans. David Farrell Krell. New York: Harper and Row, 1979.

Heidegger, Martin. *Poetry, Language, Thought*, trans. Albert Hosfstadter. New York: Harper and Row, 1971.

Hobbes, Thomas. *Leviathan*, ed. C. B. Macpherson. London: Harmondsworth, 1968.

Hume, David. *An Enquiry Concerning Human Understanding and Selections from a Treatise of Human Nature*. La Salle: Open Court, 1963.

Irigaray, Lucé. *An Ethics of Sexual Difference*, trans. Carolyn Burke and Gillian C. Gill. New York: Cornell University Press, 1993.

James, Henry. *The Aspern Papers and The Turn of the Screw*, ed. Anthony Curtis. Harmondsworth: Penguin, 1984.

Jameson, Fredric. 'Foreword', in Jean-François Lyotard, *The Postmodern Condition: A Report on Knowledge. Theory and History of Literature*, 10. Manchester: Manchester University Press, 1986, pp. vii–xxi.

Jameson, Fredric. 'Postmodernism, or The Cultural Logic of Late Capitalism'. *New Left Review*, 146 (1984), pp. 53–92.

Johnson, B. S. 'Introduction to *Aren't You Rather Young to be Writing Your Memoirs?*', in *The Novel Today: Contemporary Writers on Modern Fiction*, ed. Malcolm Bradbury. London: Fontana, 1977, pp. 151–68.

Johnson, Barbara. *The Critical Difference: Essays in the Contemporary Rhetoric of Reading*. Baltimore, MD: The Johns Hopkins University Press, 1980.

Johnson, Samuel (Dr). *The Rambler*, 60, 13 October, 1750, in *Eighteenth-Century English Literature*, ed. Geoffrey Tillotson, Paul Fussell Jr and Marshall Waingrow. New York: Harcourt, Brace & World, 1969, pp. 985–87.

Johnson, Samuel (Dr). *Rasselas*, in *Eighteenth-Century English Literature*, ed. Geoffrey Tillotson, Paul Fussell Jr and Marshall Waingrow. New York: Harcourt, Brace & World, 1969, pp. 1020–65.

Kant, Immanuel. 'An Answer to the Question: What is Enlightenment?', trans. H. B. Nisbet, in *Kant's Political Writings*, ed. Hans Reiss. Cambridge: Cambridge University Press, 1970, pp. 54–60.

Kant, Immanuel. *The Critique of Judgement*, trans. James Creed Meredith. Oxford: Clarendon Press, 1952.

Kant, Immanuel. *Critique of Practical Reason*, trans. Lewis White Beck. New York and London: Garland, 1976.

Kant, Immanuel. *Critique of Pure Reason*, trans. Vasilis Politis (based on translation by J. M. D. Meiklejohn). London: J. M. Dent, 1993.

Kant, Immanuel. 'A Renewed Attempt to Answer the Question: "Is the Human Race Continually Improving?"', trans. H. B. Nisbet, in *Kant's Political Writings*, ed. Hans Reiss. Cambridge: Cambridge University Press, 1970, pp. 176–90.

Kaplan, E. Ann and Michael Sprinker, eds. *The Althusserian Legacy*. London and New York: Verso, 1983.

Karasik, Paul and David Mazzucchelli. *Paul Auster's City of Glass*. New York: Avon, 1994.

Keats, John. *Poems*, ed. Gerald Bullett. London: J. M. Dent, 1974.

Kennedy, George. *The Art of Persuasion in Greece*. Princeton, NJ: Princeton University Press, 1963.

Klein, Melanie. *The Psycho-Analysis of Children*. London: Hogarth Press, 1949.

Kristeva, Julia. *Desire in Language: A Semiotic Approach to Literature and Art*, trans. Thomas Gora, Alice Jardine and Leon S. Roudiez, ed. Leon S. Roudiez. Oxford: Blackwell, 1981.

Kristeva, Julia. *Nations Without Nationalism*, trans. Leon S. Roudiez. New York: Columbia University Press, 1993.

Kroker, Arthur and David Cook. *The Postmodern Scene: Excremental Culture and Hyper-Aesthetics*. London: Macmillan, 1988.

Kuhn, Thomas S. *The Structure of Scientific Revolutions*, 2nd edn. Chicago, IL: University of Chicago Press, 1970.

Lacan, Jacques. 'The Insistence of the Letter in the Unconscious', trans. Jan Miel, in *Modern Criticism and Theory*, ed. David Lodge. London: Longman, 1988, pp. 79–106.

Lacoue-Labarthe, Philippe and Jean-Luc Nancy. *The Literary Absolute: The Theory of Literature in German Romanticism*, trans. Philip Barnand and Cheryl Lester. Albany: State University of New York Press, 1988.

Lacoue-Labarthe, Philippe. *The Subject of Philosophy*, trans. Claudette Sartiliot. Minneapolis: University of Minnesota Press, 1993.

Lévi-Strauss, Claude. *The Savage Mind*, trans. George Weidenfeld and Nicolson Ltd. London: Weidenfeld and Nicolson, 1966.

Lévi-Strauss, Claude. *Structural Anthropology 1*, trans. Claire Jacobson and Brooke Grundfest Schoepf. Harmondsworth: Penguin, 1968.

Lucy, Niall. *Debating Derrida*. Carlton: Melbourne University Press, 1995.

Lucy, Niall and Alec McHoul. 'The Logical Status of Searlean Discourse'. *boundary 2*, 23, 3 (1996), pp. 219–41.

Lyotard, Jean-François. *The Differend: Phrases in Dispute*, trans. Georges Van Den Abbeele. *Theory and History of Literature*, 46. Minneapolis: University of Minnesota Press, 1988.

Lyotard, Jean-François. *The Postmodern Condition: A Report on Knowledge*, trans. Geoff Bennington and Brian Massumi. *Theory and History of Literature*, 10. Manchester: Manchester University Press, 1986.

Macksey, Richard and Eugenio Donato, eds. *The Structuralist Controversy: The Languages of Criticism and the Sciences of Man*. Baltimore, MD: The Johns Hopkins University Press, 1970.

Manley, Lawrence. *Convention 1500–1750*. Cambridge, MA: Harvard University Press, 1980.

Marx, Karl. *Capital: A Critique of Political Economy*, Vol. I, trans. Ben Fowkes. London: Penguin, 1976.

Massumi, Brian. 'Translator's Foreword', in Gilles Deleuze and Félix Guattari, *A Thousand Plateaus: Capitalism and Schizophrenia*, trans. Brian Massumi. Minneapolis: University of Minnesota Press, 1987.

Massumi, Brian. *A User's Guide to Capitalism and Schizophrenia: Deviations from Deleuze and Guattari*. Cambridge, MA: Massachusetts Institute of Technology, 1992.

McCarthy, Cormac. *Child of God*. London: Picador, 1989.

McHale, Brian. *Postmodernist Fictions*. London and New York: Routledge, 1987.

McHoul, Alec. *Semiotic Investigations: Towards an Effective Semiotics*. Lincoln and London: University of Nebraska Press, 1996.

McHoul, Alec and Niall Lucy. 'That Film, This Paper – Its Body', *Southern Review*, 27, 3 (1994), pp. 303–22.

McHoul, Alec and David Wills. *Writing Pynchon: Strategies in Fictional Analysis*. London: Macmillan, 1990.

Melville, Herman. *Billy Budd, Sailor and Other Stories*, ed. Harold Beaver. Harmondsworth: Penguin, 1983.

Melville, Herman. *Moby-Dick; or, The Whale*, ed. Harold Beaver. Penguin: Harmondsworth, 1972.

Mendelson, Edward. 'The Sacred, The Profane, and *The Crying of Lot 49*', in *Pynchon: A Collection of Critical Essays*, ed. Edward Mendelson. Englewood Cliffs, NJ: Prentice-Hall, 1978, pp. 112–46.

Mickler, Steve. *Gambling on the First Race: A Comment on Racism and Talk-Back Radio, 6PR, the TAB, and the WA Government*. Perth: Centre for Research in Culture and Communication, Murdoch University, 1992.

Miller, J. Hillis. *Fiction and Repetition: Seven English Novels*. Cambridge, MA: Harvard University Press, 1982.

Milton, John. *Poetical Works*, ed. Douglas Bush. Oxford: Oxford University Press, 1969.

Nietzsche, Friedrich. *On the Genealogy of Morals*, in *Basic Writings of Nietzsche*, trans. and ed. Walter Kaufmann. New York: Modern Library, 1968.

Nietzsche, Friedrich. *The Will to Power*, trans. Walter Kaufmann and R. J. Hollingdale, ed. Walter Kaufmann. New York: Vintage, 1968.

Norris, Christopher. *The Deconstructive Turn: Essays in the Rhetoric of Philosophy*. London and New York: Methuen, 1983.

Norris, Christopher. *Derrida*. London: Fontana, 1987.

Norris, Christopher. *The Truth About Postmodernism*. Oxford: Blackwell, 1993.

Norris, Christopher. *Truth and the Ethics of Criticism*. Manchester and New York: Manchester University Press, 1994.

Norris, Christopher. *What's Wrong with Postmodernism: Critical Theory and the Ends of Philosophy*. New York and London: Harvester Wheatsheaf, 1990.

Peirce, Charles S. *Collected Papers* of Charles Sanders Peirce, ed. Charles Hartshome and Paul Weiss. Cambridge, MA: Harvard University Press, 1965.

Petrey, Sandy. *Speech Acts and Literary Theory*. New York and London: Routledge, 1990.

Podhoretz, Norman. 'The Article as Art'. *Harper's* (July 1958), pp. 74–9.

Poe, Edgar Allan. *The Fall of the House of Usher and Other Writings: Poems, Tales, Essays and Reviews*, ed. David Galloway. Harmondsworth: Penguin, 1967.

Pope, Alexander. *Selected Poetry and Prose*, 2nd edn, ed. William K. Wimsatt. New York: Holt, Rinehart and Winston, 1972.

Pynchon, Thomas. *The Crying of Lot 49*. London: Pan, 1979.

Richards, I. A. *Practical Criticism: A Study of Literary Judgement*. London and Henley: Routledge and Kegan Paul, 1964.

Rorty, Richard. *Contingency, Irony, Solidarity*. Cambridge: Cambridge University Press, 1989.

Roth, Philip. 'Writing American Fiction'. *Commentary*, 31 (March 1961), pp. 223–33.

Rousseau, Jean-Jacques. *Considerations on the Government of Poland and on its Proposed Reformation*, in *Political Writings*, trans. and ed. Frederick Watkins. Madison: University of Wisconsin Press, 1986, pp. 157–274.

Rousseau, Jean-Jacques. *Émile*, trans. Barbara Foxley. London: J. M. Dent, 1974.

Rousseau, Jean-Jacques. *The First and Second Discourses*, trans. Roger D. and Judith R. Masters, ed. Roger D. Masters. New York: St Martin's Press, 1964.

Ruthrof, Horst. *Pandora and Occam: On the Limits of Language and Literature*. Bloomington and Indianapolis: Indiana University Press, 1992.

Schiller, Friedrich. *On the Aesthetic Education of Man (in a Series of Letters)*, trans. and ed. Elizabeth M. Wilkinson and L. A. Willoughby. Oxford: Clarendon Press, 1967.

Schrag, Calvin O. 'The Transvaluation of Aesthetics and the Work of Art', in *Thinking About Being: Aspects in Heidegger's Thought*, ed. Robert W. Shahan and J. N. Mohanty. Norman: University of Oklahoma Press, 1984, pp. 109–24.

Searle, John R. *Intentionality: An Essay in the Philosophy of Mind*. Cambridge: Cambridge University Press, 1983.

Searle, John R. *Speech Acts: An Essay in the Philosophy of Language*. Cambridge: Cambridge University Press, 1969.

Shakespeare, William. *Hamlet*, ed. John Dover Wilson. Cambridge: Cambridge University Press, 1936.

Shelley, Percy Bysshe. *Selected Poetry and Prose*, ed. Harold Bloom. New York: Signet, 1966.

Strachey, James. 'Some Unconscious Factors in Reading', *International Journal of Psycho-Analysis*, 2 (1930), pp. 322–31.

Tanner, Tony. *City of Words: American Fiction 1950–1970*. London: Jonathan Cape, 1971.

Tapper, Marion. '*Ressentiment* and Power: Some Reflections on Feminist Practices', in *Nietzsche, Feminism and Political Theory*, ed. Paul Patton. St Leonards: Allen & Unwin, 1993, pp. 130–43.

Thwaites, Tony. 'Miracles: Hot Air and Histories of the Improbable', in *Futur* Fall: Excursions into Post-Modernity*, ed. E. A. Grosz, Terry Threadgold, David Kelly, Alan Cholodenko and Edward Colless. Sydney: Power Institute Publications, 1986, pp. 82–96.

Veatch, Henry B. *Rational Man: A Modern Interpretation of Aristotelian Ethics*. Bloomington and London: Indiana University Press, 1966.

Virilio, Paul. *War and Cinema*, trans. Patrick Camiller. London: Verso, 1989.

Wellek, René. *A History of Modern Criticism: 1750–1950*, Vol. 6, *American Criticism 1900–1950*. London: Jonathan Cape, 1986.

Wittgenstein, Ludwig. *The Blue and Brown Books*. Oxford: Blackwell, 1958.

Wittgenstein, Ludwig. *Philosophical Investigations*, trans. G. E. M. Anscombe. Oxford: Blackwell, 1967.

Wordsworth, William. *Selected Poems and Prefaces*, ed. Jack Stillinger. Boston: Houghton Mifflin, 1965.

Wyschogrod, Edith. *Saints and Postmodernism: Revisioning Moral Philosophy*. Chicago, IL and London: University of Chicago Press, 1990.

Zavarzadeh, Mas'ud. *The Mythopoeic Reality: The Postwar American Nonfiction Novel*. Urbana: University of Illinois Press, 1976.

Index